Thackray's 2017 Investor's Guide

THACKRAY'S
2017
INVESTOR'S GUIDE

Brooke Thackray MBA, CIM, CFP

Published in 2016 by: MountAlpha Media:

alphamountain.com

Brooke Thackray is a research analyst for Horizons ETFs Management (Canada) Inc. All of the views expressed herein are the personal views of the author and are not necessarily the views of Horizons ETFs Management (Canada) Inc., although any of the strategies/recommendations found herein may be reflected in positions or transactions in the various client portfolios managed by Horizons ETFs Management (Canada) Inc., securities (if any) discussed in this publication are meant to highlight investment strategies for educational purposes only not investment advice.

Commissions, trailing commissions, management fees and expenses all may be associated with an investment in the Horizons Seasonal Rotation ETF. The Horizons Seasonal Rotation ETF is not guaranteed, its values change frequently, and past performance may not be repeated. Please read the prospectus before investing.

ISBN13: 978-0-9918735-6-2

Printed and Bound by Webcom Inc.
10 9 8 7 6 5 4 3 2 1

To my wife Jane

Acknowledgments

This book is the product of many years of research and could not have been written without the help of many people. I would like to thank my wife, Jane Steer-Thackray, and my children Justin, Megan, Carly and Madeleine, for the help they have given me and their patience during the many hours that I have devoted to writing this book. Thanks must be given to Wade Guenther for helping me source and filter a lot of the data in this book. Special mention goes to Jane Stiegler, my proofreader and editor, for the countless hours she spent helping with formatting and editing this book.

VISIT ALPHAMOUNTAIN.COM

MATERIAL STOCKS
MATERIAL GAINS

URE MOOOVES

WITCHES' HANGOVER

SUPER SEVEN

BIOTECH
SUMM

SMALL CAP EFFECT

SEPTEMBER NOT
A FAVORABLE MONTH

THANKS &
TURNS
INFORMATION T
USE IT OR L

007 BOND

HEALTH CARE
PRESCRIPTION RENEWAL

VALUE & GROWTH

GAS FO

INDEPENDENCE DAY

AIR
IN SEPTEM

EARNINGS
TH EFFECT

MORE:
✓ **Strategies**

✓ **Graphs**

✓ **Reports**

FREE:
✓ *Subscription to the Thackray Market Letter*

ALPHAMOUNTAIN.COM

INTRODUCTION

2017 THACKRAY'S INVESTOR'S GUIDE
Technical Commentary

The seasonal strategies that I have included in my previous books have proven to be very successful. The buy and sell dates are based upon iterative comparisons of different time periods measured by gain and frequency of success. Although the buy and sell dates are the optimal dates on which seasonal investors should focus on making their investment decisions, the markets have different dynamics from year to year, shifting the optimal buy and sell dates. Combining technical analysis with seasonal trends helps to adjust the decision process, allowing seasonal investors to enter and exit trades early or late, depending on market conditions.

The universe of technical indicators and techniques is huge. It is impossible to use all of the indicators. Only a small number of indicators and techniques that suit an investment style should be used. In the case of seasonal investing, a lot of long-term indicators provide very little benefit. For example, the standard Moving Average Convergence Divergence (MACD), is far too slow to be of any use in shorter term seasonal strategies. In this book I have chosen to illustrate the use of three technical indicators that have provided a lot of value in fine-tuning the dates for seasonal investing: Full Stochastic Oscillator (FSO), Relative Strength Index (RSI) and Relative Strength. The indicators are used in conjunction with the price pattern and moving averages of the security being considered. Investors must remember that technical analysis is not absolute and there will be exceptions when utilizing indicators and price patterns.

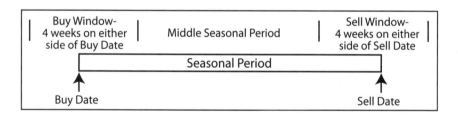

To combine technical indicators with seasonal trends, the indicators should only be used within the windows of the buy and sell dates. The indicators should be ignored outside the seasonal buy/sell windows. The only exception to this occurs when an indicator gives a signal during its middle seasonal period, which is in the seasonal period, but after the buy window and before the sell window. In this case a technical signal can support selling a full position based upon a fundamental breakdown in the price action of a security. By itself, a FSO or RSI indicator showing weakness in a security during its middle seasonal period, does not warrant action, it can only be used to support a decision being made in conjunction with underperformance relative to the broad market, or a major price action break.

Below are short descriptions of the three technical indicators that are used in this book and the metrics of how they are used with seasonal analysis. Full evaluation of the indicators and their uses with seasonal analysis is beyond the scope of this book.

Full Stochastic Oscillator (FSO)

A stochastic oscillator is a range bound momentum indicator that tracks the location of the close price relative to the high-low range, over a set number of periods. It tracks the momentum of price change and helps to indicate the strength and direction of price movement.

I have found that generally the best method to combine the FSO with seasonal trends is to buy an early partial position when the FSO turns up above 20 within four weeks of the seasonal buy date. Additionally, the best time to sell an early partial position occurs when the FSO turns below 80, within four weeks of the seasonal exit date.

For practical purposes in this book, %D, a 3 period smoothed %K, has been omitted. The standard variables are used in the FSO calculation (14 day look back period, and a 3 day simple moving average smoothing constant).

Relative Strength Index (RSI)

The RSI is a momentum oscillator that measures the speed and change of price movements. I have found that the best method to combine the RSI with seasonal trends is to buy an early partial position when the RSI turns up above 30 within four weeks of the seasonal buy date. The best time to sell an early partial position occurs when the RSI turns below 70, within four weeks of the seasonal exit date. Compared with the FSO, the RSI is less useful as it is slower and gives too few signals in the buy/sell windows.

Relative Strength

Relative strength calculates the performance of one security versus another security. When the relative strength is increasing, it indicates the seasonal security is outperforming. When the relative strength is declining, the seasonal security is underperforming. When a downward trend line is broken to the upside by the performance of the seasonal security, relative to the benchmark, this is a positive signal. This action carries a lot of weight and can justify a full early entry into a position if other technical evidence is positive. Likewise, if an upward trend line is broken to the downside, a negative technical signal is given and can justify a full early exit from a position if other technical evidence is negative.

THACKRAY'S 2017 INVESTOR'S GUIDE

You can choose great companies to invest in and still underperform the market. Unless you are in the market at the right time and in the best sectors, your investment expertise can be all for naught.

Successful investors know when they should be in the market. Very successful investors know when they should be in the market, and the best sectors in which to invest. *Thackray's 2017 Investor's Guide* is designed to provide investors with the knowledge of when and what to buy, and when to sell.

The goal of this book is to help investors capture extra profits by taking advantage of the seasonal trends in the markets. This book is straightforward. There are no complicated rules and there are no complex algorithms. The strategies put forward are intuitive and easy to understand.

It does not matter if you are a short-term or long-term investor, this book can be used to help establish entry and exit points. For the short-term investor, specific periods are identified that can provide profitable opportunities. For the long-term investor best buy dates are identified to launch new investments on a sound footing.

The stock market has its seasonal rhythms. Historically, the broad markets, such as the S&P 500, have a seasonal trend of outperforming during certain times of the year. Likewise, different sectors of the market have their own seasonal trends of outperformance. When oil stocks tend to do well in the springtime before "driving season," health care stocks tend to underperform the market. When utilities do well in the summertime, industrials do not. With different markets and different sectors having a tendency to outperform at different times of the year, there is always a place to invest.

Until recently, investors did not have access to the information necessary to analyse and create sector strategies. In recent years there have been a great number of sector Exchange Traded Funds (ETFs) and sector indexes introduced into the market. For the first time, investors are now able to easily implement a sector rotation strategy. This book provides a seasonal road map of what sectors tend to do well at different times of the year. It is a first of its kind, revealing new sector-based strategies that have never before been published.

In terms of market timing there are ample strategies in this book to help determine the times when equities should be over or underweight. During a favorable time for the market, investments can be purchased to overweight equities relative to their target weight in a portfolio (staying within risk tolerances). During an unfavorable time, investments can be sold to underweight equities relative to their target.

A large part of the book is devoted to sector seasonality – the underpinnings for a sector rotation strategy. The most practical rotation strategy is to create a core part of a portfolio that represents the broad market and then set aside an allocation to be rotated between favored sectors from one time period to the next.

It does not makes sense to apply any investment strategy only once with a large investment. Seasonal strategies are no exception. The best way to apply an investment strategy is to use a disciplined methodology that allows for diversification and a large enough number of investments to help remove the anomalies of the market. This reduces risk and increases the probability of a long term gain.

Following the specific buy and sell dates put forth in this book would have netted an investor large, above market returns. To "turbo-charge" gains, an investor can combine seasonality with technical analysis. As the seasonal periods are never exactly the same, technical analysis can help investors capture the extra gains when a sector turns up early, or momentum extends the trend.

IMPORTANT: Strategy Buy and Sell Dates
The beginning date of every strategy period in this book represents a full day in the market; therefore, investors should buy at the end of the preceding market day. For example the *Biotech Summer Solstice* seasonal period of strength is from June 23rd to September 13th. To be in the sector for the full seasonal period, an investor would enter the market before the closing bell on June 22nd. If the buy date landed on a weekend or holiday, then the buy would occur at the end of the preceding trading day.

The last day of a trading strategy is the sell date. For example, the Biotech sector investment would be sold at the end of the day on September 13th. If the sell date is a holiday or weekend, then the investment would be sold at the close on the preceding trading day.

What is Seasonal Investing?

In order to properly understand seasonal investing in the stock market, it is important to look briefly at its evolution. It may surprise investors to know that seasonal investing at the broad market level, i.e. Dow Jones or S&P 500, has been around for a long time. The initial seasonal strategies were written by Fields (1931, 1934) and Watchel (1942), who focused on the *January Effect*. Coincidentally, this strategy is still bantered about in the press every year.

Yale Yirsch Senior has been largely responsible for the next stage in the evolution, producing the *Stock Trader's Almanac* for more than forty years. This publication focuses on broad market trends such as the best six months of the year and tendencies of the market to do well depending on the political party in power and holiday trades.

In 2000, Brooke Thackray and Bruce Lindsay wrote, *Time In Time Out: Outsmart the Market Using Calendar Investment Strategies*. This work focused on a comprehensive analysis of the six month seasonal cycle and other shorter seasonal cycles in the broad markets such as the S&P 500.

Seasonal investing has changed over time. The focus has shifted from broad market strategies to taking advantage of sector rotation opportunities – investing in different sectors at different times of the year, depending on their seasonal strength. This has created a whole new set of investment opportunities. Rather than just being "in or out" of the market, investors can now always be invested by shifting between different sectors and asset classes, taking advantage of both up and down markets.

Definition – Seasonal investing is a method of investing in the market at the time of the year when it typically does well, or investing in a sector of the market when it typically outperforms the broad market such as the S&P 500.

The term seasonal investing is somewhat of a misnomer, and it is easy to see why some investors might believe that the discipline relates to investing based upon the seasons of the year – winter, spring, summer and autumn. Other than some agricultural commodities where the price is often correlated to growing seasons, generally seasonal investment strategies use the calendar as a reference for buy and sell dates. It is usually a specific event, i.e. Christmas sales, that occurs on a recurring annual basis that creates the seasonal opportunity.

The discipline of seasonal investing is not restricted to the stock market. It has been used successfully for a number of years in the commodities market. The opportunities in this market tend to be based upon changes in supply and/or demand that occur on a yearly basis. Most commodities, especially the agricultural commodities, tend to have cyclical supply cycles, i.e., crops are harvested only at certain times of the year. The supply bulge that occurs at the same time every year provides seasonal investors with profit opportunities. Recurring increased seasonal demand for commodities also plays a major part in providing opportunities for seasonal investors. This applies to most metals and many other commodities, whether the end-product is industrial or consumer based.

Seasonal investment strategies can be used with a lot of different types of investments. The premise is the same, outperformance during a certain period of the year based upon a repeating event in the markets or economy. In my past writings I have developed seasonal strategies that have been used successfully in the stock, commodity, bond and foreign exchange markets. Seasonal investing is still relatively new for most markets with a lot of new opportunities waiting to be discovered.

How Does Seasonal Investing Work?

Most stock market sector seasonal trends are the result of a recurring annual catalyst: an event that affects the sector positively. These events can range from a seasonal spike in demand, seasonal inventory lows, weather effects, conferences and other events. Mainstream investors very often anticipate a move in a sector and incorrectly try to take a position just before an event takes place that is supposed to drive a sector higher. A good example of this would be investors buying oil just before the cold weather sets in. Unfortunately, their efforts are usually unsuccessful as they are too late to the party and the opportunity has already passed.

By the time the anticipated event occurs, a substantial amount of investors have bought into the sector – fully pricing in the expected benefit. At this time there is little potential left in the short-term. Unless there is a strong positive surprise, the sector's outperformance tends to slowly roll over. If the event produces less than its desired result, the sector can be severely punished.

So how does the seasonal investor take advantage of this opportunity? "Be there" before the mainstream investors, and get out before they do. Seasonal investors usually enter a sector two or three months before an event is anticipated to have a positive effect on a sector and get out before the actual event takes place. In essence, seasonal investors are benefiting from the mainstream investor's tendency to "buy in" too late.

Seasonality in the markets occurs because of three major reasons: money flow, changing market analyst expectations and the *Anticipation-Realization Cycle*. First, money flows vary throughout the year and at different times of the month. Generally, money flows increase at the end of the year and into the start of the next year. This is a result of year end bonuses and tax related investments. In addition, money flows increase at month end from money managers "window dressing" their portfolios. As a result of these money flows, the months around the end of the year and the days around the end of the month, tend to have a stronger performance than the other times of the year.

Second, the analyst expectations cycle tends to push markets up at the end of the year and the beginning of the next year. Stock market analysts tend to be a positive bunch – the large investment houses pay them to be positive. They start the year with aggressive earnings for all of their favorite companies. As the year progresses, they generally back off their earnings forecast, which decreases their support for the market. After a lull in the summer and early autumn months, they start to focus on the next year with another rosy forecast. As a result, the stock market tends to rise once again at the end of the year.

Third, at the sector level, sectors of the market tend to be greatly influenced by the *Anticipation-Realization Cycle*. Although some investors may not be familiar with the term "anticipation-realization," they probably are familiar with the concept of "buy the rumor – sell the fact," or in the famous words of Lord Rothschild "Buy on the sound of the war-cannons; sell on the sound of the victory trumpets."

The *Anticipation-Realization Cycle* as it applies to human behavior has been much studied in psychology journals. In the investment world, the premise of this cycle rests on investors anticipating a positive event in the market to drive prices higher and buying in ahead of the event. When the event takes place, or is realized, upward pressure on prices decreases as there is very little impetus for further outperformance.

A good example of the *Anticipation-Realization Cycle* takes place with the "conference effect." Very often large industries have major conferences that occur at approximately the same time every year. Major companies in the industry often hold back positive announce-ments and product introductions to be released during the conference.

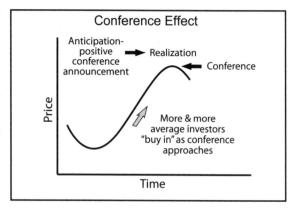

Two to three months prior to the conference, seasonal investors tend to buy into the sector. Shortly afterwards, the mainstream investors anticipate "good news" from the conference and start to buy in. As a result, prices are pushed up. Just before the conference starts, seasonal investors capture their profits by exiting their positions. As the conference unfolds, company announcements are made (realized), but as the potential good news has already been priced into the sector, there is little to push prices higher and the sector typically starts to rolls over.

The same *Anticipation-Realization Cycle* takes place with increased demand for oil to meet the "summer driving season", increased sales of goods at Christmas time, increased demand for gold jewellery to meet the autumn and winter demand, and many other events that tend to drive the outperformance of different sectors.

Does Seasonal Investing ALWAYS Work?

The simple answer to the above question is "No." There is not any investment system in the world that works all of the time. When following any investment system, it is probability of success that counts. It has often been said that "being correct in the markets 60% of the time will make you rich." Investors tend to forget this and become too emotionally attached to their losses. Just about every investment trading book states that investors typically fail to let their profits run and cut their losses quickly. I concur. In my many years in the investment industry, the biggest mistake that I have found with investors is not being able to cut their losses. Everyone wants to be right, that is how we have been raised. Investors feel that if they sell at a loss they have failed, and as a result, often suffer bigger losses by waiting for their position to trade at profit.

With any investment system, investors should let probability work for them. This means that investors should be able to enter and exit positions capturing both gains and losses without becoming emotionally attached to any positions. Emotional attachment clouds judgement, which leads to errors. When all of the trades are put together, the goal is for profits to be larger than losses in a way that minimizes risks and beats the market.

If we examine the winter oil stock trade, we can see how probability has worked in an investor's favor. This trade is based upon the premise that at the tail end of winter, the refineries drive up demand for oil in order to produce enough gas for the approaching "driving season" that starts in the spring. As a result, oil stocks tend to increase and outperform the market (from February 25th to May 9th). The oil stock sector, represented by the NYSE Arca Oil Index (XOI), has been very successful

XOI vs S&P 500 1984 to 2016		
Feb 25 to May 9	positive	
S&P 500	XOI	Diff
1984 1.7 %	5.6 %	3.9 %
1985 1.4	4.9	3.5
1986 6.0	7.7	1.7
1987 3.7	25.5	21.8
1988 -3.0	5.6	8.6
1989 6.3	8.1	1.8
1990 5.8	-0.6	-6.3
1991 4.8	6.8	2.0
1992 0.9	5.8	4.9
1993 0.3	6.3	6.0
1994 -4.7	3.2	7.9
1995 7.3	10.3	3.1
1996 -2.1	2.2	4.3
1997 1.8	4.7	2.9
1998 7.5	9.8	2.3
1999 7.3	35.4	28.1
2000 4.3	22.2	17.9
2001 0.8	10.2	9.4
2002 -1.5	5.3	6.9
2003 12.1	5.7	-6.4
2004 -3.5	4.0	7.5
2005 -1.8	-1.0	0.8
2006 2.8	9.4	6.6
2007 4.2	10.1	5.8
2008 2.6	7.6	5.0
2009 20.2	15.8	-4.4
2010 0.5	-2.3	-2.8
2011 3.1	-0.6	-3.7
2012 -0.8	-13.4	-12.5
2013 7.3	3.8	-3.5
2014 1.7	9.1	7.4
2015 0.3	1.2	1.1
2016 6.7	11.1	4.4
Avg 3.1 %	7.3 %	4.1 %
Fq > 0 79 %	85 %	79 %

at this time of year, producing an average return of 7.3% and beating the S&P 500 by 4.1%, from 1984 to 2016. In addition it has been positive 28 out of 33 times. Investors should always evaluate the strength of seasonal trades before applying them to their own portfolios.

If an investor started using the seasonal investment discipline in 1984 and chose to invest in the winter-oil trade, they would have been very happy with the results. Over the last few years, the fact that the trade did not produce a gain in 2010, 2011 and 2012, does not mean that the seasonal trade no longer works. All seasonal trades go through periods, sometimes multiple years where they do not work. An investor can start any methodology of trading at the "wrong time," and be unsuccessful in a particular trade. In fact, if an investor started the oil-winter trade in 1990 and had given up in the same year, they would have missed the following successful twelve years. Investors have to remember that it is the final score that counts, after all of the gains have been weighed against the losses.

In practical terms, investors should not put all of their investment strategies in one basket. If one or two large investments were made based upon seasonal strategies, it is possible that the seasonal methodology might be inappropriately evaluated and its use discontinued. A much more prudent strategy is to use a larger number of strategic seasonal investments with smaller investments. The end result will be to put the seasonal probability to work with a much greater chance of success.

Measuring Seasonal Performance

How do you determine if a seasonal strategy has been successful? Many people feel that ten years of data is a good sample size, others feel that fifteen years is better, and yet others feel that the more data the better. I tend to fall into the camp that, if possible, it is best to use fifteen or twenty years of data for sectors and more data for the broad markets, such as the S&P 500. Although the most recent data in almost any analytical framework is the most relevant, it is important to get enough data to reflect a sector's performance across different economic conditions. Given that historically the economy has performed on an eight year cycle, four years of expansion and then four years of contraction, using a short data set does not provide for enough exposure to different economic conditions.

A data set that is too long can run into the problem of older data having too much of an influence on the numbers when fundamental factors affecting a sector have changed. It is important to look at trends over time and assess if there has been a change that should be considered in determining the dates for a seasonal cycle. Each sector should be judged on its own merit. The analysis tables in this book illustrate the performance level for each year in order to provide the opportunity for readers to determine any relevant changes.

In order to determine if a seasonal strategy is effective there are two possible benchmarks, absolute and relative performance. Absolute performance measures if a profit is made and relative performance measures the performance of a sector in relationship to a major market. Both measurements have their merits and depending on your investment style, one measurement may be more valuable than another. This book provides both sets of measurement in tables and graphs.

It is not just the average percent gain of a sector over a certain time period that determines success. It is possible that one or two spectacular years of performance skew the results substantially (particularly with a small data set). The frequency of success is also very important: the higher the percentage of success the better. Also, the fewer large drawdowns the better. There is no magic number (percent success rate) per se of what constitutes a successful strategy. The success rate should be above fifty percent, otherwise it would be better to just invest in the broad market. Ideally speaking a strategy should have a high percentage success rate on both an absolute and relative basis. Some strategies are stronger than others, but that does not mean that the weaker strategies should not be used. Prudence should be used in determining the ideal portfolio allocation.

Illustrating the strength of a sector's seasonal performance can be accomplished through either an absolute yearly average performance graph, or a relative yearly average performance graph. The absolute graph shows the average yearly cumulative gain for a set number of years. It lets a reader visually identify the strong periods during the year. The relative graph shows the average yearly cumulative gain for the sector relative to the benchmark index.

Both graphs are useful in determining the strength of a particular seasonal strategy. In the above diagram, the top graph illustrates the average year for the NYSE Arca Oil Index (XOI) from 1984 to 2015. Essentially it illustrates the cumulative average gain if an investment were made in the index. The steep rising line starting in January/February shows the overall price rise that typically occurs in this sector at this time of year. In May the line flattens out and then rises very modestly starting in July.

The bottom graph is a ratio graph, illustrating the strength of the XOI Index relative to the S&P 500. It is derived by dividing the average year of the XOI by the average year of the S&P 500. When the line in the graph is rising, the XOI is outperforming the S&P 500, and vise versa when it is declining. This is an important graph and should be used in considering seasonal investments because the S&P 500 is a viable alternative to the energy sector. If both markets are increasing, but the S&P 500 is increasing at a faster rate, the S&P 500 represents a more attractive opportunity. This is particularly true when measuring the risk of a volatile sector relative to the broad market. If both investments were expected to produce the same rate of return, generally the broad market is a better investment because of its diversification.

Who Can Use Seasonal Investing?

Any investor from novice to expert, from short-term trader to long-term investor can benefit from using seasonal analysis. Seasonal investing is unique because it is an easy to understand system that can be used by itself or as a complement to another investment discipline. For the novice it provides an easy to follow strategy that makes intuitive sense. For the expert it can be used as a stand-alone system or as a complement to an existing system.

Seasonal investing is easily understood by all levels of investors, which allows investors to make rational decisions. This may seem obvious, but it is very common for investors to listen to a "guru of the market", be impressed and blindly follow his advice. When the advice works there is no problem. When the advice does not work investors wonder why they made the investment in the first place. When investors do not understand their investments it causes stress, bad decisions and a lack of "stick-to-it ness" with any investment discipline. Even expert investors realize the importance of understanding your investments. Peter Lynch of Fidelity Investments used to say "Never invest in any idea that you can't illustrate with a crayon." Investors do not need to go that far, but they should understand their investments.

Novice investors find seasonal strategies very easy to understand because they are intuitive. They do not have to be investing for years to understand why seasonal strategies work. They understand that an increase in demand for gold every year at the same time causes a ripple effect in the stock market pushing up gold stocks at the same time every year.

Most expert investors use information from a variety of sources in making their decisions. Even experts that primarily use fundamental analysis can benefit from using seasonal trends to get an edge in the market. Fundamental analysis is a very crude tool and provides very little in the way of timing an investment. Using seasonal trends can help with the timing of the buy and sell decisions and produce extra profit.

Seasonal investing can be used by both short-term and long-term investors, but in different ways. For short-term investors it provides a complete trade – buy and sell dates. For long-term investors it can provide a buy date for a sector of interest.

Combining Seasonal Analysis with other Investment Disciplines

Seasonal investing used by itself has historically produced above average market returns. Depending on an investor's particular style, it can be combined with one of the other three investment disciplines: fundamental, quantitative and technical analysis. There are two basic ways to combine seasonal analysis with other investment methodologies – as the primary or secondary method. If it is used as a primary method, seasonally strong time periods are established for a number of sectors and then appropriate sectors are chosen based upon fundamental, quantitative or technical screens. If it is used as a secondary method, sector selections are first made based upon one of three methods and then final sectors are chosen based upon which ones are in their seasonally strong period.

Technical analysis is an ideal mate for seasonal analysis. Unlike fundamental and quantitative analysis, which are very blunt timing tools at best, seasonal and technical analysis can provide specific trigger points to buy and sell. The combination can turbo-charge investment strategies, adding extra profits by fine-tuning entry and exit dates.

Seasonal analysis provides both buy and sell dates. Although a sector in the market can sometimes bottom on the exact seasonal buy date, it more often bottoms a bit early or a bit late. After all, the seasonal buy date is based upon an average of historical performance. Depending on the sector, buying opportunities start to develop approximately one month before and after the seasonal buy date. Using technical analysis gives an investor the advantage of buying into a sector when it turns up early or waiting when it turns up late. Likewise, technical analysis can be used to trigger a sell signal when the market turns down before or after the sell date.

The sell decision can be extended with the help of a trailing stop-loss order. If a sector has strong momentum and the technical tools do not provide a sell signal, it is possible to let the sector "run." When a trailing stop-loss is used, a profitable sell point is established. If the price continues to run, then the selling point is raised. If, on the other hand, the price falls through the stop-loss point, the position is sold.

Sectors of the Market

Standard & Poor's has done an excellent job in categorizing the U.S. stock market into its different parts. Although the demand for this service initially came from institutional investors, many individual investors now seek the same information. Knowing the sector breakdown in the market allows investors to see how different their portfolio is relative to the market. As a result, they are able to make conscious decisions on what parts of the stock market to overweight based upon their beliefs of which sectors will outperform. It also helps control the amount of desired risk.

Standard & Poor's uses four levels of detail in its Global Industry Classification Standard (GICS©) to categorize stock markets around the world. From the most specific, it classifies companies into sub-industries, industries, industry groups and finally economic sectors. All companies in the Standard & Poor's global family of indices are classified according to the GICS structure.

This book focuses on the U.S. market, analysing the trends of the venerable S&P 500 index and its economic sectors and industry groups. The following diagram illustrates the index classified according to its economic sectors.

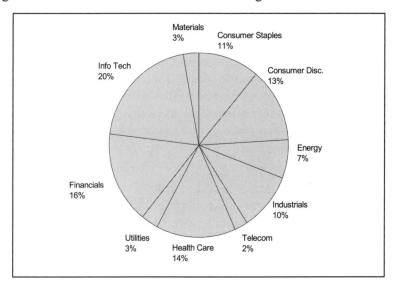

Standard and Poor's, Understanding Sectors, June 30, 2015

For more information on Standard and Poor's Global Industry Classification Standard (GICS©), refer to www.standardandpoors.com

Investment Products – Which One Is The Right One?

There are many ways to take advantage of the seasonal trends at the broad stock market and sector levels. Regardless of the investment products that you currently use, whether exchange traded funds, mutual funds, stocks or options, all can be used with the strategies in this book. Different investments offer different risk-reward relationships and return potential.

Exchange Traded Funds (ETFs)

Exchange Traded Funds (ETFs) offer the purest method of seasonal investment. The broad market ETFs are designed to track the major indices and the sector ETFs are designed to track specific sectors without using active management. Relatively new, ETFs are a great way to capture both market and sector trends. They were originally introduced into the Canadian market in 1993 to represent the Toronto stock market index. Shortly afterward they were introduced to the U.S. market and there are now hundreds of ETFs to represent almost every market, sector, style of investing and company capitalization. Originally ETFs were mainly of interest to institutional investors, but individual investors have fast realized the merits of ETF investing and have made some of the broad market ETFs the most heavily traded securities in the world.

An ETF is a single security that represents a market, such as the S&P 500; a sector of the market, such as the financial sector; or a commodity, such as gold. In the case of the S&P 500, an investor buying one security is buying all 500 stocks in the index. By investing into a financial ETF, an investor is buying the companies that make up the financial sector of the market. By investing into a gold commodity ETF, an investor is buying a security that represents the price of gold.

ETFs trade on the open market just like stocks. They have a bid and an ask, can be shorted and many are option eligible. They are a very low cost, tax efficient method of targeting specific parts of the market.

Mutual Funds

Mutual funds are a good way to combine market or sector investing with active management. In recent years, many mutual fund companies have added sector funds to accommodate an increasing appetite in this area.

As the seasonal strategies put forward in this book have a short-term nature, it is important to make sure that there are no fees (or a nominal charge) for getting into and out of a position in the market.

Stocks

Stocks provide an opportunity to make better returns than the market or sector. If the market increases during its seasonal period, some stocks will increase dramatically more than the index. Choosing one of the outperforming stocks will greatly enhance returns; choosing one of the underperforming stocks can create substantial loses. Using stocks requires increased attention to diversification and security selection.

Options

Disclaimer: Options involve risk and are not suitable for every investor. Because they are cash-settled, investors should be aware of the special risks associated with index options and should consult a tax advisor. Prior to buying or selling options, a person must receive a copy of Characteristics and Risks of Standardized Options and should thoroughly understand the risks involved in any use of options. Copies may be obtained from The Options Clearing Corporation, 440 S. LaSalle Street, Chicago, IL 60605.

Options, for more sophisticated investors, are a good tool to take advantage of both market and sector opportunities. An option position can be established with either stocks or ETFs. There are many different ways to use options for seasonal trends: establish a long position on the market during its seasonally strong period, establish a short position during its seasonally weak period, or create a spread trade to capture the superior gains of a sector over the market.

THACKRAY'S 2017 INVESTOR'S GUIDE

CONTENTS

JANUARY

	MONDAY	TUESDAY	WEDNESDAY
WEEK 01	**2** 29 CAN Market Closed - New Year's Day USA Market Closed - New Year's Day	**3** 28	**4** 27
WEEK 02	**9** 22	**10** 21	**11** 20
WEEK 03	**16** 15 USA Market Closed- Martin Luther King Jr. Day	**17** 14	**18** 13
WEEK 04	**23** 8	**24** 7	**25** 6
WEEK 05	**30** 1	**31**	1

THURSDAY		FRIDAY	
5	26	**6**	25
12	19	**13**	18
19	12	**20**	11
26	5	**27**	4
2		3	

FEBRUARY

M	T	W	T	F	S	S
		1	2	3	4	5
6	7	8	9	10	11	12
13	14	15	16	17	18	19
20	21	22	23	24	24	26
27	28					

MARCH

M	T	W	T	F	S	S
		1	2	3	4	5
6	7	8	9	10	11	12
13	14	15	16	17	18	19
20	21	22	23	24	25	26
27	28	29	30	31		

APRIL

M	T	W	T	F	S	S
					1	2
3	4	5	6	7	8	9
10	11	12	13	14	15	16
17	18	19	20	21	22	23
24	25	26	27	28	29	30

MAY

M	T	W	T	F	S	S
1	2	3	4	5	6	7
8	9	10	11	12	13	14
15	16	17	18	19	20	21
22	23	24	25	26	27	28
29	30	31				

JANUARY
S U M M A R Y

	Dow Jones	S&P 500	Nasdaq	TSX Comp
Month Rank	6	5	1	3
# Up	42	40	28	20
# Down	24	26	16	11
% Pos	64	61	64	65
% Avg. Gain	1.0	1.0	2.6	1.1

Dow & S&P 1950-2015, Nasdaq 1972-2015, TSX 1985-2015

S&P500 Cumulative Daily Gains for Avg Month 1950 to 2016

♦ Since 1950, January has been one of the better months of the year for North American stock markets. Over the last ten years, January has not lived up to its long-term reputation. ♦ In January there is typically a lot of sector rotation. ♦ Small caps tend to perform well. ♦ The technology sector finishes its seasonal period. ♦ The industrial, materials, metals and mining sectors start the second the second part of their seasonal periods. ♦ Silver starts its seasonal period. ♦ The retail sector starts its strongest seasonal period.

BEST / WORST JANUARY BROAD MKTS. 2007-2016

BEST JANUARY MARKETS
- ♦ Nasdaq (2012) 8.0%
- ♦ Nikkei 225 (2013) 7.2%
- ♦ Russell 2000 (2012) 7.0%

WORST JANUARY MARKETS
- ♦ Nikkei (2008) -11.2%
- ♦ Russell 2000 (2009) -11.2%
- ♦ Nasdaq (2008) -9.9%

Index Values End of Month

	2007	2008	2009	2010	2011	2012	2013	2014	2015	2016
Dow	12,622	12,650	8,001	10,067	11,892	12,633	13,861	15,699	17,165	16,466
S&P 500	1,438	1,379	826	1,074	1,286	1,312	1,498	1,783	1,995	1,940
Nasdaq	2,464	2,390	1,476	2,147	2,700	2,814	3,142	4,104	4,635	4,614
TSX Comp.	13,034	13,155	8,695	11,094	13,552	12,452	12,685	13,695	14,674	12,822
Russell 1000	1,507	1,444	860	1,133	1,371	1,396	1,599	1,916	2,137	2,056
Russell 2000	1,989	1,773	1,102	1,496	1,942	1,970	2,242	2,811	2,896	2,573
FTSE 100	6,203	5,880	4,150	5,189	5,863	5,682	6,277	6,510	6,749	6,084
Nikkei 225	17,383	13,592	7,994	10,198	10,238	8,803	11,139	14,915	17,674	17,518

Percent Gain for January

	2007	2008	2009	2010	2011	2012	2013	2014	2015	2016
Dow	1.3	-4.6	-8.8	-3.5	2.7	3.4	5.8	-5.3	-3.7	-5.5
S&P 500	1.4	-6.1	-8.6	-3.7	2.3	4.4	5.0	-3.6	-3.1	-5.1
Nasdaq	2.0	-9.9	-6.4	-5.4	1.8	8.0	4.1	-1.7	-2.1	-7.9
TSX Comp.	1.0	-4.9	-3.3	-5.5	0.8	4.2	2.0	0.5	0.3	-1.4
Russell 1000	1.8	-6.1	-8.3	-3.7	2.3	4.8	5.3	-3.3	-2.8	-5.5
Russell 2000	1.6	-6.9	-11.2	-3.7	-0.3	7.0	6.2	-2.8	-3.3	-8.8
FTSE 100	-0.3	-8.9	-6.4	-4.1	-0.6	2.0	6.4	-3.5	2.8	-2.5
Nikkei 225	0.9	-11.2	-9.8	-3.3	0.1	4.1	7.2	-8.5	1.3	-8.0

January Market Avg. Performance 2007 to 2016[1]

- Dow -1.8%
- S&P 500 -1.7%
- Nasdaq -1.8%
- TSX Comp (CAN) -0.6%
- Russell 1000 (Lg Cap) -1.6%
- Russell 2000 (Sm Cap) -2.2%
- FTSE 100 -1.5%
- Nikkei 225 -2.7%

Interest Corner Jan[2]

	Fed Funds % [3]	3 Mo. T-Bill % [4]	10 Yr % [5]	20 Yr % [6]
2016	0.50	0.33	1.94	2.36
2015	0.25	0.02	1.68	2.04
2014	0.25	0.02	2.67	3.35
2013	0.25	0.07	2.02	2.79
2012	0.25	0.06	1.83	2.59

(1) Russell Data provided by Russell (2) Federal Reserve Bank of St. Louis- end of month values (3) Target rate set by FOMC (4)(5)(6) Constant yield maturities.

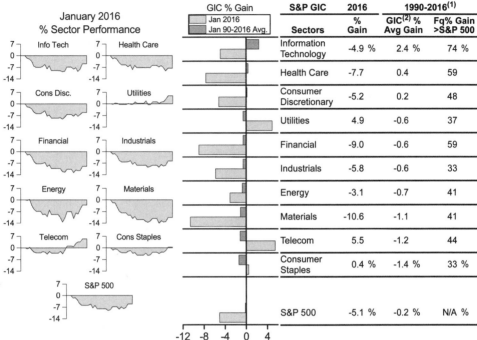

S&P GIC Sectors	2016 % Gain	1990-2016[1]	
		GIC[2] % Avg Gain	Fq% Gain >S&P 500
Information Technology	-4.9 %	2.4 %	74 %
Health Care	-7.7	0.4	59
Consumer Discretionary	-5.2	0.2	48
Utilities	4.9	-0.6	37
Financial	-9.0	-0.6	59
Industrials	-5.8	-0.6	33
Energy	-3.1	-0.7	41
Materials	-10.6	-1.1	41
Telecom	5.5	-1.2	44
Consumer Staples	0.4 %	-1.4 %	33 %
S&P 500	-5.1 %	-0.2 %	N/A %

Sector Commentary

♦ January 2016 was a weak month for the S&P 500 as it lost 5.1% Most of the major sectors in the S&P 500 were negative. The only positive sectors were three of the defensive sectors consumer staples, telecom and utilities. The utilities sector was the top performing sector as falling interest rates gave the sector an extra boost.

Sub-Sector Commentary

♦ In January 2016, the cyclical sub-sectors lost a lot of ground. ♦ The automotive and components sub-sector lost 15%, homebuilders 12.2% and metals and mining 12.1%. ♦ The biotech sub-sector was also strongly negative with a loss of 13.7%, as investors moved strongly to a risk-off mode. ♦ The U.S. banking sub-sector also had a large loss of 11.9% as investors started to anticipate that the U.S. Federal Reserve was going to further delay raising interest rates. ♦ After a negative December 2015, silver and gold produced gains as investors perceived that the precious metals were oversold in an environment of low interest rates.

SELECTED SUB-SECTORS[3]

	2016 % Gain	GIC % Avg Gain	Fq% Gain >S&P 500
Homebuilders	-12.2 %	3.6 %	68 %
SOX (1995-2016)	-7.5	3.3	55
Silver	1.9	3.0	70
Biotech (1993-2016)	-13.7	1.7	54
Gold	4.9	1.5	59
Railroads	-10.2	0.8	56
Automotive & Components	-15.0	0.5	48
Steel	-3.1	0.4	52
Pharma	-4.4	-0.1	59
Transportation	-8.8	-0.3	48
Retail	-7.2	-0.4	52
Banks	-11.9	-0.6	48
Agriculture (1994-2016)	-3.6	-0.7	39
Chemicals	-10.4	-1.0	41
Metals & Mining	-12.1	-1.5	41

(1) Sector data provided by Standard and Poors (2) GIC is short form for Global Industry Classification (3) Sub Sector data provided by Standard and Poors, except where marked by symbol.

U.S. Dollar vs. Euro – "V" Trade
①SELL SHORT (Nov17-Dec31)
②LONG (Jan1-Feb7)

The U.S. dollar tends to underperform the euro from November 17th to December 31st, and then outperform from January 1st to February 7th.

This down-and-up pattern, creates an opportunistic double-trade strategy. The first leg is a short sell trade for USD/EUR and the second leg is a long position. Both trades are contiguous and create a combination "V" shaped trade.

Most times, the transition between the trades will not take place precisely at the end of the year and technical analysis should be used to help with the appropriate timing.

88% of the time positive

What makes the "V" trade a success is that the sum of its parts is greater than the individual pieces. The first leg of the "V," represents U.S. dollar weakness. Short selling the U.S. dollar from November 17th to December 31st, during the period 1999 to 2015, has produced an average gain of 1.6% with a 59% success rate. The second leg, from January 1st to February 7th, has produced an average gain of 1.7% with a 65% success rate. Combining both legs of the trade has produced an average gain of 3.3%, but the real benefit of the combination trade is the 88% success rate, which is much higher than both individual legs by themselves.

In the first part of the "V" trade, the U.S. dollar tends to weaken at the tail end of the year as U.S. dollars flow to foreign countries at this time. The year-end outward flow is the result of two factors.

First, foreign companies repatriate their profits back to their home countries in order to settle their books.

USD/EUR vs S&P500 1999 to 2015*

Negative Short ☐   Positive Long ☐

| Year | Nov 17 to Dec 31 | | Jan 1 Feb 7 | | Compound Growth |
	S&P 500	USD/ EUR	S&P 500	USD/ EUR	USD/ EUR
1999	3.5 %	2.4 %	0.8 %	4.7 %	2.2 %
2000	-3.8	-9.1	-3.1	2.9	12.3
2001	0.8	-0.6	1.6	0.6	1.2
2002	-3.3	-3.8	-5.9	2.4	6.4
2003	5.9	-6.8	-5.7	-2.9	3.7
2004	3.1	-4.1	2.8	-0.8	3.3
2005	1.4	-1.4	-0.8	6.0	7.5
2006	1.3	-3.0	0.5	-1.1	1.8
2007	0.7	0.3	2.2	1.4	1.0
2008	3.4	-8.5	-9.0	0.8	9.4
2009	0.5	4.5	-3.8	8.1	3.3
2010	6.7	1.9	-4.4	5.3	3.4
2011	1.7	4.1	4.9	-2.1	-6.1
2012	4.9	-3.6	7.1	-2.1	1.4
2013	2.8	-2.2	5.8	-1.5	0.7
2014	0.9	3.3	-2.8	1.2	-2.1
2015	-0.5	-1.4	-0.2	6.8	8.3
Avg.	1.8 %	-1.6 %	-0.6 %	1.7 %	3.3 %
Fq>0	82 %	41 %	47 %	65 %	88 %

Second, migrants remit funds back to their home countries, an activity that happens mainly at year-end. In 2014, U.S. migrants remitted $131 billion back to their home countries versus the U.S. citizens receiving $7 billion (World Bank 2014 Annual Remittance Data). The U.S. is by far the largest net remitter compared to all other countries. Although this does not have a large impact boosting the euro, the large remittances are a factor in exerting downward pressure on the U.S. dollar.

The second part of the "V" trade, the upwards leg of the U.S. dollar outperforming the euro, occurs in the New Year as foreign companies demand U.S. dollars to enact their transactions at the start of the year.

ⓘ *Source data: Federal Reserve Bank of St. Louis. Noon buying rates in New York City for cable transfers payable in foreign currencies.*

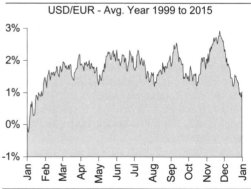

USD/EUR - Avg. Year 1999 to 2015

USD/EUR Performance

USD/EUR Monthly Performance (1999-2015)

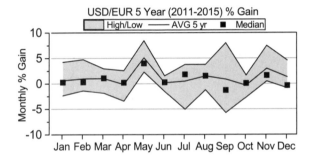

Legend: Avg % Gain | + Med % Gain

	Jan	Feb	Mar	Apr	May	Jun	Jul	Aug	Sep	Oct	Nov	Dec
Avg. % Gain	1.5	0.2	0.1	-0.5	0.8	-0.4	-0.1	0.4	-0.4	0.4	0.3	-1.3
Med. % Gain	1.5	0.1	0.2	-0.7	1.4	-0.2	0.6	-0.1	-0.6	-0.4	-0.1	-1.3
Fq %>0	65	53	59	47	65	41	59	47	41	41	41	41
Fq %>S&P 500	59	59	24	35	47	71	59	47	53	29	41	35

USD/EUR 5 Year (2011-2015) % Gain

Legend: High/Low — AVG 5 yr ■ Median

USD/EUR Performance 2015-2016

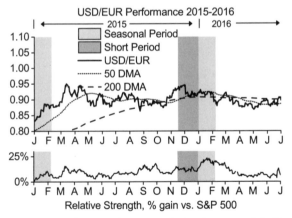

Legend: Seasonal Period | Short Period | — USD/EUR | ······ 50 DMA | – – 200 DMA

Relative Strength, % gain vs. S&P 500

The USD/EUR tends to perform poorly in the second half of November into the end of the year and then rebound at the start of the year. From 1999 to 2015, on average, the USD/EUR declined in December and then rebounded in January. On average, over the last five years, the seasonal trend of USD/EUR performing well in May (the second strongest month over the long-term) remained intact, as well as the seasonal trend of January being a stronger month than December.

In 2015, the gain on the short sell USD/EUR position at the end of the year and the gain on the long USD/EUR position at the beginning of 2016 combined together for a successful trade.

WEEK 01

Market Indices & Rates
Weekly Values**

Stock Markets	2015	2016
Dow	17,919	16,815
S&P500	2,072	1,977
Nasdaq	4,762	4,793
TSX	14,673	12,694
FTSE	6,574	6,034
DAX	9,832	10,127
Nikkei	17,590	18,096
Hang Seng	23,684	20,857

Commodities	2015	2016
Oil	53.42	34.63
Gold	1187.8	1091.8

Bond Yields	2015	2016
USA 5 Yr Treasury	1.67	1.66
USA 10 Yr T	2.18	2.19
USA 20 Yr T	2.47	2.60
Moody's Aaa	3.72	3.98
Moody's Baa	4.68	5.46
CAN 5 Yr T	1.34	0.68
CAN 10 Yr T	1.79	1.34

Money Market	2015	2016
USA Fed Funds	0.25	0.50
USA 3 Mo T-B	0.03	0.21
CAN tgt overnight rate	1.00	0.50
CAN 3 Mo T-B	0.92	0.46

Foreign Exchange	2015	2016
EUR/USD	1.21	1.08
GBP/USD	1.55	1.46
USD/CAD	1.17	1.41
USD/JPY	120.03	118.38

JANUARY

M	T	W	T	F	S	S
						1
2	3	4	5	6	7	8
9	10	11	12	13	14	15
16	17	18	19	20	21	22
23	24	25	26	27	28	29
30	31					

FEBRUARY

M	T	W	T	F	S	S
		1	2	3	4	5
6	7	8	9	10	11	12
13	14	15	16	17	18	19
20	21	22	23	24	24	26
27	28					

MARCH

M	T	W	T	F	S	S
		1	2	3	4	5
6	7	8	9	10	11	12
13	14	15	16	17	18	19
20	21	22	23	24	25	26
27	28	29	30	31		

HASBRO— Play for Gains

HAS (NEW)
①LONG (Jan21-Apr12) ②SHORT (Jun1-Jul21)
③LONG (Oct10-Nov26) ④SHORT(Nov27-Dec22)

Hasbro tends to perform well in the same time period as the retail sector from January 21st to April 12th, as it also benefits from a bounce off the weakest month of the year for retail, January.

Hasbro typically performs poorly from June 1st to July 21st as it suffers from a lack of mid-year sales. At this time of the year, investors have little interest in Hasbro as there is a lack of a strong catalyst to move the price upwards.

In autumn, Hasbro once again tends to have a strong period (October 10th to November 26th, heading into the holiday shopping season.

The busiest day of the year for Christmas holiday shopping is Black Friday in November. Average investors look to profit from the holiday shopping season by being in the retail sector, including Hasbro, in the time period leading up to Black Friday. Seasonal investors seek to enter the retail sector before the average investor, and exit around Black Friday. As a result, Hasbro has a strong seasonal period form October 10th to November 26th, and then performs poorly from November 27th to December 22nd.

HAS - stock symbol for Hasboro which trades on the NYSE, adjusted for splits.

Gain % & Fq % Positive Hasbro vs. S&P 500 1990 to 2015
Negative Short [ ]   Positive Long [ ]

Year	Jan 21 to Apr 12		Jun 1 Jul 21		Oct 10 Nov 26		Nov 27 Dec 22		Compound Growth	
	S&P 500	HAS	S&P 500	HAS	S&P 500	HAS	S&P 500	HAS	S&P 500	HAS
1990	1.5	-3.7	0.1	-21.1	3.7	17.6	4.8	3.4	10.5	32.5
1991	14.5	37.4	-1.4	-5.4	0.3	22.5	2.4	1.8	15.9	74.2
1992	-2.9	-5.6	-0.4	-3.4	6.6	10.7	2.6	-6.8	5.8	15.3
1993	3.5	-4.7	-0.7	-1.4	0.6	-5.3	0.9	-4.4	4.3	-4.6
1994	-5.8	3.6	-0.9	-10.2	-0.6	5.7	1.6	-5.4	-5.6	27.2
1995	9.1	14.5	3.8	-12.8	3.7	1.3	2.0	-1.2	19.8	32.4
1996	4.1	22.1	-4.5	-7.3	8.5	7.5	-0.9	-7.0	6.8	50.6
1997	-5.0	-2.6	7.6	0.0	-2.0	9.0	0.2	10.7	0.4	-5.1
1998	13.5	4.1	6.8	4.4	20.6	16.3	1.4	-9.7	48.2	26.9
1999	8.1	27.3	6.0	-5.4	6.0	13.6	1.4	-25.1	23.1	90.7
2000	1.5	7.2	4.2	-32.8	-4.3	-3.2	-2.7	-14.7	-1.5	58.2
2001	-11.9	-3.1	-3.6	0.0	9.5	15.6	-1.1	-5.1	-7.9	17.7
2002	-1.5	0.3	-20.6	-23.6	17.6	18.9	-1.9	-10.3	-9.7	62.6
2003	-3.7	22.6	1.6	11.1	1.9	6.2	3.3	-5.7	2.9	22.2
2004	0.6	6.4	-2.4	-6.9	5.4	1.2	2.3	-0.1	5.8	15.2
2005	1.1	5.4	3.0	5.8	6.1	6.8	0.0	-0.5	10.3	6.6
2006	2.1	-0.5	-2.4	-5.7	3.7	19.3	0.7	-0.1	4.1	25.5
2007	1.2	6.6	0.2	1.3	-10.1	-7.3	5.5	-4.4	-3.8	1.9
2008	0.6	30.1	-10.0	3.1	-2.4	-5.1	-1.8	5.6	-13.3	13.0
2009	6.4	4.0	3.9	3.8	3.7	5.0	0.7	7.8	15.3	-3.2
2010	5.1	21.2	-1.8	-2.0	2.1	4.6	5.8	4.0	11.5	24.1
2011	2.7	2.3	-0.1	-13.7	0.3	2.7	8.2	-5.8	11.3	26.4
2012	5.5	10.7	4.0	-4.5	-2.4	2.0	1.7	-6.0	8.8	25.0
2013	6.9	15.1	3.8	2.0	8.8	16.9	0.9	-2.3	21.8	34.9
2014	-1.3	3.1	2.6	-3.6	7.5	6.0	0.3	-6.6	9.2	20.6
2015	3.9	23.3	0.6	11.5	3.7	2.8	-2.4	-12.7	5.8	26.5
Avg.	2.3	9.5	0.0	-4.5	3.8	7.4	1.4	-3.9	7.7	27.6
Fq%>0	73	77	54	31	77	85	73	23	77	88

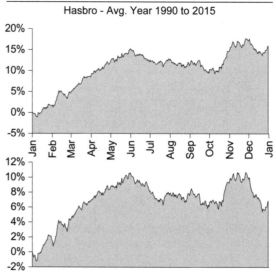

Hasbro - Avg. Year 1990 to 2015

Hasbro / S&P 500 Rel. Strength- Avg Yr. 1990-2015

Hasbro Performance

HAS Monthly Performance (1990-2015)

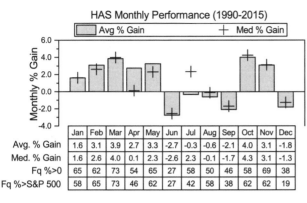

	Jan	Feb	Mar	Apr	May	Jun	Jul	Aug	Sep	Oct	Nov	Dec
Avg. % Gain	1.6	3.1	3.9	2.7	3.3	-2.7	-0.3	-0.6	-2.1	4.0	3.1	-1.8
Med. % Gain	1.6	2.6	4.0	0.1	2.3	-2.6	2.3	-0.1	-1.7	4.3	3.1	-1.3
Fq %>0	65	62	73	54	65	27	58	50	46	58	69	38
Fq %>S&P 500	58	65	73	46	62	27	42	58	38	62	62	19

HAS 5 Year (2011-2015) % Gain

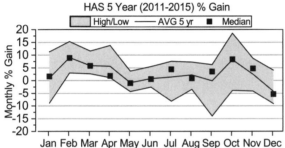

HAS Performance 2015-2016

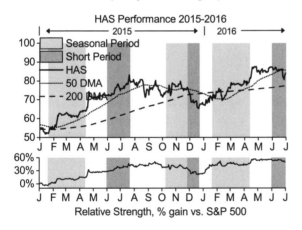

Relative Strength, % gain vs. S&P 500

Market Indices & Rates
Weekly Values**

Stock Markets	2015	2016
Dow	17,621	16,287
S&P500	2,031	1,911
Nasdaq	4,667	4,591
TSX	14,353	12,255
FTSE	6,455	5,897
DAX	9,589	9,822
Nikkei	17,108	17,331
Hang Seng	23,729	19,775

Commodities	2015	2016
Oil	48.75	30.59
Gold	1210.8	1091.3

Bond Yields	2015	2016
USA 5 Yr Treasury	1.50	1.52
USA 10 Yr T	2.00	2.10
USA 20 Yr T	2.29	2.50
Moody's Aaa	3.54	3.95
Moody's Baa	4.53	5.42
CAN 5 Yr T	1.24	0.59
CAN 10 Yr T	1.67	1.24

Money Market	2015	2016
USA Fed Funds	0.25	0.50
USA 3 Mo T-B	0.03	0.23
CAN tgt overnight rate	1.00	0.50
CAN 3 Mo T-B	0.92	0.38

Foreign Exchange	2015	2016
EUR/USD	1.19	1.09
GBP/USD	1.52	1.44
USD/CAD	1.18	1.43
USD/JPY	119.09	117.63

JANUARY

M	T	W	T	F	S	S
						1
2	3	4	5	6	7	8
9	10	11	12	13	14	15
16	17	18	19	20	21	22
23	24	25	26	27	28	29
30	31					

FEBRUARY

M	T	W	T	F	S	S
			1	2	3	4	5
6	7	8	9	10	11	12
13	14	15	16	17	18	19
20	21	22	23	24	24	26
27	28					

MARCH

M	T	W	T	F	S	S
	1	2	3	4	5
6	7	8	9	10	11	12
13	14	15	16	17	18	19
20	21	22	23	24	25	26
27	28	29	30	31		

From 1990 to 2015, March and October were on average the best months of the year for Hasbro. June, September and December were the worst months. Over the last five years, Hasbro has generally followed its long-term seasonal pattern.

In 2015 and 2016, three out of four of the seasonal periods were successful. In the June 1st to July 21st seasonal period, when Hasbro typically underperforms the S&P 500, Hasbro performed well. Nevertheless, compound growth was 27% for 2015 and 2016, versus the S&P 500 which had a return of 6%.

Silver— Shines at the Start of the Year
January 1st - March 31st

Note: The silver strategy is not new to the Thackray's Investor's Guides, as it was last included in 2013. At the time, September and November were included as seasonal periods. Although the periods do provide some seasonal value, it is nominal compared to the January 1st to March 31st period. As a result, the silver seasonal period has been adjusted to focus on the January 1st to March 31st period.

Silver is often thought of as the poor man's gold. Silver has a lot of similar properties to gold as it is a store of value and is used for jewelery and industrial purposes.

One of the major differences between silver and gold is the proportion of production that is used for industrial purposes. A very small amount of gold is used in industrial products due to its price. In comparison, a large portion of silver's production is used for industrial products because of its relatively low price.

6.8% gain &
positive 76% of the time

Silver - Avg. Year 1984 to 2015

Silver / S&P 500 Rel. Str. - Avg Yr. 1984 - 2015

Silver* vs. S&P 500 1984 to 2016			
Jan 1 to Mar 31	S&P 500	Silver	Positive Diff
1984	-3.5%	8.3%	11.8%
1985	8.0	5.9	-2.1
1986	13.1	-3.2	-16.2
1987	20.5	19.4	-1.1
1988	4.8	0.8	-4.0
1989	6.2	-4.7	-10.9
1990	-3.8	-4.8	-1.0
1991	13.6	-8.5	-22.1
1992	-3.2	6.7	10.0
1993	3.7	6.0	2.4
1994	-4.4	12.1	16.6
1995	9.0	6.4	-2.6
1996	4.8	7.3	2.5
1997	2.2	6.9	4.7
1998	13.5	5.8	-7.7
1999	4.7	0.4	-4.3
2000	2.0	-7.4	-9.4
2001	-12.1	-5.4	6.8
2002	-0.1	3.4	3.5
2003	-3.6	-4.4	-0.8
2004	1.3	31.2	29.9
2005	-2.6	5.5	8.1
2006	3.7	33.1	29.4
2007	0.2	3.5	3.3
2008	-9.9	21.9	31.8
2009	-11.7	21.5	33.2
2010	4.9	3.0	-1.9
2011	5.4	23.6	18.2
2012	12.0	15.1	3.1
2013	10.0	-4.4	-14.4
2014	1.3	2.4	1.1
2015	0.4	3.9	3.5
2016	0.8	11.3	10.5
Avg	2.8%	6.8%	4.0%
Fq > 0	70%	76%	58%

well from late January into May, which helps to drive up the price of silver because of its industrial properties. The period of seasonal strength for silver does not last as long as the period of seasonal strength for base metals, as typically gold's poor performance in late spring helps to drag the price of silver lower.

Gold and silver have a high degree of price correlation, with silver typically mirroring the direction of gold's price changes. When gold increases in price, silver typically increases in price and vice versa. Despite this relationship, the seasonal profiles for gold and silver are different. Base metals tend to perform

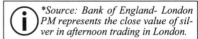

Source: Bank of England- London PM represents the close value of silver in afternoon trading in London.

Silver Performance

Silver Monthly Performance (1984-2015)

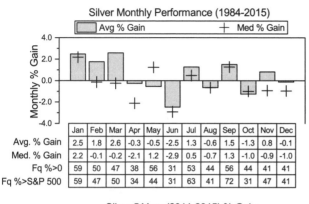

	Jan	Feb	Mar	Apr	May	Jun	Jul	Aug	Sep	Oct	Nov	Dec
Avg. % Gain	2.5	1.8	2.6	-0.3	-0.5	-2.5	1.3	-0.6	1.5	-1.3	0.8	-0.1
Med. % Gain	2.2	-0.1	-0.2	-2.1	1.2	-2.9	0.5	-0.7	1.3	-1.0	-0.9	-1.0
Fq %>0	59	50	47	38	56	31	53	44	56	44	41	41
Fq %>S&P 500	59	47	50	34	44	31	63	41	72	31	47	41

Silver 5 Year (2011-2015) % Gain

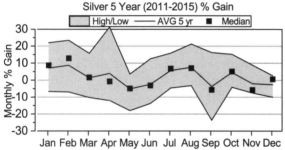

Silver Performance 2015-2016

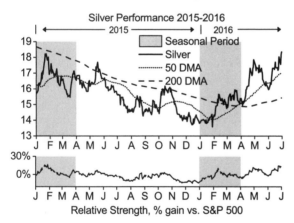

Relative Strength, % gain vs. S&P 500

Market Indices & Rates
Weekly Values**

Stock Markets	2015	2016
Dow	17,503	15,940
S&P500	2,015	1,879
Nasdaq	4,634	4,503
TSX	14,178	12,043
FTSE	6,496	5,801
DAX	9,948	9,583
Nikkei	16,964	16,679
Hang Seng	24,162	19,076

Commodities	2015	2016
Oil	47.08	28.57
Gold	1245.9	1094.0

Bond Yields	2015	2016
USA 5 Yr Treasury	1.32	1.47
USA 10 Yr T	1.86	2.04
USA 20 Yr T	2.19	2.44
Moody's Aaa	3.46	4.03
Moody's Baa	4.45	5.45
CAN 5 Yr T	1.11	0.66
CAN 10 Yr T	1.56	1.22

Money Market	2015	2016
USA Fed Funds	0.25	0.50
USA 3 Mo T-B	0.03	0.28
CAN tgt overnight rate	1.00	0.50
CAN 3 Mo T-B	0.91	0.38

Foreign Exchange	2015	2016
EUR/USD	1.17	1.09
GBP/USD	1.52	1.42
USD/CAD	1.20	1.44
USD/JPY	117.46	117.68

JANUARY

M	T	W	T	F	S	S
						1
2	3	4	5	6	7	8
9	10	11	12	13	14	15
16	17	18	19	20	21	22
23	24	25	26	27	28	29
30	31					

FEBRUARY

M	T	W	T	F	S	S
	1	2	3	4	5
6	7	8	9	10	11	12
13	14	15	16	17	18	19
20	21	22	23	24	24	26
27	28					

MARCH

M	T	W	T	F	S	S
	1	2	3	4	5
6	7	8	9	10	11	12
13	14	15	16	17	18	19
20	21	22	23	24	25	26
27	28	29	30	31		

From 1984 to 2015, January, February and March have on average been the strongest months of the year for silver. However, only January is a top ranked month on a median basis. The medians for February and March are negative. In other words, some large returns have skewed the average upwards in February and March. Over the same time period, the weakest month of the year has been June.

From 2011 to 2015 the general seasonal trend has held up, as January and February have been the strongest months and June one of the weakest months. In both 2015 and 2016, silver was positive, with the 2016 rally extending out into July.

TJX COMPANIES INC.
January 22nd to March 30th

In 2016, TJX during its seasonally strong period, out-performed the retail sector and outperformed the S&P 500. Over the long-term, TJX has typically outperformed the retail sector when the sector has been positive, making it an excellent complement to a retail sector investment during its seasonal period.

TJX is an off-price apparel and home fashion retailer that typically reports its fourth quarter earnings in approximately the third week of February. The company, like the retail sector, benefits from investors expecting positive results from the Christmas season.

TJX's period of seasonal strength is similar to the seasonal period for the retail sector. The best time to invest in TJX has been from January 22nd to March 30th. From 1990 to 2016, investing in this period has produced an average gain of 12.6%, which is substantially better than the average 2.1% performance of the S&P 500. It is also important to note that the TJX has been positive 74% of the time during this period.

12.6% gain &
positive 74% of the time

Equally impressive is the amount of times TJX has produced a large gain, versus a large loss in its seasonal period. In the last twenty-seven years, TJX has only had one loss of 10% or greater. In the same time period, TJX has had thirteen gains of 10% or greater.

TJX* vs. Retail vs. S&P 500 1990 to 2016			
			Positive
Jan 22 to Mar 30	S&P 500	Retail	TJX
1990	0.2%	6.3%	6.7%
1991	13.3	21.7	61.9
1992	-2.3	1.7	17.0
1993	3.8	3.0	21.7
1994	-6.1	-0.1	-2.8
1995	8.1	9.7	-6.9
1996	5.5	19.7	43.6
1997	-1.1	10.4	-0.3
1998	12.6	19.7	25.4
1999	5.3	16.5	18.9
2000	3.2	5.1	35.4
2001	-13.6	1.7	16.4
2002	1.8	4.7	2.9
2003	-2.7	6.6	-6.7
2004	-1.8	5.4	3.5
2005	1.2	-0.6	-1.6
2006	3.1	4.5	3.8
2007	-0.7	-2.7	-10.2
2008	-0.8	1.4	13.1
2009	-6.3	8.1	29.0
2010	5.1	12.5	17.2
2011	3.5	3.5	6.1
2012	7.1	12.9	19.3
2013	5.6	6.2	4.5
2014	0.8	-2.7	-0.2
2015	2.7	12.5	6.8
2016	10.4	10.9	16.0
Avg	2.1%	7.3%	12.6%
Fq > 0	67%	85%	74%

It is interesting to note that the seasonally strong period for TJX ends before April, one of the strongest months of the year for the stock market. It is possible that by the end of March, after a typically strong run for TJX, the full value of TJX's first quarter earnings report has already been priced into the stock and investors look to other companies in which to invest. This is particularly true if the economy and the stock market are in good shape.

On the other hand, in a soft economy, consumers favor off-price apparel companies such as TJX. In this scenario, TJX is more likely to perform strongly past the end of its seasonal period in March, allowing seasonal investors to continue holding TJX until it starts to show signs of weakness.

TJX - Avg. Year 1990 to 2015

TJX / S&P 500 Relative Strength - Avg Yr. 1990 - 2015

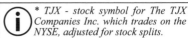
* TJX - stock symbol for The TJX Companies Inc. which trades on the NYSE, adjusted for stock splits.

TJX Performance

TJX Monthly Performance (1990-2015)

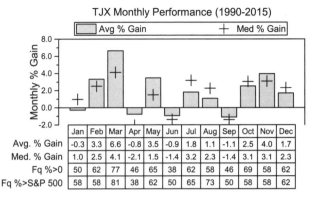

	Jan	Feb	Mar	Apr	May	Jun	Jul	Aug	Sep	Oct	Nov	Dec
Avg. % Gain	-0.3	3.3	6.6	-0.8	3.5	-0.9	1.8	1.1	-1.1	2.5	4.0	1.7
Med. % Gain	1.0	2.5	4.1	-2.1	1.5	-1.4	3.2	2.3	-1.4	3.1	3.1	2.3
Fq %>0	50	62	77	46	65	38	62	58	46	69	58	62
Fq %>S&P 500	58	58	81	38	62	50	65	73	50	58	58	62

TJX 5 Year (2011-2015) % Gain

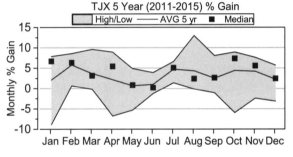

TJX Performance 2015-2016

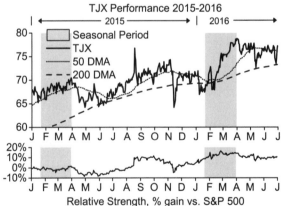

Relative Strength, % gain vs. S&P 500

Market Indices & Rates
Weekly Values**

Stock Markets	2015	2016
Dow	17,639	16,107
S&P500	2,042	1,899
Nasdaq	4,708	4,535
TSX	14,545	12,453
FTSE	6,713	5,959
DAX	10,377	9,775
Nikkei	17,300	17,109
Hang Seng	24,283	19,226

Commodities	2015	2016
Oil	46.22	31.80
Gold	1289.3	1112.5

Bond Yields	2015	2016
USA 5 Yr Treasury	1.35	1.42
USA 10 Yr T	1.85	2.00
USA 20 Yr T	2.17	2.40
Moody's Aaa	3.45	4.05
Moody's Baa	4.45	5.46
CAN 5 Yr T	0.93	0.69
CAN 10 Yr T	1.46	1.24

Money Market	2015	2016
USA Fed Funds	0.25	0.50
USA 3 Mo T-B	0.03	0.32
CAN tgt overnight rate	0.75	0.50
CAN 3 Mo T-B	0.73	0.47

Foreign Exchange	2015	2016
EUR/USD	1.15	1.09
GBP/USD	1.51	1.43
USD/CAD	1.22	1.41
USD/JPY	118.12	119.07

JANUARY

M	T	W	T	F	S	S
						1
2	3	4	5	6	7	8
9	10	11	12	13	14	15
16	17	18	19	20	21	22
23	24	25	26	27	28	29
30	31					

FEBRUARY

M	T	W	T	F	S	S
	1	2	3	4	5
6	7	8	9	10	11	12
13	14	15	16	17	18	19
20	21	22	23	24	24	26
27	28					

MARCH

M	T	W	T	F	S	S
	1	2	3	4	5
6	7	8	9	10	11	12
13	14	15	16	17	18	19
20	21	22	23	24	25	26
27	28	29	30	31		

From 1990 to 2015, March has been the best month for TJX on an average, median and frequency basis. March is the core part of the seasonal period for TJX, which lasts from January 22nd to March 30th. The seasonal trade falls off sharply in April and investors should consider exiting early if weakness is evident. Over the last five years, March has been an average month for TJX.

In 2016, TJX started by performing well in its seasonal period, but by the end of its seasonal period, TJX started to underperform the S&P 500.

ROYAL BANK— A TRADE TO BANK ON
①Oct10-Nov28　②Jan23-Apr13

Canadians love their banks and tend to hold large amounts of the bank stocks in their portfolios. Their love for the sector has remained strong, as international accolades have supported a positive viewpoint of Canadian banks. In a 2012 Bloomberg report, the Canadian banks dominated the top ten strongest banks in the world, with four banks in the top ten.

For years, Royal Bank was considered one of the most conservative banks and often attracted investors during tough times. After a few mis-steps in their expansion into the U.S., Royal Bank seems to be getting back on track.

Through its ups and downs, Royal Bank has followed the same general pattern as the banking sector: rising in autumn and then once again in the new year.

11.9% gain & positive 78% of the time

In the period from October 10th to November 28th, from 1989 to 2015, Royal Bank has produced an average gain of 5.0% and has been positive 89% of the time. The bank tends to perform well at this time, as Canadians tend to increase their bank holdings before the year-end earnings reports are released in late November. It is not a coincidence that Royal Bank's seasonally strong period ends at approximately the same time as their year-end earnings announcements. Seasonal investors benefit from buying Royal Bank before the "masses," whom are also trying to take advantage of the possibility of positive earnings.

In the second seasonal period from January 23rd to April 13, Canadian banks tend to outperform the TSX Composite, as they benefit from the typically strong economic forecasts at the beginning of the year. In addition, they "echo," or get a boost from the strong seasonal performance of the U.S banks at this time.

Royal Bank* vs. TSX Comp 1989/90 to 2015/16 Positive

Year	Oct 10 to Nov 28 TSX Comp	RY	Jan 23 to Apr 13 TSX Comp	RY	Compound Growth TSX Comp	RY
1989/90	-2.8%	2.4%	-6.3%	-10.0%	-8.9%	-7.8%
1990/91	0.2	3.5	9.8	11.6	10.0	15.5
1991/92	2.9	3.3	-6.8	-14.5	-4.1	-11.6
1992/93	1.8	5.0	10.7	17.6	12.6	23.4
1993/94	3.8	0.0	-5.6	-13.1	-2.1	-13.1
1994/95	-4.7	2.2	5.0	13.2	0.0	15.7
1995/96	4.0	3.3	3.6	0.0	7.7	3.3
1996/97	10.7	23.3	-6.2	1.3	3.9	24.9
1997/98	-8.7	7.6	19.9	24.0	9.4	33.4
1998/99	18.0	20.9	4.8	0.6	23.7	21.6
1999/00	10.9	8.6	3.8	34.5	15.1	46.0
2000/01	-14.5	5.1	-14.1	-12.0	-26.5	-7.5
2001/02	7.1	3.2	2.3	11.8	9.6	15.4
2002/03	16.4	18.1	-4.3	1.8	11.4	20.2
2003/04	3.4	0.3	2.0	1.8	5.4	2.1
2004/05	2.8	4.0	4.5	17.6	7.3	22.3
2005/06	3.1	7.3	5.5	7.0	8.8	14.8
2006/07	7.2	8.5	6.9	7.1	14.5	16.2
2007/08	-4.4	-5.1	8.2	-4.9	3.5	-9.8
2008/09	-3.4	4.3	9.4	35.0	5.7	40.8
2009/10	0.2	1.3	6.7	12.6	6.9	14.1
2010/11	2.9	0.4	4.3	12.4	7.3	12.8
2011/12	0.5	-6.3	-2.9	3.8	-2.4	-2.8
2012/13	-1.1	2.1	-3.8	-0.3	-4.8	1.9
2013/14	5.0	6.0	1.9	-0.5	7.1	5.5
2014/15	2.0	3.0	4.2	7.3	6.2	10.5
2015/16	-4.3	1.8	10.4	10.7	5.6	12.7
Avg.	2.2%	5.0%	2.7%	6.5%	4.9%	11.9%
Fq > 0	70%	89%	70%	70%	78%	78%

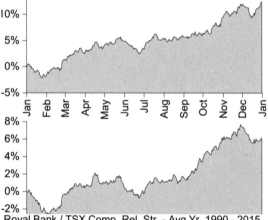

Royal Bank* Avg. Year 1990 to 2015

Royal Bank / TSX Comp. Rel. Str. - Avg Yr. 1990 - 2015

Ⓨ *Alternate Strategy—*
Investors can bridge the gap between the two positive seasonal trends for Royal Bank by holding from October 10th to April 13th. Longer term investors may prefer this strategy, shorter term investors can use technical tools to determine the appropriate strategy.

ⓘ *Royal Bank of Canada (RBC) is a diversified financial services company that trades on both the Toronto and NYSE exchanges under the symbol RY. Data from TSX Exchange, includes stock splits only.*

Royal Bank Performance

RY Monthly Performance (1990-2015)

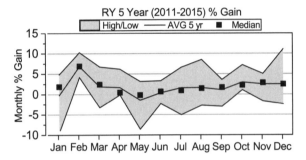

	Jan	Feb	Mar	Apr	May	Jun	Jul	Aug	Sep	Oct	Nov	Dec
Avg. % Gain	-1.9	3.3	1.3	1.3	1.1	-1.5	2.1	0.0	0.1	3.1	1.9	0.5
Med. % Gain	-1.8	4.3	1.2	0.8	1.0	-0.7	2.9	1.2	0.7	1.9	1.6	0.7
Fq %>0	38	73	58	69	62	38	77	62	54	77	69	54
Fq %>S&P 500	35	69	65	65	38	46	62	50	58	58	65	38

RY 5 Year (2011-2015) % Gain

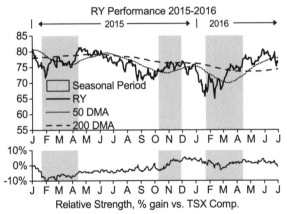

RY Performance 2015-2016

Relative Strength, % gain vs. TSX Comp.

WEEK 05

Market Indices & Rates
Weekly Values**

Stock Markets	2015	2016
Dow	17,368	16,312
S&P500	2,021	1,910
Nasdaq	4,682	4,503
TSX	14,709	12,650
FTSE	6,810	5,913
DAX	10,714	9,491
Nikkei	17,663	17,334
Hang Seng	24,736	19,301

Commodities	2015	2016
Oil	45.72	31.28
Gold	1277.4	1138.7

Bond Yields	2015	2016
USA 5 Yr Treasury	1.28	1.29
USA 10 Yr T	1.77	1.89
USA 20 Yr T	2.10	2.30
Moody's Aaa	3.36	4.03
Moody's Baa	4.36	5.40
CAN 5 Yr T	0.71	0.61
CAN 10 Yr T	1.37	1.16

Money Market	2015	2016
USA Fed Funds	0.25	0.50
USA 3 Mo T-B	0.02	0.33
CAN tgt overnight rate	0.75	0.50
CAN 3 Mo T-B	0.60	0.45

Foreign Exchange	2015	2016
EUR/USD	1.13	1.11
GBP/USD	1.51	1.45
USD/CAD	1.26	1.39
USD/JPY	117.93	118.50

JANUARY

M	T	W	T	F	S	S
						1
2	3	4	5	6	7	8
9	10	11	12	13	14	15
16	17	18	19	20	21	22
23	24	25	26	27	28	29
30	31					

FEBRUARY

M	T	W	T	F	S	S
		1	2	3	4	5
6	7	8	9	10	11	12
13	14	15	16	17	18	19
20	21	22	23	24	24	26
27	28					

From 1990 to 2015, February has been the best month for Royal Bank on an average and median basis and January has been the worst month. Given that the second leg of the seasonal strategy starts in late January, investors should use technical analysis in choosing the best entry date for Royal Bank at this time.

Over the last five years, on average, Royal Bank has followed its general seasonal trend with February being the strongest month of the year and May being the weakest month.

MARCH

M	T	W	T	F	S	S
	1	2	3	4	5	
6	7	8	9	10	11	12
13	14	15	16	17	18	19
20	21	22	23	24	25	26
27	28	29	30	31		

In the 2015 October to November seasonal period, Royal Bank outperformed the TSX Composite and then declined, only to outperform once again in its January to April seasonal period.

FEBRUARY

	MONDAY	TUESDAY	WEDNESDAY
WEEK 05	30	31	**1** 27
WEEK 06	**6** 22	**7** 21	**8** 20
WEEK 07	**13** 15	**14** 14	**15** 13
WEEK 08	**20** 8 CAN Market Closed - Family Day USA Market Closed - Presidents' Day	**21** 7	**22** 6
WEEK 09	**27** 1	**28**	1

THURSDAY		FRIDAY	
2	26	**3**	25
9	19	**10**	18
16	12	**17**	11
23	5	**24**	4
2		3	

MARCH

M	T	W	T	F	S	S
		1	2	3	4	5
6	7	8	9	10	11	12
13	14	15	16	17	18	19
20	21	22	23	24	25	26
27	28	29	30	31		

APRIL

M	T	W	T	F	S	S
					1	2
3	4	5	6	7	8	9
10	11	12	13	14	15	16
17	18	19	20	21	22	23
24	25	26	27	28	29	30

MAY

M	T	W	T	F	S	S
1	2	3	4	5	6	7
8	9	10	11	12	13	14
15	16	17	18	19	20	21
22	23	24	25	26	27	28
29	30	31				

JUNE

M	T	W	T	F	S	S
			1	2	3	4
5	6	7	8	9	10	11
12	13	14	15	16	17	18
19	20	21	22	23	24	25
26	27	28	29	30		

FEBRUARY
SUMMARY

S&P500 Cumulative Daily Gains for Avg Month 1950 to 2016

	Dow Jones	S&P 500	Nasdaq	TSX Comp
Month Rank	8	9	9	4
# Up	38	37	24	19
# Down	28	29	20	12
% Pos	58	56	55	61
% Avg. Gain	0.3	0.1	0.7	1.1

Dow & S&P 1950-2015, Nasdaq 1972-2015, TSX 1985-2015

♦ Historically over the long-term, February has been one of the weaker months of the year for the S&P 500. Initially, in February 2016, the stock market continued its January correction but managed to find a bottom mid-month. ♦ Small caps tend to outperform in February. ♦ The energy sector typically starts to outperform in late February, which helps to boost the S&P/ TSX Composite. ♦ The consumer discretionary sector tends to be one of the better performing sectors.

BEST / WORST FEBRUARY BROAD MKTS. 2007-2016

BEST FEBRUARY MARKETS
- ♦ Nikkei 225 (2012) 10.5%
- ♦ Nasdaq (2015) 7.1%
- ♦ Nikkei (2015) 6.4%

WORST FEBRUARY MARKETS
- ♦ Russell 2000 (2009) -12.3%
- ♦ Dow (2009) -11.7%
- ♦ S&P 500 (2009) -11.0%

Index Values End of Month

	2007	2008	2009	2010	2011	2012	2013	2014	2015	2016
Dow	12,269	12,266	7,063	10,325	12,226	12,952	14,054	16,322	18,133	16,517
S&P 500	1,407	1,331	735	1,104	1,327	1,366	1,515	1,859	2,105	1,932
Nasdaq	2,416	2,271	1,378	2,238	2,782	2,967	3,160	4,308	4,964	4,558
TSX Comp.	13,045	13,583	8,123	11,630	14,137	12,644	12,822	14,210	15,234	12,860
Russell 1000	1,478	1,396	768	1,168	1,415	1,454	1,617	2,002	2,256	2,050
Russell 2000	1,972	1,705	967	1,562	2,046	2,015	2,264	2,940	3,065	2,570
FTSE 100	6,172	5,884	3,830	5,355	5,994	5,872	6,361	6,810	6,947	6,097
Nikkei 225	17,604	13,603	7,568	10,126	10,624	9,723	11,559	14,841	18,798	16,027

Percent Gain for February

	2007	2008	2009	2010	2011	2012	2013	2014	2015	2016
Dow	-2.8	-3.0	-11.7	2.6	2.8	2.5	1.4	4.0	5.6	0.3
S&P 500	-2.2	-3.5	-11.0	2.9	3.2	4.1	1.1	4.3	5.5	-0.4
Nasdaq	-1.9	-5.0	-6.7	4.2	3.0	5.4	0.6	5.0	7.1	-1.2
TSX Comp.	0.1	3.3	-6.6	4.8	4.3	1.5	1.1	3.8	3.8	0.3
Russell 1000	-1.9	-3.3	-10.7	3.1	3.3	4.1	1.1	4.5	5.5	-0.3
Russell 2000	-0.9	-3.8	-12.3	4.4	5.4	2.3	1.0	4.6	5.8	-0.1
FTSE 100	-0.5	0.1	-7.7	3.2	2.2	3.3	1.3	4.6	2.9	0.2
Nikkei 225	1.3	0.1	-5.3	-0.7	3.8	10.5	3.8	-0.5	6.4	-8.5

February Market Avg. Performance 2007 to 2016[1]

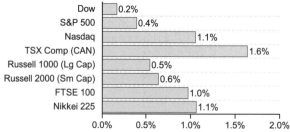

Dow	0.2%
S&P 500	0.4%
Nasdaq	1.1%
TSX Comp (CAN)	1.6%
Russell 1000 (Lg Cap)	0.5%
Russell 2000 (Sm Cap)	0.6%
FTSE 100	1.0%
Nikkei 225	1.1%

Interest Corner Feb[2]

	Fed Funds %[3]	3 Mo. T-Bill %[4]	10 Yr %[5]	20 Yr %[6]
2016	0.50	0.33	1.74	2.19
2015	0.25	0.02	2.00	2.38
2014	0.25	0.05	2.66	3.31
2013	0.25	0.11	1.89	2.71
2012	0.25	0.08	1.98	2.73

(1) Russell Data provided by Russell (2) Federal Reserve Bank of St. Louis- end of month values (3) Target rate set by FOMC (4)(5)(6) Constant yield maturities.

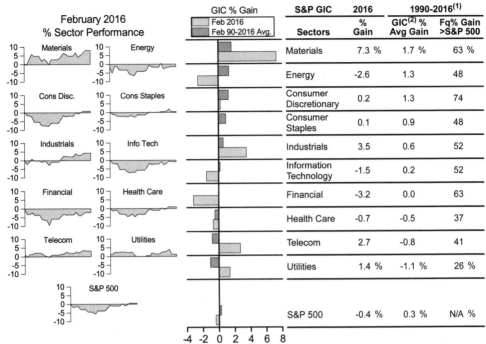

| S&P GIC | 2016 | 1990-2016[1] | |
Sectors	% Gain	GIC[2] % Avg Gain	Fq% Gain >S&P 500
Materials	7.3 %	1.7 %	63 %
Energy	-2.6	1.3	48
Consumer Discretionary	0.2	1.3	74
Consumer Staples	0.1	0.9	48
Industrials	3.5	0.6	52
Information Technology	-1.5	0.2	52
Financial	-3.2	0.0	63
Health Care	-0.7	-0.5	37
Telecom	2.7	-0.8	41
Utilities	1.4 %	-1.1 %	26 %
S&P 500	-0.4 %	0.3 %	N/A %

February 2016 % Sector Performance

GIC % Gain — Feb 2016 / Feb 90-2016 Avg.

Sector Commentary

♦ In February 2016, the cyclical sectors led the stock market. ♦ The materials sector was the best performing sector with a gain of 7.3%. ♦ Despite the strong performance of the cyclical sectors, the defensive consumer staples, telecom and utilities sectors all produced positive performances. ♦ The expectation that the U.S. Federal Reserve would delay increasing interest rates due to weak economic growth helped to push both the cyclical sectors and interest rate sectors into positive territory.

Sub-Sector Commentary

♦ In February 2016, the strong seasonal sub-sectors that typically perform well, generally outperformed the weaker seasonal sub-sectors. ♦ Metals and mining roared ahead as gold and silver miners sky-rocketed (not shown in table). Gold miners, silver miners and precious metals and minerals make up approximately one-quarter of the metals and mining sector. ♦ U.S. banks declined as investors anticipated that the U.S. Federal Reserve would hold off on raising interest rates due to slow economic growth and a volatile stock market.

SELECTED SUB-SECTORS[3]			
SOX (1995-2016)	1.4 %	2.9 %	64 %
Silver	4.8	2.6	52
Metals & Mining	23.7	2.2	56
Retail	-0.1	2.0	74
Chemicals	5.6	1.8	74
Gold	11.1	1.2	48
Automotive & Components	3.0	0.7	48
Steel	0.7	0.7	52
Agriculture (1994-2016)	-1.1	0.7	48
Transportation	7.1	0.7	56
Railroads	7.9	0.5	48
Homebuilders	-0.7	0.4	63
Banks	-6.9	0.1	56
Pharma	-1.8	-0.6	37
Biotech (1993-2016)	-1.9	-1.0	50

RETAIL – POST HOLIDAY BARGAIN
SHOP Jan 21st and RETURN Your Investment Apr 12th

Historically, the retail sector has outperformed from January 21st until April 12th. From 1990 to 2016, during its seasonally strong period, the retail sector produced an average gain of 5.9%, compared with the S&P 500's average gain of 2.6%. Not only has the retail sector had greater gains than the broad market, but it has also outperformed it on a fairly regular basis: 78% of the time.

5.9% extra & 78% of the time
better than the S&P 500

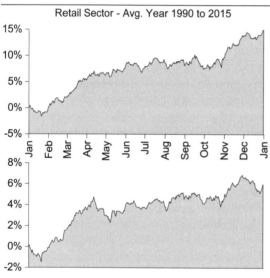

Retail Sector vs.
S&P 500 1990 to 2016

Jan 21 to Apr 12	S&P 500	Positive Retail	Diff
1990	1.5 %	9.7 %	8.1 %
1991	14.5	29.9	15.4
1992	-2.9	-2.7	0.2
1993	3.5	-0.6	-4.0
1994	-5.8	2.0	7.8
1995	9.1	7.4	-1.8
1996	4.1	19.7	15.7
1997	-5.0	6.0	11.0
1998	13.5	20.1	6.6
1999	8.1	23.4	15.2
2000	1.5	5.8	4.3
2001	-11.8	-0.5	11.3
2002	-1.5	6.7	8.2
2003	-3.7	6.5	10.3
2004	0.6	6.7	6.1
2005	1.1	-1.6	-2.7
2006	2.1	3.4	1.3
2007	1.2	-0.7	-1.9
2008	0.6	3.5	3.0
2009	6.4	25.1	18.7
2010	5.1	15.5	10.4
2011	2.7	4.4	1.7
2012	5.5	12.1	6.6
2013	6.9	10.1	3.2
2014	-1.3	-7.1	-5.8
2015	3.9	15.5	11.5
2016	10.9	9.7	-1.2
Avg.	2.6 %	8.5 %	5.9 %
Fq > 0	74 %	78 %	78 %

Retail Sector - Avg. Year 1990 to 2015

Retail / S&P 500 Relative Strength - Avg Yr. 1990 - 2015

Most investors think that the best time to invest in retail stocks is before Black Friday in November. Yes, there is a positive seasonal cycle at this time, but it is not as strong as the cycle from January to April.

The worst month for retail sales is January. Consumers are all shopped out from the holiday season. Investors start becoming attracted to the sector as the prospect of increasing spring sales unfolds. Seasonal investors enter the sector ahead of other investors in late January to take advantage of the increasing interest in the sector that unfolds over the next two to three months.

The January retail bounce coincides with the "rosy" stock market analysts' forecasts that tend to occur at the beginning of the year. These forecasts generally rely on healthy consumer spending which makes up approximately 2/3 of the GDP. The retail sector benefits from the optimistic forecasts and tends to outperform the S&P 500.

From a seasonal basis, investors have been best served by exiting the retail sector in April and then returning to it later, at the end of October (see *Retail Shop Early* strategy).

Retail SP GIC Sector # 2550:
An index designed to represent a cross section of retail companies
For more information on the retail sector, see www.standardandpoors.com.

Retail Performance

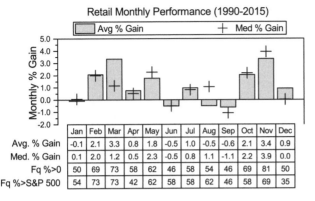

Retail Monthly Performance (1990-2015)

Avg % Gain | Med % Gain

	Jan	Feb	Mar	Apr	May	Jun	Jul	Aug	Sep	Oct	Nov	Dec
Avg. % Gain	-0.1	2.1	3.3	0.8	1.8	-0.5	1.0	-0.5	-0.6	2.1	3.4	0.9
Med. % Gain	0.1	2.0	1.2	0.5	2.3	-0.5	0.8	1.1	-1.1	2.2	3.9	0.0
Fq %>0	50	69	73	58	62	46	58	54	46	69	81	50
Fq %>S&P 500	54	73	73	42	62	58	58	62	46	58	69	35

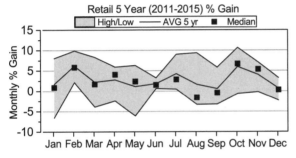

Retail 5 Year (2011-2015) % Gain

High/Low — AVG 5 yr ■ Median

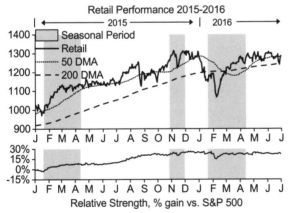

Retail Performance 2015-2016

2015 — 2016
Seasonal Period
Retail
50 DMA
200 DMA

Relative Strength, % gain vs. S&P 500

From 1990 to 2015, the two best months of the year for the retail sector were March and November. November is the core part of the autumn retail seasonal trade and March is the core part of the spring retail seasonal trade.

On average over the last five years, from 2011 to 2015, the retail sector has followed its general seasonal pattern with the strongest months being February, April, October and November. These months are part of either the spring seasonal trade or the autumn seasonal trade. In 2016, the retail sector marginally underperformed the S&P 500 in its spring seasonal period.

Market Indices & Rates
Weekly Values**

Stock Markets	2015	2016
Dow	17,682	15,918
S&P500	2,046	1,850
Nasdaq	4,726	4,288
TSX	15,034	12,294
FTSE	6,847	5,648
DAX	10,876	8,919
Nikkei	17,545	15,939
Hang Seng	24,633	18,433

Commodities	2015	2016
Oil	50.65	28.15
Gold	1261.1	1211.0

Bond Yields	2015	2016
USA 5 Yr Treasury	1.31	1.15
USA 10 Yr T	1.81	1.71
USA 20 Yr T	2.18	2.13
Moody's Aaa	3.42	3.92
Moody's Baa	4.41	5.29
CAN 5 Yr T	0.67	0.52
CAN 10 Yr T	1.33	1.05

Money Market	2015	2016
USA Fed Funds	0.25	0.50
USA 3 Mo T-B	0.02	0.30
CAN tgt overnight rate	0.75	0.50
CAN 3 Mo T-B	0.55	0.45

Foreign Exchange	2015	2016
EUR/USD	1.14	1.13
GBP/USD	1.52	1.45
USD/CAD	1.25	1.39
USD/JPY	117.81	114.00

FEBRUARY

M	T	W	T	F	S	S
		1	2	3	4	5
6	7	8	9	10	11	12
13	14	15	16	17	18	19
20	21	22	23	24	24	26
27	28					

MARCH

M	T	W	T	F	S	S
		1	2	3	4	5
6	7	8	9	10	11	12
13	14	15	16	17	18	19
20	21	22	23	24	25	26
27	28	29	30	31		

APRIL

M	T	W	T	F	S	S
					1	2
3	4	5	6	7	8	9
10	11	12	13	14	15	16
17	18	19	20	21	22	23
24	25	26	27	28	29	30

EASTMAN CHEMICAL COMPANY

①LONG (Jan28-May5)
②SELL SHORT (May30-Oct27)

In 2015, Eastman Chemical performed according to its seasonal trends, outperforming from January 28th to May 5th and underperforming from May 30th to October 27th. So far in 2016, Eastman Chemical has once again outperformed in its positive seasonal leg.

In its positive seasonal period from January 28th to May 5th, Eastman Chemical during the period from 1994 to 2015, has produced an average 13.2% gain and has been positive 86% of the time. In its short sell seasonal period from May 30th to October 27th, in the same yearly period, Eastman Chemical has produced an average loss of 6.2% and has been positive 36% of the time. The short sell seasonal period has not been as successful as the long seasonal period, especially in recent years. Nevertheless, investors should still be aware of the weaker period for Eastman Chemical in the summer months.

20.3% growth & positive 73% of the time

Eastman Chemical, in its 10-K report filed with regulators in 2013, outlines the seasonal trends in its business. "The Company's earnings are typically greater in second and third quarters." This is a bit different than many other cyclical companies, that tend to have weaker earnings over the summer months. The net result is for Eastman Chemical to outperform into May and then underperform at the tail end of Q2, and Q3, as investors anticipate a weaker Q4 earnings report. In Q4, Eastman tends to perform at market.

ⓘ *Eastman Chemical Company manufactures and sells chemicals, fibers, and plastics, globally. Its stock symbol is EMN. which trades on the NYSE, adjusted for splits.*

Eastman Chemical* vs. S&P 500 1994 to 2015

Positive Long ☐   Negative Short ☐

Year	Jan 28 to May 5 S&P 500	Jan 28 to May 5 EMN	May 30 to Oct 27 S&P 500	May 30 to Oct 27 EMN	Compound Growth S&P 500	Compound Growth EMN
1994	-5.4	7.8 %	1.9 %	8.7 %	-3.6 %	-1.6 %
1995	10.6	11.0	10.7	2.6	22.4	8.2
1996	3.2	7.1	4.9	-21.8	8.3	30.5
1997	8.5	-1.1	3.9	2.7	12.8	-3.8
1998	15.1	18.7	-2.3	-15.3	12.4	36.8
1999	8.4	32.1	-0.4	-24.5	8.0	64.4
2000	2.4	21.9	0.1	-19.3	2.6	45.3
2001	-6.5	22.7	-12.9	-33.1	-18.6	63.2
2002	-5.3	13.1	-15.9	-21.2	-20.4	37.0
2003	9.3	-11.4	8.6	-0.6	18.7	-10.9
2004	-2.0	16.4	0.4	-1.9	-1.6	18.6
2005	-0.2	10.5	-1.7	-15.7	-1.8	27.9
2006	3.3	17.3	7.6	5.5	11.1	10.9
2007	5.9	11.8	1.1	-0.1	7.1	11.9
2008	5.8	14.9	-39.3	-55.6	-35.8	78.8
2009	6.9	52.4	15.7	34.3	23.6	0.2
2010	6.2	12.4	8.5	33.0	15.3	-24.7
2011	2.7	9.2	-3.5	-23.1	-0.8	34.5
2012	4.0	0.6	6.0	21.6	10.2	-21.1
2013	7.4	-5.6	6.8	8.4	14.7	-13.5
2014	5.8	15.5	2.2	-15.6	8.1	33.4
2015	3.0	13.1	-2.0	-6.0	0.9	19.9
Avg.	4.1 %	13.2 %	0.0 %	-6.2 %	4.3 %	20.3 %
Fq>0	77 %	86 %	64 %	36 %	68 %	73 %

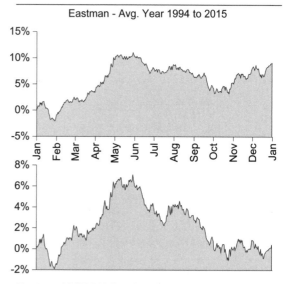

Eastman - Avg. Year 1994 to 2015

Eastman / S&P 500 Rel. Strength- Avg Yr. 1994-2015

Eastman Chemical Performance

EMN Monthly Performance (1994-2015)

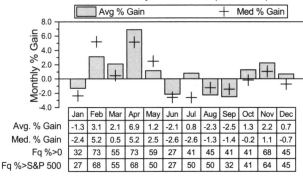

	Jan	Feb	Mar	Apr	May	Jun	Jul	Aug	Sep	Oct	Nov	Dec
Avg. % Gain	-1.3	3.1	2.1	6.9	1.2	-2.1	0.8	-2.3	-2.5	1.3	2.2	0.7
Med. % Gain	-2.4	5.2	0.5	5.2	2.5	-2.6	-2.6	-1.3	-1.4	-0.2	1.1	-0.7
Fq %>0	32	73	55	73	59	27	41	45	41	41	68	45
Fq %>S&P 500	27	68	55	68	50	27	50	50	32	41	64	45

EMN 5 Year (2011-2015) % Gain

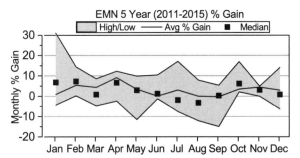

EMN Performance 2015-2016

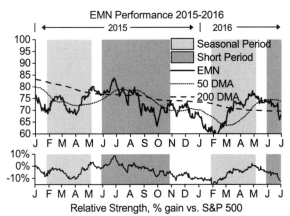

Relative Strength, % gain vs. S&P 500

Market Indices & Rates
Weekly Values**

Stock Markets	2015	2016
Dow	17,890	16,364
S&P500	2,074	1,915
Nasdaq	4,813	4,490
TSX	15,172	12,792
FTSE	6,837	5,928
DAX	10,811	9,314
Nikkei	17,814	16,015
Hang Seng	24,494	19,123

Commodities	2015	2016
Oil	51.14	30.03
Gold	1230.4	1213.8

Bond Yields	2015	2016
USA 5 Yr Treasury	1.51	1.24
USA 10 Yr T	2.00	1.78
USA 20 Yr T	2.33	2.19
Moody's Aaa	3.62	4.01
Moody's Baa	4.53	5.37
CAN 5 Yr T	0.74	0.61
CAN 10 Yr T	1.43	1.14

Money Market	2015	2016
USA Fed Funds	0.25	0.50
USA 3 Mo T-B	0.01	0.30
CAN tgt overnight rate	0.75	0.50
CAN 3 Mo T-B	0.53	0.46

Foreign Exchange	2015	2016
EUR/USD	1.14	1.11
GBP/USD	1.53	1.44
USD/CAD	1.25	1.38
USD/JPY	119.28	113.73

FEBRUARY

M	T	W	T	F	S	S
		1	2	3	4	5
6	7	8	9	10	11	12
13	14	15	16	17	18	19
20	21	22	23	24	24	26
27	28					

MARCH

M	T	W	T	F	S	S
		1	2	3	4	5
6	7	8	9	10	11	12
13	14	15	16	17	18	19
20	21	22	23	24	25	26
27	28	29	30	31		

APRIL

M	T	W	T	F	S	S
					1	2
3	4	5	6	7	8	9
10	11	12	13	14	15	16
17	18	19	20	21	22	23
24	25	26	27	28	29	30

From 1994 to 2015, the best performing months for Eastman Chemical were February and April on an average, median and frequency basis. These months are the cornerstones of the long seasonal trade. On a median basis, the worst performing contiguous months are June through October, as all five months have negative medians. These months make up the bulk of the ideal time to short Eastman Chemical.

Over the last five years, Eastman Chemical has performed well in its seasonally strong period. In 2015 and 2016, the combination of the long and short seasonal periods worked well.

AUTOMOTIVE & COMPONENTS
①LONG (Dec14-Jan7) ②LONG (Feb24-Apr24)
③SELL SHORT (Aug3-Oct3)

The automotive and components sector (auto sector) has its main seasonal period from February 24th to April 24. In this time period, from 1990 to 2015, the sector has produced an average gain of 8.1% and has been positive 73% of the time.

The total seasonal strategy of investing in the auto sector on December 14th, exiting on January 7th, reinvesting on February 24th, exiting on April 24th and shorting the sector from August 3rd to October 3rd, has produced an average gain of 20.8%.

20.8% gain & positive 81% of the time

The auto sector tends to rise in the spring, as investors look to benefit from being in this sector ahead of the peak in auto sales in May.

After the peak, auto sales generally decline from May until November (1975-2013, source: BEA). As a result, shorting the sector from August 3rd to October 3rd has proven to be profitable. The trend changes as auto sales increase in December, creating a positive seasonal period from December 14th to January 7th.

ⓘ *The SP GICS Automotive and Components Sector encompasses a wide range of automotive based companies. For more information, see www.standardandpoors.com*

Automotive & Components* vs. S&P 500 1989/90 to 2015/16

Negative Short ☐   Positive Long ▨

Year	Dec 14 to Jan 7 S&P 500	Auto	Feb 24 to Apr 24 S&P 500	Auto	Aug 3 to Oct 3 S&P 500	Auto	Compound Growth S&P 500	Auto
1989/90	-0.2 %	-0.8 %	1.9 %	4.4 %	-11.4 %	-19.3 %	-9.8 %	23.6 %
1990/91	-4.2	-4.0	4.7	6.9	-0.7	-6.3	-0.4	9.1
1991/92	8.6	15.7	-0.6	9.1	-3.2	-16.4	4.4	46.8
1992/93	-0.7	3.6	0.5	11.2	2.5	-1.8	2.3	17.3
1993/94	0.9	1.5	-4.9	-11.1	0.3	-9.5	-3.8	-1.2
1994/95	2.3	10.9	5.3	2.7	4.2	-0.5	12.3	14.4
1995/96	-0.8	1.1	-1.4	11.4	4.6	-2.1	2.3	15.0
1996/97	3.4	4.3	-3.8	-4.0	1.9	6.9	1.3	-6.7
1997/98	1.1	0.1	6.7	10.4	-10.5	-23.0	-3.5	35.9
1998/99	8.9	10.0	6.7	5.8	-3.4	-2.8	12.2	19.5
1999/00	1.9	8.5	5.1	22.9	-0.9	1.8	6.1	31.0
2000/01	-4.5	8.7	-2.9	4.0	-12.2	-27.9	-18.6	44.7
2001/02	4.1	4.6	0.3	12.2	-5.2	-12.1	-1.1	31.6
2002/03	3.8	5.2	7.5	10.1	5.1	7.2	17.2	7.5
2003/04	4.9	12.8	0.0	7.0	2.3	-2.8	7.2	24.0
2004/05	-1.0	0.7	-3.3	-22.4	-1.4	-10.5	-5.6	-13.6
2005/06	1.4	0.8	1.6	-0.8	4.4	7.9	7.6	-7.9
2006/07	-0.3	5.1	2.0	-2.5	4.6	2.0	6.4	0.4
2007/08	-4.9	-9.6	2.6	6.1	-12.8	-15.1	-14.8	10.4
2008/09	3.1	1.0	16.5	102.4	3.8	-11.4	24.7	127.8
2009/10	3.2	16.3	11.2	21.3	1.8	-3.1	16.8	45.4
2010/11	2.5	9.8	2.3	2.7	-12.4	-24.0	-8.1	39.8
2011/12	4.3	10.3	0.6	-5.8	6.3	10.8	11.5	-7.3
2012/13	3.0	13.6	4.2	6.9	-1.8	-0.3	5.3	21.8
2013/14	3.5	-1.4	2.3	1.0	2.2	-6.8	8.3	6.3
2014/15	1.2	3.5	0.4	-1.7	-7.3	-4.2	-5.8	5.9
Avg.	1.7 %	5.1 %	2.5 %	8.1 %	-1.5 %	-6.3 %	2.9 %	20.8 %
Fq>0	69 %	85 %	73	73 %	50 %	23 %	62 %	81 %

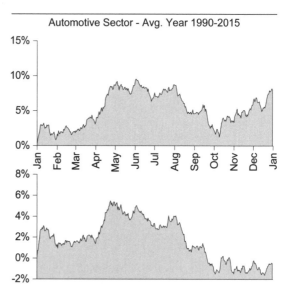

Automotive Sector - Avg. Year 1990-2015

Automotive / S&P 500 Rel. Strength- Avg Yr. 1990-2015

Automotive Performance

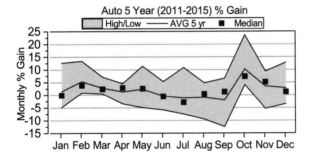

Auto Monthly Performance (1990-2015)

	Jan	Feb	Mar	Apr	May	Jun	Jul	Aug	Sep	Oct	Nov	Dec
Avg. % Gain	1.1	0.6	1.3	6.1	0.3	-1.7	1.2	-3.4	-2.5	0.7	1.6	1.3
Med. % Gain	2.0	-0.4	0.7	2.3	0.4	-0.2	0.4	-2.2	-1.9	1.9	2.2	1.7
Fq %>0	58	38	54	69	54	50	54	35	31	58	62	58
Fq %>S&P 500	50	46	54	54	27	46	50	31	38	42	54	38

Auto 5 Year (2011-2015) % Gain

High/Low — AVG 5 yr ■ Median

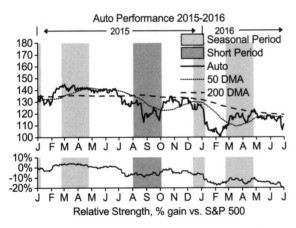

Auto Performance 2015-2016

Seasonal Period
Short Period
Auto
50 DMA
200 DMA

Relative Strength, % gain vs. S&P 500

Market Indices & Rates
Weekly Values**

Stock Markets	2015	2016
Dow	18,051	16,575
S&P500	2,102	1,939
Nasdaq	4,922	4,558
TSX	15,212	12,780
FTSE	6,891	5,995
DAX	10,966	9,401
Nikkei	18,158	16,082
Hang Seng	24,781	19,265

Commodities	2015	2016
Oil	51.79	31.38
Gold	1212.5	1229.1

Bond Yields	2015	2016
USA 5 Yr Treasury	1.58	1.22
USA 10 Yr T	2.11	1.75
USA 20 Yr T	2.49	2.17
Moody's Aaa	3.77	3.91
Moody's Baa	4.64	5.31
CAN 5 Yr T	0.79	0.63
CAN 10 Yr T	1.46	1.15

Money Market	2015	2016
USA Fed Funds	0.25	0.50
USA 3 Mo T-B	0.02	0.33
CAN tgt overnight rate	0.75	0.50
CAN 3 Mo T-B	0.50	0.47

Foreign Exchange	2015	2016
EUR/USD	1.14	1.10
GBP/USD	1.54	1.40
USD/CAD	1.25	1.36
USD/JPY	118.90	112.84

FEBRUARY

M	T	W	T	F	S	S
		1	2	3	4	5
6	7	8	9	10	11	12
13	14	15	16	17	18	19
20	21	22	23	24	24	26
27	28					

MARCH

M	T	W	T	F	S	S
		1	2	3	4	5
6	7	8	9	10	11	12
13	14	15	16	17	18	19
20	21	22	23	24	25	26
27	28	29	30	31		

APRIL

M	T	W	T	F	S	S
					1	2
3	4	5	6	7	8	9
10	11	12	13	14	15	16
17	18	19	20	21	22	23
24	25	26	27	28	29	30

From 1990 to 2015, April has been the best month of the year for the auto sector on an average, median and frequency basis. April is the core of the spring seasonal strategy.

Over the last five years, the auto sector has generally followed its seasonal trend of weakness in the summer months and strength in the autumn months. October has been uncharacteristically strong, especially given that the auto sector tends to underperform the S&P 500 at this time of the year. In 2015 and 2016, the combination of long and short trades was successful as it produced a gain of 5.9% and outperformed the S&P 500.

OIL STOCKS– WINTER/SPRING STRATEGY
February 25th to May 9th

Despite a long downtrend for energy that started in 2014, the *Energy- Winter/Spring Strategy* outperformed the S&P 500 during its 2016 winter-spring seasonal period. The *Energy- Winter/Spring Strategy* is a strong seasonal performer over the long-term. From 1984 to 2016, for the two and half months starting on February 25th and ending May 9th, the energy sector (XOI) has outperformed the S&P 500 by an average 4.1%.

What is even more impressive are the positive returns, 28 out of 33 times, and the outperformance of the S&P 500, 26 out of 33 times.

4.1% extra and 28 out of 33 times positive, in just over two months

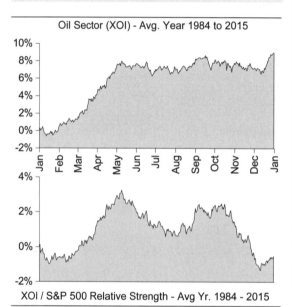

Oil Sector (XOI) - Avg. Year 1984 to 2015

XOI / S&P 500 Relative Strength - Avg Yr. 1984 - 2015

XOI* vs S&P 500 1984 to 2015			
Feb 25 to May 9	S&P 500	positive XOI	Diff
1984	1.7 %	5.6 %	3.9 %
1985	1.4	4.9	3.5
1986	6.0	7.7	1.7
1987	3.7	25.5	21.8
1988	-3.0	5.6	8.6
1989	6.3	8.1	1.8
1990	5.8	-0.6	-6.3
1991	4.8	6.8	2.0
1992	0.9	5.8	4.9
1993	0.3	6.3	6.0
1994	-4.7	3.2	7.9
1995	7.3	10.3	3.1
1996	-2.1	2.2	4.3
1997	1.8	4.7	2.9
1998	7.5	9.8	2.3
1999	7.3	35.4	28.1
2000	4.3	22.2	17.9
2001	0.8	10.2	9.4
2002	-1.5	5.3	6.9
2003	12.1	5.7	-6.4
2004	-3.5	4.0	7.5
2005	-1.8	-1.0	0.8
2006	2.8	9.4	6.6
2007	4.2	10.1	5.8
2008	2.6	7.6	5.0
2009	20.2	15.8	-4.4
2010	0.5	-2.3	-2.8
2011	3.1	-0.6	-3.7
2012	-0.8	-13.4	-12.5
2013	7.3	3.8	-3.5
2014	1.7	9.1	7.4
2015	0.3	1.2	1.1
2016	6.7	11.1	4.4
Avg	3.1 %	7.3 %	4.1 %
Fq > 0	79 %	85 %	79 %

A lot of investors assume that the time to buy oil stocks is just before the cold winter sets in. The rationale is that oil will climb in price as the temperature drops.

The results in the market have not supported this assumption. The price for a barrel of oil has more to do with oil inventory. Refineries have a choice: they can produce either gasoline or heating oil. As the winter progresses, refineries start to convert their operations from heating oil to gasoline.

In late winter and early spring, as refineries start coming off their conversion and winter maintenance programs, they increase their demand for oil, putting upward pressure on its price. In addition, later in the spring, in April and early May, investors increase their holdings in the oil sector before the driving season kicks off (Memorial Day in May), helping to drive up the price of oil stocks.

> (i) *NYSE Arca Oil Index (XOI):*
> *An index designed to represent a cross section of widely held oil corporations involved in various phases of the oil industry.*
> *For more information on the XOI index, see www.cboe.com*

NYSE Arca Oil Index (XOI) Performance

XOI Monthly Performance (1984-2015)

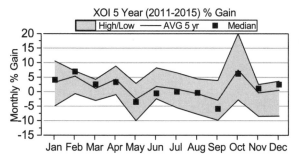

	Jan	Feb	Mar	Apr	May	Jun	Jul	Aug	Sep	Oct	Nov	Dec
Avg. % Gain	0.5	1.0	2.9	3.0	0.7	-0.9	0.4	0.8	-0.3	0.3	-0.6	1.7
Med. % Gain	0.1	1.8	2.5	2.4	0.8	-1.8	1.7	0.4	-0.2	0.5	0.6	1.0
Fq %>0	50	56	72	81	63	38	56	56	50	50	53	63
Fq %>S&P 500	34	56	66	63	41	34	50	63	56	50	34	53

XOI 5 Year (2011-2015) % Gain

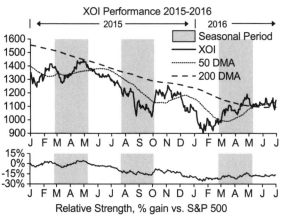

XOI Performance 2015-2016

Relative Strength, % gain vs. S&P 500

Market Indices & Rates
Weekly Values**

Stock Markets	2015	2016
Dow	18,180	16,846
S&P500	2,111	1,978
Nasdaq	4,970	4,675
TSX	15,214	13,039
FTSE	6,939	6,145
DAX	11,255	9,713
Nikkei	18,648	16,567
Hang Seng	24,818	19,728

Commodities	2015	2016
Oil	49.09	34.66
Gold	1204.8	1247.7

Bond Yields	2015	2016
USA 5 Yr Treasury	1.51	1.32
USA 10 Yr T	2.01	1.82
USA 20 Yr T	2.39	2.25
Moody's Aaa	3.65	3.89
Moody's Baa	4.48	5.32
CAN 5 Yr T	0.75	0.70
CAN 10 Yr T	1.33	1.23

Money Market	2015	2016
USA Fed Funds	0.25	0.50
USA 3 Mo T-B	0.02	0.32
CAN tgt overnight rate	0.75	0.50
CAN 3 Mo T-B	0.54	0.47

Foreign Exchange	2015	2016
EUR/USD	1.13	1.09
GBP/USD	1.55	1.41
USD/CAD	1.25	1.34
USD/JPY	119.14	113.52

FEBRUARY

M	T	W	T	F	S	S
		1	2	3	4	5
6	7	8	9	10	11	12
13	14	15	16	17	18	19
20	21	22	23	24	24	26
27	28					

MARCH

M	T	W	T	F	S	S
	1	2	3	4	5	
		1	2	3	4	5
6	7	8	9	10	11	12
13	14	15	16	17	18	19
20	21	22	23	24	25	26
27	28	29	30	31		

APRIL

M	T	W	T	F	S	S
					1	2
3	4	5	6	7	8	9
10	11	12	13	14	15	16
17	18	19	20	21	22	23
24	25	26	27	28	29	30

From 1984 to 2015, March and April have been the best performing months for the energy sector on an average, median and frequency basis. Over the last five years, the energy sector has generally followed its seasonal pattern of positive performance in early winter and weaker performance in summer. The outlier to the trend has been October's positive performance. In 2015, the energy sector performed well in its February to May seasonal period, but in its secondary seasonal period from July to October, global oversupply of oil hurt the sector. In its 2016 winter seasonal period, the energy sector, once again performed well.

MARCH

	MONDAY	TUESDAY	WEDNESDAY
WEEK09	27	28	1 30
WEEK 10	6 25	7 24	8 23
WEEK 11	13 18	14 17	15 16
WEEK 12	20 11	21 10	22 9
WEEK 13	27 4	28 3	29 2

THURSDAY	FRIDAY
2 29	**3** 28
9 22	**10** 21
16 15	**17** 14
23 8	**24** 7
30 1	**31**

APRIL

M	T	W	T	F	S	S
					1	2
3	4	5	6	7	8	9
10	11	12	13	14	15	16
17	18	19	20	21	22	23
24	25	26	27	28	29	30

MAY

M	T	W	T	F	S	S
1	2	3	4	5	6	7
8	9	10	11	12	13	14
15	16	17	18	19	20	21
22	23	24	25	26	27	28
29	30	31				

JUNE

M	T	W	T	F	S	S
			1	2	3	4
5	6	7	8	9	10	11
12	13	14	15	16	17	18
19	20	21	22	23	24	25
26	27	28	29	30		

JULY

M	T	W	T	F	S	S
					1	2
3	4	5	6	7	8	9
10	11	12	13	14	15	16
17	18	19	20	21	22	23
24	25	26	27	28	29	30
31						

MARCH
S U M M A R Y

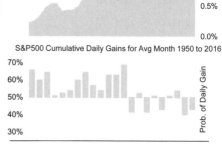

S&P500 Cumulative Daily Gains for Avg Month 1950 to 2016

	Dow Jones	S&P 500	Nasdaq	TSX Comp
Month Rank	5	4	8	5
# Up	43	43	27	18
# Down	23	23	17	13
% Pos	65	65	61	58
% Avg. Gain	1.1	1.2	0.7	1.0

Dow & S&P 1950-2015, Nasdaq 1972-2015, TSX 1985-2015

♦ March tends to be a strong month for stocks. From 1990 to 2016, the S&P 500 has produced an average gain of 1.5%. ♦ Typically, it is the cyclicals that perform well and the defensive sectors that underperform. ♦ The energy sector is typically the best performing sector in March, and in 2016 it was the top performing sector for the month with a 9.2% gain. ♦ The financial sector typically performs well in March, but investors need to be cautious as the sector finishes its seasonal run mid-April. In March 2016, the financial sector produced a 7.1% gain.

BEST / WORST MARCH BROAD MKTS. 2007-2016

BEST MARCH MARKETS
- Nasdaq (2009) 10.9%
- Nikkei 225 (2010) 9.5%
- Russell 2000 (2009) 8.7%

WORST MARCH MARKETS
- Nikkei 225 (2011) -8.2%
- Nikkei 225 (2008) -7.9%
- FTSE 100 (2014) -3.1%

Index Values End of Month

	2007	2008	2009	2010	2011	2012	2013	2014	2015	2016
Dow	12,354	12,263	7,609	10,857	12,320	13,212	14,579	16,458	17,776	17,685
S&P 500	1,421	1,323	798	1,169	1,326	1,408	1,569	1,872	2,068	2,060
Nasdaq	2,422	2,279	1,529	2,398	2,781	3,092	3,268	4,199	4,901	4,870
TSX	13,166	13,350	8,720	12,038	14,116	12,392	12,750	14,335	14,902	13,494
Russell 1000	1,492	1,385	834	1,238	1,417	1,497	1,676	2,012	2,224	2,189
Russell 2000	1,990	1,710	1,051	1,687	2,096	2,064	2,365	2,915	3,113	2,769
FTSE 100	6,308	5,702	3,926	5,680	5,909	5,769	6,412	6,598	6,773	6,175
Nikkei 225	17,288	12,526	8,110	11,090	9,755	10,084	12,398	14,828	19,207	16,759

Percent Gain for March

	2007	2008	2009	2010	2011	2012	2013	2014	2015	2016
Dow	0.7	0.0	7.7	5.1	0.8	2.0	3.7	0.8	-2.0	7.1
S&P 500	1.0	-0.6	8.5	5.9	-0.1	3.1	3.6	0.7	-1.7	6.6
Nasdaq	0.2	0.3	10.9	7.1	0.0	4.2	3.4	-2.5	-1.3	6.8
TSX	0.9	-1.7	7.4	3.5	-0.1	-2.0	-0.6	0.9	-2.2	4.9
Russell 1000	0.9	-0.8	8.5	6.0	0.1	3.0	3.7	0.5	-1.4	6.8
Russell 2000	0.9	0.3	8.7	8.0	2.4	2.4	4.4	-0.8	1.6	7.8
FTSE 100	2.2	-3.1	2.5	6.1	-1.4	-1.8	0.8	-3.1	-2.5	1.3
Nikkei 225	-1.8	-7.9	7.1	9.5	-8.2	3.7	7.3	-0.1	2.2	4.6

March Market Avg. Performance 2007 to 2016[1]

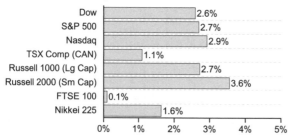

Dow	2.6%
S&P 500	2.7%
Nasdaq	2.9%
TSX Comp (CAN)	1.1%
Russell 1000 (Lg Cap)	2.7%
Russell 2000 (Sm Cap)	3.6%
FTSE 100	0.1%
Nikkei 225	1.6%

Interest Corner Mar[2]

	Fed Funds % [3]	3 Mo. T-Bill % [4]	10 Yr % [5]	20 Yr % [6]
2016	0.50	0.21	1.78	2.20
2015	0.25	0.03	1.94	2.31
2014	0.25	0.05	2.73	3.31
2013	0.25	0.07	1.87	2.71
2012	0.25	0.07	2.23	3.00

(1) Russell Data provided by Russell (2) Federal Reserve Bank of St. Louis- end of month values (3) Target rate set by FOMC (4)(5)(6) Constant yield maturities.

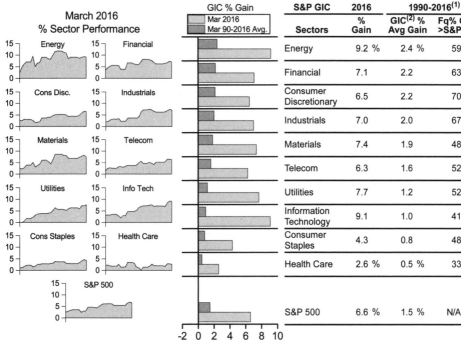

S&P GIC Sectors	2016 % Gain	1990-2016[1] GIC[2] % Avg Gain	1990-2016[1] Fq% Gain >S&P 500
Energy	9.2 %	2.4 %	59 %
Financial	7.1	2.2	63
Consumer Discretionary	6.5	2.2	70
Industrials	7.0	2.0	67
Materials	7.4	1.9	48
Telecom	6.3	1.6	52
Utilities	7.7	1.2	52
Information Technology	9.1	1.0	41
Consumer Staples	4.3	0.8	48
Health Care	2.6 %	0.5 %	33 %
S&P 500	6.6 %	1.5 %	N/A %

Sector Commentary

♦ In March 2016, generally, the sectors that are typically the top performers were the better performing sectors. ♦ The exception was the information technology sector which is usually one of the weaker sectors in March, but in 2016 it produced a 9.1% gain. ♦ The health care sector continued its weaker performance from February and only produced a gain of 2.6%.

Sub-Sector Commentary

♦ In March 2016, the cyclical sub-sectors produced very strong gains. Steel produced a gain 20.2%, metals and mining a gain 15.1% and homebuilders a gain of 12.8%. ♦ Retail is typically one of the top performing sub-sectors in March. In 2016, retail produced a strong gain of 6.9%. ♦ Gold bullion took a reprieve in March 2016 after its rapid ascent in January and February. Gold does not typically perform well in March.

SELECTED SUB-SECTORS[3]			
Retail	6.9 %	3.5 %	74 %
Steel	20.2	3.0	63
Transportation	6.6	2.2	63
Chemicals	5.7	2.2	52
Railroads	4.6	2.0	56
Banks	5.6	1.8	52
Silver	4.3	1.8	48
SOX (1995-2016)	8.8	1.7	45
Automotive & Components	9.1	1.6	56
Metals & Mining	15.1	1.2	44
Homebuilders	12.8	1.0	55
Agriculture (1994-2016)	3.9	0.8	35
Pharma	0.9	0.5	33
Biotech (1993-2016)	2.3	-0.2	38
Gold	0.2	-1.0	33

NIKE RUNS INTO EARNINGS
①Mar1-Mar20 ②Sep1-Sep25 ③Dec12-Dec24

Nike has had a strong run in the stock market since it went public in 1980. A lot of the gains in the stock price can be accounted for in the two to three week periods leading up to its first, second and third quarters earnings reports.

Nike Inc*. Seasonal Gains 1990 to 2015

Year %	Mar 1 to Mar 20	Sep 1 to Sep 25	Dec 12 to Dec 24	Positive Compound Growth
1990	51.8 %	14.7 %	2.0 %	11.6 %	30.4 %
1991	79.4	-6.0	9.0	13.0	15.7
1992	14.6	-8.3	6.2	-2.9	-5.5
1993	-44.0	5.8	-13.1	0.0	-8.1
1994	60.1	10.5	-7.0	14.2	17.3
1995	86.7	5.3	19.0	10.7	38.8
1996	72.4	22.2	13.6	13.0	56.9
1997	-34.9	-6.1	0.9	-14.2	-18.6
1998	3.9	1.1	18.0	14.7	36.8
1999	22.3	15.6	15.2	18.3	57.5
2000	12.6	16.1	1.4	16.4	37.0
2001	0.7	-2.7	-8.6	3.6	-7.8
2002	-20.9	8.7	2.8	2.0	14.0
2003	54.0	14.0	6.7	4.3	26.9
2004	32.5	4.9	5.8	5.1	16.6
2005	-4.3	-1.8	3.0	1.3	2.6
2006	14.1	-1.5	7.0	2.6	8.1
2007	29.7	4.6	3.8	4.2	13.0
2008	-20.6	11.8	7.3	0.8	20.9
2009	29.6	8.5	5.9	2.2	17.3
2010	29.3	8.8	13.5	-2.0	20.9
2011	12.8	-12.9	2.3	-0.8	-11.6
2012	7.1	3.6	-2.3	6.2	7.4
2013	52.4	0.7	9.7	1.1	11.7
2014	22.3	1.3	1.5	-0.7	2.1
2015	30.0	5.0	11.9	0.1	17.5
Avg.	22.8 %	4.8 %	5.2 %	4.8 %	16.1 %

NKE - Avg. Year 1990 to 2015

NKE / S&P 500 Relative Strength - Avg Yr. 1990 - 2015

Nike's year-end is May 31st, and although from year to year the actual report dates for Nike's earnings changes, generally speaking, Nike reports its earnings in the third or fourth week in the months of March, June, September and December.

It is interesting to note that Nike has strong seasonal runs at different times of the year. Stocks typically have similar seasonal patterns as the sector to which they belong. Nike belongs to the consumer discretionary sector and it would be expected that Nike would have a similar seasonal pattern.

There are large differences in Nike's pattern of seasonal strength compared with the consumer discretionary's seasonal pattern. First, Nike has a period of seasonal strength that includes September, a month that is not favorable to consumer discretionary stocks. Second, Nike's outperformance is focused on very short periods in the weeks leading up to three of its earnings periods. In contrast, the consumer discretionary sector has a much longer seasonal period and has a more gradual transition from its favorable seasonal period to its unfavorable seasonal period and vice versa.

From 1990 to 2015, Nike produced an average annual gain of 22.8%. In comparison, its three short seasonal periods within the year have produced an average compound gain of 16.1%. The seasonal periods in total are approximately eight weeks and yet, they have produced most of the average annual gains of Nike. Investors have been well served investing in Nike in its seasonal periods and then running to another investment during its "off-season."

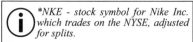

*NKE - stock symbol for Nike Inc. which trades on the NYSE, adjusted for splits.

Nike Performance

NKE Monthly Performance (1990-2015)

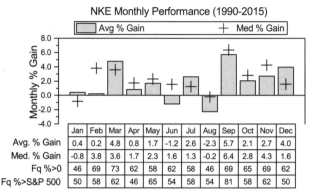

	Jan	Feb	Mar	Apr	May	Jun	Jul	Aug	Sep	Oct	Nov	Dec
Avg. % Gain	0.4	0.2	4.8	0.8	1.7	-1.2	2.6	-2.3	5.7	2.1	2.7	4.0
Med. % Gain	-0.8	3.8	3.6	1.7	2.3	1.6	1.3	-0.2	6.4	2.8	4.3	1.6
Fq %>0	46	69	73	62	58	62	58	46	69	65	69	62
Fq %>S&P 500	50	58	62	46	65	54	58	54	81	58	62	50

NKE 5 Year (2011-2015) % Gain

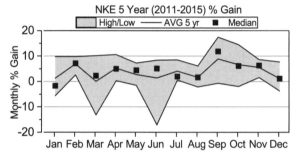

NKE Performance 2015-2016

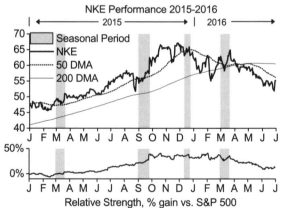

Relative Strength, % gain vs. S&P 500

Market Indices & Rates
Weekly Values**

Stock Markets	2015	2016
Dow	18,116	17,049
S&P500	2,099	1,996
Nasdaq	4,973	4,688
TSX	15,107	13,398
FTSE	6,924	6,126
DAX	11,427	9,705
Nikkei	18,814	16,826
Hang Seng	24,483	20,070

Commodities	2015	2016
Oil	50.40	37.81
Gold	1200.5	1262.5

Bond Yields	2015	2016
USA 5 Yr Treasury	1.61	1.42
USA 10 Yr T	2.13	1.91
USA 20 Yr T	2.51	2.28
Moody's Aaa	3.74	3.88
Moody's Baa	4.60	5.25
CAN 5 Yr T	0.90	0.72
CAN 10 Yr T	1.49	1.27

Money Market	2015	2016
USA Fed Funds	0.25	0.50
USA 3 Mo T-B	0.02	0.31
CAN tgt overnight rate	0.75	0.50
CAN 3 Mo T-B	0.59	0.47

Foreign Exchange	2015	2016
EUR/USD	1.11	1.11
GBP/USD	1.53	1.43
USD/CAD	1.25	1.33
USD/JPY	120.10	113.30

MARCH

M	T	W	T	F	S	S
		1	2	3	4	5
6	7	8	9	10	11	12
13	14	15	16	17	18	19
20	21	22	23	24	25	26
27	28	29	30	31		

APRIL

M	T	W	T	F	S	S
					1	2
3	4	5	6	7	8	9
10	11	12	13	14	15	16
17	18	19	20	21	22	23
24	25	26	27	28	29	30

MAY

M	T	W	T	F	S	S
1	2	3	4	5	6	7
8	9	10	11	12	13	14
15	16	17	18	19	20	21
22	23	24	25	26	27	28
29	30	31				

From 1990 to 2015, on average, the three best months for Nike were March, September and December, which are all part of the *Nike Runs Into Earnings* strategy. September has been the best month of the three as it has a higher average and median than the other two months. Performing well in September is particularly valuable as the S&P 500 tends not to perform well in this month. On average, over the last five years, Nike has performed extremely well in the month of September.

In 2015 and 2016, the Nike combination strategy was positive and outperformed the S&P 500.

LNR | LINAMAR
February 24th to May 12th

Linamar is a parts supplier to the automotive business and, as a result, is largely affected by its seasonal cycle. The automotive segment is not the only division in Linamar, but it is a major driving force.

The automotive sector has its main strong seasonal period from February 24th to April 24th (see *Automotive & Components* strategy). If the auto sector is performing well in its seasonal period, it would be expected that Linamar should also perform well. As expected, Linamar has a similar strong seasonal period as the auto sector and outperforms the TSX Composite from February 24th to May 12th.

19.4% gain &
positive 71% of the time

In its seasonal period, from 1996 to 2016, Linamar has produced an average rate of return of 19.4% and has been positive 71% of the time. Even more impressive is the 81% frequency that Linamar has outperformed the TSX Composite in its seasonal period. During its seasonal period in 2009, Linamar performed extremely well, as did many other automotive companies, after the 2008 financial crisis.

Feb 24 to May 12	TSX Comp	LNR	Diff
1996	4.3%	23.1%	18.8%
1997	0.7	29.5	28.8
1998	11.2	-4.3	-15.5
1999	8.5	-12.4	-20.9
2000	-1.1	24.4	25.5
2001	-0.1	13.6	13.6
2002	2.3	6.0	3.7
2003	2.4	-4.7	-7.1
2004	-4.9	1.8	6.7
2005	-3.6	-0.7	2.8
2006	2.6	13.0	10.4
2007	5.0	26.9	22.0
2008	8.0	14.4	6.5
2009	31.8	178.5	146.7
2010	5.8	43.5	37.7
2011	-4.1	-0.2	3.8
2012	-8.1	18.2	26.3
2013	-0.9	8.1	9.0
2014	3.2	33.0	29.8
2015	-1.0	4.6	5.7
2016	8.0	-8.5	-16.5
Avg	3.3%	19.4%	16.1%
Fq > 0	62%	71%	81%

LNR* vs. TSX Composite 1996 to 2016 — Positive

formed extremely well in its seasonal period.

In its 2014 annual report, Linamar acknowledged a seasonally weak period for its business: "The third and fourth quarters are generally negatively impacted by the scheduled shutdowns at automotive customers and seasonal slowdowns in the aerial work platform and agricultural businesses."

The third and fourth quarter seasonal weakness for business shows up in Linamar's stock price. From 1996 to 2015, for all of the months from August to November, Linamar both underperformed the TSX Composite more than half of the time and was positive less than half of the time.

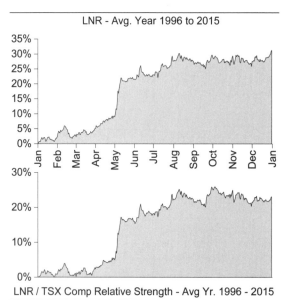

LNR - Avg. Year 1996 to 2015

LNR / TSX Comp Relative Strength - Avg Yr. 1996 - 2015

There is no question that the exceptionally strong results in 2009 skewed the seasonal results, but even with the 2009 results removed, Linamar has per-

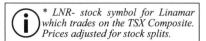

* LNR- stock symbol for Linamar which trades on the TSX Composite. Prices adjusted for stock splits.

Linamar Performance

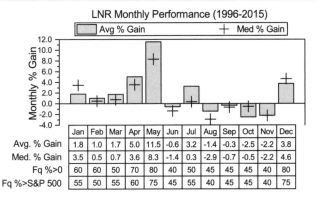

LNR Monthly Performance (1996-2015)

Legend: Avg % Gain | Med % Gain

	Jan	Feb	Mar	Apr	May	Jun	Jul	Aug	Sep	Oct	Nov	Dec
Avg. % Gain	1.8	1.0	1.7	5.0	11.5	-0.6	3.2	-1.4	-0.3	-2.5	-2.2	3.8
Med. % Gain	3.5	0.5	0.7	3.6	8.3	-1.4	0.3	-2.9	-0.7	-0.5	-2.2	4.6
Fq %>0	60	60	50	70	80	40	50	45	45	45	40	80
Fq %>S&P 500	55	50	55	60	75	45	55	40	45	45	40	75

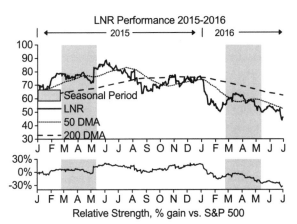

LNR 5 Year (2011-2015) % Gain

Legend: High/Low — AVG 5 yr ■ Median

Jan Feb Mar Apr May Jun Jul Aug Sep Oct Nov Dec

LNR Performance 2015-2016

2015 → | 2016 →

Seasonal Period
LNR
50 DMA
200 DMA

J F M A M J J A S O N D J F M A M J J

Relative Strength, % gain vs. S&P 500

Stock Markets	2015	2016
Dow	17,788	17,378
S&P500	2,057	2,031
Nasdaq	4,883	4,763
TSX	14,748	13,495
FTSE	6,760	6,176
DAX	11,718	9,950
Nikkei	18,885	16,997
Hang Seng	23,872	20,431

Commodities	2015	2016
Oil	47.67	38.32
Gold	1157.0	1244.4

Bond Yields	2015	2016
USA 5 Yr Treasury	1.61	1.43
USA 10 Yr T	2.14	1.93
USA 20 Yr T	2.50	2.30
Moody's Aaa	3.70	3.80
Moody's Baa	4.59	5.13
CAN 5 Yr T	0.91	0.74
CAN 10 Yr T	1.52	1.31

Money Market	2015	2016
USA Fed Funds	0.25	0.50
USA 3 Mo T-B	0.03	0.31
CAN tgt overnight rate	0.75	0.50
CAN 3 Mo T-B	0.56	0.46

Foreign Exchange	2015	2016
EUR/USD	1.06	1.12
GBP/USD	1.50	1.43
USD/CAD	1.27	1.31
USD/JPY	121.28	112.50

MARCH

M	T	W	T	F	S	S
		1	2	3	4	5
6	7	8	9	10	11	12
13	14	15	16	17	18	19
20	21	22	23	24	25	26
27	28	29	30	31		

APRIL

M	T	W	T	F	S	S
					1	2
3	4	5	6	7	8	9
10	11	12	13	14	15	16
17	18	19	20	21	22	23
24	25	26	27	28	29	30

MAY

M	T	W	T	F	S	S
1	2	3	4	5	6	7
8	9	10	11	12	13	14
15	16	17	18	19	20	21
22	23	24	25	26	27	28
29	30	31				

From 1996 to 2015, the best month for Linamar has been May on an average, median and frequency basis. The seasonal period for Linamar finishes on May 12th, but the remainder of the month can still provide solid gains. Care must be taken as June is typically a weak month.

Over the last five years, on average, Linamar has followed its seasonal trend with May being the strongest month and November performing poorly.

In 2015, Linamar outperformed the TSX Composite during its seasonal period. In 2016, Linamar substantially underperformed the TSX Composite.

BBBY BED BATH & BEYOND
①Feb25-Apr8   ②Aug23-Sep29

Bed Bath & Beyond is a retailer with a focus on selling house merchandise. As the majority of its revenue comes from selling products for the home, the company's seasonal performance is not only affected by retail sales, but also by home sales and starts. According to the company's 2014 annual report, "The company's sales exhibit seasonality with sales levels generally higher in the calendar months of August, November and December, and generally lower in February."

23.6% gain & positive 83% of the time

Bed Bath & Beyond has a two periods of seasonal strength. The first period is from February 25th to April 8th and the second from August 23rd to September 29th.

The first period of seasonal strength from late February to early April is the core part of the retail sector's seasonal trend. The tendency is for Bed Bath and Beyond to perform well into the first week in April, leading up to the day the company releases in full-year earnings report.

The second period of seasonal strength is from late August into late September. This period of strength is driven mainly by investors taking a position in the stock ahead of the company's Q2 earnings announcement that typically takes place towards the end of September. This seasonal period tends to perform particularly well if Bed Bath & Beyond has corrected in the summer months relative to the S&P 500.

ⓘ *BBBY- stock symbol for Bed Bath and Beyond which trades on the Nasdaq exchange. Prices adjusted for stock splits.*

BBBY* vs. S&P 500 1993 to 2015 Positive ▢

Year	Feb 25 to Apr 8 S&P 500	Feb 25 to Apr 8 BBBY	Aug 23 to Sep 29 S&P 500	Aug 23 to Sep 29 BBBY	Compound Growth S&P 500	Compound Growth BBBY
1993	0.2	23.1 %	0.9	40.1 %	1.1	72.5 %
1994	-3.7	13.8	0.0	-5.0	-3.7	8.1
1995	3.8	-12.1	4.5	8.9	8.4	-4.3
1996	-2.3	13.9	2.3	32.6	0.0	50.9
1997	-5.5	2.8	3.2	10.6	-2.4	13.7
1998	6.9	22.3	-3.0	25.3	3.7	53.2
1999	7.2	31.0	-5.1	7.7	1.8	41.1
2000	12.0	70.2	-4.1	36.4	7.4	132.2
2001	-9.4	3.9	-10.7	-10.6	-19.1	-7.1
2002	3.3	9.7	-14.1	0.2	-11.3	9.9
2003	5.5	11.2	1.4	-8.9	6.9	1.3
2004	0.0	-2.7	1.5	4.0	1.5	1.2
2005	-1.6	6.4	0.5	-4.1	-1.1	2.1
2006	0.5	13.0	2.9	8.5	3.3	22.6
2007	-0.5	-3.2	4.3	-1.2	3.7	-4.3
2008	0.9	6.8	-14.4	1.8	-13.6	8.7
2009	6.7	47.3	3.4	5.1	10.3	54.8
2010	7.4	11.5	6.8	13.6	14.7	26.6
2011	1.7	13.6	3.3	15.0	5.0	30.6
2012	2.4	19.1	1.9	-5.4	4.3	12.6
2013	3.1	12.9	2.1	3.8	5.3	17.2
2014	0.2	2.7	-0.5	3.4	-0.3	6.2
2015	-1.6	2.0	-4.4	-8.7	-5.9	-6.8
Avg.	1.6 %	13.9 %	-0.8 %	7.5 %	0.9 %	23.6 %
Fq>0	70 %	87 %	61 %	70 %	65 %	83 %

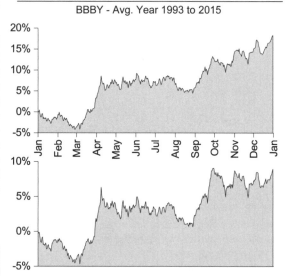

BBBY - Avg. Year 1993 to 2015

BBBY / S&P 500 Rel. Strength- Avg Yr. 1993-2015

Bed Bath & Beyond Performance

BBBY Monthly Performance (1993-2015)

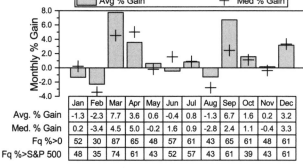

	Jan	Feb	Mar	Apr	May	Jun	Jul	Aug	Sep	Oct	Nov	Dec
Avg. % Gain	-1.3	-2.3	7.7	3.6	0.6	-0.4	0.8	-1.3	6.7	1.6	0.2	3.2
Med. % Gain	0.2	-3.4	4.5	5.0	-0.2	1.6	0.9	-2.8	2.4	1.1	-0.4	3.3
Fq %>0	52	30	87	65	48	57	61	43	65	61	48	61
Fq %>S&P 500	48	35	74	61	43	52	57	43	61	39	43	61

BBBY 5 Year (2011-2015) % Gain

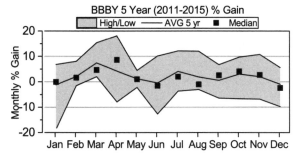

BBBY Performance 2015-2016

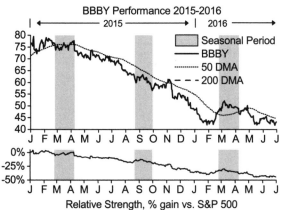

Relative Strength, % gain vs. S&P 500

Market Indices & Rates
Weekly Values**

Stock Markets	2015	2016
Dow	17,998	17,556
S&P500	2,090	2,044
Nasdaq	4,974	4,793
TSX	14,908	13,448
FTSE	6,914	6,171
DAX	12,002	9,953
Nikkei	19,453	16,986
Hang Seng	24,163	20,578
Commodities	2015	2016
Oil	44.34	39.08
Gold	1159.6	1234.0
Bond Yields	2015	2016
USA 5 Yr Treasury	1.49	1.39
USA 10 Yr T	2.00	1.91
USA 20 Yr T	2.36	2.29
Moody's Aaa	3.62	3.78
Moody's Baa	4.51	5.01
CAN 5 Yr T	0.77	0.73
CAN 10 Yr T	1.36	1.28
Money Market	2015	2016
USA Fed Funds	0.25	0.50
USA 3 Mo T-B	0.03	0.30
CAN tgt overnight rate	0.75	0.50
CAN 3 Mo T-B	0.53	0.45
Foreign Exchange	2015	2016
EUR/USD	1.07	1.12
GBP/USD	1.49	1.42
USD/CAD	1.27	1.32
USD/JPY	120.73	112.54

MARCH

M	T	W	T	F	S	S
	1	2	3	4	5	
6	7	8	9	10	11	12
13	14	15	16	17	18	19
20	21	22	23	24	25	26
27	28	29	30	31		

APRIL

M	T	W	T	F	S	S
					1	2
3	4	5	6	7	8	9
10	11	12	13	14	15	16
17	18	19	20	21	22	23
24	25	26	27	28	29	30

MAY

M	T	W	T	F	S	S
1	2	3	4	5	6	7
8	9	10	11	12	13	14
15	16	17	18	19	20	21
22	23	24	25	26	27	28
29	30	31				

From 1993 to 2015, on average, the best month for Bed Bath & Beyond has been March. April is also a strong month, but the returns have mostly come at the beginning of the month. September is also a strong month for Bed Bath & Beyond and is the core part of the second seasonal period from late August to late September.

Over the last five years, Bed Bath & Beyond has followed its general seasonal trend with March and April being the strongest months. In 2015, Bed Bath & Beyond was only positive in its Spring seasonal period. In 2016, Bed Bath & Beyond was negative in its spring seasonal period.

CANADIANS GIVE 3 CHEERS FOR AMERICAN HOLIDAYS

When I used to work on the retail side of the investment business, I was always amazed at how often the Canadian stock market increased on U.S. holidays, when the U.S. stock market was closed.

The Canadian stock market on U.S. holidays always had light volume, tended not to have large increases or decreases, but usually ended the day with a gain.

1% average gain

How the trade works

For the three big holidays in the United States that do not exist in Canada (Memorial, Independence and U.S. Thanksgiving Days), buy at the end of the market day before the holiday (TSX Composite) and sell at the end of the U.S. holiday when the U.S markets are closed.

For U.S. investors to take advantage of this trade, they must have access to the TSX Composite. Unfortunately, SEC regulations do not allow Americans to purchase foreign ETFs.

Generally, markets perform well around most major U.S. holidays, hence the trading strategies for U.S holidays included in this book. The typical U.S. holiday trade is to get into the stock market the day before the holiday and then exit the day after the holiday.

The main reason for the strong performance around these holidays is a lack of institutional involvement in the markets, allowing bullish retail investors to push up the markets.

On the actual American holidays, economic reports are not released in the U.S. and are very seldom released in Canada. During market hours on U.S. holidays, without any strong influences, the TSX Composite tends to float, preferring to wait until the next day before making any significant moves. Despite this laxidasical action during the day, the TSX Composite tends to end the day on a gain. This is true for the three major U.S. holidays that are covered in this book: Memorial Day, Independence Day and U.S. Thanksgiving.

From a theoretical perspective, a lot of the gain that is captured on the U.S. holidays in the Canadian stock market is realized the next day when the U.S stock market is open. This does not invalidate the *Canadians Give 3 Cheers* trade – it presents more alternatives for the astute investor.

For example, an investor can allocate a portion of money to a standard U.S. holiday trade and another portion to the *Canadian Give 3 Cheers* version. By spreading out the exit days, the overall risk in the trade is reduced.

S&P/TSX Comp
Gain 1977-2015   Positive

	Memorial	Independence	Thanksgiving	Compound Growth
1977	0.10 %	-0.08 %	0.61 %	0.63 %
1978	-0.05	-0.16	0.57	0.36
1979	1.11	0.23	0.58	1.93
1980	1.64	0.76	0.89	3.32
1981	0.51	-0.15	1.03	1.40
1982	-0.18	-0.01	0.35	0.17
1983	0.29	0.53	0.15	0.97
1984	0.86	-0.11	0.73	1.48
1985	0.61	0.31	0.31	1.24
1986	0.23	-0.02	0.22	0.44
1987	-0.11	1.08	1.57	2.55
1988	0.44	0.08	0.58	1.11
1989	0.10	-0.12	-0.11	-0.13
1990	0.11	0.43	0.02	0.57
1991	0.02	0.18	-0.09	0.11
1992	-0.06	0.35	0.36	0.65
1993	0.42	-0.18	0.14	0.38
1994	-0.19	0.70	0.91	1.43
1995	0.14	0.25	0.29	0.68
1996	0.11	0.25	0.54	0.90
1997	1.08	-0.04	-0.85	0.18
1998	0.56	0.18	0.51	1.25
1999	0.57	1.63	1.14	3.39
2000	0.43	1.04	0.91	2.40
2001	-0.02	-0.23	0.70	0.45
2002	-0.01	0.08	0.38	0.45
2003	0.03	0.03	0.26	0.31
2004	0.84	-0.02	0.55	1.39
2005	0.56	0.39	1.48	2.45
2006	0.70	1.04	0.70	2.46
2007	0.35	-0.03	0.76	1.08
2008	0.24	-0.94	1.28	0.56
2009	0.76	0.36	-1.29	-0.18
2010	0.78	-0.92	0.34	0.19
2011	0.23	0.64	-0.75	0.12
2012	-0.09	0.55	0.44	0.90
2013	0.23	0.17	0.07	0.47
2014	0.05	0.05	-0.77	-0.67
2015	-0.09	0.30	0.16	0.38
Avg	0.34 %	0.22 %	0.40 %	0.97 %
Fq > 0	77 %	64 %	85 %	92 %

Canadians Give 3 Cheers Performance

Market Indices & Rates
Weekly Values**

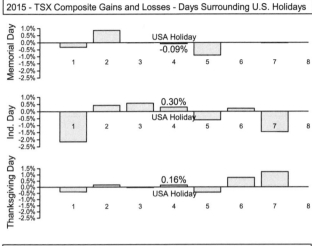

2015 - TSX Composite Gains and Losses - Days Surrounding U.S. Holidays

2016 - TSX Composite Gains and Losses - Days Surrounding U.S. Holidays

Stock Markets	2015	2016
Dow	17,847	17,673
S&P500	2,075	2,058
Nasdaq	4,927	4,853
TSX	14,930	13,451
FTSE	6,976	6,158
DAX	11,903	9,924
Nikkei	19,594	16,808
Hang Seng	24,481	20,611

Commodities	2015	2016
Oil	47.87	38.22
Gold	1195.2	1228.2

Bond Yields	2015	2016
USA 5 Yr Treasury	1.42	1.27
USA 10 Yr T	1.94	1.82
USA 20 Yr T	2.29	2.22
Moody's Aaa	3.55	3.73
Moody's Baa	4.47	4.91
CAN 5 Yr T	0.78	0.68
CAN 10 Yr T	1.35	1.23

Money Market	2015	2016
USA Fed Funds	0.25	0.50
USA 3 Mo T-B	0.03	0.24
CAN tgt overnight rate	0.75	0.50
CAN 3 Mo T-B	0.55	0.45

Foreign Exchange	2015	2016
EUR/USD	1.09	1.13
GBP/USD	1.49	1.43
USD/CAD	1.25	1.30
USD/JPY	119.46	112.57

MARCH

M	T	W	T	F	S	S
		1	2	3	4	5
6	7	8	9	10	11	12
13	14	15	16	17	18	19
20	21	22	23	24	25	26
27	28	29	30	31		

APRIL

M	T	W	T	F	S	S
					1	2
3	4	5	6	7	8	9
10	11	12	13	14	15	16
17	18	19	20	21	22	23
24	25	26	27	28	29	30

MAY

M	T	W	T	F	S	S
1	2	3	4	5	6	7
8	9	10	11	12	13	14
15	16	17	18	19	20	21
22	23	24	25	26	27	28
29	30	31				

Canadians Give 3 Cheers Performance

In 2015, the TSX Composite suffered a nominal loss on Memorial Day. The loss was more than offset by the gains on Independence Day and Thanksgiving Day.

In 2016, the TSX Composite was slightly negative on Memorial Day. On Independence Day, the TSX was up sharply as it benefited from the Brexit bounce. The TSX rallied sharply in the last few days of June and into July. After Independence Day, the TSX Composite fell back moderately before once again rallying.

APRIL

	MONDAY	TUESDAY	WEDNESDAY
WEEK 13	27	28	29
WEEK 14	**3** 27	**4** 26	**5** 25
WEEK 15	**10** 20	**11** 19	**12** 18
WEEK 16	**17** 13	**18** 12	**19** 11
WEEK 17	**24** 6	**25** 5	**26** 4

THURSDAY	FRIDAY
30	31
6 24	**7** 23
13 17	**14** 16
	USA Market Closed- Good Friday CAN Market Closed- Good Friday
20 10	**21** 9
27 3	**28** 2

MAY

M	T	W	T	F	S	S
1	2	3	4	5	6	7
8	9	10	11	12	13	14
15	16	17	18	19	20	21
22	23	24	25	26	27	28
29	30	31				

JUNE

M	T	W	T	F	S	S
			1	2	3	4
5	6	7	8	9	10	11
12	13	14	15	16	17	18
19	20	21	22	23	24	25
26	27	28	29	30		

JULY

M	T	W	T	F	S	S
					1	2
3	4	5	6	7	8	9
10	11	12	13	14	15	16
17	18	19	20	21	22	23
24	25	26	27	28	29	30
31						

AUGUST

M	T	W	T	F	S	S
	1	2	3	4	5	6
7	8	9	10	11	12	13
14	15	16	17	18	19	20
21	22	23	24	25	26	27
28	29	30	31			

APRIL SUMMARY

	Dow Jones	S&P 500	Nasdaq	TSX Comp
Month Rank	1	3	4	7
# Up	44	45	28	18
# Down	22	21	16	13
% Pos	67	68	64	58
% Avg. Gain	1.9	1.5	1.3	0.7

Dow & S&P 1950-2015, Nasdaq 1972-2015 TSX 1985-2015

S&P500 Cumulative Daily Gains for Avg Month 1950 to 2016

♦ April, on average, from 1950 to 2016 has been the third strongest month for the S&P 500 with an average gain of 1.5% and a positive frequency of 68%. ♦ The first part of April tends to be the strongest (see *18 Day Earnings Month Effect strategy*). ♦ The last part of April tends to be "flat." ♦ Overall, April tends to be a volatile month with the cyclical sectors outperforming. When the defensive sectors outperform in April, it often indicates market weakness ahead.

BEST / WORST APRIL BROAD MKTS. 2007-2016

BEST APRIL MARKETS
- Russell 2000 (2009) 15.3%
- Nasdaq (2009) 12.3%
- Nikkei 225 (2013) 11.8%

WORST APRIL MARKETS
- Nikkei 225 (2012) -5.6%
- Russell 2000 (2014) -3.9%
- Nikkei 225 (2014) -3.5%

Index Values End of Month

	2007	2008	2009	2010	2011	2012	2013	2014	2015	2016
Dow	13,063	12,820	8,168	11,009	12,811	13,214	14,840	16,581	17,841	17,774
S&P 500	1,482	1,386	873	1,187	1,364	1,398	1,598	1,884	2,086	2,065
Nasdaq	2,525	2,413	1,717	2,461	2,874	3,046	3,329	4,115	4,941	4,775
TSX	13,417	13,937	9,325	12,211	13,945	12,293	12,457	14,652	15,225	13,951
Russell 1000	1,553	1,453	917	1,259	1,458	1,487	1,705	2,019	2,238	2,199
Russell 2000	2,024	1,780	1,212	1,781	2,150	2,030	2,355	2,801	3,032	2,810
FTSE 100	6,449	6,087	4,244	5,553	6,070	5,738	6,430	6,780	6,961	6,242
Nikkei 225	17,400	13,850	8,828	11,057	9,850	9,521	13,861	14,304	19,520	16,666

Percent Gain for April

	2007	2008	2009	2010	2011	2012	2013	2014	2015	2016
Dow	5.7	4.5	7.3	1.4	4.0	0.0	1.8	0.7	0.4	0.5
S&P 500	4.3	4.8	9.4	1.5	2.8	-0.7	1.8	0.6	0.9	0.3
Nasdaq	4.3	5.9	12.3	2.6	3.3	-1.5	1.9	-2.0	0.8	-1.9
TSX	1.9	4.4	6.9	1.4	-1.2	-0.8	-2.3	2.2	2.2	3.4
Russell 1000	4.1	5.0	10.0	1.8	2.9	-0.7	1.7	0.4	0.6	0.4
Russell 2000	1.7	4.1	15.3	5.6	2.6	-1.6	-0.4	-3.9	-2.6	1.5
FTSE 100	2.2	6.8	8.1	-2.2	2.7	-0.5	0.3	2.8	2.8	1.1
Nikkei 225	0.7	10.6	8.9	-0.3	1.0	-5.6	11.8	-3.5	1.6	-0.6

April Market Avg. Performance 2007 to 2016[1]

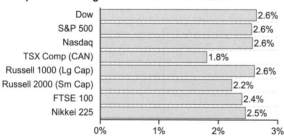

Dow	2.6%
S&P 500	2.6%
Nasdaq	2.6%
TSX Comp (CAN)	1.8%
Russell 1000 (Lg Cap)	2.6%
Russell 2000 (Sm Cap)	2.2%
FTSE 100	2.4%
Nikkei 225	2.5%

Interest Corner Apr[2]

	Fed Funds % [3]	3 Mo. T-Bill % [4]	10 Yr % [5]	20 Yr % [6]
2016	0.50	0.22	1.83	2.26
2015	0.25	0.01	2.05	2.49
2014	0.25	0.03	2.67	3.22
2013	0.25	0.05	1.70	2.49
2012	0.25	0.10	1.95	2.73

(1) Russell Data provided by Russell (2) Federal Reserve Bank of St. Louis- end of month values (3) Target rate set by FOMC (4)(5)(6) Constant yield maturities.

APRIL SECTOR PERFORMANCE

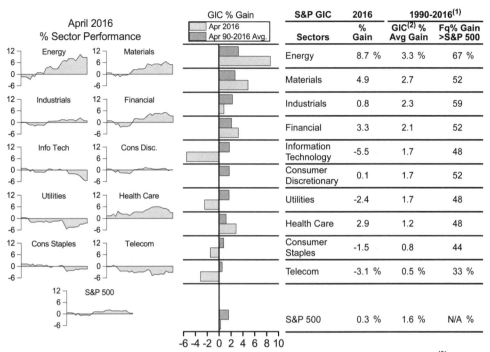

S&P GIC Sectors	2016 % Gain	1990-2016[1] GIC[2] % Avg Gain	Fq% Gain >S&P 500
Energy	8.7 %	3.3 %	67 %
Materials	4.9	2.7	52
Industrials	0.8	2.3	59
Financial	3.3	2.1	52
Information Technology	-5.5	1.7	48
Consumer Discretionary	0.1	1.7	52
Utilities	-2.4	1.7	48
Health Care	2.9	1.2	48
Consumer Staples	-1.5	0.8	44
Telecom	-3.1 %	0.5 %	33 %
S&P 500	0.3 %	1.6 %	N/A %

Sector Commentary

♦ On average, April is one of the strongest months of the year for commodities. ♦ In 2016, the energy sector once again led the major sectors of the stock market with a gain of 8.7%. ♦ The information technology sector typically finishes its seasonal period in March. After having an uncharacteristically strong run in March 2016, the information technology sector turned down and was the weakest sector in April with a loss of 5.5%.

Sub-Sector Commentary

♦ In April 2016, the cyclical sub-sectors continued their strong performance. One of the leading sub-sectors was metals and mining which produced a strong gain of 21.8%. ♦ Gold and silver typically do not perform well in April. After a weaker month in March, gold and silver resumed their climb in April with strong results. Generally, as the U.S. dollar declined in value, the commodity sectors appreciated.

SELECTED SUB-SECTORS[3]

Automotive & Components	-0.2 %	5.8 %	52 %
Railroads	8.7	3.4	59
SOX (1995-2016)	-4.7	3.3	50
Chemicals	2.7	3.2	70
Banks	6.8	2.6	56
Metals & Mining	21.8	2.3	44
Transportation	-0.9	2.2	56
Pharma	2.7	1.8	56
Steel	5.2	1.6	48
Retail	0.9	0.8	44
Homebuilders	-2.9	0.6	47
Agriculture (1994-2016)	10.0	0.4	57
Gold	3.9	0.3	44
Silver	16.1	0.3	41
Biotech (1993-2016)	3.0	0.3	42

(1) Sector data provided by Standard and Poors (2) GIC is short form for Global Industry Classification (3) Sub Sector data provided by Standard and Poors, except where marked by symbol.

18 DAY EARNINGS MONTH EFFECT
Markets Outperform 1st 18 Calendar Days of Earnings Months

Earnings season occurs the first month of every quarter. At this time, public companies report their financials for the previous quarter and give guidance on future expectations. As a result, investors tend to bid up stocks, anticipating good earnings. Earnings are a major driver of stock market prices as investors generally get in the stock market early, in anticipation of favorable results, which helps to run stock prices up in the first half of the month.

18th Day Line

January (% axis: 1.2, 1.0, 0.8, 0.6, 0.4, 0.2, 0.0, -0.2)

1st to 18th Day 1950-2015

Avg Gain 0.6%	Fq Pos 62%

The first month of the year generally has a good start. Investors and money managers generally push the market upward as they try to lock in their new positions for the year. The result is that the market tends to increase for the first eighteen days, pause, and then accelerate through the end of the month.

April (% axis: 1.6, 1.4, 1.2, 1.0, 0.8, 0.6, 0.4, 0.2, 0.0)

Avg Gain 1.4%	Fq Pos 68%

This month has a reputation of being a strong month. If you look at the graph, you can see that almost all of the gains have come in the first half of the month. It is interesting to note that the month returns tend to peak just after the last day to file tax returns.

July (% axis: 1.2, 1.0, 0.8, 0.6, 0.4, 0.2, 0.0)

Avg Gain 0.9%	Fq Pos 65%

This is the month in which the market can peak in strong bull markets. The returns in the first half of the month can be positive, but investors should be cautious, as the time period following in August and September has a tendency towards negative returns.

October (% axis: 1.0, 0.8, 0.6, 0.4, 0.2, 0.0)

Avg Gain 0.9%	Fq Pos 65%

This is the month with a bad reputation. Once again, the first part of the month tends to do well. It is the middle segment, centered around the notorious Black Monday, that brings down the results. Toward the end of the month, investors realize that the world has not ended and start to buy stocks again, providing a strong finish to the month.

1st to 18th Day Gain S&P500

	JAN	APR	JUL	OCT
1950	0.36 %	4.28 %	-3.56 %	2.88 %
1951	4.75	3.41	4.39	1.76
1952	2.02	-3.57	-0.44	-1.39
1953	-2.07	-2.65	0.87	3.38
1954	2.50	3.71	2.91	-1.49
1955	-3.28	4.62	3.24	-4.63
1956	-2.88	-1.53	4.96	2.18
1957	-4.35	2.95	2.45	-4.93
1958	2.78	1.45	1.17	2.80
1959	1.09	4.47	1.23	0.79
1960	-3.34	2.26	-2.14	1.55
1961	2.70	1.75	-0.36	2.22
1962	-4.42	-1.84	2.65	0.12
1963	3.30	3.49	-1.27	2.26
1964	2.05	1.99	2.84	0.77
1965	2.05	2.31	1.87	1.91
1966	1.64	2.63	2.66	2.77
1967	6.80	1.84	3.16	-1.51
1968	-0.94	7.63	1.87	2.09
1969	-1.76	-0.27	-2.82	3.37
1970	-1.24	-4.42	6.83	-0.02
1971	1.37	3.17	0.42	-1.01
1972	1.92	2.40	-1.22	-2.13
1973	0.68	0.02	2.00	1.46
1974	-2.04	0.85	-2.58	13.76
1975	3.50	3.53	-2.09	5.95
1976	7.55	-2.04	0.38	-3.58
1977	-3.85	2.15	0.47	-3.18
1978	-4.77	4.73	1.40	-2.00
1979	3.76	0.11	-1.19	-5.22
1980	2.90	-1.51	6.83	4.83
1981	-0.73	-0.96	-0.34	2.59
1982	-4.35	4.33	1.33	13.54
1983	4.10	4.43	-2.20	1.05
1984	1.59	-0.80	-1.16	1.20
1985	2.44	0.10	1.32	2.72
1986	-1.35	1.46	-5.77	3.25
1987	9.96	-1.64	3.48	-12.16
1988	1.94	0.12	-1.09	2.75
1989	3.17	3.78	4.20	-2.12
1990	-4.30	0.23	1.73	-0.10
1991	0.61	3.53	3.83	1.20
1992	0.42	3.06	1.83	-1.45
1993	0.26	-0.60	-1.06	2.07
1994	1.67	-0.74	2.46	1.07
1995	2.27	0.93	2.52	0.52
1996	-1.25	-0.29	-4.04	3.42
1997	4.78	1.22	3.41	-0.33
1998	-0.92	1.90	4.67	3.88
1999	1.14	2.54	3.36	-2.23
2000	-0.96	-3.80	2.69	-6.57
2001	2.10	6.71	-1.36	2.66
2002	-1.79	-2.00	-10.94	8.48
2003	2.50	5.35	1.93	4.35
2004	2.51	0.75	-3.46	-0.05
2005	-1.32	-2.93	2.50	-4.12
2006	2.55	1.22	0.51	3.15
2007	1.41	4.33	-3.20	1.48
2008	-9.75	5.11	-1.51	-19.36
2009	-5.88	8.99	2.29	2.89
2010	1.88	1.94	3.32	3.81
2011	2.97	-1.56	-1.15	8.30
2012	4.01	-1.66	0.78	1.16
2013	4.2	-1.76	5.17	3.74
2014	-0.52	-0.4	0.92	-4.34
2015	-1.92	0.64	3.08	5.89
Avg	0.64 %	1.37 %	0.86 %	0.87 %

Earnings Month Effect Performance

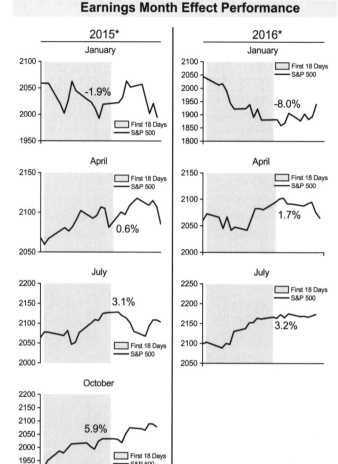

*Last day of previous month included in graph only, displayed return is for first 18 calendar days of month

Market Indices & Rates Weekly Values**

Stock Markets	2015	2016
Dow	17,803	17,635
S&P500	2,070	2,053
Nasdaq	4,904	4,871
TSX	14,945	13,330
FTSE	6,827	6,152
DAX	12,005	9,633
Nikkei	19,280	15,829
Hang Seng	25,029	20,255

Commodities	2015	2016
Oil	48.88	37.26
Gold	1192.0	1230.8

Bond Yields	2015	2016
USA 5 Yr Treasury	1.34	1.18
USA 10 Yr T	1.91	1.74
USA 20 Yr T	2.28	2.14
Moody's Aaa	3.49	3.63
Moody's Baa	4.46	4.82
CAN 5 Yr T	0.75	0.68
CAN 10 Yr T	1.33	1.20

Money Market	2015	2016
USA Fed Funds	0.25	0.50
USA 3 Mo T-B	0.03	0.23
CAN tgt overnight rate	0.75	0.50
CAN 3 Mo T-B	0.56	0.46

Foreign Exchange	2015	2016
EUR/USD	1.08	1.14
GBP/USD	1.48	1.41
USD/CAD	1.26	1.31
USD/JPY	119.73	109.55

APRIL

M	T	W	T	F	S	S
					1	2
3	4	5	6	7	8	9
10	11	12	13	14	15	16
17	18	19	20	21	22	23
24	25	26	27	28	29	30

MAY

M	T	W	T	F	S	S
1	2	3	4	5	6	7
8	9	10	11	12	13	14
15	16	17	18	19	20	21
22	23	24	25	26	27	28
29	30	31				

JUNE

M	T	W	T	F	S	S
		1	2	3	4	
5	6	7	8	9	10	11
12	13	14	15	16	17	18
19	20	21	22	23	24	25
26	27	28	29	30		

Earnings Month Effect Performance

In 2015, the first eighteen calendar days of the earnings months were positive three out of four times. The biggest gain occurred in October, as the S&P 500 was still rallying from its summertime correction.

In 2016, the first eighteen calendar days for earnings months phenomenon started off on a negative note as January corrected sharply as investors questioned the impact of the first Federal Reserve interest rate increase since 2006.

The first eighteen calendar days in April and July of 2016, were very strong, but not enough to overcome the negative impact of the S&P 500 correcting 8.0% in January.

CONSUMER SWITCH
Consumer Staples Outperform Apr 23 to Oct 27

The *Consumer Switch* strategy has allowed investors to use a set portion of their account to switch between the two related consumer sectors. To use this strategy, investors invest in the consumer discretionary sector from October 28th to April 22nd, and then use the proceeds to invest in the consumer staples sector from April 23rd to October 27th, and then repeat the cycle.

The end result has been outperformance compared with buying and holding both consumer sectors, or buying and holding the broad market.

3863% total aggregate gain

The basic premise of the strategy is that the consumer discretionary sector tends to outperform during the favorable six month period for stocks (October 28th to May 5th), when more money flows into the stock market, pushing up stock prices. On the other hand, the consumer staples sector tends to outperform when investors are looking for safety and stability of earnings in the other six months when the market tends to move into a defensive mode.

Consumer Staples & Discretionary Switch Strategy*

Investment Period		Buy @ Beginning of Period	% Gain @ End of Period	% Gain Cumulative
90 Apr23 - 90 Oct29		Staples	7.7%	8%
90 Oct29 - 91 Apr23		Discretionary	41.7	53
91 Apr23 - 91 Oct28		Staples	2.1	56
91 Oct28 - 92 Apr23		Discretionary	15.9	81
92 Apr23 - 92 Oct27		Staples	6.3	92
92 Oct27 - 93 Apr23		Discretionary	6.3	104
93 Apr23 - 93 Oct27		Staples	5.8	116
93 Oct27 - 94 Apr25		Discretionary	-3.7	108
94 Apr25 - 94 Oct27		Staples	10.2	129
94 Oct27 - 95 Apr24		Discretionary	4.4	139
95 Apr24 - 95 Oct27		Staples	15.3	176
95 Oct27 - 96 Apr23		Discretionary	17.3	227
96 Apr23 - 96 Oct27		Staples	12.6	265
96 Oct27 - 97 Apr23		Discretionary	5.1	283
97 Apr23 - 97 Oct27		Staples	2.5	293
97 Oct27 - 98 Apr23		Discretionary	35.9	434
98 Apr23 - 98 Oct27		Staples	-0.7	423
98 Oct27 - 99 Apr23		Discretionary	41.8	651
99 Apr23 - 99 Oct27		Staples	-9.7	578
99 Oct27 - 00 Apr24		Discretionary	11.9	659
00 Apr24 - 00 Oct27		Staples	16.5	785
00 Oct27 - 01 Apr23		Discretionary	9.8	872
01 Apr23 - 01 Oct29		Staples	4.0	910
01 Oct29 - 02 Apr23		Discretionary	16.1	1073
02 Apr23 - 02 Oct28		Staples	-13.9	910
02 Oct28 - 03 Apr23		Discretionary	3.0	941
03 Apr23 - 03 Oct27		Staples	8.4	1028
03 Oct27 - 04 Apr23		Discretionary	9.6	1137
04 Apr23 - 04 Oct27		Staples	-7.4	1045
04 Oct27 - 05 Apr25		Discretionary	-2.0	1021
05 Apr25 - 05 Oct27		Staples	-0.5	1016
05 Oct27 - 06 Apr24		Discretionary	9.2	1119
06 Apr24 - 06 Oct27		Staples	10.6	1249
06 Oct27 - 07 Apr23		Discretionary	6.3	1334
07 Apr23 - 07 Oct29		Staples	4.6	1400
07 Oct29 - 08 Apr23		Discretionary	-13.7	1194
08 Apr23 - 08 Oct27		Staples	-21.5	916
08 Oct27 - 09 Apr23		Discretionary	17.7	1096
09 Apr23 - 09 Oct27		Staples	20.6	1342
09 Oct27 - 10 Apr23		Discretionary	29.7	1770
10 Apr23 - 10 Oct27		Staples	2.4	1815
10 Oct27 - 11 Apr25		Discretionary	13.7	2079
11 Apr25 - 11 Oct27		Staples	2.2	2126
11 Oct27 - 12 Apr23		Discretionary	10.9	2368
12 Apr23 - 12 Oct31		Staples	4.7	2485
12 Oct31 - 13 Apr23		Discretionary	17.5	2938
13 Apr23 - 13 Oct28		Staples	2.3	3006
13 Oct28 - 14 Apr23		Discretionary	1.7	3060
14 Apr23 - 14 Oct27		Staples	5.9	3248
14 Oct27 - 15 Apr23		Discretionary	15.2	3758
15 Apr23 - 15 Oct27		Staples	3.1	3878
15 Oct27 - 16 Apr22		Discretionary	-0.4	3863

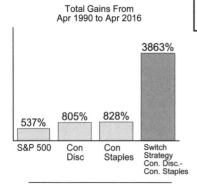

Total Gains From
Apr 1990 to Apr 2016

3863%

537% — S&P 500
805% — Con Disc
828% — Con Staples
3863% — Switch Strategy Con. Disc.- Con. Staples

* If buy date lands on weekend or holiday, then next day is used

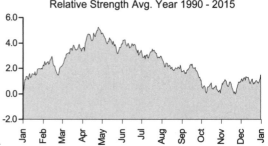

Consumer Discretionary / Consumer Staples
Relative Strength Avg. Year 1990 - 2015

Consumer Switch Performance

2015

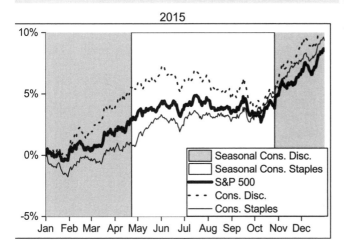

Legend:
- Seasonal Cons. Disc.
- Seasonal Cons. Staples
- S&P 500
- - - - Cons. Disc.
- —— Cons. Staples

2016

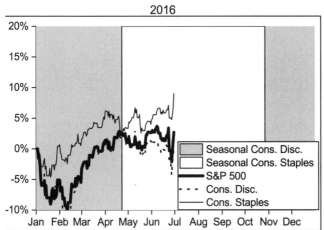

Legend:
- Seasonal Cons. Disc.
- Seasonal Cons. Staples
- S&P 500
- - - - Cons. Disc.
- —— Cons. Staples

Market Indices & Rates
Weekly Values**

Stock Markets	2015	2016
Dow	17,935	17,802
S&P500	2,086	2,070
Nasdaq	4,950	4,907
TSX	15,244	13,596
FTSE	7,001	6,303
DAX	12,175	9,923
Nikkei	19,735	16,364
Hang Seng	26,818	20,952

Commodities	2015	2016
Oil	51.79	41.23
Gold	1205.1	1243.2

Bond Yields	2015	2016
USA 5 Yr Treasury	1.36	1.22
USA 10 Yr T	1.93	1.77
USA 20 Yr T	2.31	2.16
Moody's Aaa	3.50	3.61
Moody's Baa	4.47	4.78
CAN 5 Yr T	0.77	0.75
CAN 10 Yr T	1.35	1.27

Money Market	2015	2016
USA Fed Funds	0.25	0.50
USA 3 Mo T-B	0.03	0.22
CAN tgt overnight rate	0.75	0.50
CAN 3 Mo T-B	0.58	0.48

Foreign Exchange	2015	2016
EUR/USD	1.08	1.13
GBP/USD	1.48	1.42
USD/CAD	1.25	1.28
USD/JPY	120.15	108.80

APRIL

M	T	W	T	F	S	S
					1	2
3	4	5	6	7	8	9
10	11	12	13	14	15	16
17	18	19	20	21	22	23
24	25	26	27	28	29	30

MAY

M	T	W	T	F	S	S
1	2	3	4	5	6	7
8	9	10	11	12	13	14
15	16	17	18	19	20	21
22	23	24	25	26	27	28
29	30	31				

JUNE

M	T	W	T	F	S	S
			1	2	3	4
5	6	7	8	9	10	11
12	13	14	15	16	17	18
19	20	21	22	23	24	25
26	27	28	29	30		

Consumer Switch Strategy Performance

In 2015, the consumer discretionary sector outperformed the S&P 500 in its seasonal period at the beginning of the year and the end of the year. In both instances, the S&P 500 was rallying sharply. The consumer staples sector outperformed both the S&P 500 and the consumer discretionary sector in its seasonal period. Overall the consumer switch strategy in 2015 was a strong success.

So far in 2016, the consumer discretionary sector has performed at market in its seasonal period. The consumer staples sector has outperformed the S&P 500 in the first half of its seasonal period, as investors have favored companies with stable growth and higher than average dividends.

NATURAL GAS FIRES UP AND DOWN
①LONG (Mar22-Jun19) ②LONG (Sep5-Dec21)
③SELL SHORT (Dec22-Dec31)

There are two high consumption times for natural gas: winter and summer. The colder it gets in winter, the more natural gas is consumed to keep the furnaces going. The warmer it gets in summer, the more natural gas is used to produce power for air conditioners.

On the supply side, weather plays a large factor in determining price. During the hurricane season in the Gulf of Mexico, the price of natural gas is affected by the number and severity of hurricanes.

Natural Gas (Cash) Henry Hub LA*
Seasonal Gains 1995 to 2015

		Pos.	Pos.	Neg. (Short)	Pos.
Year	Mar 22	Sep 5	Dec 22	Compound
%	to Jun 19	to Dec 21	to Dec 31	Growth
1995	99.4	13.0 %	103.0 %	1.2 %	126.7
1996	-27.4	-6.6	170.4	-46.2	269.2
1997	-9.4	16.8	-13.1	-6.3	7.9
1998	-13.0	-2.6	20.9	-6.7	25.7
1999	18.6	28.9	5.3	-11.2	50.9
2000	356.5	57.1	121.9	0.7	246.3
2001	-74.3	-24.1	21.5	1.5	-9.2
2002	70.0	0.6	61.3	-9.1	77.1
2003	26.4	9.5	47.1	-16.3	87.4
2004	3.6	18.2	54.6	-11.6	103.9
2005	58.4	6.3	14.5	-29.6	57.7
2006	-42.2	-1.8	17.4	-9.5	26.3
2007	30.2	9.2	32.7	2.0	42.1
2008	-21.4	52.2	-21.4	-0.9	20.6
2009	3.6	1.5	208.0	0.7	210.4
2010	-27.4	28.6	10.4	2.4	38.6
2011	-29.6	10.0	-26.1	-1.7	-17.3
2012	15.4	18.7	21.7	0.6	43.7
2013	26.3	-1.4	18.2	-0.2	16.8
2014	-31.1	7.7	-11.8	-12.9	7.2
2015	-22.8	-0.5	-36.1	35.6	-59.0
Avg.	19.5	11.5 %	39.1 %	-5.6 %	65.4

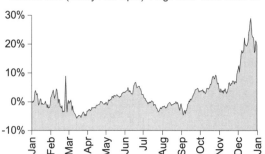

Natural Gas (Henry Hub Spot)- Avg. Year 1995 to 2015

Natural gas prices tend to rise from mid-March to mid-June ahead of the cooling season demands in the summer. From 1995 to 2015, during the period of March 22nd to June 19th, the spot price of natural gas has on average increased 11.5% and has been positive 71% of the time. The price of natural gas also tends to rise between September 5th and December 21st, due to the demands of the heating season. In this period, from 1995 to 2015, natural gas has produced an average gain of 39.1% and has been positive 76% of the time.

Positive 86% of the time

Natural gas tends to fall in price from December 22nd to December 31st. Although this is a short time period, for the years from 1995 to 2015, natural gas has produced an average loss of 5.6% and has only been positive 38% of the time. Also, in this period, when gains did occur, they were relatively small. The poor performance of natural gas at this time is largely driven by southern U.S. refiners dumping inventory on the market to help mitigate year-end taxes on their inventory.

Applying a strategy of investing in natural gas from March 22nd to June 19th, reinvesting the proceeds from September 5th to December 21st, reinvesting the proceeds again to short natural gas from December 22nd to December 31st, has produced a compounded average return of 65.4% and has been positive 86% of the time.

Using the natural gas compound strategy has produced returns that are over three times greater than the average annual gain in natural gas. By using the strategy, an investor would have caught most of the large gains and missed most of the large losses.

> ⚠ *Caution: The cash price for natural gas is extremely volatile and extreme caution should be used. Care must be taken to ensure that investments are within risk tolerances.*

> ⓘ *Source: New York Mercantile Exchange. NYMX is an exchange provider of futures and options.*

Natural Gas Performance

NatGas Monthly Performance (1995-2015)

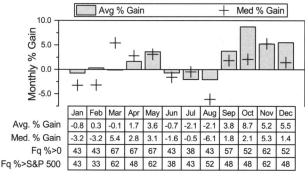

Avg % Gain · Med % Gain

	Jan	Feb	Mar	Apr	May	Jun	Jul	Aug	Sep	Oct	Nov	Dec
Avg. % Gain	-0.8	0.3	-0.1	1.7	3.6	-0.7	-2.1	-2.1	3.8	8.7	5.2	5.5
Med. % Gain	-3.2	-3.2	5.4	2.8	3.1	-1.6	-0.5	-6.1	1.8	2.1	5.3	1.4
Fq %>0	43	43	67	67	67	43	38	43	57	52	62	52
Fq %>S&P 500	43	33	62	48	62	38	43	52	48	48	62	48

NatGas 5 Year (2011-2015) % Gain

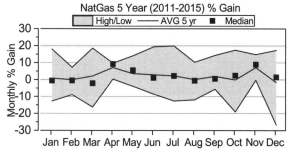

High/Low — AVG 5 yr ■ Median

NatGas Performance 2015-2016

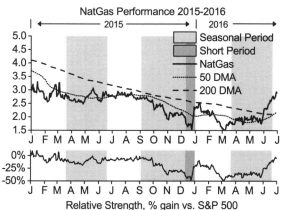

Relative Strength, % gain vs. S&P 500

Market Indices & Rates
Weekly Values**

Stock Markets	2015	2016
Dow	18,012	18,028
S&P500	2,096	2,096
Nasdaq	4,983	4,940
TSX	15,394	13,851
FTSE	7,058	6,372
DAX	12,097	10,340
Nikkei	19,845	16,999
Hang Seng	27,718	21,385

Commodities	2015	2016
Oil	54.81	41.68
Gold	1198.9	1246.8

Bond Yields	2015	2016
USA 5 Yr Treasury	1.33	1.31
USA 10 Yr T	1.90	1.84
USA 20 Yr T	2.30	2.24
Moody's Aaa	3.47	3.57
Moody's Baa	4.44	4.77
CAN 5 Yr T	0.79	0.82
CAN 10 Yr T	1.36	1.39

Money Market	2015	2016
USA Fed Funds	0.25	0.50
USA 3 Mo T-B	0.02	0.22
CAN tgt overnight rate	0.75	0.50
CAN 3 Mo T-B	0.62	0.55

Foreign Exchange	2015	2016
EUR/USD	1.07	1.13
GBP/USD	1.48	1.43
USD/CAD	1.24	1.27
USD/JPY	119.32	109.82

APRIL

M	T	W	T	F	S	S
					1	2
3	4	5	6	7	8	9
10	11	12	13	14	15	16
17	18	19	20	21	22	23
24	25	26	27	28	29	30

MAY

M	T	W	T	F	S	S
1	2	3	4	5	6	7
8	9	10	11	12	13	14
15	16	17	18	19	20	21
22	23	24	25	26	27	28
29	30	31				

JUNE

M	T	W	T	F	S	S
		1	2	3	4	
5	6	7	8	9	10	11
12	13	14	15	16	17	18
19	20	21	22	23	24	25
26	27	28	29	30		

From 1995 to 2015, on average, September through to December has been the best cluster of positive months for natural gas. Natural gas is a very volatile commodity and as a result there is a large difference between the mean and median performances on a month to month basis.

April and May are also strong months and make up the core of the spring trade. In the last five years, natural gas has generally followed its seasonal trend, with a strong performance in April, a weak summer and a strong autumn. In 2015/2016, the overall return for the combination of natural gas periods was negative.

![CA][$] CANADIAN DOLLAR STRONG– TWICE
①April ②Aug20-Sep25

All other things being equal, if oil increases in price, investors favor the Canadian dollar over the U.S. dollar. They do so with good reason, as Canada is a net exporter of oil and benefits from its rising price.

Oil tends to do well in the month of April, which is the core of the main energy seasonal strategy that lasts from February 25th to May 9th.

April has been a strong month for the Canadian dollar relative to the U.S. dollar. The largest losses have had a tendency to occur in years when the Fed Reserve has been aggressively hiking its target rate.

At some point during the years 1987, 2000, 2004 and 2005, the Fed increased their target rate by a total of at least 1% in each year. Since 1971, three of these

CAD vs USD Avg. % Gain 1971 to 2015

years (1987, 2004 and 2005) were three of the biggest losers for the Canadian dollar in the month of April.

The Canadian dollar also has a second period of seasonality, August 20th to September 25th. It is not a coincidence that oil also has a second period of seasonal strength at this time. Although the August 20th to September 25th seasonal period is not as strong as the April seasonal period, it is still a trade worth considering.

CAD vs USD Apr & Aug 20 to Sep 25 % Gain (1971-2016) Source: Bloomberg   Positive ☐

	Apr1- Apr30	Aug20 -Sep25		Apr1- Apr30	Aug20 -Sep25		Apr1- Apr30	Aug20 -Sep25		Apr1- Apr30	Aug20 -Sep25		Apr1- Apr30	Aug20 -Sep25
			1980	0.29%	-0.15%	1990	0.44%	-0.43%	2000	-1.89%	-0.96%	2010	0.44%	1.32%
1971	-0.10%	0.46%	1981	-0.74	1.08	1991	0.65	0.86	2001	2.76	-1.76	2011	2.44	-4.20
1972	0.53	0.01	1982	0.89	0.78	1992	-0.48	-3.37	2002	1.77	-0.61	2012	1.05	1.16
1973	-0.41	-0.32	1983	0.64	0.17	1993	-1.02	-0.08	2003	2.50	3.95	2013	1.01	0.39
1974	1.27	-0.40	1984	-0.62	-1.01	1994	0.14	2.22	2004	-4.46	1.57	2014	0.88	-1.58
1975	-1.56	1.33	1985	0.04	-0.32	1995	2.91	0.96	2005	-3.77	3.75	2015	4.67	-1.18
1976	0.55	1.41	1986	1.69	0.35	1996	0.15	0.48	2006	4.17	0.64	2016	3.40	
1977	0.91	0.31	1987	-2.38	1.41	1997	-0.97	0.79	2007	4.17	6.30			
1978	0.09	-3.22	1988	0.41	0.43	1998	-0.85	1.37	2008	1.81	2.59			
1979	1.61	0.15	1989	0.60	0.55	1999	3.53	1.36	2009	5.59	0.46			
Avg.	0.32%	-0.03%		0.06%	0.38%		0.45%	0.51%		1.62%	1.88%		1.98%	-0.68%

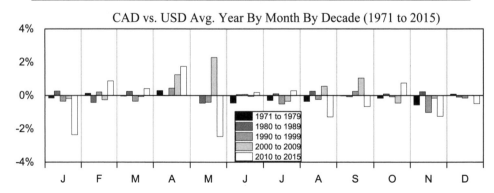

CAD vs. USD Avg. Year By Month By Decade (1971 to 2015)

1971 to 1979
1980 to 1989
1990 to 1999
2000 to 2009
2010 to 2015

CAD/USD Performance

CAD/USD Monthly Performance (1971-2015)

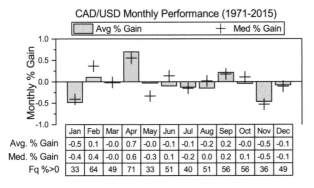

	Jan	Feb	Mar	Apr	May	Jun	Jul	Aug	Sep	Oct	Nov	Dec
Avg. % Gain	-0.5	0.1	-0.0	0.7	-0.0	-0.1	-0.1	-0.2	0.2	-0.0	-0.5	-0.1
Med. % Gain	-0.4	0.4	-0.0	0.6	-0.3	0.1	-0.2	0.0	0.2	0.1	-0.5	-0.1
Fq %>0	33	64	49	71	33	51	40	51	56	56	36	49

CAD/USD 5 Year (2011-2015) % Gain

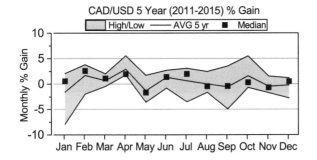

CAD/USD Performance 2015-2016

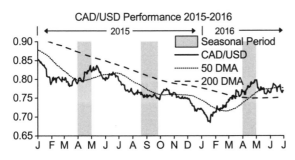

Market Indices & Rates
Weekly Values**

Stock Markets	2015	2016
Dow	18,032	17,923
S&P500	2,107	2,083
Nasdaq	5,038	4,846
TSX	15,373	13,866
FTSE	7,054	6,277
DAX	11,847	10,294
Nikkei	19,977	17,187
Hang Seng	27,754	21,306

Commodities	2015	2016
Oil	55.82	44.13
Gold	1191.0	1253.4

Bond Yields	2015	2016
USA 5 Yr Treasury	1.35	1.35
USA 10 Yr T	1.93	1.89
USA 20 Yr T	2.36	2.30
Moody's Aaa	3.55	3.63
Moody's Baa	4.48	4.75
CAN 5 Yr T	0.90	0.89
CAN 10 Yr T	1.46	1.52

Money Market	2015	2016
USA Fed Funds	0.25	0.50
USA 3 Mo T-B	0.03	0.23
CAN tgt overnight rate	0.75	0.50
CAN 3 Mo T-B	0.66	0.56

Foreign Exchange	2015	2016
EUR/USD	1.08	1.13
GBP/USD	1.50	1.46
USD/CAD	1.22	1.26
USD/JPY	119.47	109.72

APRIL

M	T	W	T	F	S	S
					1	2
3	4	5	6	7	8	9
10	11	12	13	14	15	16
17	18	19	20	21	22	23
24	25	26	27	28	29	30

MAY

M	T	W	T	F	S	S
1	2	3	4	5	6	7
8	9	10	11	12	13	14
15	16	17	18	19	20	21
22	23	24	25	26	27	28
29	30	31				

JUNE

M	T	W	T	F	S	S
		1	2	3	4	
5	6	7	8	9	10	11
12	13	14	15	16	17	18
19	20	21	22	23	24	25
26	27	28	29	30		

Canadian Dollar Performance (CAD/USD)

From 1971 to 2015, April has been the strongest month of the year for CAD/USD on an average, median and frequency basis. On an average basis, September is the second strongest month and its gains makes up the bulk of the second seasonal period of performance for the Canadian dollar. Over the last five years, May and August have been the worst performing months, with July being the best performing month.

In 2015, the Canadian dollar started the year on a negative note and generally continued its downward trend except for the time period around its April seasonal period. In 2016, the Canadian dollar started to rally in January, performed well in April and then started a period of consolidation after its seasonal period.

MAY

	MONDAY	TUESDAY	WEDNESDAY
WEEK 18	**1** 30	**2** 29	**3** 28
WEEK19	**8** 23	**9** 22	**10** 21
WEEK 20	**15** 16	**16** 15	**17** 14
WEEK 21	**22** 9 CAN Market Closed- Victoria Day	**23** 8	**24** 7
WEEK 22	**29** 2 USA Market Closed- Memorial Day	**30** 1	**31**

THURSDAY		FRIDAY	
4	27	**5**	26
11	20	**12**	19
18	13	**19**	12
25	6	**26**	5
1		2	

JUNE

M	T	W	T	F	S	S
			1	2	3	4
5	6	7	8	9	10	11
12	13	14	15	16	17	18
19	20	21	22	23	24	25
26	27	28	29	30		

JULY

M	T	W	T	F	S	S
					1	2
3	4	5	6	7	8	9
10	11	12	13	14	15	16
17	18	19	20	21	22	23
24	25	26	27	28	29	30
31						

AUGUST

M	T	W	T	F	S	S
	1	2	3	4	5	6
7	8	9	10	11	12	13
14	15	16	17	18	19	20
21	22	23	24	25	26	27
28	29	30	31			

SEPTEMBER

M	T	W	T	F	S	S
				1	2	3
4	5	6	7	8	9	10
11	12	13	14	15	16	17
18	19	20	21	22	23	24
25	26	27	28	29	30	

MAY
S U M M A R Y

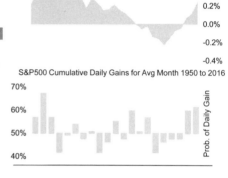

0.6%
0.4%
0.2%
0.0%
-0.2%
-0.4%

S&P500 Cumulative Daily Gains for Avg Month 1950 to 2016

	Dow Jones	S&P 500	Nasdaq	TSX Comp
Month Rank	9	8	5	2
# Up	34	38	27	19
# Down	32	28	17	12
% Pos	52	58	61	61
% Avg. Gain	0.0	0.2	1.0	1.4

Dow & S&P 1950-2015, Nasdaq 1972-2015, TSX 1985-2015

♦ The S&P 500 often peaks in May and as a result, seasonal investors should start to be more cautious with their investments at this time. ♦ Defensive sectors often perform well in May♦ The first few days and the last few days in May tend to be strong and the period in between tends to negative. ♦ A lot of the cyclical sectors finish their seasonal periods at the beginning of May. ♦ The month of May starts the six month unfavorable period for stocks, which has historically been the weaker six months of the year.

BEST / WORST MAY BROAD MKTS. 2007-2016

BEST MAY MARKETS
- ♦ TSX Comp. (2009) 11.2%
- ♦ Nikkei 225 (2009) 7.9%
- ♦ TSX Comp (2008) 5.6%

WORST MAY MARKETS
- ♦ Nikkei 225 (2010) -11.7%
- ♦ Nikkei 225 (2012) -10.3%
- ♦ Nikkei 225 (2006) -8.5%

Index Values End of Month

	2007	2008	2009	2010	2011	2012	2013	2014	2015	2016
Dow	13,628	12,638	8,500	10,137	12,570	12,393	15,116	16,717	18,011	17,787
S&P 500	1,531	1,400	919	1,089	1,345	1,310	1,631	1,924	2,107	2,097
Nasdaq	2,605	2,523	1,774	2,257	2,835	2,827	3,456	4,243	5,070	4,948
TSX Comp.	14,057	14,715	10,370	11,763	13,803	11,513	12,650	14,604	15,014	14,066
Russell 1000	1,605	1,477	965	1,157	1,439	1,392	1,739	2,061	2,262	2,232
Russell 2000	2,105	1,860	1,247	1,644	2,108	1,893	2,446	2,820	3,098	2,870
FTSE 100	6,622	6,054	4,418	5,188	5,990	5,321	6,583	6,845	6,984	6,231
Nikkei 225	17,876	14,339	9,523	9,769	9,694	8,543	13,775	14,632	20,563	17,235

Percent Gain for May

	2007	2008	2009	2010	2011	2012	2013	2014	2015	2016
Dow	4.3	-1.4	4.1	-7.9	-1.9	-6.2	1.9	0.8	1.0	0.1
S&P 500	3.3	1.1	5.3	-8.2	-1.4	-6.3	2.1	2.1	1.0	1.5
Nasdaq	3.1	4.6	3.3	-8.3	-1.3	-7.2	3.8	3.1	2.6	3.6
TSX Comp.	4.8	5.6	11.2	-3.7	-1.0	-6.3	1.6	-0.3	-1.4	0.8
Russell 1000	3.4	1.6	5.3	-8.1	-1.3	-6.4	2.0	2.1	1.1	1.5
Russell 2000	4.0	4.5	2.9	-7.7	-2.0	-6.7	3.9	0.7	2.2	2.1
FTSE 100	2.7	-0.6	4.1	-6.6	-1.3	-7.3	2.4	1.0	0.3	-0.2
Nikkei 225	2.7	3.5	7.9	-11.7	-1.6	-10.3	-0.6	2.3	5.3	3.4

May Market Avg. Performance 2007 to 2016[1]

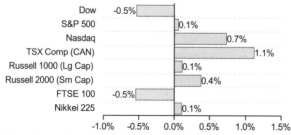

Dow	-0.5%
S&P 500	0.1%
Nasdaq	0.7%
TSX Comp (CAN)	1.1%
Russell 1000 (Lg Cap)	0.1%
Russell 2000 (Sm Cap)	0.4%
FTSE 100	-0.5%
Nikkei 225	0.1%

Interest Corner May[2]

	Fed Funds % [3]	3 Mo. T-Bill % [4]	10 Yr % [5]	20 Yr % [6]
2016	0.50	0.34	1.84	2.23
2015	0.25	0.01	2.12	2.63
2014	0.25	0.04	2.48	3.05
2013	0.25	0.04	2.16	2.95
2012	0.25	0.07	1.59	2.27

(1) Russell Data provided by Russell (2) Federal Reserve Bank of St. Louis- end of month values (3) Target rate set by FOMC (4)(5)(6) Constant yield maturities.

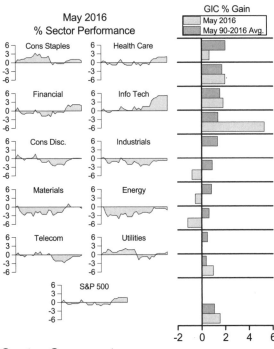

S&P GIC Sectors	2016 % Gain	1990-2016[1]	
		GIC[2] % Avg Gain	Fq% Gain >S&P 500
Consumer Staples	0.6 %	2.0 %	56 %
Health Care	2.0	1.7	56
Financial	1.8	1.5	48
Information Technology	5.3	1.4	59
Consumer Discretionary	0.0	1.3	59
Industrials	-0.8	0.9	33
Materials	-0.6	0.8	33
Energy	-1.2	0.6	33
Telecom	0.0	0.5	48
Utilities	1.0 %	0.4 %	41 %
S&P 500	1.5 %	1.0 %	N/A %

SELECTED SUB-SECTORS[3]			
Agriculture (1994-2016)	7.1 %	2.6 %	57 %
Biotech (1993-2016)	2.5	2.3	71
Banks	2.0	2.1	52
Retail	1.4	1.8	59
Pharma	2.2	1.3	48
Railroads	-3.9	1.3	56
Chemicals	0.6	1.0	48
SOX (1995-2016)	8.4	0.8	55
Steel	-2.5	0.6	48
Transportation	-2.2	0.4	48
Metals & Mining	-11.9	0.4	44
Automotive & Components	-1.0	0.3	26
Gold	-5.7	0.1	52
Home-builders	1.4	-0.3	35
Silver	-10.1	-0.6	44

Sector Commentary

♦ In May 2016, the information technology sector continued with its rally from previous months, producing a 5.3% gain. ♦ The energy sector is typically one of the weaker performing sectors in May. ♦ In May 2016, the energy sector was the worst performing sector with a loss of 1.2%. ♦ Two other sectors with losses were industrials and materials.

Sub-Sector Commentary

♦ In May 2016, the metals and mining sub-sector produced a large loss of 11.9%. This occurred after a very strong multi-month rally. ♦ Gold and silver also produced large losses of 5.7% and 10.1%, respectively. ♦ The semi-conductors produced a strong 8.4% gain in May. Typically, semi-conductors do not perform strongly in May. ♦ The agriculture sector is typically one of the better performing sub-sectors in May. In 2016, agriculture produced a strong gain of 7.1%.

U.S. Government Bonds (7-10 Years)
May 6th to Oct 3rd

The following government bond seasonal period analysis has been broken down into two contiguous periods in order to demonstrate the relative strength of first part of the trade compared with the second part. Although both the May 6th to August 8th and the August 9th to October 3rd periods provide value, the sweet spot to the government bond trade is in the latter period from August 9th to October 3rd.

Bonds outperform from late spring into autumn for three reasons. First, governments and companies tend to raise more money through bond issuance at the beginning of the year to meet their needs for the rest of the year. With more bonds competing in the market for money, bond prices tend to decrease. Less bonds tend to be issued in late spring and early summer during their seasonal period, helping to support bond prices.

4.3% gain & positive 78% of the time

Second, optimistic forecasts at the beginning of the year for stronger GDP growth tend to increase inflation expectations and as a result interest rates respond by increasing. As economic growth expectations tend to decrease in the summer, interest rates respond by retreating.

Third, the stock market often peaks in May and investors rotate their money into bonds. As the demand for bonds increases, interest rates decrease and bonds increase in value. For seasonal investors looking to put their money to work in the unfavora-

ble six months of the year, buying bonds in the summer months fits perfectly.

Although the beginning of May has been a good time to increase an allocation to bonds, when the stock market has continued higher into July, the bond market's entry point can be correspondingly delayed. Nevertheless, May has proven to be a good entry point for government bonds.

Investors should note that government bonds have a track record of appreciating in November and December, but despite their typical positive performance at this time, there are other investments, such as high yield bonds, corporate bonds and equities that have a better return profile.

	U.S. Gov. Bonds* vs. S&P 500 1998 to 2015				Positive ☐	
	May 6 to Aug 8		Aug 9 to Oct 3		Total Growth	
Year	S&P 500	Gov. Bonds	S&P 500	Gov. Bonds	S&P 500	Gov. Bonds
1998	-2.3	3.0 %	-8.0	8.7 %	-10.1	11.9 %
1999	-3.5	-3.0	-1.3	0.9	-4.8	-2.1
2000	2.1	5.7	-2.5	0.9	-0.4	6.7
2001	-5.2	1.9	-10.7	5.1	-15.3	7.1
2002	-19.9	6.5	-4.7	5.0	-23.7	11.9
2003	4.4	-1.7	6.5	1.7	11.2	0.0
2004	-5.1	3.6	6.4	0.8	0.9	4.4
2005	4.6	-0.8	0.0	0.6	4.6	-0.2
2006	-3.5	2.7	4.3	2.6	0.6	5.3
2007	-2.5	0.5	4.9	2.5	2.3	3.0
2008	-8.4	0.1	-14.7	3.3	-21.9	3.4
2009	10.3	-3.3	2.8	4.6	13.4	1.1
2010	-3.8	7.1	2.2	2.6	-1.7	9.8
2011	-10.2	6.0	-8.4	6.3	-17.7	12.6
2012	1.8	3.0	4.1	0.3	6.0	3.3
2013	5.1	-5.7	-1.1	0.8	4.0	-4.9
2014	1.9	1.8	2.5	0.5	4.4	2.4
2015	-0.3	0.1	-6.3	2.5	-6.6	2.6
Avg.	-1.9 %	1.5 %	-1.3 %	2.7 %	-3.1 %	4.3 %
Fq>0	39 %	72 %	50 %	100 %	50 %	78 %

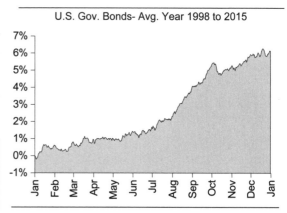

U.S. Gov. Bonds- Avg. Year 1998 to 2015

Source: Barclays Capital Inc.
The U.S. Treasury: 7-10 Year is a total return index, which includes both interest and capital appreciation. For more information on fixed income indices, see www.barcap.com.

U.S. Government Bonds - Performance

U.S Gov Bonds 7-10yr Monthly Performance (1998-2015)

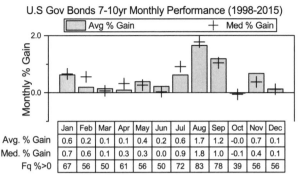

	Jan	Feb	Mar	Apr	May	Jun	Jul	Aug	Sep	Oct	Nov	Dec
Avg. % Gain	0.6	0.2	0.1	0.1	0.4	0.2	0.6	1.7	1.2	-0.0	0.7	0.1
Med. % Gain	0.7	0.6	0.1	0.3	0.3	0.0	0.9	1.8	1.0	-0.1	0.4	0.1
Fq %>0	67	56	50	61	56	50	72	83	78	39	56	56

U.S. Gov Bonds 7-10yr (2011-2015) % Gain

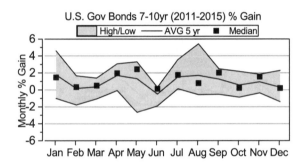

U.S. Gov Bonds 7-10yr Performance 2015-2016

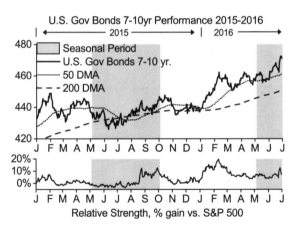

Relative Strength, % gain vs. S&P 500

Market Indices & Rates
Weekly Values**

Stock Markets	2015	2016
Dow	18,010	17,739
S&P500	2,105	2,061
Nasdaq	5,017	4,752
TSX	15,320	13,708
FTSE	6,981	6,135
DAX	11,642	9,920
Nikkei	19,773	16,127
Hang Seng	28,352	20,441

Commodities	2015	2016
Oil	58.28	44.24
Gold	1194.8	1286.6

Bond Yields	2015	2016
USA 5 Yr Treasury	1.42	1.25
USA 10 Yr T	2.03	1.81
USA 20 Yr T	2.47	2.23
Moody's Aaa	3.68	3.66
Moody's Baa	4.61	4.66
CAN 5 Yr T	0.97	0.78
CAN 10 Yr T	1.57	1.42

Money Market	2015	2016
USA Fed Funds	0.25	0.50
USA 3 Mo T-B	0.01	0.20
CAN tgt overnight rate	0.75	0.50
CAN 3 Mo T-B	0.66	0.53

Foreign Exchange	2015	2016
EUR/USD	1.11	1.15
GBP/USD	1.53	1.45
USD/CAD	1.21	1.28
USD/JPY	119.29	106.88

MAY

M	T	W	T	F	S	S
1	2	3	4	5	6	7
8	9	10	11	12	13	14
15	16	17	18	19	20	21
22	23	24	25	26	27	28
29	30	31				

JUNE

M	T	W	T	F	S	S
			1	2	3	4
5	6	7	8	9	10	11
12	13	14	15	16	17	18
19	20	21	22	23	24	25
26	27	28	29	30		

JULY

M	T	W	T	F	S	S
					1	2
3	4	5	6	7	8	9
10	11	12	13	14	15	16
17	18	19	20	21	22	23
24	25	26	27	28	29	30
31						

From 1998 to 2015 U.S. government bonds have performed well from May until October, particularly in August and September which is the sweet spot for the seasonal U.S. Government Bond Trade. From 2011 to 2015, the magnitude of the relative gains in the seasonal period compared to the rest of the year have not been as strong as the long-term trend.

In 2015, U.S. government bonds performed well as investors sought safety when the stock market corrected in August and September. In 2016, at the beginning of the seasonal period, once again U.S. government bonds provided value.

Although some children receive Disney stock as a gift to hold onto for life, using a seasonal investment approach to owning the stock has proven to be a better strategy. Disney's stock price has performed like a seasonal roller coaster: up strongly in the late autumn, into the winter; and down in the summer.

Gain of 28.7%

Disney's year-end occurs at the end of September and they typically report their results in the first week of November. Investors start to increase their positions at the beginning of October in anticipation of positive year-end news.

Investors are particularly attracted to Disney at this time of the year as Q4 tends to be a big revenue reporting quarter.

According to their Form 10-K filed with the Securities and Exchange Commission for the year ended September 29, 2012: "Revenues in our Media Networks segment are subject to seasonal advertising patterns... these commitments are typically satisfied during the second half of the Company's fiscal year." The media segment is the biggest driver of revenue for Disney. In addition, their other business segments are skewed towards revenue generation in the summer.

Do not visit the Disney stock from June 5th to September 30th. For the period from 1990 to 2015, Disney produced an average loss of 8.2% and only beat the S&P 500, 13% of the time.

ⓘ *DIS - stock symbol for Walt Disney Company which trades on the NYSE. is a diversified worldwide entertainment company. Price is adjusted for stock splits.*

Disney vs. S&P 500 1990/91 to 2015/16

Negative Short □   Positive Long ▢

Year	Jun 5 to Sep 30 S&P 500	Jun 5 to Sep 30 Disney	Oct 1 to Feb 15 S&P 500	Oct 1 to Feb 15 Disney	Compound Growth S&P 500	Compound Growth Disney
1990/91	-16.7 %	-29.4 %	20.6 %	30.1 %	40.7 %	68.4 %
1991/92	0.0	-3.0	6.4	25.4	6.3	29.1
1992/93	1.1	-2.7	6.4	29.7	5.2	33.1
1993/94	2.0	-14.7	3.0	23.9	0.9	42.1
1994/95	0.6	-13.2	4.7	38.5	4.1	56.7
1995/96	9.8	2.7	11.5	11.3	0.6	8.3
1996/97	2.2	5.2	17.6	23.6	15.1	17.1
1997/98	12.8	0.9	7.7	38.2	-6.1	36.9
1998/99	-7.1	-30.4	21.0	39.6	29.6	82.1
1999/00	-3.4	-15.1	9.3	41.9	13.0	63.3
2001/01	-2.8	-5.4	-7.7	-15.3	-5.1	-10.7
2001/02	-17.9	-41.1	6.1	28.4	25.0	81.1
2002/03	-21.7	-31.9	2.4	10.5	24.6	45.8
2003/04	1.0	-2.7	15.0	33.5	13.9	37.1
2004/05	-0.7	-6.3	8.6	31.2	9.3	39.4
2005/06	2.7	-11.7	4.2	11.4	1.3	24.4
2006/07	3.7	1.0	9.1	12.2	5.0	11.1
2007/08	-0.8	-3.7	-11.6	-5.5	-10.9	-2.1
2008/09	-15.3	-10.7	-29.1	-39.7	-18.3	-33.2
2009/10	12.2	9.2	1.7	9.5	-10.6	0.6
2010/11	7.2	-1.8	16.4	30.2	8.0	32.5
2011/12	-13.0	-23.4	18.7	36.8	34.1	68.8
2012/13	12.7	17.7	5.5	6.4	-7.9	-12.5
2013/14	3.1	0.2	9.3	22.9	6.0	22.6
2014/15	2.3	5.7	6.3	17.0	3.9	10.4
2015/16	-8.4	-7.3	-2.9	-10.8	5.3	-4.3
Avg.	-1.3 %	-8.2 %	6.2 %	18.5 %	7.4 %	28.7 %
Fq>0	58 %	31 %	85 %	85 %	77 %	77 %

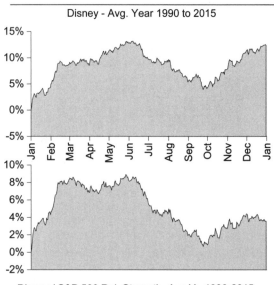

Disney - Avg. Year 1990 to 2015

Disney / S&P 500 Rel. Strength- Avg Yr. 1990-2015

Disney Performance

DIS Monthly Performance (1990-2015)

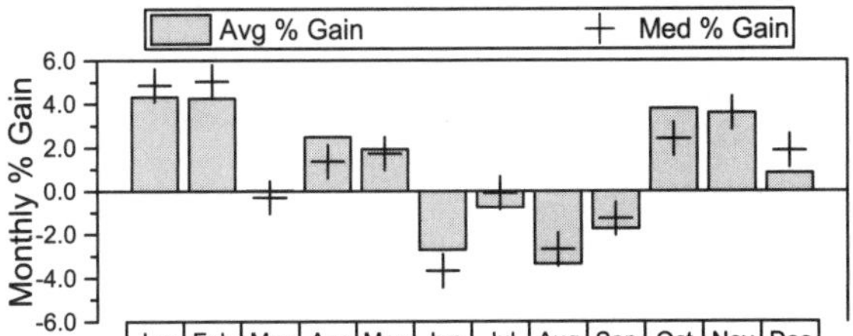

	Jan	Feb	Mar	Apr	May	Jun	Jul	Aug	Sep	Oct	Nov	Dec
Avg. % Gain	4.3	4.3	0.0	2.5	1.9	-2.7	-0.8	-3.4	-1.7	3.8	3.6	0.8
Med. % Gain	4.8	5.0	-0.3	1.4	1.7	-3.7	-0.1	-2.7	-1.3	2.4	3.6	1.9
Fq %>0	77	77	46	65	73	31	50	35	46	81	77	69
Fq %>S&P 500	69	73	31	42	54	38	42	38	42	69	73	42

DIS 5 Year (2011-2015) % Gain

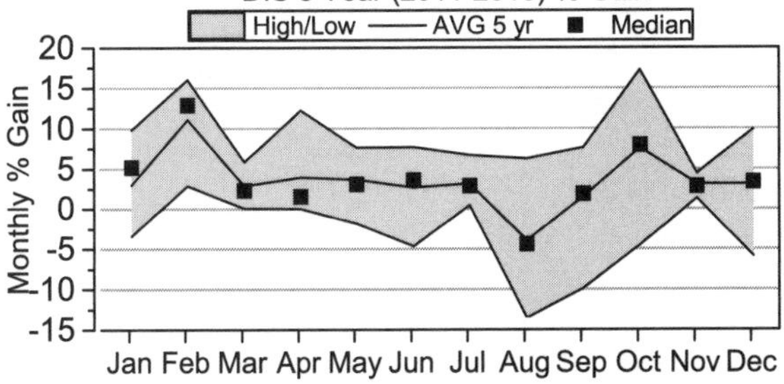

DIS Performance 2015-2016

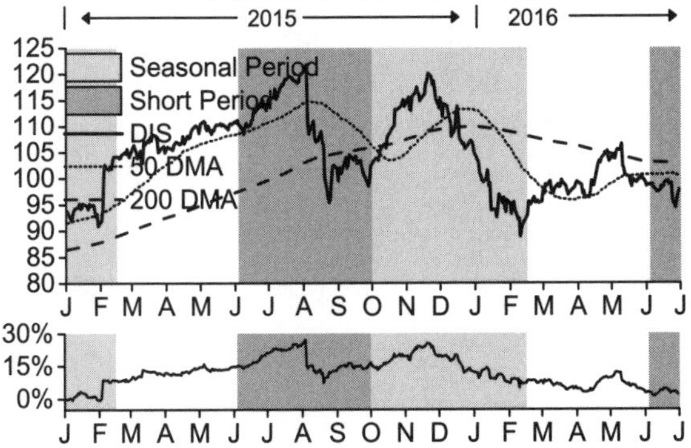

Relative Strength, % gain vs. S&P 500

From 1990 to 2015, Disney has on average been negative from June to September and positive from October into February. These two time periods represent the long and short seasonal periods and are juxtaposed. The transition from the short period to the long period is best navigated with technical analysis. Over the last five years, Disney has generally followed its seasonal trend. October and February have been the strongest months (included in the long seasonal period) and August has been the weakest month (included in the short seasonal period). In 2015, Disney in the short seasonal period produced a gain. In 2016, Disney was negative in its seasonal period. Overall, the combined trade lost ground.

WEEK 19

Market Indices & Rates
Weekly Values**

Stock Markets	2015	2016
Dow	17,991	17,720
S&P500	2,098	2,064
Nasdaq	4,965	4,755
TSX	15,165	13,733
FTSE	6,949	6,135
DAX	11,483	9,963
Nikkei	19,336	16,484
Hang Seng	27,678	20,018
Commodities	**2015**	**2016**
Oil	59.72	45.45
Gold	1191.1	1270.0
Bond Yields	**2015**	**2016**
USA 5 Yr Treasury	1.54	1.21
USA 10 Yr T	2.19	1.75
USA 20 Yr T	2.65	2.17
Moody's Aaa	3.91	3.63
Moody's Baa	4.82	4.64
CAN 5 Yr T	1.08	0.69
CAN 10 Yr T	1.74	1.31
Money Market	**2015**	**2016**
USA Fed Funds	0.25	0.50
USA 3 Mo T-B	0.01	0.26
CAN tgt overnight rate	0.75	0.50
CAN 3 Mo T-B	0.67	0.51
Foreign Exchange	**2015**	**2016**
EUR/USD	1.12	1.14
GBP/USD	1.52	1.44
USD/CAD	1.21	1.29
USD/JPY	119.79	108.73

MAY

M	T	W	T	F	S	S
1	2	3	4	5	6	7
8	9	10	11	12	13	14
15	16	17	18	19	20	21
22	23	24	25	26	27	28
29	30	31				

JUNE

M	T	W	T	F	S	S
			1	2	3	4
5	6	7	8	9	10	11
12	13	14	15	16	17	18
19	20	21	22	23	24	25
26	27	28	29	30		

JULY

M	T	W	T	F	S	S
					1	2
3	4	5	6	7	8	9
10	11	12	13	14	15	16
17	18	19	20	21	22	23
24	25	26	27	28	29	30
31						

CANADIAN SIX 'N' SIX
Take a Break for Six Months - May 6th to October 27th

In analyzing long-term trends for the broad markets such as the S&P 500 or the TSX Composite, a large data set is preferable because it incorporates various economic cycles. The daily data set for the TSX Composite starts in 1977.

Over this time period, investors have been rewarded for following the six month cycle of investing from October 28th to May 5th, versus the other unfavorable six months, May 6th to October 27th.

Starting with an investment of $10,000 in 1977, investing in the unfavorable six months has produced a loss of $3,865, versus investing in the favorable six months which has produced a gain of $211,307.

$211,307 gain on $10,000 since 1977

The TSX Composite Average Year 1977 to 2014 (graph below) indicates that the market tended to peak in mid-July or the end of August. In our book *Time In Time Out, Outsmart the Stock Market Using Calendar Investment Strategies*, Bruce Lindsay and I analyzed a number of market trends and peaks over different decades.

What we found was that the markets tend to peak at the beginning of May or mid-July. The mid-July peak was usually the result of a strong bull market in place that had a lot of momentum.

The main reason that the TSX Composite data shows a peak occurring in July-August is that the data is primarily from the biggest bull market in history, starting in 1982.

TSX Composite % Gain Avg. Year 1977 to 2015

Does a later average peak in the stock market mean that the best six month cycle does not work? No. Dividing the year up into six month intervals, the period from October to May is far superior compared with the other half of the year.

The table below illustrates the superiority of the best six months over the worst six months. Going down the table year by year, the period from October 28 to May 5th outperforms the period from May 6th to October 27 on a regular basis.

In a strong bull market, investors always have the choice of using a stop loss or technical indicators to help extend the exit point past the May date.

	TSX Comp May 6 to Oct 27	$10,000 Start	TSX Comp Oct 28 to May 5	$10,000 Start
1977/78	-3.9%	9,608	13.1%	11,313
1978/79	12.1	10,775	21.3	13,728
1979/80	2.9	11,084	23.0	16,883
1980/81	22.5	13,579	-2.4	16,479
1981/82	-17.0	11,272	-18.2	13,488
1982/83	16.6	13,138	34.6	18,150
1983/84	-0.9	13,015	-1.9	17,811
1984/85	1.6	13,226	10.7	19,718
1985/86	0.5	13,299	16.5	22,978
1986/87	-1.9	13,045	24.8	28,666
1987/88	-23.4	9,992	15.3	33,050
1988/89	2.7	10,260	5.7	34,939
1989/90	7.9	11,072	-13.3	30,294
1990/91	-8.4	10,148	13.1	34,266
1991/92	-1.6	9,982	-2.0	33,571
1992/93	-2.3	9,750	15.3	38,704
1993/94	10.8	10,801	1.7	39,365
1994/95	-0.1	10,792	0.3	39,483
1995/96	1.3	10,936	18.2	46,671
1996/97	8.3	11,843	10.8	51,725
1997/98	7.3	12,707	17.0	60,510
1998/99	-22.3	9,870	17.1	70,871
1999/00	-0.2	9,853	36.9	97,009
2000/01	-2.9	9,570	-14.4	83,062
2001/02	-12.2	8,399	9.4	90,875
2002/03	-16.4	7,020	4.0	94,476
2003/04	15.1	8,079	10.3	104,252
2004/05	3.9	8,398	7.8	112,379
2005/06	8.1	9,080	19.8	134,587
2006/07	0.0	9,079	12.2	151,053
2007/08	3.8	9,426	-0.2	150,820
2008/09	-40.2	5,638	15.7	174,551
2009/10	11.9	6,307	7.4	187,526
2010/11	5.8	6,674	7.1	200,778
2011/12	-7.4	6,183	-4.8	191,207
2012/13	3.6	6,407	1.1	193,348
2013/14	7.7	6,902	9.7	212,072
2014/15	-1.6	6,795	4.9	222,404
2015/16	-9.7	6,135	-4.9	221,307
Total Gain (Loss)	**($-3,865)**			**$211,307**

6n6 Canada Strategy Performance

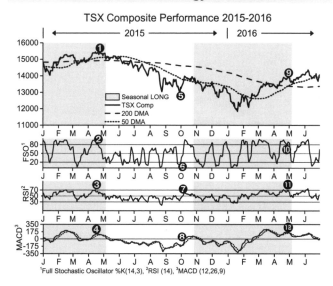

TSX Composite Performance 2015-2016

¹Full Stochastic Oscillator %K(14,3), ²RSI (14), ³MACD (12,26,9)

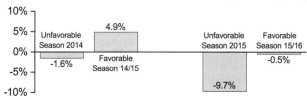

Favorable vs. Unfavorable Seasons 2015-2016 (TSX Composite)

Market Indices & Rates
Weekly Values**

Stock Markets	2015	2016
Dow	18,152	17,541
S&P500	2,109	2,051
Nasdaq	5,010	4,742
TSX	15,063	13,875
FTSE	6,969	6,139
DAX	11,501	9,886
Nikkei	19,663	16,629
Hang Seng	27,497	19,875

Commodities	2015	2016
Oil	60.01	48.03
Gold	1207.4	1267.2

Bond Yields	2015	2016
USA 5 Yr Treasury	1.54	1.34
USA 10 Yr T	2.24	1.82
USA 20 Yr T	2.74	2.22
Moody's Aaa	4.02	3.65
Moody's Baa	4.94	4.69
CAN 5 Yr T	1.08	0.74
CAN 10 Yr T	1.79	1.34

Money Market	2015	2016
USA Fed Funds	0.25	0.50
USA 3 Mo T-B	0.02	0.30
CAN tgt overnight rate	0.75	0.50
CAN 3 Mo T-B	0.65	0.51

Foreign Exchange	2015	2016
EUR/USD	1.13	1.13
GBP/USD	1.57	1.45
USD/CAD	1.20	1.30
USD/JPY	119.51	109.69

MAY

M	T	W	T	F	S	S
1	2	3	4	5	6	7
8	9	10	11	12	13	14
15	16	17	18	19	20	21
22	23	24	25	26	27	28
29	30	31				

JUNE

M	T	W	T	F	S	S
		1	2	3	4	
5	6	7	8	9	10	11
12	13	14	15	16	17	18
19	20	21	22	23	24	25
26	27	28	29	30		

JULY

M	T	W	T	F	S	S
				1	2	
3	4	5	6	7	8	9
10	11	12	13	14	15	16
17	18	19	20	21	22	23
24	25	26	27	28	29	30
31						

TSX Composite Performance– May 6th to October 27, 2015
The TSX Composite had a positive start to 2015 in its seasonal period. In April, the TSX Composite was trading above its 200 and 50 day moving averages❶. An early exit signal in the favorable period was triggered when the FSO crossed below 80❷. The RSI corroborated the signal by bouncing off 70❸. At the same time, the MACD turned lower❹.

October 28th to May 5th, 2016
***Entry Strategy* –Buy Position Early–**

In late September, the TSX Composite corrected sharply and then rallied❺, triggering an early buy signal when the FSO crossed above 20❻. At the time, the RSI was slightly above 30 and turned upwards❼. The MACD was below zero and started to increase❽.

***Exit Strategy* –Sell Position Early–**

In late April, the TSX Composite was trading above its 200 and 50 day moving averages❾. An early signal was triggered as the FSO crossed below 80❿. The RSI was just below 70 and also started to turn down⓫. The MACD also turned down at the time⓬.

Special Report

6n6

An Analysis of a Six Month Seasonal Strategy

Introduction

The objective of this report is to examine the efficacy of Thackray's *6n6* seasonal trading strategy, which is based on the premise that the best six months of the year for the stock market is from October 28th to May 5th. This report will initially discuss the *Sell in May* strategy that advocates selling or decreasing stock positions in May and returning to the stock market in November. The *Sell in May* strategy is sometimes referred to as the *Halloween Indicator* as the buy date for the strategy is October 31st.

The *6n6* seasonal trading strategy differs from the *Sell in May* strategy as it uses specific entry and exit dates that include the last few days in October and the first few days in May. The best six month period for stocks in the *6n6* trade, October 28th to May 5th, is referred to as the favorable period for stocks, or favorable period. The other six months of the year in the *6n6* trade, from May 6th to October 27th is referred to as the unfavorable period for stocks, or unfavorable period. This report will incorporate various metrics including risk measurement and return analysis. In order to effectively demonstrate the value of the *6n6* trade, the analysis will take the position of either being 100% invested in the stock market during the favorable period for stocks, or 100% invested in cash during the unfavorable period for stocks. This report will also briefly present sector investments that tend to perform well in the unfavorable period and a short-term broad market strategy that has performed well within the unfavorable period.

Sell in May (Halloween Indicator)

When investors think of seasonal investing, they generally think of the *Sell in May* trade that is often discussed in the media at the end of April and the beginning of May. The premise of the trade is that the stock market tends to perform poorly from May to October.

The media tends to focus its attention on the first half of the trade, selling in May, rather than the second half of the trade, buying at the end of October in order to be invested at the beginning of November. Selling in May is an easy headline generator for the press, as it plays upon investor's fears that the stock market may be set up for a correction.

The *Sell in May* trade has its roots in Britain, where many stock brokers advocated the saying "Sell in May and go away and don't come back until St Leger Day." Established in 1776, the St Leger Stakes is the last of the five British classic horse races and takes place in late September. Many brokers would sell their stocks in May, enjoy the summer and get back into the stock market just after St Leger Day.

Today, the *Sell in May* trade generally refers to selling in May and then being invested from November to April. The data that analysts use to access the merits of the trade focuses on the returns of the stock market in the six month period from May to October. The media often judges the success or failure of the *Sell in May* strategy based upon the frequency of how often the stock market has risen in this period. Given that from May to October (1950 to 2015), the S&P 500 has been positive 62% of the time, some stock market pundits incorrectly conclude that the *Sell in May* strategy does not work. This simplistic view does not properly incorporate the amount of risk taken for nominal returns.

Jacobsen and Bouman (2001) examined the relationship between stock market returns in the November to April time period compared to the May to October time period. They found that the returns from November to April were higher in thirty-six of thirty seven countries. Jacobsen and Zhang (2014) illustrated the merits of investing during the November to April time period. They examined more than 300 years of market data in 108 countries. The study found stock market returns from November through April were on average 4.5% greater than those over the other six months of the year.

In their articles, collectively, Jacobsen, Bouman and Zhang illustrate the strength of the *Halloween Indicator* by making performance comparisons between November to April and May to October. The *Halloween Indicator* states that over the long-term, the period from November to April is a better period for stock markets compared to the period from May to October, as it has a higher average gain and a greater positive frequency.

Possible Causes of Six Month Cycle for Stocks

There has been a number of possible causes put forward for the six month stock cycle. The oldest and generally most accepted causation factor for the stock market's poor performance from May to October has been that stock brokers, money managers and investors take time off from the stock markets in the summer and reduce their risk accordingly. In autumn, when they return to the markets, they sell positions that have become undesirable, putting negative pressure on the stock market in September and into October. Once the selling pressure abates in late October, the market starts to rise.

Another possible cause for the six month cycle is the impact of analysts adjusting their recommendations for stocks downward in the summer months. Typically, analysts start the year with an overly optimistic bias for the stocks which they are responsible for making recommendations. Collectively as a group, summing all of their recommendations together to get a S&P 500 earnings outlook tends to produce an overly optimistic expectation for the stock market. There is a tendency for the analysts to make downward adjustments in the summer months as they realize that their forecasts are probably not attainable. Statistically, it is difficult to determine if it is the underperforming markets that cause analysts to lower their recommendations, or if it is the analyst's downward earnings adjustments that contribute to stock market underperformance. It is also possible that both of the above scenarios have a negative cybernetic feedback loop where both factors reinforce a negative downward trend in the stock market.

Despite the large amount of research and publications on the *Sell in May* strategy, there has not been conclusive research on the possible causes. Authors on the subject have generally pointed to possible causes and referred to anecdotal evidence. It is difficult to quantitatively prove the causes of the six month cycle for stocks as the generally accepted theories are largely based upon human emotion. In addition, there are a large number of variables that affect stock market valuation.

It is always prudent to look for causation factors for seasonal trends, as sometimes correlation can exist without causation. Nevertheless, statistical evidence should not be ignored. Many different researchers and writers have shown the validity of investing during the six month period from November to April. Overall, the results show a net benefit from investing during the November to April time-frame.

6n6 - A Variation on "Sell in May"

Thackray and Lindsay wrote *Time In Time Out, Outsmart the Stock Market Using Calendar Strategies* (Thackray and Lindsay 2000). Most of the book is dedicated to examining the benefits of investing in the favorable six month period for stocks from October 28th to May 5th, compared to the other six month unfavorable period. At the time, it was probably one of the most seminal books on the topic as it examined variables such as survivor bias, transaction slippage, commissions, dividends and interest.

Through their research, Thackray and Lindsay came up with slightly different entry and exit dates for the favorable/unfavorable six month periods compared to the *Halloween Indicator*. Thackray and Lindsay found that over the long-term, the best six month period for the stock market started on October 28th versus waiting until the first day in November, and the average optimal exit date for the stock market was May 5th versus the last day in April. In years following the publication of *Time In Time Out, Outsmart the Stock Market Using Calendar Strategies*, Thackray went on to call the October 28th to May 5th strategy, the *6n6* strategy.

The beginning date of the *6n6* strategy represents a full day in the market; therefore, investors should buy at the end of the market day preceding the *6n6* period. For example, the *6n6* strategy is from October 28th to May 5th, and to be invested in the stock market for the full seasonal period, an investor would enter the market before the closing bell on October 27th. If the buy date landed on a weekend or holiday, the buy would occur at the end of the preceding trading day. The last day of a trading strategy is the sell date. For example, with the *6n6* strategy the stock market would be exited at the end of the day on May 5th. If the sell date is a holiday or weekend, the investment would be sold at the close on the preceding trading day.

The standard academic protocol for examining returns in different time periods is to use complete discrete months (monthly performance). Thackray and Lindsay opted to forgo the standard discrete month protocol in choosing a start date a few days before the end of October and an exit date a few days into May. Adding the extra days at the end of October and the beginning of May to the standard *Halloween Indicator* period has historically increased the returns of the six month seasonal cycle.

Adding the last few days of October to the standard *Halloween Indicator* period is justified as, on average, the last few days of the month have historically performed better than the rest of the month. There is a body of research analyzing this phenomenon, often called *Turn of the Month Effect* or *End of the Month Effect*. The research measures the performance of the days before and after month end for all months of the year. Hensel Sick, and Ziemba (1994) examined the significance of the last day of the month and the first four days of the next month. Liu (2014) looked at a different time period and established the best dates to be invested are the last four days of the month and the first day of the next month.

Thackray and Lindsay (2000, 145) found that over the long-term, from 1950 to 1998, the last four days of the month and the first three of the next month have produced above average gains. Entering into the stock market a few days before October month end and exiting a few days into May, is in line with the phenomenon of superior market returns around month ends.

Number of Years in Study

For the purpose of the *6n6* study, the starting point for the analysis is 1950. This start date is a generally accepted point in time for most academic studies as it coincides with the start of the post World War II economy. It also incorporates an acceptable number of business cycles.

According to the National Bureau of Economic Research (NBER), from 1945 to 2009, the average length of a business cycle was 68.5 months, or almost six years (2016). Using data starting in 1950 allows for the incorporation of over eleven business cycles in the analysis. Not every business cycle is the same and using a large number of business cycles allows for a robust analysis of the *6n6* strategy in different economic environments.

Investors should be weary of pundits trying to use a substantially shorter period of time to analyze broad market trends. For example, using twenty years of data incorporates only three business cycles and falls short of providing a valid multi-business cycle analysis. For broad markets, such as the S&P 500, a longer period is necessary to establish seasonal trends.

Six Month Seasonal Cycle is Evident in Monthly Average Gains

If S&P 500 returns are examined on a monthly basis, it can be seen that the best six month contiguous period is from November to April (Figure 1). The months in the six month unfavorable period are not necessarily negative or in the bottom half of the performance for all of the months of the year, but collectively, they make up the worst contiguous monthly period.

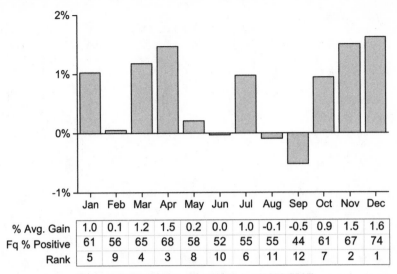

	Jan	Feb	Mar	Apr	May	Jun	Jul	Aug	Sep	Oct	Nov	Dec
% Avg. Gain	1.0	0.1	1.2	1.5	0.2	0.0	1.0	-0.1	-0.5	0.9	1.5	1.6
Fq % Positive	61	56	65	68	58	52	55	55	44	61	67	74
Rank	5	9	4	3	8	10	6	11	12	7	2	1

Figure 1. S&P 500 Avg. Monthly Gains (1950-2015)
Source Data: Bloomberg

There are a few monthly anomalies within the "best six month period" and the "worst six month period." Anomalies do not negate the validity of the six month cycle, but they should be recognized.

From 1950 to 2015, February has on average been the weakest performing month within the favorable period for the S&P 500. February has produced an average gain of 0.1% and has been positive 56% of the time. Given its relative weakness compared to the other months in the favorable period, some investors may attempt to navigate the favorable period by reducing equities in February. Although this is possible, it may not be practical for most investors, especially considering that the months on either side of February (January and March) over the long-term from 1950, have been two of the better performing months of the year.

From 1950 to 2015, July has on average been an anomaly within the unfavorable period as it is the strongest month in the "worst six month period." It has produced an average positive return of 1.0% and has been positive 55% of the time. Because the return profile is strong, for more active traders, it is possible to enter back into the stock market for a brief period of time to capitalize on this interim seasonal anomaly. It should be noted that almost all of the gains that have been made in July have been the result of superior performance in the first eighteen calendar days of the month. Figure 2 breaks July down into two parts (Part 1- July 1st to 18th and Part 2- July 19th to 31st). The rally that tends to take place at the beginning of July occurs because July is an earnings month. Investors tend to take positions in the stock market in early July, anticipating the positive effect of earnings releases, before the bulk of the companies release their earnings reports. For more information on this seasonal phenomenon, see *July– (1st half) Aberration – Eye of the Storm*, later in this report.

From 1950 to 2015, April has produced an average gain of 1.5% and has been positive 68% of the time. This is a very strong performance profile. Although April is part of the "best six months," its strong performance can spill over into the beginning of May. The end result is that the first five calendar days of May have on average been responsible for a 0.5% gain, which is more than the average gain for the total month. In other words, the S&P 500 on average lost 0.2% in the remainder of May (Figure 2).

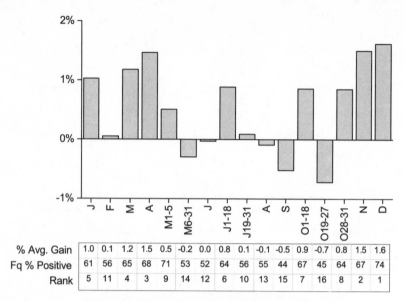

	J	F	M	A	M1-5	M6-31	J	J1-18	J19-31	A	S	O1-18	O19-27	O28-31	N	D
% Avg. Gain	1.0	0.1	1.2	1.5	0.5	-0.2	0.0	0.8	0.1	-0.1	-0.5	0.9	-0.7	0.8	1.5	1.6
Fq % Positive	61	56	65	68	71	53	52	64	56	55	44	67	45	64	67	74
Rank	5	11	4	3	9	14	12	6	10	13	15	7	16	8	2	1

Figure 2. S&P 500 Monthly Avg. Gain Including Part Months (1950-2015) Source Data: Bloomberg

From 1950 to 2015, October has produced an average 0.9% gain and has been positive 61% of the time. These are strong results, particularly for a month that is part of the "worst six months." October is mainly included in the "worst six month period" because in earlier decades, October was on average not a strong month and very volatile.

Should October still be included in the "worst six month period?" Yes, but with a twist. If you break October into three parts (Part 1- October 1st to 18th, Part 2- October 19th to 27th and Part 3- October 28th to 31st), an intra month seasonal trend is evident. The stock market tends to perform well at the beginning of the month, perform poorly mid-month and perform well in the last few days of the month. Although some critics may say that treating a month in such a fashion is too granular, the delineation is justified based upon seasonal trends. Stocks tend to perform well in Part 1 of October (October 1st to October 18th) due to the fact that October is an earnings month. From 1950 to 2015, the S&P 500 in Part 1 of October has produced an average gain of 0.9% and has been positive 67% of the time (Figure 2). The first part of all of the earnings months January, April, July and October tends to be positive times for the stock market (Thackray, 2016,43).

Part 2 of October (October 19th to 27th) tends to be negative and from 1950 to 2015, the S&P 500 has produced an average loss of 0.7% and has only been positive 45% of the time. The stock market tends to pull back at this time as the October *Earnings Month Effect* wanes mid-month (Thackray, 2016,43).

Part 3 of October (October 28th to 31st) has produced an average gain of 0.8% and has been positive 64% of the time. The last few days of the month tend to be stronger than the rest of the month and is part of the *Turn-of-the-Month Effect* or *End-of-Month Effect*. Part 3 of October is included in the *6n6* favorable period for stocks as it is contiguous with the "best six months" and is accretive to the six month period.

Examining the yearly cumulative returns of the S&P 500 illustrates the strength of the six month favorable period for stocks compared to the unfavorable period. Figure 3 shows the average annual cumulative growth in the S&P 500 from 1950 to 2015. The shaded bars represent the strong seasonal period, or favorable period for the stock market from October 28th to May 5th. On average, over the long-term, the difference of investing in the six month favorable period is positively discernible compared to the six month unfavorable period.

Cumulative % Gains Average Year S&P 500 (1950-2015)

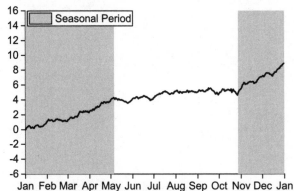

Performance S&P 500 1950-2015*

	May 6 - Oct 27	Oct 28 - May 5
Avg. %	0.1	8.3
Med. %	0.7	8.4
% Fq. Pos.	62	80

*First buy date May 6, 1950
Last sell date May 5, 2016

Figure 3. S&P 500 Yearly Avg. % Cumulative Gain
(1950-2015) Source Data: Bloomberg

Figure 3 is an average year graph. Every year is different, but when all of the years from 1950 to 2015 are averaged together, the end result is the above graph. The following average decade graphs illustrate the persistence of the trend over time. Specific yearly returns for the favorable and unfavorable periods that are discussed in this section, are found in Table 1 later in this report. All averages in this section of the report are arithmetic averages.

Cumulative % Gains Average Year S&P 500– 1950's

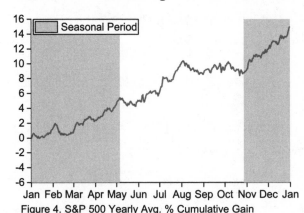

Performance S&P 500 1950-1959*

	May 6 - Oct 27	Oct 28 - May 5
Avg. %	3.0	10.4
Med. %	1.0	11.2
% Fq. Pos.	60	91

*First buy date May 6, 1950
Last sell date May 5, 1960

Figure 4. S&P 500 Yearly Avg. % Cumulative Gain
(1950-1959) Source Data: Bloomberg

The 1950's were boom years as soldiers returned home and started families. As the baby boom increased demand for American goods, the economy expanded.

Overall, the 1950's was a good time to be invested. The unfavorable period for stocks produced an average gain of 3.0% and was positive 60% of the time. The median gain of 1.0% was lower than the average gain, as large gains skewed the results to the upside. The favorable period for stocks performed significantly better than the unfavorable period, producing an average gain of 10.4% and positive 91% of the time. The median was higher than the average as a few larger losses skewed the average results to the downside.

Cumulative % Gains Average Year S&P 500– 1960's

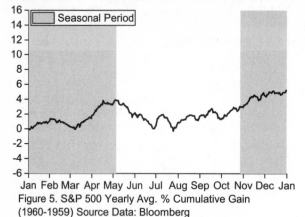

Performance S&P 500 1960-1969*

	May 6 - Oct 27	Oct 28 - May 5
Avg. %	-1.2	7.8
Med. %	1.6	4.7
% Fq. Pos.	60	73

*First buy date May 6, 1960
Last sell date May 5, 1970

Figure 5. S&P 500 Yearly Avg. % Cumulative Gain
(1960-1959) Source Data: Bloomberg

The baby boom continued into the 1960's as did economic expansion. The S&P 500 respond-ed by rising. After a few corrections along the way, the S&P 500 had an intra-decade peak in late 1968.

In the 1960's, the difference in performance between the unfavorable and favorable periods was large as the unfavorable period lost an average 1.2% and the favorable period gained 7.8%. In the unfavorable period, the median was positive, indicating that a few large losses were mainly responsible for the negative average. In particular, the 1962 loss of 17.7% had a large negative impact. In the favorable period, the median was lower than the average, indi-cating that a few large gains were responsible for the strong performance. In particular, the 1962 gain of 28.4% had a large positive impact.

Unfavorable Six Month Period vs. Favorable Six Month Period– 1970's

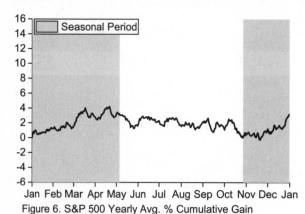

Performance S&P 500 1970-1979*

	May 6 - Oct 27	Oct 28 - May 5
Avg. %	-3.2	7.1
Med. %	-0.3	5.2
% Fq. Pos.	40	82

*First buy date May 6, 1970
Last sell date May 5, 1980

Figure 6. S&P 500 Yearly Avg. % Cumulative Gain
(1970-1979) Source Data: Bloomberg

The S&P 500 peaked in late 1972 as the 1970's suffered from stagflation. The last few years of the decade were challenging as the U.S. Federal Reserve raised its discount rate aggres-sively in order to combat inflation. This was done at a time of high unemployment and as a result, hurt overall economic growth.

Like the 1960's, the 1970's had a large performance difference between the unfavorable and favorable periods, with the unfavorable period having an average loss of 3.2% and the favorable period having an average gain of 7.1%. The median for the unfavorable period was higher than the average, as a few years with weaker performance skewed the average performance results. The median for the favorable period was lower than the average, as a few years of above average performance skewed the average number positively.

Unfavorable Six Month Period vs. Favorable Six Month Period - 1980's

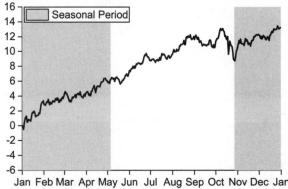

Figure 7. S&P 500 Yearly Avg. % Cumulative Gain
(1980-1989) Source Data: Bloomberg

Performance S&P 500 1980-1989*

	May 6 - Oct 27	Oct 28 - May 5
Avg. %	3.1	11.4
Med. %	4.0	11
% Fq. Pos.	80	82

*First buy date May 6, 1980
Last sell date May 5, 1990

The 1980's kicked off the "greatest" bull market of all time, as the U.S. Federal Reserve decreased its discount rate and interest rates followed. The S&P 500 did not peak in the decade until late 1989.

Although both the unfavorable and favorable periods produced average positive returns, the favorable period's average 11.4% gain was substantially larger than the unfavorable period's average 3.1% gain. The medians for both periods were close to their averages for the decade.

Unfavorable Six Month Period vs. Favorable Six Month Period - 1990's

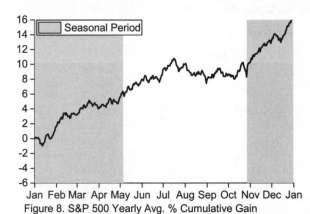

Figure 8. S&P 500 Yearly Avg. % Cumulative Gain
(1990-1999) Source Data: Bloomberg

Performance S&P 500 1990-1999*

	May 6 - Oct 27	Oct 28 - May 5
Avg. %	1.7	12.1
Med. %	2.0	10.6
% Fq. Pos.	70	82

*First buy date May 6, 1990
Last sell date May 5, 2000

The bull market continued into the 1990's. In the second half of the decade, the S&P 500 increased as the internet gained wide spread use and productivity increased dramatically in companies. Despite a few declines along the way, the S&P 500 finished the decade peaking in late 1999.

Once again, the favorable six month period outperformed the unfavorable period, with average gains of 12.1% and 1.7% respectively. The medians were not dramatically different than the averages.

Unfavorable Six Month Period vs. Favorable Six Month Period - 2000's

Performance S&P 500 2000-2009*

	May 6 - Oct 27	Oct 28 - May 5
Avg. %	-3.7	4.3
Med. %	0.4	7.6
% Fq. Pos.	60	73

*First buy date May 6, 2000
Last sell date May 5, 2010

Figure 9. S&P 500 Yearly Avg. % Cumulative Gain
(2000-2009) Source Data: Bloomberg

The 2000's started off the decade correcting from the internet bubble of the 1990's and bottomed in 2003. After another strong multi-year rally, the S&P 500 peaked for the decade in 2007. It then subsequently corrected again as a result of the financial crisis in 2007-2008. At the end of the decade, the S&P 500 was lower than when it started.

On average, the losses occurred mostly in the unfavorable period which posted an average loss of 3.7%. The large loss in the unfavorable period in 2008, skewed the average down. The median for the decade was 0.4%. The favorable period produced an average gain of 4.3% with a median of 7.6%.

Unfavorable Six Month Period vs. Favorable Six Month Period - 2010-2015

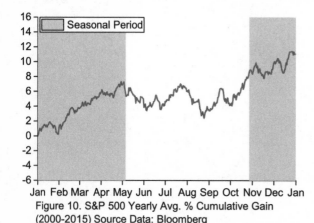

Performance S&P 500 2010-2015*

	May 6 - Oct 27	Oct 28 - May 5
Avg. %	2.1	7.8
Med. %	2.3	6.8
% Fq. Pos.	67	83

*First buy date May 6, 2010
Last sell date May 5, 2016

Figure 10. S&P 500 Yearly Avg. % Cumulative Gain
(2000-2015) Source Data: Bloomberg

The U.S. Federal Reserve has managed to engineer the stock market rally since 2009. Both the economy and corporate earnings have had anemic growth, and yet because of declining interest rates for the first part of the decade, the stock market responded positively.

The unfavorable six month period has produced a small average gain of 2.1%, while the favorable six month period has produced a much stronger gain of 7.8%. The medians for both the unfavorable and favorable periods have not been significantly dissimilar from their averages.

Unfavorable Six Month Period vs. Favorable Six Month Period - Decade Cumulative Gains

Figure 11 illustrates the results of investing in only the favorable period or the unfavorable period by decade. For each decade, the gain or loss is calculated by compounding the gain from each favorable or unfavorable period collectively up until the end of the decade. In other words, the total amount of the principal and gain from the first favorable period is invested in the second favorable period and the process is repeated until the end of the decade. The returns for the unfavorable period are calculated in the same manner.

In every decade, the cumulative returns for the favorable period are greater than the unfavorable period. The returns from the favorable period in the 1990's are substantially higher than the unfavorable period. Smaller differences between cumulative decade gains have occurred since the year 2000. The fact that differences between the favorable and unfavorable periods have not been as great as in the past, does not necessarily mean that the six month seasonal investment cycle is diminishing. It is possible that a set of unique factors could be applicable, especially with such a small sample size (number of years being analyzed). For example, the impact of the U.S. Federal Reserve's quantitative easing programs from 2009 to 2015 have had a disproportionate positive impact on the stock market during the unfavorable periods compared with the favorable periods.

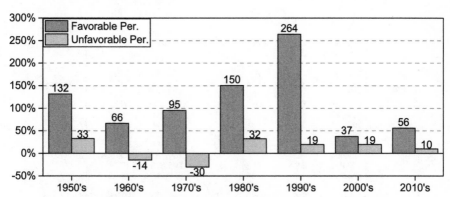

Figure 11. S&P 500 Favorable vs. Unfavorable Period Decade Total % Gain
(May 6, 1950 to May 5, 2016) Source Data: Bloomberg

Favorable Period vs Unfavorable Period Cumulative Gains from May 6, 1950 to May 5, 2016

Table 1 illustrates the difference in returns of investing in the favorable period compared with the unfavorable period. From 1950 to 2016, investing $10,000 on October 27th (to be in the market on October 28th), selling on May 5th, investing the proceeds back into the stock market on the next October 27th, selling on the next May 5th and following this process up until 2016, has generated a profit of $1,463,351. This compares to investing in the opposite six months from May 6th to October 27th, which has generated a loss of $2,362.

Table 1: Favorable Period Returns vs Unfavorable Period Returns and Growth of $10,000 (May 6, 1950 to May 5, 2016)

	S&P 500 % May 6 to Oct 27	$10,000 Start	S&P 500 % Oct 28 to May 5	$10,000 Start	Oct28- May5 > May6- Oct27
1950/51	8.5%	10,851	15.2%	11,517	YES
1951/52	0.2	10,870	3.7	11,947	YES
1952/53	1.8	11,067	3.9	12,413	YES
1953/54	-3.1	10,727	16.6	14,475	YES
1954/55	13.2	12,141	18.1	17,097	YES
1955/56	11.4	13,528	15.1	19,681	YES
1956/57	-4.6	12,903	0.2	19,711	YES
1957/58	-12.4	11,302	7.9	21,265	YES
1958/59	15.1	13,013	14.5	24,356	
1959/60	-0.6	12,939	-4.5	23,270	
1960/61	-2.3	12,647	24.1	28,869	YES
1961/62	2.7	12,993	-3.1	27,982	
1962/63	-17.7	10,698	28.4	35,929	YES
1963/64	5.7	11,306	9.3	39,264	YES
1964/65	5.1	11,882	5.5	41,440	YES
1965/66	3.1	12,253	-5.0	39,388	
1966/67	-8.8	11,180	17.7	46,364	YES
1967/68	0.6	11,241	3.9	48,171	YES
1968/69	5.6	11,872	0.2	48,249	
1969/70	-6.2	11,141	-19.7	38,722	
1970/71	5.8	11,782	24.9	48,346	YES
1971/72	-9.6	10,647	13.7	54,965	YES
1972/73	3.7	11,046	0.3	55,154	
1973/74	0.3	11,084	-18.0	45,205	
1974/75	-23.2	8,513	28.5	58,073	YES
1975/76	-0.4	8,480	12.4	65,290	YES
1976/77	0.9	8,554	-1.6	64,231	
1977/78	-7.8	7,890	4.5	67,146	YES
1978/79	-2.0	7,732	6.4	71,476	YES
1979/80	-0.1	7,723	5.8	75,605	YES
1980/81	20.2	9,283	1.9	77,047	
1981/82	-8.5	8,498	-1.4	76,001	YES
1982/83	15.0	9,769	21.4	92,293	YES
1983/84	0.3	9,803	-3.5	89,085	
1984/85	3.9	10,183	8.9	97,057	YES
1985/86	4.1	10,604	26.8	123,044	YES
1986/87	0.4	10,651	23.7	152,196	YES
1987/88	-21.0	8,409	11.0	168,904	YES
1988/89	7.1	9,010	10.9	187,380	YES
1989/90	8.9	9,814	1.0	189,242	
1990/91	-10.0	8,837	25.0	236,498	YES
1991/92	0.9	8,916	8.5	256,590	YES
1992/93	0.4	8,952	6.2	272,550	YES
1993/94	4.5	9,356	-2.8	264,789	
1994/95	3.2	9,656	11.6	295,636	YES
1995/96	11.5	10,762	10.7	327,219	
1996/97	9.2	11,757	18.5	387,591	YES
1997/98	5.6	12,419	27.2	493,003	YES
1998/99	-4.5	11,860	26.5	623,489	YES
1999/00	-3.8	11,415	10.5	688,842	YES
2000/01	-3.7	10,992	-8.2	632,435	
2001/02	-12.8	9,586	-2.8	614,583	YES
2002/03	-16.4	8,016	3.2	634,369	YES
2003/04	11.3	8,921	8.8	689,985	
2004/05	0.3	8,952	4.2	718,942	YES
2005/06	0.5	9,000	12.5	808,503	YES
2006/07	3.9	9,350	9.3	883,804	YES
2007/08	2.0	9,534	-8.3	810,240	
2008/09	-39.7	5,750	6.5	862,619	YES
2009/10	17.7	6,766	9.6	934,470	
2010/11	1.4	6,862	12.9	1,067,851	YES
2011/12	-3.8	6,602	6.6	1,138,103	YES
2012/13	3.1	6,809	14.3	1,301,313	YES
2013/14	9.0	7,422	7.1	1,393,667	
2014/15	4.1	7,725	6.5	1,484,478	YES
2015/16	-1.1	7,638	-0.7	1,473,351	YES
Total Gain (Loss)		($2,362)		$1,463,351	

Table 1 also shows how many times the favorable period has outperformed the unfavorable period in the same year, from 1950 to 2016. In the last column of the table, the "YES" value represents the years when the favorable period has outperformed the unfavorable period, 71% of the time. The outperformance has been fairly consistent from 1950. On a geometric average basis, the favorable six month period has produced a gain of 7.6% per year from 1950 to 2016. This compares to the unfavorable period which has produced a loss of 0.5% per year.

It is not just averages that are important, but also frequencies of success. Sometimes, an average result can be skewed by one or two outliers in the data. The favorable six month period has been positive 80% of the time, compared with the unfavorable period which has been positive 62% of the time.

A lot of investors focus on the 62% of positive returns in the six month unfavorable period and see the more than 50% success rate as ample evidence that an investor should stay in the stock market for the unfavorable period. The rationale is that if the stock market is positive most of the time in the six month unfavorable period, then it is best to remain invested. The counter argument is that despite the stock market being positive most of the time, does it matter if on average a loss is incurred? The reason that a greater than 50% positive frequency of success co-exists with an average loss is that the losses in the six month unfavorable period have on average been greater than the gains. Although the average loss per year seems small, making it seem innocuous and not worth the effort of exiting the stock market; an average loss, year after year, compounded produces destructive results in the long-term.

Large Gains/Losses Risk Analysis

Risk management is an important part of a long-term successful investment strategy. Without properly assessing risk, steady returns over time are less likely and there is a greater chance of capital loss. There are a large number of metrics that can be used to assess risk. One practical method is to measure the occurrences of large losses or gains. Generally speaking, investors can tolerate missing small gains or participating in small losses over the short-term. Nevertheless, they find it very difficult to be out of the stock market when it produces large returns or being in the stock market when it produces large losses.

By measuring large losses and large gains in the favorable and unfavorable periods for the stock market, a measurement of return versus risk is achieved. A large loss or gain is defined at the 10% threshold.

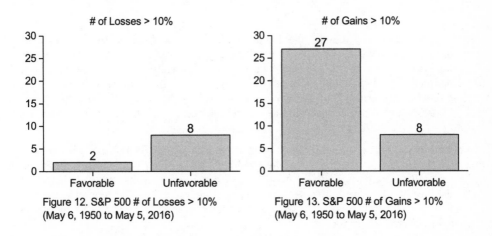

Figure 12. S&P 500 # of Losses > 10%
(May 6, 1950 to May 5, 2016)

Figure 13. S&P 500 # of Gains > 10%
(May 6, 1950 to May 5, 2016)

From 1950 to 2016, the unfavorable period has produced loses greater than 10%, eight times and gains greater than 10%, also eight times (Figure 12 and 13). This compares to the favorable period which has produced losses greater than 10% twice and gains greater than 10%, twenty-seven times. Clearly, the favorable period has a track record of producing large gains more often and fewer large losses.

There have been large corrections in the stock market within the favorable period, but most of the time the stock market has managed to bounce back. The largest loss in the last decade in the favorable period occurred in 2008/2009. Within the favorable time period, the S&P 500 corrected a total of 33%, but managed to bounce back substantially in March, April and May to produce a total gain of 6.5% in the unfavorable period. Even more recently, in 2016, the S&P 500 fell by more than 11% in January and the first part of February. A few months later the S&P 500 was once again at a new high level. In the favorable period, the stock market has a greater propensity to increase, including bouncing off corrections. Trying to avoid corrections in the favorable period is difficult. Attempting to avoid corrections is typically best left to the unfavorable period when gains tend not to be as strong.

Every year in May, some media publications posit the position that this time is different and the S&P 500 has a good chance of producing a strong rally during the upcoming unfavorable period for stocks. Historical results do not support this position. Although there has been eight times from 1950 to 2015 that the S&P 500 has produced a gain of greater than 10%, these instances have occurred under unique circumstances. The conditions for large increases in the unfavorable period have essentially been either a bounce off a recession or from an environment of weak economic growth rising quickly to strong economic growth (Table 2).

Table 2. Unfavorable Period % Gains > 10% (1950-2015)

Year	Environment Factor
1954	Recession 1953/54 bounce
1955	Recession bounce continued
1958	Recession 1957/58 bounce
1980	Recession 1980 bounce
1982	Recession 1981/82 bounce
1995	Weak growth 1995 Q1&Q2 to strong growth Q3
2003	Weak growth 2002 Q4 (0.3%) to strong growth Q3 (6.9%)
2009	Recession 2008 bounce

Very often in the summer months, the media puts forward the position that the stock market is set for a summer rally. Stock markets can rally at any time, including in the summer months. The question in the end is how sustainable is a summertime rally? In the unfavorable period, the rallies tend not to last as long, or be as strong. Typically, if there is a rally, it tends to occur starting the last few days of June and into the first couple of weeks of July. The possibility of trading this period is discussed later in this report under the section titled: *July– (1st half) Aberration – Eye of the Storm.*

It is always possible that the S&P 500 may have a strong rally in the unfavorable period, but investors should at least check to see if the conditions are similar to the past in supporting an off-season rally. Ideally, it would be good to have a stock market that has had a substantial correction heading into the unfavorable period and at the same time, the economy was showing indications of rapid growth. These conditions are best found at the end of a recession or similar slow growth environment.

Dispersion of returns- Favorable and Unfavorable Period Risk Analysis -

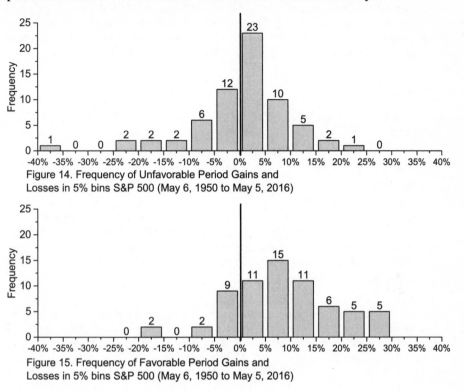

Figure 14. Frequency of Unfavorable Period Gains and
Losses in 5% bins S&P 500 (May 6, 1950 to May 5, 2016)

Figure 15. Frequency of Favorable Period Gains and
Losses in 5% bins S&P 500 (May 6, 1950 to May 5, 2016)

Another way of looking at the risk-return relationship is to look at the dispersion of returns over time in both the unfavorable and favorable periods. Figure 14 illustrates the returns in the unfavorable period from 1950 to 2016. The unfavorable period has its highest frequency of returns in the 0 to 5% bin with twenty-three occurrences (bins are a grouping of results between specified maximum and minimum boundaries). This compares to the favorable period over the same time period which has its highest frequency of returns in the 5 to 10% bin (Figure 15). The favorable period also has far fewer returns in the negative bins. In addition, the favorable period has a greater amount of occurrences in the bins representing higher returns. This includes five occurrences of returns in the 25-30% bin, compared to the unfavorable period with no returns in the same bin.

Measuring risk by the day

Being in the stock market entails risk. The stock market can correct at any time and investors can lose money. Investors tolerate risk because of the expectation of returns. Generally, the greater the expectation of return, the more risk investors are willing to take. Although seasonal investing is not typically structured to take advantage of daily gains, comparing average daily metrics helps to illustrate the difference in the risk/reward relationship between the favorable and unfavorable periods for the stock market.

One of the appropriate methods for measuring risk when investing based upon seasonal trends is to measure returns versus days in the market. Being in the stock market is risky: being out of the stock market and in cash is not risky. Based upon historical trends, if the expectation is for negative returns or even nominal returns in the unfavorable period why stay invested? By staying invested, an investor is exposing themselves to the risk of capital loss.

Comparing average daily gains between the favorable and unfavorable periods allows for a common denominator, and adjusts for the difference in the number of days in each period. Figure 16 illustrates the difference in the average daily gains between the two periods. The difference is substantial. Although any one day can produce gains or losses, the average daily percent gain in the unfavorable period has been nominally positive.

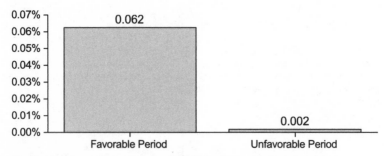

Figure 16. Average Daily % Gains S&P 500 in Favorable Period and Unfavorable Periods (Start May 6, 1950 and End May 5, 2016)

The frequency of positive occurrences between the favorable and unfavorable periods is not dramatically different, but it is enough to make a difference. Figure 17 shows both periods to have positive frequencies greater than 50%, with the favorable period being two percent greater than the unfavorable period.

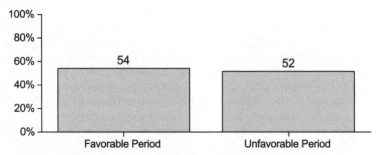

Figure 17. Fq % Gains > 0 for S&P 500 in Favorable Period and Unfavorable Periods (Start May 6, 1950 and End May 5, 2016)

Volatility- Highest in the unfavorable period

Historically, volatility has increased in the unfavorable period, starting in July and peaking in October. Generally, higher volatility means a greater risk of investment losses. Most investors have a propensity to avoid volatility.

Volatility tends to increase in mid-July, just after earnings season gets into full swing. It tends to increase through August, September and finally peaking in October (Figure 18). As a result, investing in August and September typically means investing in a period of higher volatility, exposing investments to a greater chance of a loss. On average, volatility tends to be lower in the favorable period for stocks compared with the unfavorable period.

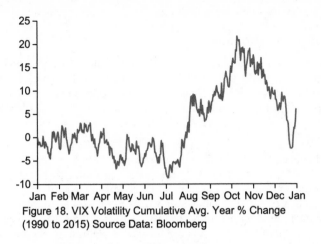
Figure 18. VIX Volatility Cumulative Avg. Year % Change
(1990 to 2015) Source Data: Bloomberg

Favorable period– ideal combination of returns and risk

Successful investing isn't just about maximum returns. It is about producing maximum returns with the least amount of risk. In other words, the best risk adjusted returns. Focusing on the favorable period for an investment into the stock market has produced an ideal combination of risk adjusted returns. Historically, the favorable period has significantly outperformed the unfavorable period and has had the least amount of volatility.

Criticisms of the 6n6

Every trading strategy has its critics, and seasonal investing is no exception. There is no such thing as a perfect strategy, one that works all of the time. Of course there are the generic criticisms that are thrown at almost every strategy. The most common generic criticism of the *6n6* strategy is trading costs. At one time, this was a major criticism as trading costs were substantial. Today, trading costs have plummeted as technology has made it extremely cheap to trade. In addition, slippage costs, the difference between the bid and the ask price, has shrunk with increased trading and decimalization. These costs still exist, but they are a lot less than in previous decades.

Even though seasonal investing is considered a relatively high turnover strategy, trading costs are still fairly nominal. Seasonal trades tend to be large trades, especially with the broad market *6n6* trade. If an investment product that represents the S&P 500 is used during the favorable six month period for stocks, then all that is required is one trade to exit the position. With a lot of brokerages having caps on the amount that they charge per trade, the costs can be nominal.

Investors are concerned about reducing their total returns with the amount of taxes that will be charged on their trades. Everyone should have a goal to mitigate their tax payments, but it should not be the major driving force on all trades. Too many investors have not sold positions for tax reasons and have lost out as their positions have declined, sometimes over a multi-year period. Taxes should be a consideration, but they should not be the only consideration. If an investor is overly sensitive to potential taxes, then it is always possible to use the *6n6* strategy in a non-taxable account.

Some investors criticize the *6n6* strategy, by stating that the strategy does not work all of the time. No investment strategy works all of the time and it is unrealistic to expect otherwise. Some investors criticize the *6n6* because more than half of the time the S&P 500 rises in the unfavorable period (1950 to 2016). This criticism is not valid as the more important consideration is if an investor made or lost money. Given that investing in only the unfavorable period has been a money losing venture, the frequency of success is not a major consideration.

Additional Strategies to Maximize the 6n6

Over the long-term, if an investor had followed the *6n6* strategy by investing in the stock market every year from October 28th to May 5th and holding cash for the other six months of the year, they would have been rewarded with strong risk adjusted returns. Nevertheless, there are opportunities to adjust the strategy to potentially maximize returns (detailed below).

May– Let it Ride

If the stock market is performing well at the beginning of May, an investor could potentially continue to hold equity positions and use trailing stop losses as an exit strategy. A trailing stop loss is defined as the process of raising stops as a position advances. Using trailing stop losses is a better process compared to absolute stop losses in this situation. With an absolute stop loss, an investment could continue to perform well in May and if it peaked and went back through the stop loss, all of the gains between the peak and the stop loss (or greater) would be forgone. Given that the preference at this time of the year is to be out of the stock market, it is better to use an exit strategy that is "trigger" sensitive.

In the opposite scenario, when the stock market starts to perform negatively in April, an investor could always exit positions early. This is particularly applicable as, on average, most of April's gains have been made in the first half of the month from 1950 to 2016.

October– Positive but volatile

Most of October is not included in the favorable period and for a good reason. October is a volatile month. Nevertheless, it is possible to use the opportunities created by the volatility to enter the stock market.

October is an earnings month (one of the four months of the year when new quarterly reports are released). The first eighteen calendar days in October have, on average, been positive for the S&P 500 from 1950 to 2015. On average, this period has been positive 65% of the time and has produced a gain of 0.9%. The positive performance can be explained by the *Earnings Month Effect* (Thackray 2016, 43).

The *Earnings Month Effect* is the result of investor's tendency to push up the stock market in the first eighteen calendar days of the earnings months January, April, July and October. Investors put upward pressure on stock prices at this time as they desire to be in the stock market ahead of the period when earnings season hits its busiest time and possible good news could be released. The stock market in the first eighteen calendar days of October is a beneficiary of this effect.

Although the first part of October tends to be positive, the period just after the *Earnings Month Effect* can be volatile. After a large number of companies have reported earnings in the first part of October, investors tend to be influenced by other factors which can lead to increased volatility and decreases in the stock market. These drops in the stock market can be good opportunities to enter positions before the start of the six month favorable period for stocks.

The volatility in October often leads to good buying opportunities as the stock market tends to bottom at this time. October has a reputation of being a bear killer and correction killer. A bear market is defined as a drop in the stock market of 20% or more. A correction is defined as a drop in the stock market of 10% or more. Compared to all of the other months of the year, October has the highest number of instances of stock market bottoms (Figure 19), which represented ideal times to enter the stock market.

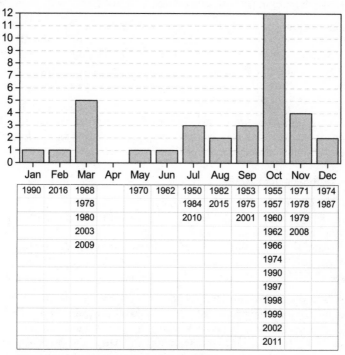

Jan	Feb	Mar	Apr	May	Jun	Jul	Aug	Sep	Oct	Nov	Dec
1990	2016	1968		1970	1962	1950	1982	1953	1955	1971	1974
		1978				1984	2015	1975	1957	1978	1987
		1980				2010		2001	1960	1979	
		2003							1962	2008	
		2009							1966		
									1974		
									1990		
									1997		
									1998		
									1999		
									2002		
									2011		

Figure 19. Frequency of Corrections > 10%
Ended in Month S&P 500 (1950-2016 July)

October has a reputation for large corrections. Given that most of October is a part of the un-favorable period, a large drop in the stock market in the first part of the month can provide a good opportunity to enter early. In addition, if the stock market has had a substantial correc-tion in September, this can also lead to a good opportunity to enter early in October.

On the other hand, if the stock market is fully valued and has not had a recent correction, it is often best to wait and enter the stock market on October 27th (to be invested on October 28th). Given that the last few days in October and the month of November tend to be very strong, it is typically best to enter the stock market at this time, even if the stock market is showing weakness. On average, the last four trading days in October have produced an average 1% gain from 1950 to 2015 (Thackray 2012). Given the strong seasonal tendencies at the start of the favorable six month period, an investor sitting on the sidelines waiting for the stock mar-ket to show improved technical performance can miss out on large returns very quickly.

July– (1st half) Aberration – Eye of the Storm

On a short-term multi-week basis, one of the best times to be invested is close to the middle of the unfavorable period. The stock market tends to increase in the last few days of June and then perform well until July 18th. This strong performance is actually two seasonal strategies meshed together: *Independence Day* and the *Earnings Month Effect* (Thackray 2016,43). Us-ing this blended strategy approach incorporates the last two trading days in June and the first eighteen calendar days in July.

Thackray and Lindsay noticed a bimodal distribution of market peaks in May and July and that in strong bull markets the S&P 500 tends to peak in July shortly after the earnings season gets underway (Thackray and Lindsay 2000). They also stated that the S&P 500 tends to peak a few days into May in normal market conditions. They went on to state that the May 5th date was a conservative date for exiting the stock market and July 19th was an aggressive date.

A practical method to incorporate both exit dates is to lower the amount of equities at the beginning of May and then increase the amount of equities in the last few days of June until mid-July. This process lowers the amount of equities for most of May and June when market returns tend to be nominal, and increases the amount of equities in a time period that typically performs well.

It is difficult for most investors to take advantage of short-term trading strategies. More nimble investors taking advantage of the July aberration would be advised to use tight stops, especially towards the end of the strong period in July, as this aberration is followed by two of the most negative months of the year: August and September.

Practical Portfolio Considerations

Most investors are not going to be 100% invested in the stock market, or 100% out of the stock market. A practical approach is to decrease equity exposure during the unfavorable period and increase it during the favorable period. Overall, if an investor were 100% invested during the favorable period and less than 100% invested during the unfavorable period, given a constant risk level for the investment assets, the amount of risk would be lower than being invested all year.

There are still positive seasonal investment opportunities during the unfavorable period. Government bonds have their strong seasonal period in the unfavorable period and there are sectors of the stock market that tend to perform well at this time. The sectors of the stock market that tend to perform well in the unfavorable period are mainly the defensive sectors. The list of seasonal investment opportunities in the unfavorable period also includes some commodity sectors and other sectors such as biotech.

In the six month favorable period for stocks, there are a large number of sectors that tend to perform well and outperform the S&P 500. The sectors are mainly the cyclical sectors and generally have a higher beta than the S&P 500. Although, some sectors will not outperform in any one year, on average, over the long-term, on a seasonal basis it is expected that most sectors would outperform during their strong seasonal period.

Following a *6n6* strategy with sector investments, allows for equities to be held for most of the year, although there typically would be a higher percentage of equity investments during the favorable six months of the year. Generally, this strategy has a higher beta in the six month favorable period for stocks and a lower beta in the unfavorable period. Using such an approach, it is theoretically possible to construct a portfolio that is, on average, beta neutral for the whole year, but have less seasonal risk than the stock market.

Combining the six month cycle with other indicators

The *6n6* strategy is based upon specified entry and exit dates every year. Technical analysis can be used to help fine tune the entry and exit dates. The goal of using technical analysis with seasonal investing is to enter the stock market early if it is showing strength before the seasonal entry date, or delay entry if it is showing weakness heading into the entry date. Likewise, technical analysis can be used to exit the stock market early or late.

One of the more well known investors/investment writers that deployed a technical indicator to the "best/worst" six month period was the late Sy Harding (1999). In his book *Riding the Bear*, Harding advocated using the MACD indicator to determine the timing of an investment in the market around the transition times of the "best/worst" six months. Like any investment strategy, it is best to establish the entry/exit rules before the event. Doing so will help to take the emotion of out of the decision to invest.

Conclusion

The *Sell in May* seasonal phenomenon has been analyzed over the decades by many researchers and often discussed in the media in the spring time. The time to buy in October is not widely discussed in the media, but it has been written about in academic journals and is referred to as the *Halloween Indicator*. Most recently, Jacobsen, Bouman and Zhang have written a number of articles on the subject and have shown that the six month period from November to April has outperformed the other six months of the year in thirty-six out of thirty seven countries and over the long-term. Thackray and Lindsay have shown the benefits of adjusting the dates to include the last few days of October and the first few days in May. They referred to the six months to be in the stock market (October 28th to May 5th) as the favorable period and the other six months as the unfavorable period. Most recently, Thackray has named the strategy of investing in the six month favorable period as the "*6n6*." Using a variety of different metrics, this report has illustrated that the favorable period is a better time to be invested in the stock market compared to the unfavorable period. It also discussed the nuances of investing in both the favorable and unfavorable periods as well as applicable strategies.

References:

Harding, S. (1999). Riding the bear: How to prosper in the coming bear market. Holbrook, MA: Adams Media Corporation.

Hensel, C.R., Sick, G. & Ziemba, W.T. (1994). The Turn of the Month Effect in the S&P 500, 1926-1992. Review of Futures Markets, 13 (3) 827-856.

Jacobsen, Ben and Bouman, Sven, The Halloween Indicator, 'Sell in May and Go Away': Another Puzzle (July 1, 2001). Available at SSRN: http://ssrn.com/abstract=76248 or http://dx.doi.org/10.2139/ssrn.76248

Jacobsen, Ben and Zhang, Cherry Yi, The Halloween indicator, 'Sell in May and go Away': An Even Bigger Puzzle (October 1, 2014). Available at SSRN: http://ssrn.com/abstract=2154873 or http://dx.doi.org/10.2139/ssrn.2154873

Liu, L. (2013). The Turn-of-the-Month Effect in the S&P 500, 2001-2011. Journal of Business & Economics Research, 11(6), 269-276.

"The National Bureau Of Economic Research". Nber.org. N.p., 2016. Web. 19 Aug. 2016.

Thackray, B., (2012). Thackray's 2013 Investor's Guide: How to Profit from Seasonal Market Trends. Oakville, ON: MountAlpha Media, 129.

Thackray, B., (2015). Thackray's 2016 Investor's Guide: How to Profit from Seasonal Market Trends. Oakville, ON: MountAlpha Media.

Thackray, B., & Lindsay, B. (2000). Time in, time out: Outsmart the market using calendar investment strategies. Penfield, NY: Upwave Media.

Special Report

Small Cap Effect

An Analysis of the Best Times
to Invest in Small Capitalized Companies

Small Cap Sector Introduction

One of the most analyzed sectors of the stock market is the small company sector, which is often referred to as the small cap sector. This sector is defined differently by different institutions, but generally includes companies with a small market capitalization compared to the average company in a broad market index. The venerable Russell 2000 Index (Russell 2000) is a small cap index that includes companies with a capitalization of under five billion dollars.

By the very nature of their composition, small caps represent better long-term growth opportunities compared to large caps. Trees do not grow to the sky, and eventually large fast growing companies mature with slower growth rates. It is much easier for a small company to grow compared to a large company. There are exceptions, as some large companies in the past have managed to maintain a high growth rate for an extended period of time.

Generally speaking, most analysts agree that the small cap sector provides the potential for larger returns over time, compared to large caps. The price for the expected higher returns is greater volatility. Small caps have typically had greater volatility as they tend to have earnings that are less stable, not be as well capitalized and have a higher chance of going bankrupt. Investors demand a risk premium (higher returns over the long-term) for investing in the more volatile small cap sector.

Over the years, many academics have tried to establish the best mix of small caps and large caps in order to establish an "efficient" portfolio that maximizes returns with the least amount of risk. The discussion is primarily focused on the value that small caps can add to a diversified portfolio.

There have also been some studies on effectively timing the best periods to hold small caps compared to an investment that tracks the S&P 500 or some other broad market index. The studies have focused on finding correlation and causation by examining different variables in different economic environments.

Past studies have found that small caps tend to outperform broad market at different parts of the economic cycle, with the relative performance related to the value of the U.S. dollar, inflation rate, change in the yield on the U.S. government ten year bond, change in GDP growth, and other variables. Although these indicators may provide some value, a lot of the variables are coincident indicators reducing their value as a timing mechanism.

Most analysts favor the small cap sector in times of economic expansion as the sector can typically grow at a fast rate at this time. Figure 1 shows the absolute yearly performance of the Russell 2000 (small caps) from 1979 to 2015. The Russell dataset starts in 1979. Figure 2 shows the yearly performance of the small cap sector (Russell 2000) relative to the large cap sector (Russell 1000 Index or Russell 1000), calculated as the average monthly percent gain for the Russell 2000 minus the average monthly percent gain for the Russell 1000. Positive columns on the graph represent small cap outperformance. Negative columns, represent small cap underperformance.

In the beginning of the 1980's, the economy was boosted by rapid interest rate cuts, and the small cap sector outperformed the large cap sector (Figure 2). As growth slowed in the later 1980's the small cap sector underperformed. After the recession in 1990, the small cap sector once again outperformed as the economy expanded in the early 1990's. In the second half of the 1990's the small cap sector underperformed as the large cap sector was growing at a rapid rate due to the implementation of the internet creating productivity gains that disproportionately benefited large companies. Investors reasoned that since large cap stocks were growing rapidly, why invest in small caps. In the early 2000's, the small cap sector outperformed the large cap sector as small caps had become relatively cheap. For the rest of the 2000's and up until 2015, the small cap sector has outperformed the large cap sector intermittently as there has not been a long-term trend of outperformance of either small or large caps.

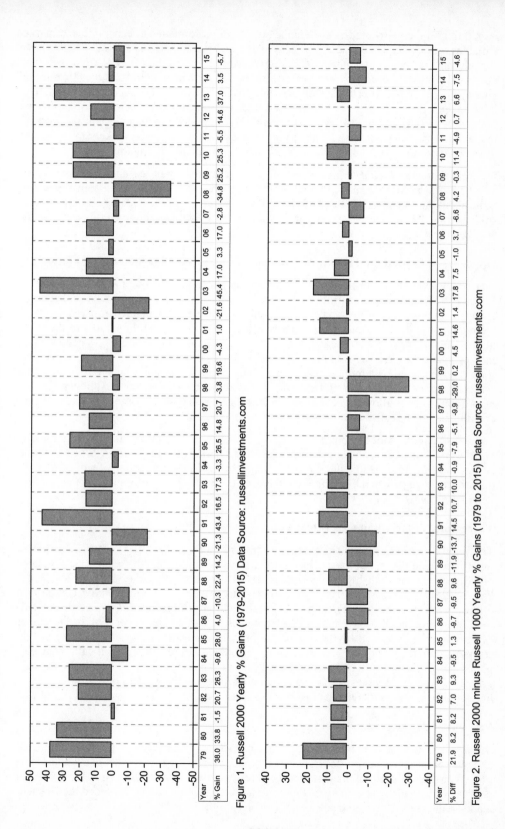

Year	79	80	81	82	83	84	85	86	87	88	89	90	91	92	93	94	95	96	97	98	99	00	01	02	03	04	05	06	07	08	09	10	11	12	13	14	15
% Gain	38.0	33.8	-1.5	20.7	26.3	-9.6	28.0	4.0	-10.3	22.4	14.2	-21.3	43.4	16.5	17.3	-3.3	26.5	14.8	20.7	-3.8	19.6	-4.3	1.0	-21.6	45.4	17.0	3.3	17.0	-2.8	-34.8	25.2	25.3	-5.5	14.6	37.0	3.5	-5.7

Figure 1. Russell 2000 Yearly % Gains (1979-2015) Data Source: russellinvestments.com

Year	79	80	81	82	83	84	85	86	87	88	89	90	91	92	93	94	95	96	97	98	99	00	01	02	03	04	05	06	07	08	09	10	11	12	13	14	15
% Diff	21.9	8.2	8.2	7.0	9.3	-9.5	1.3	-9.7	-9.5	9.6	-11.9	-13.7	14.5	10.7	10.0	-0.9	-7.9	-5.1	-9.9	-29.0	0.2	4.5	14.6	1.4	17.8	7.5	-1.0	3.7	-6.6	4.2	-0.3	11.4	-4.9	0.7	6.6	-7.5	-4.6

Figure 2. Russell 2000 minus Russell 1000 Yearly % Gains (1979 to 2015) Data Source: russellinvestments.com

In addition to the many studies correlating small cap performance to economic and market variables, academics have studied the seasonal tendency of small caps to outperform large caps during the month of January. This researched tendency is an offshoot from the much published *January Effect*, first put forward by Sidney B. Wachtel (1942). Later Rozeff and Kinney (1976) helped to bring the strategy into the mainstream. The *January Effect* strategy is based upon the tendency of investors to sell stocks in December for tax loss reasons, driving prices down to artificially low levels, and setting stocks up for a rebound in January. This effect applies particularly to small caps as these stocks are the ones most likely to be sold to generate losses in order to offset any capital gains accumulated during the year.

In recent years, the *January Effect* is one of the most written about seasonal anomalies in academic journals. Many brokerage houses across North America make it an annual event to write about the *January Effect* and often put their own angle on the trade by ranking the best small cap stocks that are set up well for the trade or by actively promoting a sub-sector of the small cap sector, such as value stocks.

Opportunity beyond the January Effect - Small Cap Effect (December 19th-March 7th)

Investors looking to profit from the *January Effect* phenomenon, invest at the beginning of January and seek to realize a profit at the end of the month. The theory postulates that at the end of January any value created by tax loss selling in December will have been realized over the month. The examination of the *January Effect* trade focuses on the returns of the stock market on a monthly basis. The generally accepted protocol for academic research on stock market calendar anomalies is to compare performance across months as discrete units (performance measured on a monthly basis only). This myopic viewpoint fails to recognize that seasonal anomalies exist with start and end on dates other than month ends. Although discrete month comparisons allow for general seasonal trend examinations, it forgos the potential benefits that could be realized by investing on intra-month dates.

Small caps have historically outperformed large caps from December 19th to March 7th. The *Small Cap Effect* trade includes a period before and a period after the *January Effect* trade and is a much longer trade. Although tax loss selling may account for a portion of why small caps outperform large caps at the beginning of the year, the average outperformance is not just limited to the month of January.

Three Parts to the Small Cap Effect Trade

The *Small Cap Effect* trade is one continuous trade from December 19th to March 7th. In this report, the trade has been broken down into three parts to illustrate the relative performance of the small cap sector in different periods (Part 1- December 19th to the 31st, Part 2- January, Part 3- February 1st to March 7th). Comparing the three parts allows for a relative comparison of the pre and post *January Effect* periods, to the traditional *January Effect* period. The outperformance of small caps compared to large caps in Part 1 (December 19th to December 31st) cannot be explained by the tax loss selling phenomenon as investors are still selling stocks up until the end of the year in order to generate losses to offset capital gains. The outperformance of small caps compared to large caps in Part 3 (February 1st to March 7th), also cannot be explained by the tax loss phenomenon as this is well past the December 31st deadline for U.S. investors to generate losses for tax purposes.

Beta out of the gate and coast

Beta Definition: a measure of the risk potential of a stock or an investment portfolio expressed as a ratio of the stock's or portfolio's volatility to the volatility of the market as a whole (Merriam-Webster). Beta out of the gate and coast, refers to the act of money managers increasing their beta (risk) at the beginning of the year and then once they have exceeded their benchmarks, reducing their risk and coasting for the rest of the year.

A possible explanation of why the periods before and after January are strong periods for the small cap sector relies on investment manager behavior. A lot of investment managers create portfolios that are close to their benchmark index and look for incremental gains compared to their benchmarks. At the beginning of the year, investment managers are willing to take bigger risks in order to get ahead of the market. This is the least risky time (career risk) of the year to take on market risk. Career risk occurs if a portfolio manager underperforms their benchmark and as a result could potentially lose their job. If a portfolio manager is able to take on more market risk at the beginning of the year and is successful in outperforming their benchmark, they will have reduced their career risk. If they perform at market for the rest of the year, they will still have beaten their benchmark for the year. On the other hand, if they are unsuccessful at the beginning of the year and underperform their benchmark, they still have almost a full year to make up the difference and even beat the benchmark. The investment manager's risk adjustment at the beginning of the year is an act of "beta out of the gate and coast."

Small caps are the good choice to beat the market at the beginning of the year. Most portfolio managers are mandated to invest only in American stocks and cannot change risk levels except through stock and sector selection. Moving down the capitalization scale and choosing small caps, allows portfolio managers to be discrete in their strategy to increase beta as they do not have to explain a tactical increase in higher risk sectors. For portfolio managers that do have the flexibility to increase non-American assets in order to increase beta in their portfolios, making an allocation change between countries may not be desirable as other factors come into play, such as currency risk. In addition, increasing an allocation to higher risk countries at the beginning of the year on a shorter-term basis is an action that would be frowned upon in the investment industry.

The *Small Cap Effect* starts before year-end as it takes advantage of investors who are in turn trying to take advantage of the *January Effect*. The *January Effect* is probably the most published calendar anomaly and as a result draws a lot of interest in December as brokerage houses produce their reports early in the month. Investors strive to take advantage of the increased interest in the sector by taking positions in the broad stock market and the small cap sector ahead of other investors in the second half of December. Investment managers act in a similar manner by increasing exposure to the broad stock market and the small cap sector in mid-December not only to try and get a bit of a boost at the end of the year, but also to position their portfolios for the start of the next year and before the Christmas holidays. The result is that on average, both the broad market and the small cap sector tend to perform well in the second half of December. Historically, the best time to enter the stock market around year-end has been December 19th, the start of the *Small Cap Effect*.

Small cap seasonal performance

The goal of investing is to produce a high rate of return with minimum risk. If risky investments end up producing the same rate of return as a less risky investment, the end result may be the same, but in choosing an investment with a higher risk rating, the investor is exposed to the possibility of greater losses. Although the return may be the same in a particular year, the risky investment has a higher chance of large losses in the future. No rational investor would make an investment decision that has a high risk rating and expect the same return over time as a lower risk investment. Why take on the extra risk?

Smaller capitalized companies tend to be riskier than large companies. Although they have a higher growth potential, they have a greater risk of going bankrupt or suffering from adverse economic conditions. As a result of the increased volatility, investors expect an increased return from investing in the small cap sector in order to compensate for the extra risk. Although the small cap sector may underperform in any one particular year, investors taking on the additional risk of small caps would expect outperformance over the long-term.

From a seasonal perspective, it is rational to invest in the small cap sector at times when it is expected to outperform the large cap sector. If both sectors are positive, and are expected to have equal performance, the rational position would be an investment in the large cap sector. To do otherwise would be taking on too much risk relative to the expected return. On a portfolio management basis, some investors may desire to have a fully diversified portfolio at all times, but still follow the tenets of seasonal investing. In this case, a rational investor would look to overweight the small cap sector when the sector is expected to outperform the large cap sector in the period from December 19th to March 7th.

Figure 3 shows the average yearly absolute performance of the small cap sector over thirty-seven years from 1979 to 2015. On a prima facie basis, it looks like the small cap sector performs well into June and then performs well from late October until the end of the year. This particular graph is informative, but does not answer the question of whether there is a strong seasonal period for small caps as it does not incorporate relative performance compared to large caps. Figure 3 is an average year graph, with every year being different. The graph does not reveal whether the average cumulative growth is skewed because of one or two years of strong performance at a certain time of the year. In establishing a seasonal pattern, frequencies of success are very important, in fact, more important than the average size of gain. A low frequency of success exposes an investor to a higher risk level.

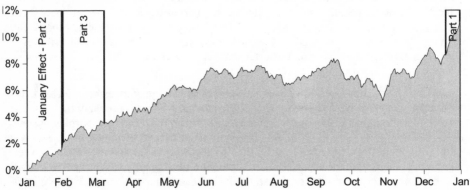

Figure 3. Russell 2000 Cumulative Avg. Year % Gain (1979-2015) Data Source: russellinvestments.com

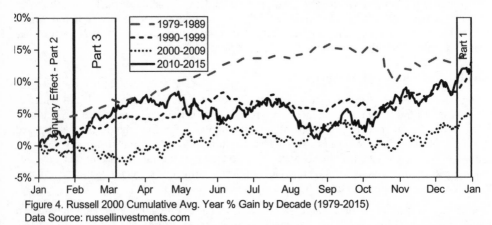

Figure 4. Russell 2000 Cumulative Avg. Year % Gain by Decade (1979-2015)
Data Source: russellinvestments.com

Figure 4 shows the seasonal trend broken down by decade (1979 is included with the 1980's and 2010 to 2015 is a shortened period). What is interesting to note is that the seasonal trend of the 1980's is different than that of the other decades, as its positive absolute performance extends into June, similar to the average trend for the entire period in Figure 4. The 1980's were a period of falling interest rates and price to earnings (P/E) multiple expansion. Overall, the stock market and the small cap sector performed well in this decade on a full year basis. The other three decades produced an average gain on a full year basis, but not as strong as the 1980's. In the other three decades a seasonal trend of average flat performance from March until October existed. In other words, on average, other than in the 1980's the returns in the small cap sector were fairly muted from early March to late October.

Seasonal Relative Performance

Figure 5 represents the relative trend for the Russell 2000 vs. the Russell 1000. A rising line indicates that the Russell 2000 is outperforming the Russell 1000 and vice versa. Figure 5 has a similar trend as Figure 3, except the average cumulative gain is muted and average relative underperformance of the Russell 2000 exists between July and October.

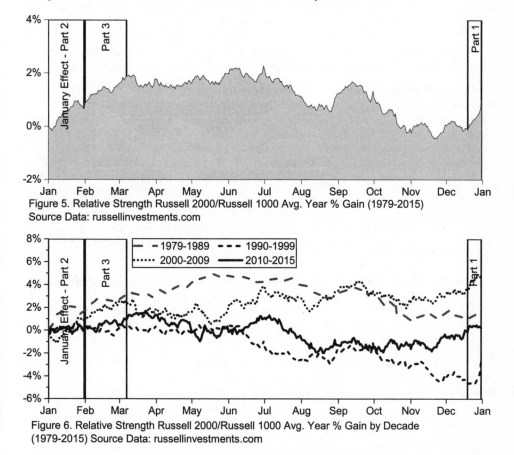

Figure 5. Relative Strength Russell 2000/Russell 1000 Avg. Year % Gain (1979-2015)
Source Data: russellinvestments.com

Figure 6. Relative Strength Russell 2000/Russell 1000 Avg. Year % Gain by Decade
(1979-2015) Source Data: russellinvestments.com

In Figure 5, the consistently rising portion of the graph that exists between late November and the beginning of March, represents the average outperformance of the small cap sector at this time. November is not included in the *Small Cap Effect* due to lower frequencies of success. The period between March and July represents flat relative performance between Russell 2000 and Russell 1000. In other words, if an investment has to be made on a seasonal basis and the choice is between small and large cap sectors from March to July, the rational choice is the large cap sector, as it represents less risk. The weakness of the small cap sector in this period has been masked by the strong positive performance of the small cap sector from March to July in the 1980's, which has pulled the overall average performance of the sector higher.

An overall negative trend exists for the small cap sector relative to the large cap sector from July to October. In this period, the preference between small cap and large cap sectors defers to the large cap sector as a declining trend line represents large cap relative outperformance. There is one small interim aberration that has on average persisted across the decades: the outperformance of small caps towards the end of August into mid-September. At this time there does not appear to be a reasonable explanation for this aberration.

Towards the end of the year, in mid-December, small caps start to outperform large caps until the end of the year (Part 1 of the *Small Cap Effect* trade). This trend has persisted across the decades from 1979 to 2015, but was particularly strong in the 1990's and the 2000's. It is interesting to note that small caps underperformed large caps on average in the 1990's over the full year and yet small caps outperformed on average in the second half of the year. The 1990's was a decade of large technology, health care and financial companies outperforming as investors bought into the benefits of mergers and acquisitions helping to propel valuations to historic levels. With large companies growing rapidly, investors saw less rationale to invest in small companies. It is possible that with small caps underperforming during the average year, investors snapped up small caps at the end of the year as they represented good bargains and as a result small caps outperformed from December 19th to December 31st.

Small caps on average also performed strongly at the end of the year in the 2000's. Overall, the 2000's were on average a strong year for small caps as they outperformed large caps. After the correction in the stock market that started in the year 2000, investors started to move their focus away from large caps to small caps. In addition, investors tend to perceive that small caps outperform large caps as the economy rapidly expands after a major downturn, such as in the early 2000's. It is possible that investors drove the small cap sector up on average at the end of the year in order to lock in positions with greater growth potential ahead of the upcoming year.

In the month of January (Part 2 of the *Small Cap Effect* trade), the 1980's and the 2000's were on average the strongest for the small cap sector. It is interesting to note that the performance of small caps relative to large caps on a full year basis was the strongest in both of these decades.

In February and into March 7th (Part 3 of the *Small Cap Effect* trade), the 1980's and the 2000's were on average the strongest for the small cap sector. These were the same decades that the small cap sector outperformed on average in January. February tends to be a weaker month of the year for the broad stock market, and as a result, the outperformance of the small cap sector is positively contrasted.

Table 1 illustrates that from 1979 to 2016, in the period from December 19th to March 7th, small caps (Russell 2000) produced an average gain of 5.5% and were positive 76% of the time. In addition, the Russell 2000 outperformed the large cap sector (Russell 1000) 68% of the time and produced an extra 3.0%. Although the large cap sector produced a strong return, the small cap sector on average produced a higher gain and had a higher frequency of positive occurrences.

On an absolute basis, the weakest performance string occurred for the small cap sector in its *Small Cap Effect* trade period, from 2006/2007 to 2008/2009. This would be expected given the impact of the Financial Crisis. Even so, the small cap sector faired relatively well compared to the large cap sector and only underperformed in the 2007/2008 and 2008/2009 time periods. The largest relative loss compared to the large cap sector in this time period was 4.5% in 2008/2009.

On a relative basis, the largest string of underperformance of the small cap sector compared to the large cap sector within the *Small Cap Effect* period, occurred from 1995/1996 to 1999/1999. This was a fairly unique time as there was a large number of merger and acquisitions in the large cap sector. In addition the large cap sector was producing very strong returns based upon an increase in productivity, which in turn was due to the implementation of the internet in business operations. In other words, investors saw a huge opportunity with large caps and did not see the benefit of investing in small caps.

It is interesting to note that the strongest part of the *Small Cap Effect* trade is Part 1. Compared to Part 2 and Part 3, small caps in Part 1 have the highest average absolute gain, highest average outperformance compared to large caps, highest frequency of positive occurrences and highest frequency of outperformance relative to large caps. From 1979/80 to 2015/16, Part1 has produced an average gain of 2.2% and has been positive 89% of the time. These are extremely strong numbers. Equally impressive is the relative performance of the small cap sector compared to the large cap sector. In the same period, the small cap sector outperformed the large cap sector by an average of 1.2% and 76% of the time.

Table 1. Small Cap Effect % Gain/Loss - Russell 2000 and Russell 1000
(Dec 19/1979 to Mar 7/2016) Data Source: russellinvestments.com

Russell 2000 Positive

	Part 1 (Dec19-Dec31)			Part 2 Jan1-Jan31			Part 3 Feb1-Mar7			Total Dec19-Mar7		
	R1000	R2000	Diff	R1000	R2000	Diff	R1000	R2000	Diff	R1000	R2000	Diff
1979/80	-0.2	1.8	2.0	5.9	8.2	2.3	-6.6	-9.6	-3.0	-1.3	-0.4	0.9
1980/81	1.9	3.2	1.2	-4.6	-0.6	4.0	-0.1	1.5	1.6	-2.8	4.0	6.8
1981/82	-1.2	-0.2	1.0	-2.7	-3.7	-1.0	-9.0	-8.6	0.4	-12.4	-12.1	0.3
1982/83	2.3	2.3	0.0	3.2	7.5	4.2	5.8	9.0	3.1	11.8	19.8	8.1
1983/84	1.5	0.7	-0.8	-1.9	-1.8	0.0	-6.0	-6.4	-0.5	-6.4	-7.5	-1.1
1984/85	-0.3	1.3	1.6	7.8	13.1	5.3	0.3	2.3	2.0	7.7	17.1	9.5
1985/86	0.5	1.8	1.3	0.9	1.5	0.6	6.8	8.2	1.4	8.2	11.7	3.5
1986/87	-1.9	-0.6	1.3	12.7	11.5	-1.3	6.0	9.7	3.7	17.2	21.5	4.3
1987/88	-0.6	0.8	1.4	4.3	4.2	-0.1	4.4	11.2	6.8	8.3	16.8	8.5
1988/89	0.8	2.1	1.3	6.7	4.4	-2.4	-0.7	2.4	3.1	6.9	9.1	2.2
1989/90	2.9	2.7	-0.2	-7.3	-8.9	-1.5	2.8	4.9	2.1	-2.0	-1.8	0.2
1990/91	0.1	1.7	1.6	4.6	8.9	4.3	9.6	16.3	6.8	14.7	28.8	14.2
1991/92	8.8	7.1	-1.6	-1.4	8.0	9.4	-1.2	0.9	2.1	6.0	16.8	10.8
1992/93	-0.5	2.6	3.1	0.6	3.3	2.7	1.4	-0.8	-2.1	1.5	5.2	3.7
1993/94	0.5	2.5	2.0	2.9	3.1	0.2	-2.8	0.0	2.8	0.6	5.7	5.1
1994/95	0.4	3.9	3.5	2.4	-1.4	-3.8	2.5	3.0	0.5	5.4	5.5	0.1
1995/96	2.0	4.1	2.1	3.1	-0.2	-3.3	3.0	3.8	0.8	8.3	7.9	-0.4
1996/97	1.5	2.7	1.2	5.8	1.9	-3.9	2.0	-1.1	-3.1	9.5	3.5	-6.0
1997/98	1.9	3.9	2.1	0.7	-1.7	-2.3	7.5	7.7	0.2	10.2	10.1	-0.2
1998/99	4.2	6.1	1.9	3.5	1.3	-2.2	-0.5	-6.9	-6.4	7.3	0.1	-7.2
1999/00	3.4	8.3	4.8	-4.2	-1.7	2.5	-0.9	19.9	20.8	-1.7	27.7	29.4
2000/01	-0.3	4.4	4.7	3.2	5.1	1.9	-7.8	-4.6	3.2	-5.2	4.7	9.8
2001/02	0.5	0.6	0.2	-1.4	-1.1	0.3	2.5	2.5	-0.1	1.6	1.9	0.4
2002/03	-1.2	-0.2	0.9	-2.6	-2.9	-0.3	-3.2	-4.8	-1.7	-6.7	-7.8	-1.0
2003/04	2.1	1.8	-0.2	1.8	4.3	2.5	2.4	3.2	0.8	6.4	9.6	3.3
2004/05	1.6	1.5	-0.1	-2.6	-4.2	-1.6	3.9	3.2	-0.7	2.8	0.3	-2.5
2005/06	-1.4	-1.4	0.0	2.7	8.9	6.2	-0.4	-1.7	-1.2	0.8	5.6	4.7
2006/07	-0.3	0.7	1.0	1.8	1.6	-0.2	-3.1	-3.1	0.1	-1.6	-0.8	0.9
2007/08	1.0	1.6	0.6	-6.1	-6.9	-0.8	-6.1	-7.5	-1.4	-10.9	-12.5	-1.6
2008/09	2.2	4.2	2.0	-8.3	-11.2	-2.9	-17.0	-20.9	-3.8	-22.2	-26.7	-4.5
2009/10	1.2	2.4	1.3	-3.7	-3.7	0.0	6.3	10.6	4.3	3.6	9.1	5.5
2010/11	1.1	0.5	-0.6	2.3	-0.3	-2.6	1.9	4.0	2.0	5.5	4.2	-1.3
2011/12	3.1	2.6	-0.5	4.8	7.0	2.3	3.1	0.4	-2.7	11.3	10.2	-1.1
2012/13	-1.3	0.2	1.5	5.3	6.2	0.9	3.1	3.6	0.5	7.1	10.3	3.1
2013/14	2.1	2.6	0.5	-3.3	-2.8	0.5	5.5	6.4	0.9	4.2	6.1	2.0
2014/15	0.0	1.1	1.0	-2.8	-3.3	-0.4	4.0	4.5	0.5	1.0	2.1	1.1
2015/16	1.9	1.3	-0.6	-5.5	-8.9	-3.4	3.5	5.7	2.2	-0.3	-2.4	-2.1
Average	1.1	2.2	1.2	0.8	1.2	0.4	0.6	1.9	1.2	2.5	5.5	3.0
Fq % > 0	70	89	76	59	51	49	59	68	68	68	76	68

On an absolute and relative drawdown basis, small caps have performed well in Part 1. The small cap sector's largest drawdown occurred in the 2005/2006 period and was equal to the large cap sector's drawdown of 1.4%. On a relative basis, the small cap sector had its largest drawdown of 1.6% relative to the large cap sector in 1991/1992. In this time period both the large cap and small cap sectors had large gains of 8.8% and 7.1% respectively.

Daily Gains Comparison

What makes the superior results of Part 1 even more impressive is that the number of trade days in Part 1 is substantially less than the number of trade days in Part 2 and 3 (Figure 7). The duration of Part 1 is less than two weeks and on average has eight trading days. This compares to Part 2 which is one month and has an average of twenty-one trading days, and Part 3 which is longer than one month and has on average twenty-four trading days.

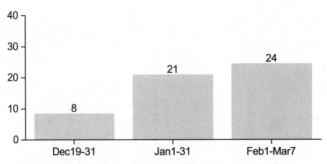

Figure 7. Avg # of Trading Days (Dec 19, 1979 to Mar 7, 2016)

The average daily gain over the period, from December 19th, 1979 to March 7th, 2015 for the small cap sector, is 0.041% and is slightly better than the average daily gain for the large cap sector at 0.038% (Figure 8). The average daily gain of the small cap sector is stronger than the large cap sector in all three parts of the trade.

The strength of Part 1 of the trade (December 19th to December 31st), is clearly realized as the small cap sector daily average gain is more than twice as large as the large cap daily average gain. The strength of small caps in Part 1 is also shown by comparing the average daily gain of the small cap sector at this time to the average daily gain of the small cap sector in Part 2 of the trade. The average daily gain of the small cap sector in Part 1 of the trade is more than four times greater than the average daily gain in Part 2 of the trade.

Part 1 is the strongest part of the *Small Cap Effect* trade for both the Russell 2000 and the Russell 1000. On an average daily basis, the Russell 2000's gain of 0.266% is over six times the average daily gain for the full year. The Russell 1000's average daily gain of 0.129% is more than three times the average daily gain for the full year. In this time period, the Russell 2000 and 1000 have positive daily average gain frequencies of 64% and 59% respectively, which are greater than the full year frequencies (Figure 9).

Part 2 is the weakest part of the *Small Cap Effect* trade for both the small and large cap sectors. The small cap sector outperforms the large cap sector and has a better relative performance compared to the full year. The average daily gain of the small cap sector is 0.057% compared with 0.038% for the full year. The average daily gain of the large cap sector is 0.038% for both Part 2 and for the full year.

Part 3 of the trade also favors the performance of small caps relative to large caps. The Russell 2000 strongly outperforms its full year daily average gain. In comparison, the Russell 1000 underperforms its full year average daily gain. On a daily positive frequency basis, the Russell 2000 is positive 58% of the time, compared with 55% of the time for the full year. The daily positive frequency of the Russell 1000, is the same rate as the full year. Given that the Russell 2000's daily performance in Part 3 is superior to its full year daily performance and the Russell 1000's daily average gain is less than its full year daily average gain, investing in small caps at this time provides additional value over large caps.

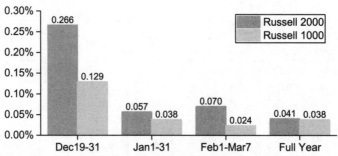

Figure 8. Russell 2000 and Russell 1000 Daily Avg. % Gain
(Dec. 19th 1979 to Mar. 7th 2016) Data Source: russellinvestments.com

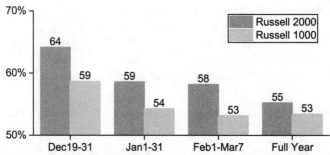

Figure 9. Russell 2000 and Russell 1000 Daily Avg. % Fq Positive
(Dec19/1979 to Mar 7/2016) Data Source: russellinvestments.com

Upside & Downside Daily Gains Analysis

Looking at the upside and downside average days can provide additional information on the nature of the average daily gains. In Figure 10, the upside numbers are all of the positive daily gains averaged together and likewise the downside numbers are all of the daily losses averaged together.

In Part 1, the Russell 2000 average daily upside gain of 0.73% is not as strong as its full year average daily upside gain of 0.77%. On the other hand, the average daily downside loss of 0.59% is substantially less than the average daily downside loss of 0.87% for the full year. In other words, it is the lack of large negative days that has the largest impact on the Russell 2000's strong performance. The same phenomenon also applies to the Russell 1000.

In Part 2, the Russell 2000's average daily upside gain of 0.76% and the Russell 1000's average daily gain of 0.74% are both greater than the full year numbers. The Russell 2000's average daily downside loss of 0.96% is greater than its full year average daily downside loss of 0.87%. The Russell 2000 outperforms in Part 2 as it has a much higher frequency of daily average gains compared with the full year.

In Part 3, the Russell 2000 has a lower daily average gain compared to the full year, but the daily average losses are less. Once again, it is the relative frequency of daily gains that provides the outperformance for the Russell 2000 relative to the rest of the year. The Russell 1000 underperforms the full year daily average gains mainly as a result of having a lower daily average gain.

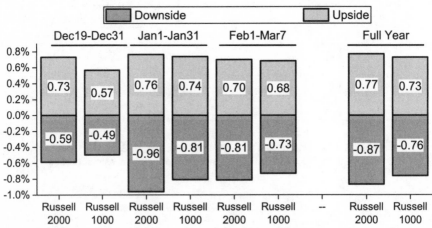

Figure 10. Russell 2000 & 1000 Day % Gain Upside/Downside (Dec 19/1979 to Mar 7/2016)
Upside calculated as average % gain of all positive days in period
Downside calculated as average % gain of all negative days in period

Small Caps and Large Caps January Monthly Rank has Slipped Over Time

The reason that the *January Effect* trade became a much written about phenomenon in the 1980's was that at the time, small caps performed very well in January, which was one of the best months of the year.

Since the 1980's, on average, January has progressed from being the strongest month of the year to one of the weaker months of the year. Table 2 illustrates the rank of both small and large caps sectors in the month of January versus the other months of the year (1 is the best and 12 is the worst). The performance of the Russell 2000 in January is compared against the performance of the Russell 2000 in the other months of the year and the performance of the Russell 1000 is compared against the performance of the Russell 1000 in the other months of the year. The small cap sector's performance in January has never been the worst month of the year from 1979 to 2015. It has been the best month of the year seven times with most of those occurrences taking place in the 1980's.

Figure 11 shows the ten year rolling average of January's rank against the other months of the year. What is interesting is that the performance of both small caps and large caps has deteriorated in January versus the other months of the year from 1979 to 2015. January was one of the better months of the year in the 1980's and has been one of the weaker months in recent years. It is not to say that January will continue to be a weak month for the stock market. It is possible that a multi-year aberration has taken place and January will return to its long-term trend of being one of the better months of the year.

Table 2: January Rank vs. All Months in Year (1 Best, 12 Worst)
Russell 2000 and 1000 (1979-2015) Data Source: russellinvestments.com

	Russell 2000	1000		Russell 2000	1000		Russell 2000	1000		Russell 2000	1000
1979	2	5									
1980	2	3	1990	10	11	2000	5	10	2010	9	9
1981	7	10	1991	2	4	2001	5	3	2011	6	4
1982	10	10	1992	1	9	2002	6	6	2012	1	1
1983	1	3	1993	3	6	2003	11	12	2013	3	1
1984	7	10	1994	2	3	2004	3	3	2014	9	12
1985	1	1	1995	11	8	2005	11	12	2015	9	10
1986	6	8	1996	9	3	2006	1	2			
1987	1	1	1997	6	3	2007	5	4			
1988	4	2	1998	9	9	2008	8	8			
1989	1	2	1999	7	6	2009	11	11			

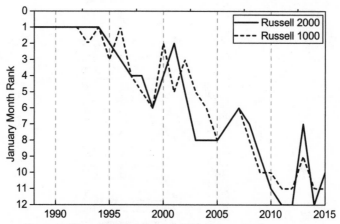

Figure 11. Russell 2000 & Russell 1000 January Rank
Compared to all other months (10 Year Rolling Average)
(1979-2015) Data Source: russellinvestments

Seasonal Period of Weakness for Small Caps

Knowing when to invest in a sector is important as well as knowing when to avoid it. Avoiding potential losses is always good. The one time of the year to avoid small caps is from September 14th to October 27th. In this period, from 1979 to 2015, on average the sector has produced a loss of 2.5% and has produced a loss 57% of the time (Table 3). Although large caps have also produced losses at this time, they have only had an average loss of 1% and produced a loss 46% of the time. In addition, small caps have been weak against large caps as they have underperformed the Russell 1000 two-thirds of the time.

The seasonally weak period for small caps occurs at the time of the year when investors typically get nervous about possible stock market corrections. As a result, investors tend to shift their holdings to more conservative positions, including favoring large caps over small caps. Out of the twelve times that the Russell 2000 outperformed the Russell 1000 from 1979 to 2015 in the period from September 14th to October 27th, only three of those occurrences took place when the Russell 1000 was negative. In other words, when the large cap sector was negative, on average, investors shunned small caps more than large caps.

Table 3: Russell 2000 and 1000 Gain / Loss %
September 14th to Oct 27th
(1979 to 2015) Data Source: russellinvestments.com

	Russell 1000	Russell 2000	Diff
1979	-7.1	-11.6	-4.5
1980	2.1	1.8	-0.2
1981	-1.8	-0.2	1.7
1982	11.2	14.8	3.6
1983	-0.7	-6.2	-5.6
1984	-1.4	-2.5	-1.1
1985	2.5	0.8	-1.7
1986	3.7	3.3	-0.4
1987	-27.9	-36.3	-8.4
1988	3.2	-0.2	-3.5
1989	-3.4	-6.5	-3.1
1990	-4.8	-12.8	-8.0
1991	0.6	1.7	1.1
1992	-0.1	1.9	2.0
1993	0.3	3.9	3.7
1994	-0.5	-2.0	-1.5
1995	-0.1	-6.8	-6.8
1996	2.8	0.7	-2.1
1997	-4.6	-4.4	0.1
1998	6.0	5.1	-0.9
1999	-3.5	-5.2	-1.7
2000	-7.2	-10.1	-3.0
2001	0.9	-0.5	-1.3
2002	0.5	-4.5	-4.9
2003	1.4	1.2	-0.2
2004	0.2	2.5	2.3
2005	-4.4	-7.3	-3.0
2006	4.5	4.8	0.4
2007	3.7	5.3	1.6
2008	-33.2	-37.7	-4.6
2009	1.8	-1.1	-3.0
2010	5.7	8.0	2.3
2011	9.2	10.7	1.4
2012	-3.3	-5.0	-1.7
2013	4.4	6.1	1.7
2014	-1.5	-3.7	-2.2
2015	4.6	-1.1	-5.7
Average	-1.0	-2.5	-1.5
Fq % > 0	54	43	32

Russell 2000 Negative ☐

Conclusion - Investing in Small Caps

For years, the investment industry has concentrated its efforts on the *January Effect* trade, putting forward the positive tendencies of stock market performance in January, especially for small caps. Using data from 1979 to 2016, it is evident that the *January Effect* is not as strong as previously purported, at least for the broad market or the large cap sector. The performance for large cap sector is not significantly different than the rest of the year when measured on daily average gain basis. On the other hand, the small cap sector has provided value during *January Effect* period.

Investing only to take advantage of the *January Effect* trade has been short-sighted. The period before January (December 19th to December 31st) has produced much better results, as has the period after January (February 1st to March 7th). Out of all three parts of the *Small Cap Effect* trade, the period before January provides the best return profile. From 1979 to 2015, the best time to invest in small caps has been the last part of December, from December 19th to December 31st. The next best time has been the period from February 1st to March 7th. Lastly, the month of January, which is the time period for the *January Effect* is by default the weakest time period within the *Small Cap Effect* trade. Regardless of January being the weakest part of the Small Cap Effect trade, on a practical basis, it is still worthwhile to be in the stock market at this time, especially the small cap sector.

For those wishing to avoid the seasonal weak spot for the small cap sector, on average, they are best to avoid the period between September 14th and October 27th, particularly the last two weeks in September. This is the time period when investors typically strive to reduce risk in their portfolios and as a result small caps are generally weak at this time.

The relative performance of the small cap sector compared to the large cap sector is influenced by a lot of different variables, such as GDP growth, U.S. dollar strength, inflation and interest rates. The fact that the variables can overcome seasonal trends in any year does not negate the benefit of using the small cap sector's seasonal trend as a road-map with which to invest. Over the long-term, through many different business cycles, the small cap sector has been persistent in its outperformance compared to the large cap sector during the *Small Cap Effect* trade period.

Small Cap Seasonal Performance

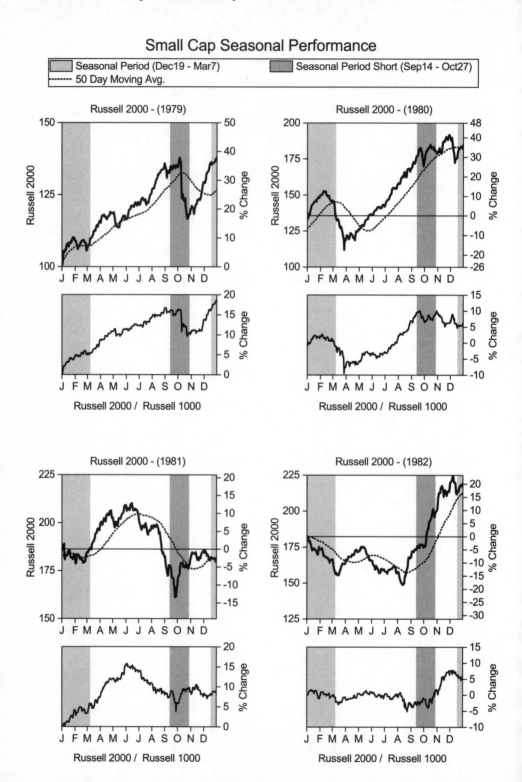

Small Cap Seasonal Performance

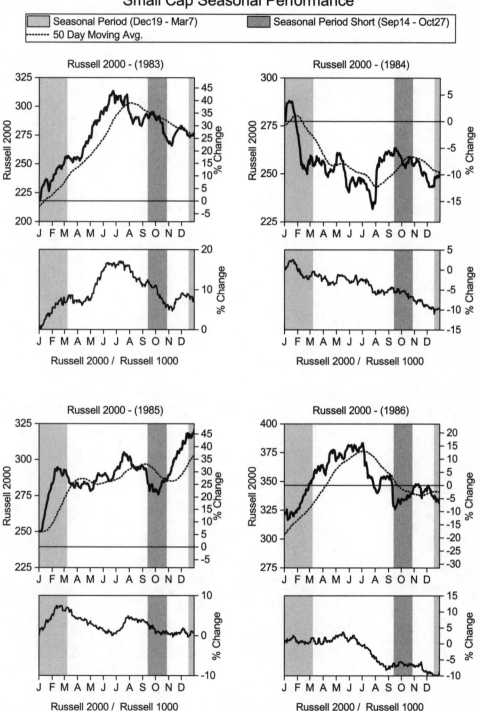

Seasonal Period (Dec19 - Mar7)   Seasonal Period Short (Sep14 - Oct27)
------- 50 Day Moving Avg.

Russell 2000 - (1983)

Russell 2000 - (1984)

Russell 2000 / Russell 1000

Russell 2000 / Russell 1000

Russell 2000 - (1985)

Russell 2000 - (1986)

Russell 2000 / Russell 1000

Russell 2000 / Russell 1000

Small Cap Seasonal Performance

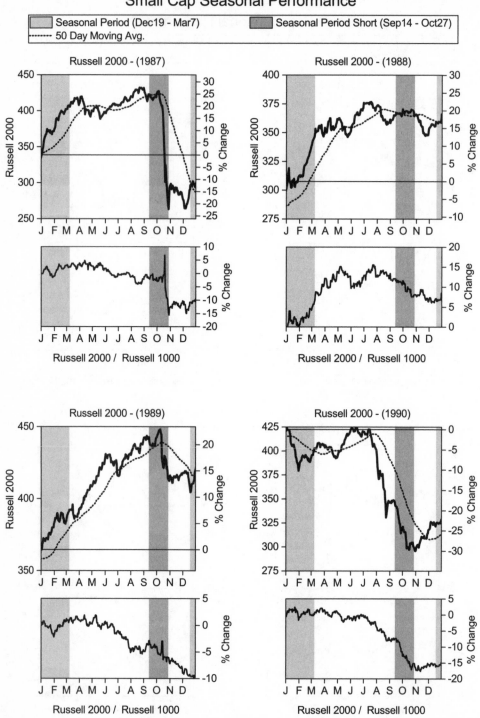

Small Cap Seasonal Performance

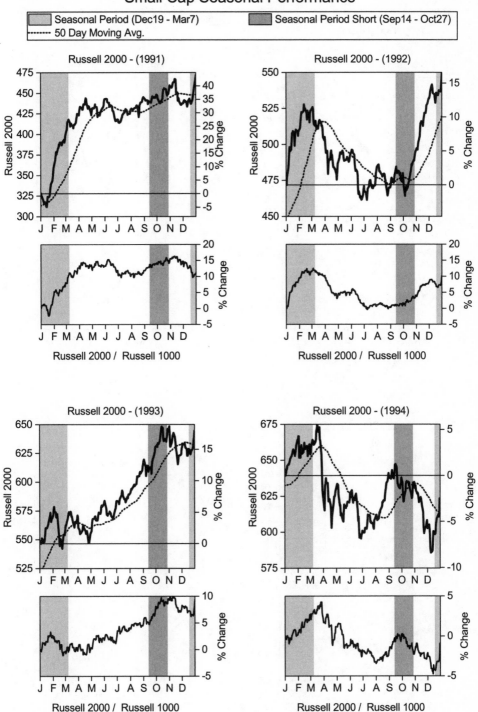

Seasonal Period (Dec19 - Mar7)   Seasonal Period Short (Sep14 - Oct27)

-------- 50 Day Moving Avg.

Russell 2000 - (1991)

Russell 2000 - (1992)

Russell 2000 / Russell 1000

Russell 2000 / Russell 1000

Russell 2000 - (1993)

Russell 2000 - (1994)

Russell 2000 / Russell 1000

Russell 2000 / Russell 1000

Small Cap Seasonal Performance

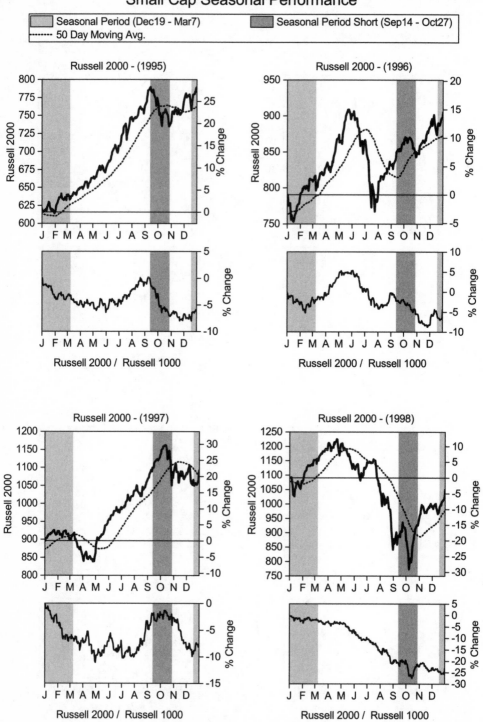

Small Cap Seasonal Performance

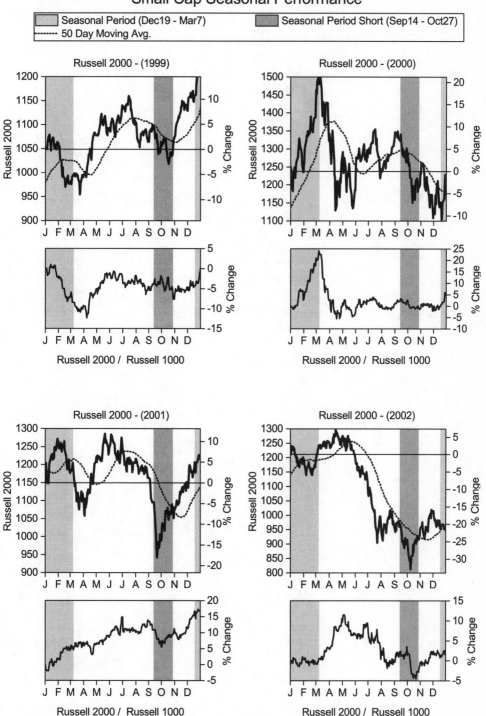

Seasonal Period (Dec19 - Mar7)   Seasonal Period Short (Sep14 - Oct27)
-------- 50 Day Moving Avg.

Russell 2000 - (1999)

Russell 2000 - (2000)

Russell 2000 / Russell 1000

Russell 2000 / Russell 1000

Russell 2000 - (2001)

Russell 2000 - (2002)

Russell 2000 / Russell 1000

Russell 2000 / Russell 1000

Small Cap Seasonal Performance

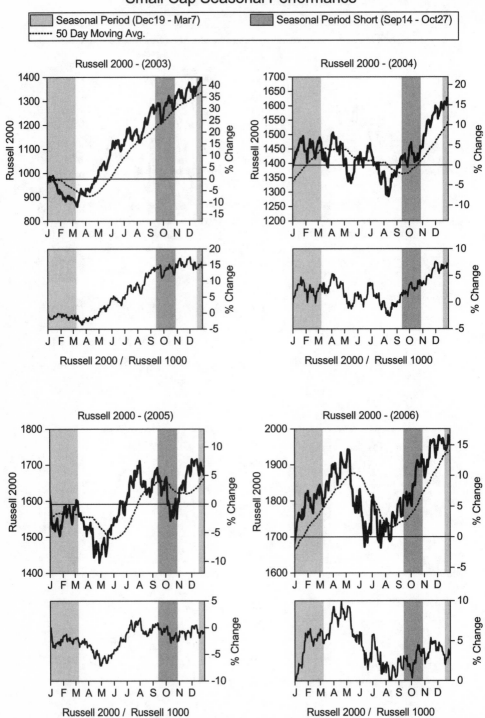

Small Cap Seasonal Performance

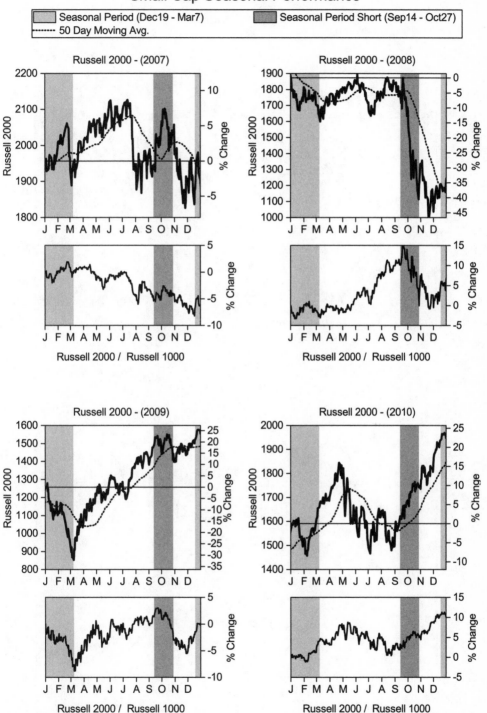

Small Cap Seasonal Performance

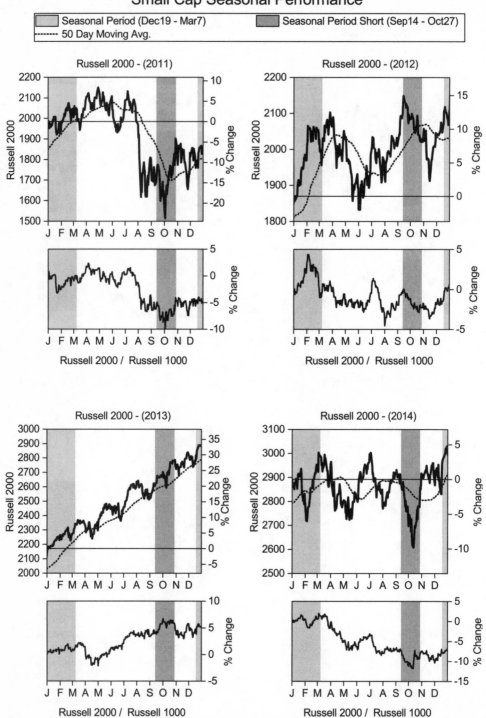

Small Cap Seasonal Performance

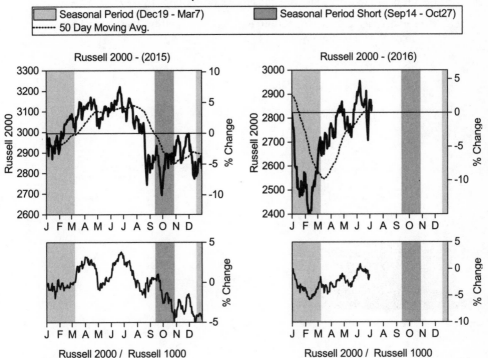

References:

Watchel, S.B., "Certain Observations on Seasonal Movements in Stock Prices," The Journal of Business of the University of Chicago, 15 (1942), pp. 184-193.

Rozeff, M.S., and W.R. Kinney, Jr., "Capital Market Seasonality: The Case of Stock Returns, " Journal of Financial Economics, 3 (1976), pp. 379-402.

COSTCO– BUY AT A DISCOUNT
①May26-Jun30　②Oct4-Dec1

Shoppers are attracted to Costco because of its consistently low prices. They take comfort in the fact that although the prices may not always be the lowest, they are consistently in the lower range.

Costco performs well in the late spring and early summer, and in the autumn and early winter. These two periods are considered to be transition periods where the stock market is moving to and from its unfavorable and favorable seasons. Companies such as Costco that have stable earnings are desirable at these times.

There are two times when Costco is a seasonal bargain: May 26th to June 30th and October 4th to December 1st. From 1990 to 2015, during the period of May 26th to June 30th, Costco has averaged a gain of 5.1% and has been positive 65% of the time. From October 4th to December 1st, Costco has averaged a gain of 10.0% and has been positive 81% of the time.

15.9% gain & positive 92% of the time

Putting both seasonal periods together has produced a 92% positive success rate and an average gain of 15.9%. Although the earlier strong years in the 1990's skews the data to the high-side, Costco has still maintained its strong seasonal performances in both the May to June and the October to December time periods. When investors go shopping for stocks, Costco is one consumer staples company that should be on their list. They should also remember not to bulk up with too much, even if it is selling at a discount.

*COST - stock symbol for Costco which trades on the Nasdaq exchange. Stock data adjusted for stock splits.

Costco* vs. S&P 500 1990 to 2015 Positive

Year	May 26 to Jun 30 S&P 500	COST	Oct 4 to Dec 1 S&P 500	COST	Compound Growth S&P 500	COST
1990	1.0	16.5%	3.5	26.5%	4.5	47.4%
1991	-1.7	-2.1	-2.4	-3.7	-4.0	-5.7
1992	-1.4	-2.2	5.0	22.7	3.5	20.1
1993	0.4	17.2	0.1	13.4	0.5	32.9
1994	-2.6	10.7	-2.8	-6.3	-5.3	3.7
1995	3.1	19.2	4.2	-2.1	7.4	16.7
1996	-1.2	9.4	9.3	15.5	8.0	26.4
1997	4.5	3.1	1.0	16.6	5.6	20.2
1998	2.1	17.6	17.2	41.1	19.7	65.9
1999	6.9	8.1	9.0	30.7	16.5	41.2
2000	5.3	10.0	-7.8	-3.6	-2.9	6.1
2001	-4.2	9.3	6.3	12.3	1.8	22.6
2002	-8.7	-0.8	14.3	4.6	4.4	3.8
2003	4.4	5.3	3.9	13.5	8.5	19.4
2004	2.5	10.3	5.3	17.3	7.9	29.4
2005	0.1	-1.5	3.1	13.9	3.2	12.2
2006	-0.2	5.0	4.7	6.0	4.5	11.3
2007	-0.8	3.8	-3.8	8.9	-4.6	12.9
2008	-7.0	-1.7	-25.8	-23.5	-30.9	-24.7
2009	3.6	-5.2	8.2	7.5	12.1	1.9
2010	-4.0	-3.0	5.2	5.0	1.0	1.9
2011	0.0	1.2	13.2	6.7	13.2	7.9
2012	3.4	12.5	-2.4	4.3	0.9	17.3
2013	-2.6	-3.3	7.6	9.6	4.7	6.0
2014	3.1	0.2	4.4	11.7	7.6	11.9
2015	-3.0	-6.0	7.8	10.6	4.6	3.9
Avg.	0.1%	5.1%	3.4%	10.0%	3.5%	15.9%
Fq>0	54%	65%	77%	81%	81%	92%

Costco - Avg. Year 1990 to 2015

Costco / S&P 500 Rel. Strength- Avg Yr. 1990-2015

Costco Performance

COST Monthly Performance (1990-2015)

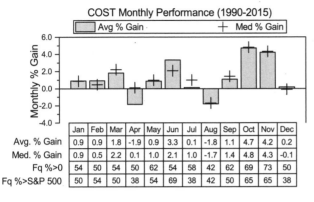

	Jan	Feb	Mar	Apr	May	Jun	Jul	Aug	Sep	Oct	Nov	Dec
Avg. % Gain	0.9	0.9	1.8	-1.9	0.9	3.3	0.1	-1.8	1.1	4.7	4.2	0.2
Med. % Gain	0.9	0.5	2.2	0.1	1.0	2.1	1.0	-1.7	1.4	4.8	4.3	-0.1
Fq %>0	54	50	54	50	62	54	58	42	62	69	73	50
Fq %>S&P 500	50	54	50	38	54	69	38	42	50	65	65	38

COST 5 Year (2011-2015) % Gain

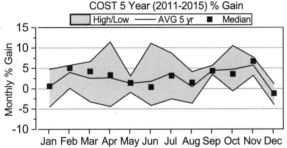

COST Performance 2015-2016

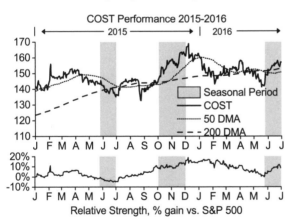

Relative Strength, % gain vs. S&P 500

Market Indices & Rates
Weekly Values**

Stock Markets	2015	2016
Dow	18,283	17,750
S&P500	2,128	2,081
Nasdaq	5,080	4,871
TSX	15,150	14,040
FTSE	7,003	6,221
DAX	11,795	10,133
Nikkei	20,116	16,704
Hang Seng	27,677	20,196

Commodities	2015	2016
Oil	58.83	48.54
Gold	1211.5	1231.8

Bond Yields	2015	2016
USA 5 Yr Treasury	1.56	1.40
USA 10 Yr T	2.23	1.86
USA 20 Yr T	2.75	2.25
Moody's Aaa	4.07	3.66
Moody's Baa	4.96	4.71
CAN 5 Yr T	1.05	0.77
CAN 10 Yr T	1.77	1.36

Money Market	2015	2016
USA Fed Funds	0.25	0.50
USA 3 Mo T-B	0.02	0.33
CAN tgt overnight rate	0.75	0.50
CAN 3 Mo T-B	0.65	0.52

Foreign Exchange	2015	2016
EUR/USD	1.11	1.12
GBP/USD	1.56	1.46
USD/CAD	1.22	1.31
USD/JPY	120.92	109.90

From 1990 to 2015, October and November have been the best two contiguous months for Costco on an average, median and frequency basis. This has been mainly driven by Costco releasing its year-end earnings at the end of September. The other strong month is June, which occurs right after Costco typically announces its Q3 results. Over the last five years, on average, November has been Costco's best month followed by December being its worst month.

In 2015, Costco outperformed the S&P 500 in its Oct. 4th to Dec. 1st seasonal period, and also more recently in its first seasonal period in 2016.

MAY

M	T	W	T	F	S	S
1	2	3	4	5	6	7
8	9	10	11	12	13	14
15	16	17	18	19	20	21
22	23	24	25	26	27	28
29	30	31				

JUNE

M	T	W	T	F	S	S
			1	2	3	4
5	6	7	8	9	10	11
12	13	14	15	16	17	18
19	20	21	22	23	24	25
26	27	28	29	30		

JULY

M	T	W	T	F	S	S
					1	2
3	4	5	6	7	8	9
10	11	12	13	14	15	16
17	18	19	20	21	22	23
24	25	26	27	28	29	30
31						

MEMORIAL DAY – BE EARLY & STAY LATE
Positive 2 Market Days Before Memorial Day to 5 Market Days into June

A lot of strategies that focus on investing around holidays concentrate on the market performance the day before and the day after a holiday.

1.0% average gain and positive 61% of the time

Not all holidays are created equal. The typical *Memorial Day* trade put forward by most market pundits is to invest the day before the holiday and sell the day after. If you invested in the stock market for just these two days, you would be missing out on a lot of gains.

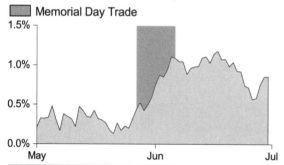

S&P 500% Gain May to June Avg. Year- 1971 to 2016
■ Memorial Day Trade

Historically, the best strategy has been to invest two market days before Memorial Day and exit five market days into June. Extending the investment into June makes sense. The first few days in June tend to be positive– so why sell early?

The graph shows the average performance of the S&P 500 on a calendar basis for the months of May and June from 1971 to 2016.

The increase from the end of May into June represents the opportunity with the "*Memorial Day - Be Early & Stay Late*" trade.

The graph clearly shows a spike in the market that occurs at the end of the month and carries on into June.

Investors using the typical Memorial Day trade of investing just for the day before and the day after Memorial Day, have missed out on potential gains. The *Memorial Day - Be Early & Stay Late* strategy has produced an average gain of 1.0% and has been positive 61% of the time (S&P 500, 1971 to 2016). Not a bad gain for being invested an average of ten market days.

The *Memorial Day - Be Early & Stay Late* trade can be extended into June primarily because the first market days of the month tend to be positive. These days are part of the end of the month effect. (see *Super Seven* strategy).

2 Market Days Before Memorial Day to 5 Market Days Into June - S&P 500   Positive ▢

		1980	5.1 %	1990	1.1 %	2000	5.2 %	2010	-1.6 %
1971	1.5 %	1981	0.2	1991	0.9	2001	-0.9	2011	-2.7
1972	-2.4	1982	-2.6	1992	-0.5	2002	-5.4	2012	-0.3
1973	1.7	1983	-2.1	1993	-1.3	2003	7.0	2013	-0.7
1974	6.3	1984	1.2	1994	0.4	2004	2.3	2014	3.3
1975	3.8	1985	4.3	1995	0.9	2005	0.6	2015	-1.6
1976	-0.7	1986	4.3	1996	0.0	2006	-0.2	2016	0.0
1977	1.0	1987	5.5	1997	2.2	2007	-2.1		
1978	3.1	1988	4.5	1998	-0.5	2008	-2.2		
1979	1.9	1989	2.4	1999	2.3	2009	4.1		
Avg.	1.8 %		2.3 %		0.6 %		0.8 %		-0.6 %

History of Memorial Day:
Originally called Decoration Day in remembrance of those who died in the nation's service. Memorial Day was first observed on May 30th 1868 when flowers were placed on the graves of Union and Confederate soldiers at Arlington National Cemetery. The South acknowledged the day after World War I, when the holiday changed from honoring just those who died fighting in the Civil War to honoring Americans who died fighting in any war. In 1971 Congress passed the National Holiday Act recognizing Memorial Day as the last Monday in May.

Memorial Day Strategy Performance

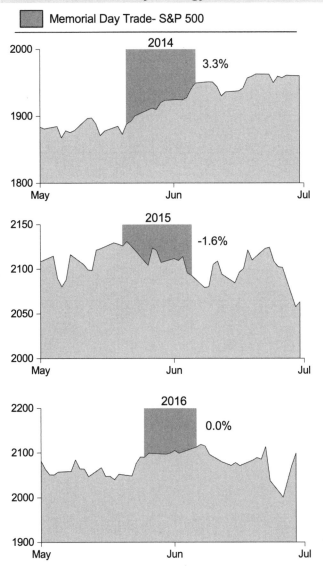

Memorial Day Trade- S&P 500

Market Indices & Rates
Weekly Values**

Stock Markets	2015	2016
Dow	18,085	17,806
S&P500	2,114	2,100
Nasdaq	5,077	4,954
TSX	15,094	14,116
FTSE	7,002	6,204
DAX	11,622	10,195
Nikkei	20,488	16,893
Hang Seng	27,802	20,802

Commodities	2015	2016
Oil	58.38	48.98
Gold	1186.9	1219.9

Bond Yields	2015	2016
USA 5 Yr Treasury	1.52	1.34
USA 10 Yr T	2.13	1.80
USA 20 Yr T	2.64	2.18
Moody's Aaa	3.95	3.59
Moody's Baa	4.86	4.64
CAN 5 Yr T	0.97	0.71
CAN 10 Yr T	1.69	1.28

Money Market	2015	2016
USA Fed Funds	0.25	0.50
USA 3 Mo T-B	0.01	0.31
CAN tgt overnight rate	0.75	0.50
CAN 3 Mo T-B	0.63	0.53

Foreign Exchange	2015	2016
EUR/USD	1.09	1.12
GBP/USD	1.54	1.45
USD/CAD	1.24	1.31
USD/JPY	123.28	109.36

MAY

M	T	W	T	F	S	S
1	2	3	4	5	6	7
8	9	10	11	12	13	14
15	16	17	18	19	20	21
22	23	24	25	26	27	28
29	30	31				

JUNE

M	T	W	T	F	S	S
			1	2	3	4
5	6	7	8	9	10	11
12	13	14	15	16	17	18
19	20	21	22	23	24	25
26	27	28	29	30		

JULY

M	T	W	T	F	S	S
					1	2
3	4	5	6	7	8	9
10	11	12	13	14	15	16
17	18	19	20	21	22	23
24	25	26	27	28	29	30
31						

In 2014, the S&P 500 had a strong run starting in mid-May and continued its upward trend through the *Memorial Day Trade* seasonal period, producing a gain of 3.3% in its seasonal period.

In 2015, the S&P 500 started to decline at the beginning of the *Memorial Day Trade* and ended up producing a loss of 1.6% in its seasonal period.

In 2016, the S&P 500 was flat in its *Memorial Day Trade* seasonal period and then declined shortly after the trade finished.

JUNE

	MONDAY	TUESDAY	WEDNESDAY
WEEK 22	29	30	31
WEEK 23	5 25	6 24	7 23
WEEK 24	12 18	13 17	14 16
WEEK 25	19 11	20 10	21 9
WEEK 26	26 4	27 3	28 2

THURSDAY		FRIDAY	
1	29	**2**	28
8	22	**9**	21
15	15	**16**	14
22	8	**23**	7
29	1	**30**	

JULY

M	T	W	T	F	S	S
					1	2
3	4	5	6	7	8	9
10	11	12	13	14	15	16
17	18	19	20	21	22	23
24	25	26	27	28	29	30
31						

AUGUST

M	T	W	T	F	S	S
	1	2	3	4	5	6
7	8	9	10	11	12	13
14	15	16	17	18	19	20
21	22	23	24	25	26	27
28	29	30	31			

SEPTEMBER

M	T	W	T	F	S	S
				1	2	3
4	5	6	7	8	9	10
11	12	13	14	15	16	17
18	19	20	21	22	23	24
25	26	27	28	29	30	

OCTOBER

M	T	W	T	F	S	S
						1
2	3	4	5	6	7	8
9	10	11	12	13	14	15
16	17	18	19	20	21	22
23	24	25	26	27	28	29
30	31					

JUNE
SUMMARY

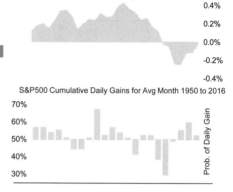

0.6%
0.4%
0.2%
0.0%
-0.2%
-0.4%

S&P500 Cumulative Daily Gains for Avg Month 1950 to 2016

70%
60%
50%
40%
30%

Prob. of Daily Gain

	Dow Jones	S&P 500	Nasdaq	TSX Comp
Month Rank	11	10	7	11
# Up	30	34	25	14
# Down	36	32	19	17
% Pos	45	52	57	45
% Avg. Gain	-0.3	0.0	0.8	-0.4

Dow & S&P 1950-2015, Nasdaq 1972-2015, TSX 1985-2015

♦ On average, June is not a strong month for the S&P 500. From 1950 to 2016, it was the third worst month of the year, producing a flat return of 0.0%. ♦ From year to year, different sectors of the market tend to lead in June as there is not a strong consistent outperforming major sector. ♦ On average, the bio-tech sector starts its seasonal run in late June. ♦ The last few days of June, the start the successful *Independence Day Trade,* tends to be positive. ♦ In June 2016, the S&P 500 produced a nominal gain of 0.1%.

BEST / WORST JUNE BROAD MKTS. 2007-2016

BEST JUNE MARKETS
♦ Nikkei 225 (2012) 5.4%
♦ Russell 2000 (2014) 5.2%
♦ Russell 2000 (2012) 4.8%

WORST JUNE MARKETS
♦ Dow (2008) -10.2%
♦ Nikkei 225 (2016) - 9.6%
♦ Nasdaq (2008) -9.1%

Index Values End of Month

	2007	2008	2009	2010	2011	2012	2013	2014	2015	2016
Dow	13,409	11,350	8,447	9,774	12,414	12,880	14,910	16,827	17,620	17,930
S&P 500	1,503	1,280	919	1,031	1,321	1,362	1,606	1,960	2,063	2,099
Nasdaq	2,603	2,293	1,835	2,109	2,774	2,935	3,403	4,408	4,987	4,843
TSX Comp.	13,907	14,467	10,375	11,294	13,301	11,597	12,129	15,146	14,553	14,065
Russell 1000	1,573	1,352	966	1,091	1,412	1,443	1,712	2,104	2,216	2,233
Russell 2000	2,072	1,714	1,263	1,515	2,056	1,984	2,429	2,965	3,116	2,863
FTSE 100	6,608	5,626	4,249	4,917	5,946	5,571	6,216	6,744	6,521	6,504
Nikkei 225	18,138	13,481	9,958	9,383	9,816	9,007	13,677	15,162	20,236	15,576

Percent Gain for June

	2007	2008	2009	2010	2011	2012	2013	2014	2015	2016
Dow	-1.6	-10.2	-0.6	-3.6	-1.2	3.9	-1.4	0.7	-2.2	0.8
S&P 500	-1.8	-8.6	0.0	-5.4	-1.8	4.0	-1.5	1.9	-2.1	0.1
Nasdaq	0.0	-9.1	3.4	-6.5	-2.2	3.8	-1.5	3.9	-1.6	-2.1
TSX Comp.	-1.1	-1.7	0.0	-4.0	-3.6	0.7	-4.1	3.7	-3.1	0.0
Russell 1000	-2.0	-8.5	0.1	-5.7	-1.9	3.7	-1.5	2.1	-2.0	0.1
Russell 2000	-1.6	-7.8	1.3	-7.9	-2.5	4.8	-0.7	5.2	0.6	-0.2
FTSE 100	-0.2	-7.1	-3.8	-5.2	-0.7	4.7	-5.6	-1.5	-6.6	4.4
Nikkei 225	1.5	-6.0	4.6	-4.0	1.3	5.4	-0.7	3.6	-1.6	-9.6

June Market Avg. Performance 2007 to 2016[1]

Dow	-1.5%
S&P 500	-1.5%
Nasdaq	-1.2%
TSX Comp (CAN)	-1.3%
Russell 1000 (Lg Cap)	-1.6%
Russell 2000 (Sm Cap)	-0.9%
FTSE 100	-2.2%
Nikkei 225	-0.5%

Interest Corner Jun[2]

	Fed Funds %[3]	3 Mo. T-Bill %[4]	10 Yr %[5]	20 Yr %[6]
2016	0.50	0.26	1.49	1.86
2015	0.25	0.01	2.35	2.83
2014	0.25	0.04	2.53	3.08
2013	0.25	0.04	2.52	3.22
2012	0.25	0.09	1.67	2.38

(1) Russell Data provided by Russell (2) Federal Reserve Bank of St. Louis- end of month values (3) Target rate set by FOMC (4)(5)(6) Constant yield maturities.

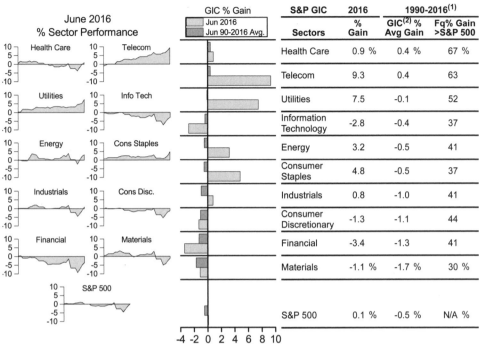

S&P GIC Sectors	2016 % Gain	1990-2016[1] GIC[2] % Avg Gain	Fq% Gain >S&P 500
Health Care	0.9 %	0.4 %	67 %
Telecom	9.3	0.4	63
Utilities	7.5	-0.1	52
Information Technology	-2.8	-0.4	37
Energy	3.2	-0.5	41
Consumer Staples	4.8	-0.5	37
Industrials	0.8	-1.0	41
Consumer Discretionary	-1.3	-1.1	44
Financial	-3.4	-1.3	41
Materials	-1.1 %	-1.7 %	30 %
S&P 500	0.1 %	-0.5 %	N/A %

SELECTED SUB-SECTORS[3]

Pharma	3.3 %	0.6 %	67 %
Gold	9.0	-0.1	52
Retail	-1.1	-0.5	56
Metals & Mining	6.7	-0.8	56
SOX (1995-2016)	-1.1	-1.0	36
Railroads	1.7	-1.0	41
Biotech (1993-2016)	-7.0	-1.1	46
Steel	1.9	-1.2	44
Transportation	-2.8	-1.4	30
Agriculture (1994-2016)	0.3	-1.6	35
Silver	14.3	-1.8	41
Chemicals	-2.7	-1.8	30
Automotive & Components	-6.6	-1.9	44
Homebuilders	2.6	-2.2	38
Banks	-7.3	-2.3	30

Sector Commentary

♦ In June 2016, the defensive sectors lead the S&P 500. ♦ The telecom sector produced a return of 9.3%, consumer staples 4.8% and utilities 7.5%. ♦ On the downside, the financial sector was the worst performer with a loss of 3.4%. ♦ The financial sector underperformed as investors were anticipating the U.S. Federal Reserve to delay raising interest rates. ♦ As the stock market started to shift into a risk-off mode, the information technology sector lost 2.8%.

Sub-Sector Commentary

♦ In June 2016, silver and gold once again produced strong results with gains of 14.3% and 9.0% respectively. ♦ Banks produced a large loss of 7.3%. ♦ The biotech sector produced a large loss of 7.0%. This loss largely occurred before the start of biotech's seasonally strong period which starts on June 23rd.

(1) Sector data provided by Standard and Poors (2) GIC is short form for Global Industry Classification (3) Sub Sector data provided by Standard and Poors, except where marked by symbol.

BIOTECH SUMMER SOLSTICE
June 23rd to September 13th

The *Biotech Summer Solstice* trade starts on June 23rd and lasts until September 13th. The trade is aptly named as its outperformance starts approximately when summer solstice starts– the longest day of the year.

There are two main drivers of the trade: biotech is a good substitute for technology stocks in the summer, and investors want to take a position in the biotech sector before the autumn conferences.

11.1% extra & 88% of the time better than the S&P 500

Biotech* vs. S&P 500 1992 to 2015

Jun 23 to Sep 13	S&P 500	Biotech	Diff
1992	4.0 %	17.9 %	13.8 %
1993	3.6	3.6	0.0
1994	3.2	24.2	21.0
1995	5.0	31.5	26.5
1996	2.1	7.0	4.9
1997	2.8	-18.9	-21.7
1998	-8.5	20.6	29.1
1999	0.6	64.3	63.7
2000	2.3	7.6	5.4
2001	-10.8	-3.6	7.2
2002	-10.0	8.1	18.2
2003	2.3	6.4	4.1
2004	-0.8	8.9	9.6
2005	1.4	26.0	24.5
2006	5.8	7.4	1.6
2007	-1.2	6.0	7.2
2008	-5.0	11.4	16.5
2009	16.8	7.7	-9.1
2010	2.4	2.8	0.4
2011	-8.9	-3.7	5.2
2012	9.4	15.6	6.2
2013	6.0	24.9	18.9
2014	1.2	14.8	13.6
2015	-7.6	-7.2	0.5
Avg	0.7 %	11.8 %	11.1 %
Fq>0	67 %	83 %	88 %

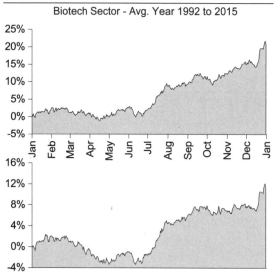

Biotech Sector - Avg. Year 1992 to 2015

Biotech / S&P 500 Relative Strength - Avg Yr. 1992 - 2015

The biotechnology sector is often considered the cousin of the technology sector, a good place for speculative investments. The sectors are similar as both include concept companies (companies without a product but with good potential).

Despite their similarity, investors view the sectors differently. The technology sector is viewed as being much more dependent on the economy compared with the biotech sector. The end product of biotechnology companies is mainly medicine, which is not economically sensitive.

As a result, in the summer months when investors tend to be more cautious, they are more willing to commit speculative money into the biotech sector, compared with the technology sector.

The biotech sector is one of the few sectors that starts its outperformance in June. This is in part because of the biotech conferences that occur in autumn and with the possibility of positive announcements, the price of biotech companies on the stock market can increase dramatically. As a result, investors try to lock in positions early.

*Biotech SP GIC Sector # 352010: Companies primarily engaged in the research, development, manufacturing and/or marketing of products based on genetic analysis and genetic engineering. This includes companies specializing in protein-based therapeutics to treat human diseases.

Biotech Performance

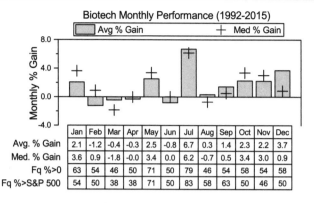

Biotech Monthly Performance (1992-2015)

	Jan	Feb	Mar	Apr	May	Jun	Jul	Aug	Sep	Oct	Nov	Dec
Avg. % Gain	2.1	-1.2	-0.4	-0.3	2.5	-0.8	6.7	0.3	1.4	2.3	2.2	3.7
Med. % Gain	3.6	0.9	-1.8	-0.0	3.4	0.0	6.2	-0.7	0.5	3.4	3.0	0.9
Fq %>0	63	54	46	50	71	50	79	46	54	58	54	58
Fq %>S&P 500	54	50	38	38	71	50	83	58	63	50	46	50

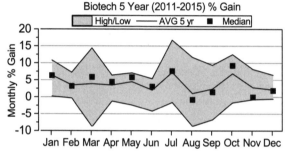

Biotech 5 Year (2011-2015) % Gain

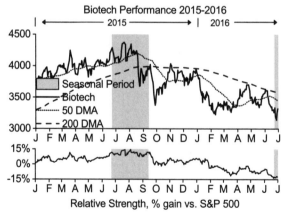

Biotech Performance 2015-2016

Relative Strength, % gain vs. S&P 500

Market Indices & Rates
Weekly Values**

Stock Markets	2015	2016
Dow	17,977	17,943
S&P500	2,105	2,110
Nasdaq	5,077	4,952
TSX	15,062	14,246
FTSE	6,899	6,241
DAX	11,344	10,110
Nikkei	20,507	16,671
Hang Seng	27,507	21,175

Commodities	2015	2016
Oil	59.65	50.18
Gold	1184.7	1257.5

Bond Yields	2015	2016
USA 5 Yr Treasury	1.65	1.22
USA 10 Yr T	2.31	1.70
USA 20 Yr T	2.80	2.07
Moody's Aaa	4.13	3.51
Moody's Baa	5.04	4.55
CAN 5 Yr T	0.97	0.62
CAN 10 Yr T	1.74	1.20

Money Market	2015	2016
USA Fed Funds	0.25	0.50
USA 3 Mo T-B	0.02	0.27
CAN tgt overnight rate	0.75	0.50
CAN 3 Mo T-B	0.61	0.50

Foreign Exchange	2015	2016
EUR/USD	1.11	1.13
GBP/USD	1.53	1.44
USD/CAD	1.25	1.28
USD/JPY	124.62	107.20

JUNE

M	T	W	T	F	S	S
		1	2	3	4	
5	6	7	8	9	10	11
12	13	14	15	16	17	18
19	20	21	22	23	24	25
26	27	28	29	30		

JULY

M	T	W	T	F	S	S
				1	2	
3	4	5	6	7	8	9
10	11	12	13	14	15	16
17	18	19	20	21	22	23
24	25	26	27	28	29	30
31						

AUGUST

M	T	W	T	F	S	S
	1	2	3	4	5	6
7	8	9	10	11	12	13
14	15	16	17	18	19	20
21	22	23	24	25	26	27
28	29	30	31			

From 1992 to 2015, the best month for the biotech sector has been July on an average, median and frequency basis. The start of the seasonal period for the sector is late June and runs into the middle of September. On the whole, June is actually a negative month, but the tail end of the month often provides a good buying opportunity. Although August has been positive on an average absolute basis, it can be a weaker month and investors should be prepared to exit the sector before the seasonal period finishes. Over the last five years, the sector has demonstrated superior performance in July. In 2015, the sector nominally outperformed the S&P 500 during its seasonal period.

SUPER SEVEN DAYS
7 Best Days of the Month

The end of the month tends to be an excellent time to invest: portfolio managers "window dress" (adjust their portfolios to look good for month end reports), investors stop procrastinating and invest their extra cash, and brokers try to increase their commissions by investing their clients' extra cash.

From 1950 to 2015
All 7 days better
than market average

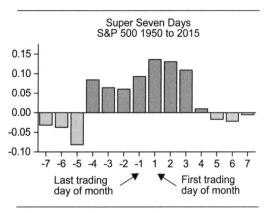

Super Seven Days
S&P 500 1950 to 2015

Last trading day of month / First trading day of month

All of these factors tend to produce above average returns in the market during the days on either side of month end.

The above graph illustrates the strength of the *Super Seven* days. The *Super Seven* days are the last four trading days of the month and the first three trading days of the next month, represented by the dark columns from day -4 to day 3. All of the *Super Seven* days have daily average gains above the daily market average gain of 0.03% since 1950.

% Gain Super Seven Day Period From 2006 to 2015

	2006	2007	2008	2009	2010	2011	2012	2013	2014	2015	Avg.
Jan	-0.1 %	1.6 %	-4.5 %	-0.5 %	0.0 %	1.2 %	1.4 %	0.6 %	-1.7 %	-0.8	-0.3 %
Feb	-0.4	-5.6	-2.8	4.1	1.0	1.2	0.1	1.6	1.4	-0.5	-0.8
Mar	0.8	0.1	1.2	3.5	2.0	1.4	-1.2	-0.2	1.2	0.9	1.0
Apr	0.0	1.5	1.3	4.3	-3.8	0.9	1.4	2.3	0.3	-1.3	0.7
May	0.5	1.6	0.1	5.0	2.7	-1.2	-2.7	-2.5	1.4	-0.6	0.4
Jun	1.9	1.8	-3.9	-0.2	-4.2	5.6	4.1	2.7	1.8	-1.9	0.8
Jul	0.9	-5.6	2.2	2.1	1.1	-5.8	4.0	1.0	-2.9	1.6	-0.2
Aug	0.4	0.8	-2.4	-2.4	4.7	0.5	1.5	-0.1	0.0	4.5	0.7
Sep	1.8	1.4	-7.3	-1.0	1.1	-1.6	-0.4	-1.1	-1.5	2.8	-0.6
Oct	-1.3	-0.8	12.2	-1.9	1.0	2.6	0.3	0.2	3.2	1.5	1.7
Nov	1.0	5.5	8.8	-0.6	3.7	8.2	0.2	-0.7	0.5	-1.8	2.5
Dec	-0.1	-5.7	7.7	0.9	1.5	1.2	2.8	-0.4	-3.8	-3.4	0.1
Avg.	0.5 %	-0.3 %	1.1 %	0.4 %	0.9 %	1.2 %	1.0 %	0.3 %	0.0 %	0.1	0.5 %

From 2006 to 2015, the *Super Seven* strategy has worked very well and has produced an average gain of 0.5% per month. On an annualized basis, this return is greater than 6% per year.

Given that the *Super Seven* strategy has seven trading days and the average month has twenty-two trading days, the *Super Seven* strategy has investors in the market for less than one third of the time. Adjusting returns for the amount of time in the market, the strategy has produced much greater gains per day than a buy and hold discipline.

If there is one time of the month that investors should be concentrating on investing, it is the last four trading days of the current month and the first three of the next month.

Super Seven Strategy Performance

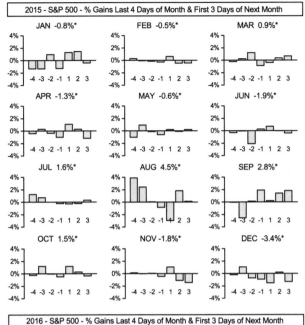

2015 - S&P 500 - % Gains Last 4 Days of Month & First 3 Days of Next Month

JAN -0.8%*   FEB -0.5%*   MAR 0.9%*

APR -1.3%*   MAY -0.6%*   JUN -1.9%*

JUL 1.6%*   AUG 4.5%*   SEP 2.8%*

OCT 1.5%*   NOV -1.8%*   DEC -3.4%*

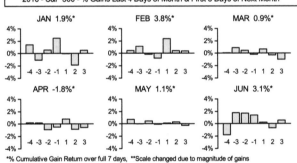

2016 - S&P 500 - % Gains Last 4 Days of Month & First 3 Days of Next Month

JAN 1.9%*   FEB 3.8%*   MAR 0.9%*

APR -1.8%*   MAY 1.1%*   JUN 3.1%*

*% Cumulative Gain Return over full 7 days, **Scale changed due to magnitude of gains

Super Seven Performance

The *Super Seven* strategy produced nominal gains in 2015 and started 2016 with every month being positive except April.

In 2015, the S&P 500 was successful five out of twelve *Super Seven* trades. On average, the positive results were slightly larger than the negative results, leading to an overall nominal gain.

In 2016, so far the *Super Seven* strategy has been positive five out of the six times. April has been the only negative month as the stock market turned down at the end of the month as it transitioned into the unfavorable period that lasts from May 6th to October 27th.

Market Indices & Rates
Weekly Values**

Stock Markets	2015	2016
Dow	17,894	17,691
S&P500	2,094	2,075
Nasdaq	5,049	4,834
TSX	14,804	13,917
FTSE	6,801	5,981
DAX	11,172	9,593
Nikkei	20,278	15,766
Hang Seng	27,036	20,315

Commodities	2015	2016
Oil	60.09	47.91
Gold	1180.0	1290.5

Bond Yields	2015	2016
USA 5 Yr Treasury	1.75	1.12
USA 10 Yr T	2.42	1.61
USA 20 Yr T	2.88	1.99
Moody's Aaa	4.20	3.45
Moody's Baa	5.13	4.49
CAN 5 Yr T	1.04	0.57
CAN 10 Yr T	1.84	1.11

Money Market	2015	2016
USA Fed Funds	0.25	0.50
USA 3 Mo T-B	0.02	0.27
CAN tgt overnight rate	0.75	0.50
CAN 3 Mo T-B	0.62	0.51

Foreign Exchange	2015	2016
EUR/USD	1.13	1.13
GBP/USD	1.55	1.42
USD/CAD	1.23	1.29
USD/JPY	123.66	105.36

JUNE

M	T	W	T	F	S	S
			1	2	3	4
5	6	7	8	9	10	11
12	13	14	15	16	17	18
19	20	21	22	23	24	25
26	27	28	29	30		

JULY

M	T	W	T	F	S	S
					1	2
3	4	5	6	7	8	9
10	11	12	13	14	15	16
17	18	19	20	21	22	23
24	25	26	27	28	29	30
31						

AUGUST

M	T	W	T	F	S	S
	1	2	3	4	5	6
7	8	9	10	11	12	13
14	15	16	17	18	19	20
21	22	23	24	25	26	27
28	29	30	31			

INDEPENDENCE DAY – THE FULL TRADE
PROFIT BEFORE & AFTER FIREWORKS
Two Market Days Before June Month End
To 5 Market Days After Independence Day

The beginning of July is a time for celebration and the markets tend to agree.

Based on previous market data, the best way to take advantage of this trend is to be invested for the two market days prior to June month end and hold until five market days after Independence Day. This time period has produced above average returns on a fairly consistent basis.

Since 1950, 0.9% avg. gain & 72% of the time positive

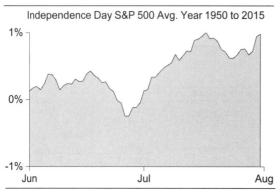

Independence Day S&P 500 Avg. Year 1950 to 2015

The typical *Independence Day Trade* put forward by quite a few pundits has been to invest one or two days before the holiday and take profits one or two days after the holiday.

Although this strategy has produced profits, it has left a lot of money on the table. This strategy misses out on the positive days at the end of June and on the full slate of positive days after Independence Day.

The beginning part of the *Independence Day Trade* positive trend is driven by two combining factors.

First, portfolio managers "window dress" (buy stocks that have a favorable perception in the market); thereby pushing stock prices up at the end of the month.

Second, investors have become "wise" to the *Independence Day Trade* and try to jump in before other investors.

Depending on market conditions at the time, investors should consider extending the exit date until eighteen calendar days in July. With July being an earnings month, the market can continue to rally until mid-month (see *18 Day Earnings Month Strategy*).

> (i) History of Independence Day:
> *Independence Day is celebrated on July 4th because that is the day when the Continental Congress adopted the final draft of the Declaration of Independence in 1776. Independence Day was made an official holiday at the end of the War of Independence in 1783. In 1941 Congress declared the 4th of July a federal holiday.*

S&P 500, 2 Market Days Before June Month End To 5 Market Days after Independence Day % Gain 1950 to 2016   Positive [ ]

Year	%	Year	%	Year	%	Year	%	Year	%	Year	%	Year	%
1950	-4.4 %	1960	-0.1 %	1970	1.5 %	1980	1.4 %	1990	1.7 %	2000	1.8 %	2010	0.4 %
1951	1.5	1961	1.7	1971	3.2	1981	-2.4	1991	1.4	2001	-2.6	2011	1.8
1952	0.9	1962	9.8	1972	0.3	1982	-0.6	1992	2.8	2002	-4.7	2012	0.7
1953	0.8	1963	0.5	1973	2.1	1983	1.5	1993	-0.6	2003	1.2	2013	4.5
1954	2.9	1964	2.3	1974	-8.8	1984	-0.7	1994	0.4	2004	-1.7	2014	0.5
1955	4.9	1965	5.0	1975	-0.2	1985	1.5	1995	1.8	2005	1.5	2015	-1.2
1956	3.4	1966	2.1	1976	2.4	1986	-2.6	1996	-2.8	2006	2.1	2016	5.0
1957	3.8	1967	1.3	1977	-0.6	1987	0.4	1997	3.7	2007	0.8		
1958	2.0	1968	2.3	1978	0.6	1988	-0.6	1998	2.7	2008	-3.4		
1959	3.3	1969	-1.5	1979	1.3	1989	0.9	1999	5.1	2009	-4.3		
Avg.	1.9 %		2.3 %		0.2 %		-0.1 %		1.8 %		-0.9 %		1.7 %

Independence Day Strategy Performance

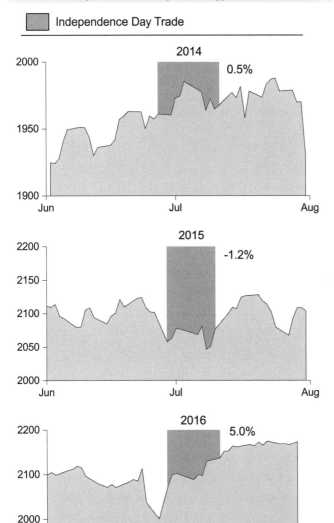

Independence Day Trade

2014 — 0.5%

2015 — -1.2%

2016 — 5.0%

Stock Markets	2015	2016
Dow	17,953	17,765
S&P500	2,102	2,082
Nasdaq	5,080	4,826
TSX	14,733	14,011
FTSE	6,704	6,234
DAX	11,029	9,973
Nikkei	20,206	15,878
Hang Seng	26,727	20,620

Commodities	2015	2016
Oil	59.89	48.56
Gold	1188.5	1279.4

Bond Yields	2015	2016
USA 5 Yr Treasury	1.65	1.18
USA 10 Yr T	2.32	1.68
USA 20 Yr T	2.81	2.05
Moody's Aaa	4.17	3.56
Moody's Baa	5.10	4.56
CAN 5 Yr T	0.95	0.69
CAN 10 Yr T	1.75	1.23

Money Market	2015	2016
USA Fed Funds	0.25	0.50
USA 3 Mo T-B	0.01	0.28
CAN tgt overnight rate	0.75	0.50
CAN 3 Mo T-B	0.62	0.50

Foreign Exchange	2015	2016
EUR/USD	1.13	1.13
GBP/USD	1.58	1.45
USD/CAD	1.23	1.28
USD/JPY	123.18	104.30

In 2014, the S&P 500 rallied in June and continued its momentum into July for a successful *Independence Day Trade*.

In 2015, the S&P 500 declined in June and continued its decline into the *Independence Day Trade* to produce a loss of 1.2%.

In 2016, the S&P 500 benefited from the post Brexit rally. The rally started a few days before the end of June, but tapered off after the *Independence Day Trade*.

JUNE

M	T	W	T	F	S	S
			1	2	3	4
5	6	7	8	9	10	11
12	13	14	15	16	17	18
19	20	21	22	23	24	25
26	27	28	29	30		

JULY

M	T	W	T	F	S	S
					1	2
3	4	5	6	7	8	9
10	11	12	13	14	15	16
17	18	19	20	21	22	23
24	25	26	27	28	29	30
31						

AUGUST

M	T	W	T	F	S	S
	1	2	3	4	5	6
7	8	9	10	11	12	13
14	15	16	17	18	19	20
21	22	23	24	25	26	27
28	29	30	31			

Ryder— Rolls Down & Up
①SELL SHORT (June 3-Oct27)
②LONG (Jan1-Jun2)

Ryder System Inc. is a supplier of transportation and supply chain management products. It is mainly known for its fleet of rental trucks.

A large part of its revenue is derived from its services and products that are provided when its customers need to be able to meet their busy seasonal demands.

19.2% growth & positive 77% of the time

The first few months of the year tend to be positive for Ryder as the economy tends to expand at this time and many companies outsource their logistical needs.

From 1990 to 2015, in the period from January 1st to June 2nd, Ryder has produced an average gain of 10.9% and been positive 73% of the time.

For most of the second half of the year, Ryder tends to perform poorly. At this time, expectations for economy growth tend to moderate. The fourth quarter of the year tends to be the weakest revenue producer for Ryder.

The end result is that Ryder tends to underperform from June 3rd to October 27th. In this period, from 1990 to 2015, Ryder has produced an average loss of 6.2% and has only been positive 27% of the time.

Short selling Ryder in its weak seasonal period and buying it in its strong seasonal period, from 1990 to 2015 has produced an average gain of 19.2% and has been positive 77% of the time.

(i) *Ryder is in the transportation sector. Its stock symbol is R. which trades on the NYSE, adjusted for splits.*

Ryder vs. S&P 500 1990 to 2015

Positive Long   Negative Short

Year	Jun 3 to Oct 27 S&P 500	R	Jan 1 to Jun 2 S&P 500	R	Compound Growth S&P 500	R
1990	-16.1	-44.8 %	2.8 %	12.3 %	-13.8 %	62.6 %
1991	-1.4	-7.3	18.1	37.5	16.4	47.5
1992	1.2	-8.2	-0.9	28.4	0.3	38.9
1993	2.4	-1.8	4.2	3.2	6.6	5.0
1994	1.8	-1.0	-1.9	-8.5	-0.1	-7.5
1995	8.9	-3.0	16.0	13.6	26.2	17.0
1996	4.8	-0.9	8.6	18.2	13.8	19.2
1997	3.6	2.2	14.3	19.1	18.4	16.5
1998	-2.6	-28.7	12.7	5.2	9.8	35.3
1999	0.2	-19.0	5.3	-2.2	5.5	16.4
2000	-6.6	-16.3	0.6	-18.4	-6.1	-5.1
2001	-12.4	-10.2	-4.5	32.0	-16.3	45.5
2002	-15.9	-20.9	-7.1	35.0	-21.8	63.2
2003	6.6	10.7	9.9	18.7	17.2	6.0
2004	0.0	31.1	1.2	9.1	1.2	-24.9
2005	-2.1	0.1	-0.6	-22.7	-2.7	-22.8
2006	6.9	-3.1	3.2	34.2	10.3	38.2
2007	-0.1	-12.4	8.3	5.9	8.2	19.0
2008	-38.7	-49.5	-5.6	55.4	-42.2	132.4
2009	12.6	44.8	4.6	-23.7	17.7	-57.9
2010	7.7	-2.0	-1.5	8.1	6.0	10.2
2011	-2.2	-3.5	4.4	1.2	2.1	4.7
2012	10.5	7.5	1.6	-21.6	12.3	-27.4
2013	7.9	3.7	14.3	26.3	23.4	21.7
2014	1.9	-2.4	4.1	18.0	6.1	20.8
2015	-2.1	-25.9	2.5	-0.8	0.3	24.9
Avg.	-0.9 %	-6.2 %	4.4 %	10.9 %	3.8 %	19.2 %
Fq>0	58 %	27 %	73 %	73 %	73 %	77 %

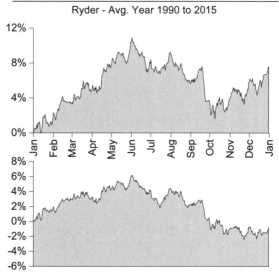

Ryder - Avg. Year 1990 to 2015

Ryder / S&P 500 Rel. Strength- Avg Yr. 1990-2015

Ryder Strategy Performance

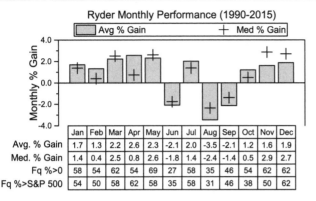

Ryder Monthly Performance (1990-2015)

Avg % Gain   + Med % Gain

	Jan	Feb	Mar	Apr	May	Jun	Jul	Aug	Sep	Oct	Nov	Dec
Avg. % Gain	1.7	1.3	2.2	2.6	2.3	-2.1	2.0	-3.5	-2.1	1.2	1.6	1.9
Med. % Gain	1.4	0.4	2.5	0.8	2.6	-1.8	1.4	-2.4	-1.4	0.5	2.9	2.7
Fq %>0	58	54	62	54	69	27	58	35	46	54	62	62
Fq %>S&P 500	54	50	58	62	58	35	58	31	46	38	50	62

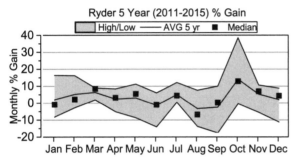

Ryder 5 Year (2011-2015) % Gain

High/Low   —— AVG 5 yr   ■ Median

Jan Feb Mar Apr May Jun Jul Aug Sep Oct Nov Dec

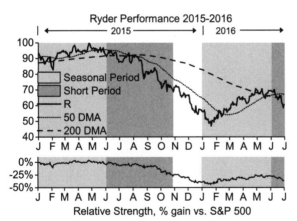

Ryder Performance 2015-2016

2015 → | 2016 →

Seasonal Period
Short Period
R
50 DMA
200 DMA

J F M A M J J A S O N D J F M A M J J

Relative Strength, % gain vs. S&P 500

Market Indices & Rates
Weekly Values**

Stock Markets	2015	2016
Dow	18,013	17,625
S&P500	2,112	2,062
Nasdaq	5,126	4,754
TSX	14,870	13,908
FTSE	6,813	6,313
DAX	11,488	9,557
Nikkei	20,717	15,492
Hang Seng	27,126	20,408

Commodities	2015	2016
Oil	59.95	48.28
Gold	1176.1	1323.3

Bond Yields	2015	2016
USA 5 Yr Treasury	1.71	1.01
USA 10 Yr T	2.41	1.47
USA 20 Yr T	2.90	1.84
Moody's Aaa	4.26	3.39
Moody's Baa	5.22	4.39
CAN 5 Yr T	0.99	0.58
CAN 10 Yr T	1.82	1.08

Money Market	2015	2016
USA Fed Funds	0.25	0.50
USA 3 Mo T-B	0.01	0.27
CAN tgt overnight rate	0.75	0.50
CAN 3 Mo T-B	0.58	0.49

Foreign Exchange	2015	2016
EUR/USD	1.12	1.11
GBP/USD	1.58	1.33
USD/CAD	1.23	1.30
USD/JPY	123.73	102.66

JUNE

M	T	W	T	F	S	S
			1	2	3	4
5	6	7	8	9	10	11
12	13	14	15	16	17	18
19	20	21	22	23	24	25
26	27	28	29	30		

JULY

M	T	W	T	F	S	S
					1	2
3	4	5	6	7	8	9
10	11	12	13	14	15	16
17	18	19	20	21	22	23
24	25	26	27	28	29	30
31						

AUGUST

M	T	W	T	F	S	S
	1	2	3	4	5	6
7	8	9	10	11	12	13
14	15	16	17	18	19	20
21	22	23	24	25	26	27
28	29	30	31			

From 1990 to 2015, Ryder has been positive from January to May, negative from June to September (other than July) and positive from October to December. Although October to December has been positive, Ryder has not strongly outperformed the S&P 500 at this time.

From 2011 to 2015, the summer months have generally been weak. Uncharacteristically, the strongest month has been October. In its 2015 long seasonal period, Ryder slightly underperformed the S&P 500. In its short sell seasonal period, the trade was successful as Ryder was strongly negative.

JULY

	MONDAY	TUESDAY	WEDNESDAY
WEEK 27	**3** 28 CAN Market Closed- Canada Day	**4** 27 USA Market Closed - Independence Day	**5** 26
WEEK 28	**10** 21	**11** 20	**12** 19
WEEK 29	**17** 14	**18** 13	**19** 12
WEEK 30	**24** 7	**25** 6	**26** 5
WEEK 31	**31**	1	2

THURSDAY	FRIDAY
6 25	**7** 24
13 18	**14** 17
20 11	**21** 10
27 4	**28** 3
3	4

AUGUST

M	T	W	T	F	S	S
	1	2	3	4	5	6
7	8	9	10	11	12	13
14	15	16	17	18	19	20
21	22	23	24	25	26	27
28	29	30	31			

SEPTEMBER

M	T	W	T	F	S	S
				1	2	3
4	5	6	7	8	9	10
11	12	13	14	15	16	17
18	19	20	21	22	23	24
25	26	27	28	29	30	

OCTOBER

M	T	W	T	F	S	S
						1
2	3	4	5	6	7	8
9	10	11	12	13	14	15
16	17	18	19	20	21	22
23	24	25	26	27	28	29
30	31					

NOVEMBER

M	T	W	T	F	S	S
		1	2	3	4	5
6	7	8	9	10	11	12
13	14	15	16	17	18	19
20	21	22	23	24	25	26
27	28	29	30			

JULY
SUMMARY

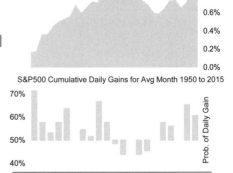

S&P500 Cumulative Daily Gains for Avg Month 1950 to 2015

	Dow Jones	S&P 500	Nasdaq	TSX Comp
Month Rank	4	6	10	6
# Up	41	36	23	20
# Down	25	30	21	11
% Pos	62	55	52	65
% Avg. Gain	1.1	1.0	0.3	0.8

Dow & S&P 1950-2015, Nasdaq 1972-2015, TSX 1985-2015

♦ When a summer rally occurs in the stock market, the gains are usually made in July. ♦ Typically, it is the first part of July that produces the gains as the market rallies before Independence Day and into the first eighteen calendar days (see the *18 Days Earnings Month Effect*). In 2015, July produced a strong gain of 2.0% during its first eighteen calendar days. ♦ On average, volatility starts to increase in July and continues this trend into October. ♦ August and September, the two months following July tend to be seasonally weak.

BEST / WORST JULY BROAD MKTS. 2006-2015

BEST JULY MARKETS
♦ Russell 2000 (2009) 9.5%
♦ Dow (2009) 8.6%
♦ FTSE 100 (2009) 8.5%

WORST JULY MARKETS
♦ Russell 2000 (2007) -6.9%
♦ Russell 2000 (2014) -6.1%
♦ TSX Comp (2008) -6.0%

Index Values End of Month

	2006	2007	2008	2009	2010	2011	2012	2013	2014	2015
Dow	11,186	13,212	11,378	9,172	10,466	12,143	13,009	15,500	16,563	17,690
S&P 500	1,277	1,455	1,267	987	1,102	1,292	1,379	1,686	1,931	2,104
Nasdaq	2,091	2,546	2,326	1,979	2,255	2,756	2,940	3,626	4,370	5,128
TSX Comp.	11,831	13,869	13,593	10,787	11,713	12,946	11,665	12,487	15,331	14,468
Russell 1000	1,331	1,523	1,334	1,038	1,165	1,380	1,458	1,802	2,068	2,256
Russell 2000	1,741	1,929	1,776	1,384	1,618	1,981	1,956	2,598	2,784	3,078
FTSE 100	5,928	6,360	5,412	4,608	5,258	5,815	5,635	6,621	6,730	6,696
Nikkei 225	15,457	17,249	13,377	10,357	9,537	9,833	8,695	13,668	15,621	20,585

Percent Gain for July

	2006	2007	2008	2009	2010	2011	2012	2013	2014	2015
Dow	0.3	-1.5	0.2	8.6	7.1	-2.2	1.0	4.0	-1.6	0.4
S&P 500	0.5	-3.2	-1.0	7.4	6.9	-2.1	1.3	4.9	-1.5	2.0
Nasdaq	-3.7	-2.2	1.4	7.8	6.9	-0.6	0.2	6.6	-0.9	2.8
TSX Comp.	1.9	-0.3	-6.0	4.0	3.7	-2.7	0.6	2.9	1.2	-0.6
Russell 1000	0.1	-3.2	-1.3	7.5	6.8	-2.3	1.1	5.2	-1.7	1.8
Russell 2000	-3.3	-6.9	3.6	9.5	6.8	-3.7	-1.4	6.9	-6.1	-1.2
FTSE 100	1.6	-3.7	-3.8	8.5	6.9	-2.2	1.2	6.5	-0.2	2.7
Nikkei 225	-0.3	-4.9	-0.8	4.0	1.6	0.2	-3.5	-0.1	3.0	1.7

July Market Avg. Performance 2006 to 2015[1]

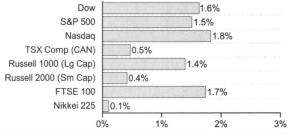

Dow	1.6%
S&P 500	1.5%
Nasdaq	1.8%
TSX Comp (CAN)	0.5%
Russell 1000 (Lg Cap)	1.4%
Russell 2000 (Sm Cap)	0.4%
FTSE 100	1.7%
Nikkei 225	0.1%

Interest Corner Jul[2]

	Fed Funds %[3]	3 Mo. T-Bill %[4]	10 Yr %[5]	20 Yr %[6]
2015	0.25	0.08	2.20	2.61
2014	0.25	0.03	2.58	3.07
2013	0.25	0.04	2.60	3.34
2012	0.25	0.11	1.51	2.21
2011	0.25	0.10	2.82	3.77

(1) Russell Data provided by Russell (2) Federal Reserve Bank of St. Louis- end of month values (3) Target rate set by FOMC (4)(5)(6) Constant yield maturities.

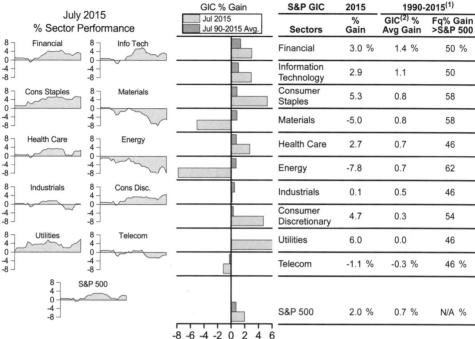

S&P GIC Sectors	2015 % Gain	1990-2015[1] GIC[2] % Avg Gain	Fq% Gain >S&P 500
Financial	3.0 %	1.4 %	50 %
Information Technology	2.9	1.1	50
Consumer Staples	5.3	0.8	58
Materials	-5.0	0.8	58
Health Care	2.7	0.7	46
Energy	-7.8	0.7	62
Industrials	0.1	0.5	46
Consumer Discretionary	4.7	0.3	54
Utilities	6.0	0.0	46
Telecom	-1.1 %	-0.3 %	46 %
S&P 500	2.0 %	0.7 %	N/A %

Sector Commentary

♦ July is an earnings month and the S&P 500 performed positively into the start of the earnings season in July 2015 ♦ Shortly after mid-month the S&P 500 corrected, but most sectors still ended up in positive territory. ♦ The worst performing major sector was the energy sector which produced a loss of 7.8%. ♦ The utilities sector was the top performing sector as investors sought companies with stable earnings and high dividends.

Sub-Sector Commentary

♦ In July 2015, the retail sub-sector produced an uncharacteristically large gain of 7.9% ♦ Likewise, homebuilders produced a large gain of 5.3%. ♦ Biotech produced a large gain of 3.5%, but was still short of its 6.7% average gain for July since 1990. ♦ Although the metals and mining sub-sector tends to be one of the weaker sub-sectors in July, it produced a loss far greater than its average since 1990. The sub-sector was down 19.9% for the month of July. ♦Silver, typically one of the better performing sub-sectors in July, produced a large loss of 7.3%.

SELECTED SUB-SECTORS[3]

Biotech (1993-2015)	3.5 %	6.7 %	83 %
Railroads	0.4	2.3	62
Banks	3.1	1.4	65
Silver	-7.3	1.3	62
Automotive & Components	-4.6	1.2	50
Transportation	2.9	1.2	46
Chemicals	-4.5	1.1	54
Retail	7.9	1.0	58
Homebuilders	5.3	0.9	44
Gold	-6.2	0.2	50
Pharma	3.6	0.2	50
SOX (1995-2015)	-5.0	0.0	38
Metals & Mining	-19.9	-0.4	46
Steel	-0.1	-0.5	46
Agriculture (1994-2015)	-1.7	-1.1	45

(1) Sector data provided by Standard and Poors (2) GIC is short form for Global Industry Classification (3) Sub Sector data provided by Standard and Poors, except where marked by symbol.

GOLD SHINES

(Metal) Gold (Metal) Outperforms – July 12th to October 9th

For many years, gold was thought to be a dead investment. It was only the "gold bugs" that espoused the virtues of investing in the precious metal. Investors were mesmerized with technology stocks, and central bankers confident of their currencies, were selling gold, "left, right and center."

3.7% gain & positive 66% of the time

Gold Bullion - Avg. Year 1984 to 2015

Gold / S&P 500 Relative Strength - Avg Yr. 1984 - 2015

Gold (Metal) London PM* vs S&P 500 1984 to 2015			
Jul 12 to Oct 9th	S&P 500	Positive Gold	Diff
1984	7.4 %	0.5 %	-6.9 %
1985	-5.4	4.1	9.5
1986	-2.6	25.2	27.8
1987	0.9	3.9	3.0
1988	2.8	-7.5	-10.3
1989	9.4	-4.2	-13.6
1990	-15.5	12.1	27.6
1991	0.0	-2.9	-2.8
1992	-2.9	0.4	3.3
1993	2.7	-8.8	-11.5
1994	1.6	1.6	0.0
1995	4.3	-0.1	-4.3
1996	7.9	-0.4	-8.3
1997	5.9	4.4	-1.5
1998	-15.5	2.8	18.2
1999	-4.8	25.6	30.4
2000	-5.3	-4.5	0.8
2001	-10.5	8.4	18.8
2002	-16.2	1.7	17.9
2003	4.1	7.8	3.8
2004	0.8	3.8	2.9
2005	-1.9	11.4	13.4
2006	6.1	-8.8	-14.9
2007	3.1	11.0	8.0
2008	-26.6	-8.2	18.4
2009	21.9	15.2	- 6.7
2010	8.1	11.0	2.9
2011	-12.4	6.2	18.6
2012	7.5	12.5	5.0
2013	-1.1	1.5	2.6
2014	-2.0	-8.1	-6.1
2015	-3.0	-0.7	2.3
Avg.	-1.0 %	3.7 %	4.6 %
Fq > 0	50 %	66 %	66 %

In the early 2000's, investors started to take a shine to gold, boosting its returns. On a seasonal basis, on average from 1984 to 2015, gold has performed well relative to the stock market from July 12th to October 9th. The reasons for gold's seasonal changes in price are largely related to jewelery production and European Central banks selling cycles (see *Golden Times* strategy page).

The movement of gold stock prices, represented by the index (XAU) on the Philadelphia Exchange, coincides closely with the price of gold. Although there is a strong correlation between gold and gold stocks, there are other factors, such as company operations and hedging policies, which determine each company's price in the market. Gold has typically started its seasonal strong period a few weeks earlier than gold miners and finished just after gold miners have turned down.

Investors should know that gold can have a run in the month of November. Although this is a positive time for gold, producing an average gain of 1.5% and being positive 66% of the time (1984 to 2015), the trouble is in the following month. December has a history of being negative for gold, producing an average loss of 0.5% and only being positive 41% of the time. This compares with the S&P 500, which over the same time period has produced a 1.8% average gain and has been positive 78% in December.

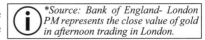

Source: Bank of England- London PM represents the close value of gold in afternoon trading in London.

Gold Performance

Gold Monthly Performance (1984-2015)

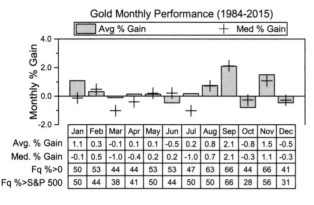

	Jan	Feb	Mar	Apr	May	Jun	Jul	Aug	Sep	Oct	Nov	Dec
Avg. % Gain	1.1	0.3	-0.1	0.1	0.1	-0.5	0.2	0.8	2.1	-0.8	1.5	-0.5
Med. % Gain	-0.1	0.5	-1.0	-0.4	0.2	0.2	-1.0	0.7	2.1	-0.3	1.1	-0.3
Fq %>0	50	53	44	44	53	53	47	63	66	44	66	41
Fq %>S&P 500	50	44	38	41	50	44	50	50	66	28	56	31

Gold 5 Year (2011-2015) % Gain

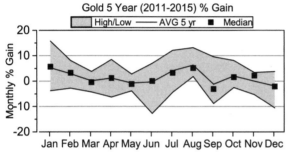

Gold Performance 2015-2016

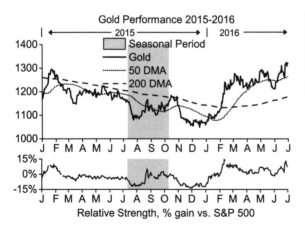

Relative Strength, % gain vs. S&P 500

From 1984 to 2015, the best month for gold bullion on a average, median and frequency basis has been September. On average the worst month of the year has been October. With the juxtaposition of the best and worst months, investors have to be cautious.

Over the last five years, gold has performed above average in July and August, but has performed poorly in September.

In 2015, gold was slightly negative in its seasonal period, but managed to outperform the S&P 500.

JULY

M	T	W	T	F	S	S
					1	2
3	4	5	6	7	8	9
10	11	12	13	14	15	16
17	18	19	20	21	22	23
24	25	26	27	28	29	30
31						

AUGUST

M	T	W	T	F	S	S
	1	2	3	4	5	6
7	8	9	10	11	12	13
14	15	16	17	18	19	20
21	22	23	24	25	26	27
28	29	30	31			

SEPTEMBER

M	T	W	T	F	S	S
			1	2	3
4	5	6	7	8	9	10
11	12	13	14	15	16	17
18	19	20	21	22	23	24
25	26	27	28	29	30	

GOLDEN TIMES

(Stocks) Gold Miners Outperform – July 27th to September 25th

Gold miners were shunned for many years. It is only recently that interest in the sector has increased again. What few investors know is that even during the twenty year bear market in gold that started in 1981, it was possible to make money in gold miners.

5.5% gain

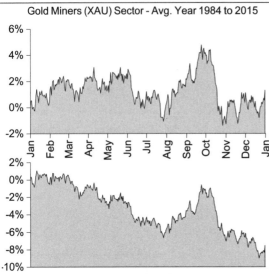

Gold Miners (XAU) Sector - Avg. Year 1984 to 2015

XAU / S&P 500 Relative Strength - Avg Yr. 1984-2015

On average from 1984 (start of the XAU index) to 2015, gold miners as represented by the XAU index, have outperformed the S&P 500 from July 27th to September 25th. One factor that has led to a rise in the price of gold miners in August and September is the Indian festival and wedding season that starts in October and finishes in November during Diwali. The Indian culture places a great emphasis on gold as a store of value and a lot of it is "consumed" as jewelery during the festival and wedding season. The price of gold tends to increase in the months preceding this season as the jewelery fabricators purchase gold to make their final product.

The August-September increase in gold miners coincides with the time that a lot of investors are pulling their money out of the broad market and are looking for a place to invest. This makes gold a very attractive investment at this time of the year.

Be careful. Just as the gold miners tend to go up in August and September, they also tend to go down in October. Historically, this negative trend has been

	XAU (Gold Miners)* vs S&P 500 and Gold (1984 to 2015)		
	XAU>S&P 500		
	XAU>Gold		
Jul 27 to Sep 25	S&P 500	Gold	XAU
1984	10.4 %	0.3 %	20.8 %
1985	-6.1	3.6	-5.5
1986	-3.5	23.0	36.9
1987	3.5	1.9	23.0
1988	1.7	-7.2	-11.9
1989	1.8	-1.3	10.5
1990	-13.4	9.5	3.8
1991	1.6	-3.1	-11.9
1992	0.7	-2.2	-3.8
1993	1.9	-8.7	-7.3
1994	1.4	2.5	18.2
1995	3.6	-0.8	-1.0
1996	7.9	-0.7	-1.0
1997	-0.1	0.2	8.7
1998	-8.4	1.2	12.0
1999	-5.2	6.5	16.9
2000	-0.9	-2.3	-2.8
2001	-15.8	7.7	3.2
2002	-1.5	6.6	29.8
2003	0.5	7.6	11.0
2004	2.4	4.4	16.5
2005	-1.3	9.3	20.5
2006	4.6	-4.8	-11.9
2007	2.3	8.7	14.0
2008	-3.9	-3.5	-18.5
2009	6.7	4.2	6.0
2010	3.0	9.6	14.7
2011	-14.7	4.7	-13.7
2012	6.0	9.5	23.4
2013	0.1	-0.6	-5.5
2014	-0.6	-6.3	-16.4
2015	-7.1	6.1	-2.6
Avg.	-0.7 %	2.7 %	5.5 %
Fq > 0	56 %	63 %	56 %

caused by European Central banks selling some of their gold holdings in autumn when their annual allotment of possible sales is renewed yearly. In recent years, European Central banks have reduced gold sales and have even become net buyers. This has muted gold's negative trend in October. Nevertheless, gold miners have still underperformed. From October 1st to October 27th, for the period 1984 to 2015, XAU has produced an average loss of 3.3% and has only been positive 31% of the time.

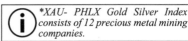 *XAU- PHLX Gold Silver Index consists of 12 precious metal mining companies.*

Gold Miners Performance

XAU Monthly Performance (1984-2015)

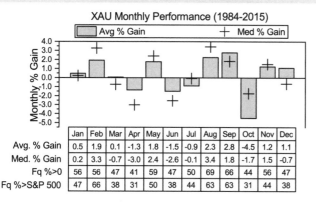

	Jan	Feb	Mar	Apr	May	Jun	Jul	Aug	Sep	Oct	Nov	Dec
Avg. % Gain	0.5	1.9	0.1	-1.3	1.8	-1.5	-0.9	2.3	2.8	-4.5	1.2	1.1
Med. % Gain	0.2	3.3	-0.7	-3.0	2.4	-2.6	-0.1	3.4	1.8	-1.7	1.5	-0.7
Fq %>0	56	56	47	41	59	47	50	69	66	44	56	47
Fq %>S&P 500	47	66	38	31	50	38	44	63	63	31	44	38

XAU 5 Year (2011-2015) % Gain

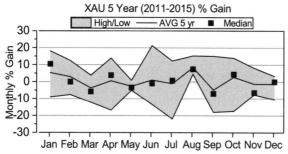

XAU Performance 2015-2016

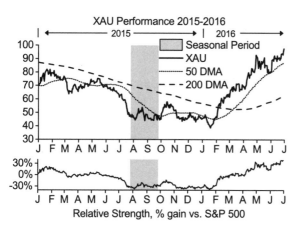

Relative Strength, % gain vs. S&P 500

Market Indices & Rates
Weekly Values**

Stock Markets	2014	2015
Dow	16,955	17,657
S&P500	1,969	2,065
Nasdaq	4,415	4,964
TSX	15,153	14,464
FTSE	6,729	6,543
DAX	9,762	10,925
Nikkei	15,275	19,972
Hang Seng	23,346	24,604

Commodities	2014	2015
Oil	102.60	52.41
Gold	1326.8	1160.9

Bond Yields	2014	2015
USA 5 Yr Treasury	1.69	1.57
USA 10 Yr T	2.57	2.31
USA 20 Yr T	3.11	2.78
Moody's Aaa	4.19	4.15
Moody's Baa	4.76	5.17
CAN 5 Yr T	1.56	0.73
CAN 10 Yr T	2.25	1.60

Money Market	2014	2015
USA Fed Funds	0.25	0.25
USA 3 Mo T-B	0.03	0.02
CAN tgt overnight rate	1.00	0.75
CAN 3 Mo T-B	0.94	0.54

Foreign Exchange	2014	2015
EUR/USD	1.36	1.11
GBP/USD	1.71	1.55
USD/CAD	1.07	1.27
USD/JPY	101.54	121.99

JULY

M	T	W	T	F	S	S
					1	2
3	4	5	6	7	8	9
10	11	12	13	14	15	16
17	18	19	20	21	22	23
24	25	26	27	28	29	30
31						

AUGUST

M	T	W	T	F	S	S
1	2	3	4	5	6	
7	8	9	10	11	12	13
14	15	16	17	18	19	20
21	22	23	24	25	26	27
28	29	30	31			

From 1984 to 2015, gold miners have outperformed in September on an average, median and frequency basis.

Over the last five years, August has been one of the strongest months and September one of the weakest, making an early exit from the seasonal strategy the best course of action.

In 2015, gold miners corrected substantially in the spring and early summer. The sector produced a small loss in its seasonal period.

SEPTEMBER

M	T	W	T	F	S	S
			1	2	3	
4	5	6	7	8	9	10
11	12	13	14	15	16	17
18	19	20	21	22	23	24
25	26	27	28	29	30	

Volatility Index
July 3rd to October 9th

The Chicago Board Options Exchange Market Volatility Index (VIX) is often referred to as a fear index as it measures investors' expectations of market volatility over the next thirty day period. The higher the VIX value, the greater the expectation of volatility and vice versa.

From 1990 to June 2016, the long-term average of the VIX is 19.8. In this time period, the VIX has bottomed at approximately 10 in the mid-90's, and the mid-00's. In both cases, the VIX dropped below 10 for a few days.

VIX* vs. S&P 500
1990 to 2015

July 3 to Oct 9	S&P 500	Positive VIX %Gain
1990	-15.1%	88.9%
1991	-0.2	5.2
1992	-2.2	47.8
1993	3.3	6.3
1994	2.0	3.9
1995	6.2	30.5
1996	3.4	13.4
1997	7.4	13.3
1998	-14.1	138.8
1999	-4.0	9.8
2000	-3.6	22.9
2001	-14.6	85.7
2002	-18.1	45.5
2003	4.5	-1.1
2004	-0.3	-0.2
2005	0.1	28.0
2006	6.3	-10.7
2007	3.0	4.7
2008	-27.9	146.6
2009	19.5	-17.3
2010	13.9	-31.2
2011	-13.8	128.1
2012	5.6	-2.6
2013	2.6	19.2
2014	-2.4	73.4
2015	-2.9	1.7
Avg	-1.6%	32.7%
Fq > 0	50%	77%

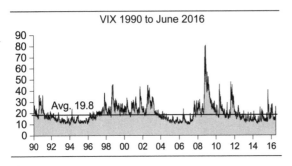

VIX 1990 to June 2016

Avg. 19.8

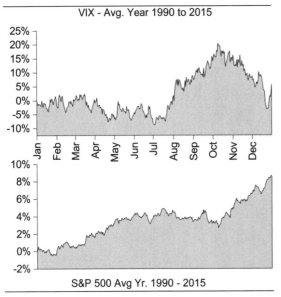

VIX - Avg. Year 1990 to 2015

S&P 500 Avg Yr. 1990 - 2015

From 1990 to 2015, during the period of July 3rd to October 9th, the VIX has increased 77% of the time. On average, the VIX tends to start increasing in July, particularly after the earnings season gets underway. After mid-July, without the expectation of strong earnings ahead, investors tend to focus on the economic forecasts that often become more dire in the second half of the year. In addition, stock market analysts tend to reduce their earnings forecasts at this time. Both of these effects tend to add volatility in the markets, increasing the VIX. The VIX tends to peak in October as the stock market often starts to establishing a rising trend at this time.

Levels below 15 are often associated with investor complacency, as investors are expecting very little volatility. Very often when a stock market correction occurs in this state, it can be sharp and severe. Knowing the trends of the VIX can be useful in adjusting the amount of risk in a portfolio.

(i) *VIX - ticker symbol for the Chicago Board Options Exchange Market Volatility Index, measure implied volatility of S&P 500 index options*

VIX Performance

2015

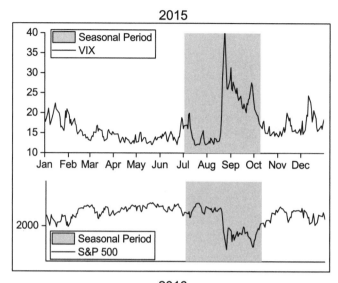

2016

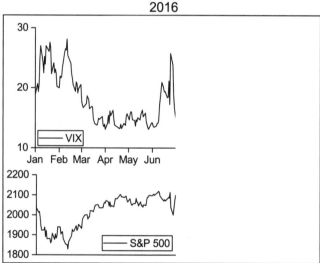

Market Indices & Rates
Weekly Values**

Stock Markets	2014	2015
Dow	17,066	18,058
S&P500	1,974	2,113
Nasdaq	4,416	5,130
TSX	15,190	14,634
FTSE	6,746	6,763
DAX	9,767	11,586
Nikkei	15,331	20,438
Hang Seng	23,461	25,196

Commodities	2014	2015
Oil	101.68	51.69
Gold	1305.4	1147.2

Bond Yields	2014	2015
USA 5 Yr Treasury	1.69	1.67
USA 10 Yr T	2.53	2.38
USA 20 Yr T	3.06	2.85
Moody's Aaa	4.16	4.22
Moody's Baa	4.73	5.27
CAN 5 Yr T	1.50	0.73
CAN 10 Yr T	2.19	1.62

Money Market	2014	2015
USA Fed Funds	0.25	0.25
USA 3 Mo T-B	0.02	0.02
CAN tgt overnight rate	1.00	0.50
CAN 3 Mo T-B	0.94	0.49

Foreign Exchange	2014	2015
EUR/USD	1.36	1.09
GBP/USD	1.71	1.56
USD/CAD	1.07	1.29
USD/JPY	101.48	123.77

JULY

M	T	W	T	F	S	S
					1	2
3	4	5	6	7	8	9
10	11	12	13	14	15	16
17	18	19	20	21	22	23
24	25	26	27	28	29	30
31						

AUGUST

M	T	W	T	F	S	S
	1	2	3	4	5	6
7	8	9	10	11	12	13
14	15	16	17	18	19	20
21	22	23	24	25	26	27
28	29	30	31			

SEPTEMBER

M	T	W	T	F	S	S
			1	2	3
4	5	6	7	8	9	10
11	12	13	14	15	16	17
18	19	20	21	22	23	24
25	26	27	28	29	30	

An increase in volatility typically occurs at the beginning of July, just ahead of earnings season. Despite the pickup in volatility ahead of earnings, the S&P 500 tends to perform well for the first half of the month.

In 2015, volatility spiked in late August to a high level of 40. Very often the stock market starts to rally when the VIX hits 40 which was the case in the 2015.

In 2016, the VIX started at a high level and then dissipated to levels below 15 in March. In June the VIX once again rose as the stock market pulled off from its April highs.

OIL STOCKS– SUMMER/AUTUMN STRATEGY
July 24th to October 3rd
(Stocks)

Oil stocks tend to outperform the market from July 24th to October 3rd. Earlier in the year, there is another seasonal period of outperformance from late February to early May. Although the first seasonal period has had an incredible record of outperformance, the second seasonal period in July is still noteworthy.

While the seasonal period has more to do with inventories during the switch from producing heating oil to gasoline, the second seasonal period is more related to the conversion of production from gasoline to heating oil and the effects of the hurricane season.

1.4% extra

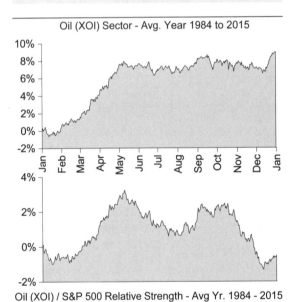

Oil (XOI) Sector - Avg. Year 1984 to 2015

Oil (XOI) / S&P 500 Relative Strength - Avg Yr. 1984 - 2015

XOI* vs. S&P 500 1984 to 2015			
Jul 24 to Oct 3	S&P 500	Positive XOI	Diff
1984	9.1 %	9.0 %	-0.1 %
1985	-4.3	6.7	11.0
1986	-2.1	15.7	17.7
1987	6.6	-1.2	-7.8
1988	3.0	-3.6	-6.6
1989	5.6	5.7	0.1
1990	-12.4	-0.5	11.8
1991	1.3	0.7	-0.7
1992	-0.4	2.9	3.3
1993	3.2	7.8	4.6
1994	1.9	-3.6	-5.5
1995	5.2	-2.2	-7.4
1996	10.5	7.7	-2.8
1997	3.0	8.9	5.9
1998	-12.0	1.4	13.5
1999	-5.5	-2.1	3.3
2000	-3.6	12.2	15.8
2001	-10.0	-5.1	4.8
2002	2.7	7.3	4.6
2003	4.2	5.5	1.4
2004	4.2	10.9	6.7
2005	-0.6	14.3	14.9
2006	7.6	-8.5	-16.9
2007	-0.1	-4.2	-4.1
2008	-14.3	-18.1	-3.8
2009	5.0	3.0	-2.0
2010	4.0	8.5	4.5
2011	-18.3	-26.0	-7.7
2012	7.4	6.1	-1.3
2013	-0.8	-0.8	0.0
2014	-1.0	-10.8	-9.8
2015	-7.2	-9.6	-2.4
Avg	-0.3 %	1.2 %	1.4 %
Fq > 0	53 %	56 %	53 %

First, there is a large difference between how heating oil and gasoline are stored and consumed. For individuals and businesses, gasoline is consumed in an immediate fashion. It is stored by the local distributor and the supplies are drawn upon as needed. Heating oil, on the other hand, is largely inventoried by individuals, farms and business operations in rural areas.

The inventory process starts before the cold weather arrives. The production facilities have to start switching from gasoline to heating oil, dropping their inventory levels and boosting prices. Second, the hurricane season can play havoc with the production of oil and drive up prices substantially. The official duration of the hurricane season in the Gulf of Mexico is from June 1st to November 30th, but most major hurricanes occur in September and early October.

The threat of a strong hurricane can shut down the oil platforms temporarily, interrupting production. If a strong hurricane strikes the platforms, it can do significant damage and put the them out of commission for an extended period of time.

(i) *NYSE Arca Oil Index (XOI): An index designed to represent a cross section of widely held oil corporations involved in various phases of the oil industry. For more information on the XOI index, see www.cboe.com

NYSE Arca Oil Index (XOI) Performance

XOI Monthly Performance (1984-2015)

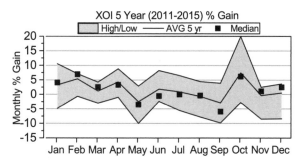

	Jan	Feb	Mar	Apr	May	Jun	Jul	Aug	Sep	Oct	Nov	Dec
Avg. % Gain	0.5	1.0	2.9	3.0	0.7	-0.9	0.4	0.8	-0.3	0.3	-0.6	1.7
Med. % Gain	0.1	1.8	2.5	2.4	0.8	-1.8	1.7	0.4	-0.2	0.5	0.6	1.0
Fq %>0	50	56	72	81	63	38	56	56	50	50	53	63
Fq %>S&P 500	34	56	66	63	41	34	50	63	56	50	34	53

XOI 5 Year (2011-2015) % Gain

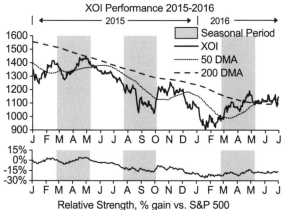

XOI Performance 2015-2016

Relative Strength, % gain vs. S&P 500

From 1984 to 2015, oil stocks have had a secondary seasonal period from late July to early October. The returns in this secondary seasonal period have largely been focused in August.

Over the last five years, the returns in the secondary seasonal period have been negative, particularly as August has been a weaker month.

In 2015, oil stocks declined during the secondary seasonal period. After a rally in October, oil stocks corrected once again into January.

Market Indices & Rates
Weekly Values**

Stock Markets	2014	2015
Dow	17,059	17,834
S&P500	1,982	2,109
Nasdaq	4,455	5,167
TSX	15,362	14,312
FTSE	6,787	6,692
DAX	9,708	11,544
Nikkei	15,354	20,666
Hang Seng	23,900	25,350

Commodities	2014	2015
Oil	105.66	49.12
Gold	1303.5	1095.4

Bond Yields	2014	2015
USA 5 Yr Treasury	1.69	1.68
USA 10 Yr T	2.49	2.32
USA 20 Yr T	3.01	2.73
Moody's Aaa	4.12	4.13
Moody's Baa	4.68	5.18
CAN 5 Yr T	1.48	0.73
CAN 10 Yr T	2.13	1.54

Money Market	2014	2015
USA Fed Funds	0.25	0.25
USA 3 Mo T-B	0.03	0.04
CAN tgt overnight rate	1.00	0.50
CAN 3 Mo T-B	0.94	0.42

Foreign Exchange	2014	2015
EUR/USD	1.35	1.09
GBP/USD	1.70	1.56
USD/CAD	1.08	1.30
USD/JPY	101.60	123.97

JULY

M	T	W	T	F	S	S
					1	2
3	4	5	6	7	8	9
10	11	12	13	14	15	16
17	18	19	20	21	22	23
24	25	26	27	28	29	30
31						

AUGUST

M	T	W	T	F	S	S
	1	2	3	4	5	6
7	8	9	10	11	12	13
14	15	16	17	18	19	20
21	22	23	24	25	26	27
28	29	30	31			

SEPTEMBER

M	T	W	T	F	S	S
			1	2	3
4	5	6	7	8	9	10
11	12	13	14	15	16	17
18	19	20	21	22	23	24
25	26	27	28	29	30	

AUGUST

	MONDAY	TUESDAY	WEDNESDAY
WEEK 31	31	**1** 30	**2** 29
WEEK 32	**7** 24 CAN Market Closed- Civic Day	**8** 23	**10** 22
WEEK 33	**14** 17	**15** 16	**16** 15
WEEK 34	**21** 10	**22** 9	**23** 8
WEEK 35	**28** 3	**29** 2	**30** 1

THURSDAY	FRIDAY
3 28	**4** 27
10 21	**11** 20
17 14	**18** 13
24 7	**25** 6
31	1

SEPTEMBER

M	T	W	T	F	S	S
				1	2	3
4	5	6	7	8	9	10
11	12	13	14	15	16	17
18	19	20	21	22	23	24
25	26	27	28	29	30	

OCTOBER

M	T	W	T	F	S	S
						1
2	3	4	5	6	7	8
9	10	11	12	13	14	15
16	17	18	19	20	21	22
23	24	25	26	27	28	29
30	31					

NOVEMBER

M	T	W	T	F	S	S
		1	2	3	4	5
6	7	8	9	10	11	12
13	14	15	16	17	18	19
20	21	22	23	24	25	26
27	28	29	30			

DECEMBER

M	T	W	T	F	S	S
				1	2	3
4	5	6	7	8	9	10
11	12	13	14	15	16	17
18	19	20	21	22	23	24
25	26	27	28	29	30	31

AUGUST
S U M M A R Y

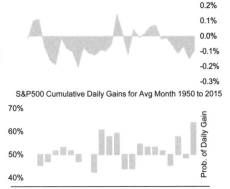

S&P500 Cumulative Daily Gains for Avg Month 1950 to 2015

	Dow Jones	S&P 500	Nasdaq	TSX Comp
Month Rank	10	11	11	10
# Up	37	36	23	17
# Down	29	30	21	14
% Pos	56	55	52	55
% Avg. Gain	-0.2	-0.1	0.0	-0.2

Dow & S&P 1950-2015, Nasdaq 1972-2015, TSX 1985-2015

♦ August is typically a marginal month and has been the fourth worst month for the S&P 500 from 1950 to 2015, producing a slight loss of 0.1%. ♦ If there is a summer rally in July, it is often in jeopardy in August. ♦ In July 2015, the S&P 500's rally faded at the beginning of August, and then corrected sharply at the end of the month. In August, the S&P 500 ended up producing a large loss of 6.3% ♦ The TSX Composite is usually one of the better performing markets in August, but its strength is largely dependent on oil and gold stocks.

BEST / WORST AUGUST BROAD MKTS. 2006-2015

BEST AUGUST MARKETS
- ♦ FTSE 100 (2009) 6.5%
- ♦ Russell 2000 (2014) 4.8%
- ♦ Nasdaq (2014) 4.8%

WORST AUGUST MARKETS
- ♦ Nikkei 225 (2011) -8.9%
- ♦ Russell 2000 (2011) -8.8%
- ♦ Nikkei 225 (2015) - 8.2%

Index Values End of Month

	2006	2007	2008	2009	2010	2011	2012	2013	2014	2015
Dow	11,381	13,358	11,544	9,496	10,015	11,614	13,091	14,810	17,098	16,528
S&P 500	1,304	1,474	1,283	1,021	1,049	1,219	1,407	1,633	2,003	1,972
Nasdaq	2,184	2,596	2,368	2,009	2,114	2,579	3,067	3,590	4,580	4,777
TSX Comp.	12,074	13,660	13,771	10,868	11,914	12,769	11,949	12,654	15,626	13,859
Russell 1000	1,360	1,540	1,350	1,073	1,110	1,297	1,490	1,748	2,149	2,116
Russell 2000	1,791	1,970	1,838	1,422	1,496	1,806	2,018	2,512	2,919	2,882
FTSE 100	5,906	6,303	5,637	4,909	5,225	5,395	5,712	6,413	6,820	6,248
Nikkei 225	16,141	16,569	13,073	10,493	8,824	8,955	8,840	13,389	15,425	18,890

Percent Gain for August

	2006	2007	2008	2009	2010	2011	2012	2013	2014	2015
Dow	1.7	1.1	1.5	3.5	-4.3	-4.4	0.6	-4.4	3.2	-6.6
S&P 500	2.1	1.3	1.2	3.4	-4.7	-5.7	2.0	-3.1	3.8	-6.3
Nasdaq	4.4	2.0	1.8	1.5	-6.2	-6.4	4.3	-1.0	4.8	-6.9
TSX Comp.	2.1	-1.5	1.3	0.8	1.7	-1.4	2.4	1.3	1.9	-4.2
Russell 1000	2.2	1.1	1.2	3.4	-4.7	-6.0	2.2	-3.0	3.9	-6.2
Russell 2000	2.8	2.2	3.5	2.8	-7.5	-8.8	3.2	-3.3	4.8	-6.4
FTSE 100	-0.4	-0.9	4.2	6.5	-0.6	-7.2	1.4	-3.1	1.3	-6.7
Nikkei 225	4.4	-3.9	-2.3	1.3	-7.5	-8.9	1.7	-2.0	-1.3	-8.2

August Market Avg. Performance 2006 to 2015[1]

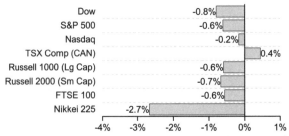

Dow	-0.8%
S&P 500	-0.6%
Nasdaq	-0.2%
TSX Comp (CAN)	0.4%
Russell 1000 (Lg Cap)	-0.6%
Russell 2000 (Sm Cap)	-0.7%
FTSE 100	-0.6%
Nikkei 225	-2.7%

Interest Corner Aug[2]

	Fed Funds % [3]	3 Mo. T-Bill % [4]	10 Yr % [5]	20 Yr % [6]
2015	0.25	0.08	2.21	2.64
2014	0.25	0.03	2.35	2.83
2013	0.25	0.03	2.78	3.46
2012	0.25	0.09	1.57	2.29
2011	0.25	0.02	2.23	3.19

(1) Russell Data provided by Russell (2) Federal Reserve Bank of St. Louis- end of month values (3) Target rate set by FOMC (4)(5)(6) Constant yield maturities.

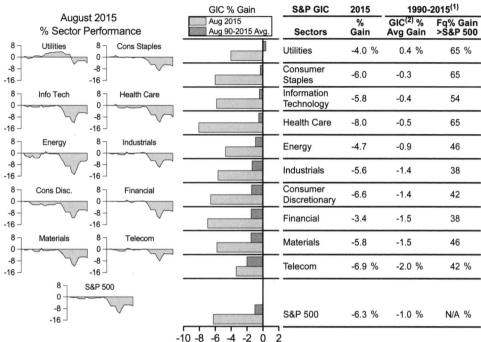

August 2015
% Sector Performance

S&P GIC Sectors	2015 % Gain	1990-2015[1] GIC[2] % Avg Gain	1990-2015[1] Fq% Gain >S&P 500
Utilities	-4.0 %	0.4 %	65 %
Consumer Staples	-6.0	-0.3	65
Information Technology	-5.8	-0.4	54
Health Care	-8.0	-0.5	65
Energy	-4.7	-0.9	46
Industrials	-5.6	-1.4	38
Consumer Discretionary	-6.6	-1.4	42
Financial	-3.4	-1.5	38
Materials	-5.8	-1.5	46
Telecom	-6.9 %	-2.0 %	42 %
S&P 500	-6.3 %	-1.0 %	N/A %

Sector Commentary

♦ In August 2015, the S&P 500 lost 6.3% and all of its major sectors produced losses. ♦ The health care sector produced the biggest loss at 8.0% as it suffered from the media coverage on the rapid increases in drug prices. With an election just over a year away, investors became concerned that drug prices were going to become a political target. ♦ Despite its defensive characteristics, the telecom sector lost 6.9%. ♦ The best performing sector in August was the financial sector, but it still lost 3.4%.

Sub-Sector Commentary

♦ In August 2015, the railroad sub-sector produced a large loss of 11.0%. ♦ Biotech, which is often one of the best performing sub-sectors in August, corrected sharply with a 10.0% loss, as high drug prices became a hot news topic. ♦ The steel sub-sector, typically a poor sector in August, had a relatively small loss of 1.9%. ♦ Homebuilders, another sub-sector that typically underperforms in the month of August, also had a relatively small loss of 0.6%.

SELECTED SUB-SECTORS[3]

Gold	3.3 %	0.7 %	50 %
Biotech (1993-2015)	-10.0	0.5	61
Agriculture (1994-2015)	-5.1	0.3	55
Silver	-0.8	-0.4	50
Retail	-2.7	-0.5	62
SOX (1995-2015)	-5.5	-0.5	52
Pharma	-8.4	-0.6	58
Homebuilders	-0.6	-1.2	47
Metals & Mining	-4.2	-1.2	50
Banks	-7.6	-1.4	35
Chemicals	-6.5	-1.7	42
Railroads	-11.0	-2.6	42
Transportation	-7.2	-2.9	31
Steel	-1.9	-3.3	50
Automotive & Components	-6.6	-3.4	31

(1) Sector data provided by Standard and Poors (2) GIC is short form for Global Industry Classification (3) Sub Sector data provided by Standard and Poors, except where marked by symbol.

ARCHER-DANIELS-MIDLAND
PLANT YOUR SEEDS FOR GROWTH
August 7th to December 31st

The agriculture sector generally performs well in the last five months of the year and ADM is no exception. If you had to choose just one part of the year in which to invest in ADM, it would have to be the last five months. From August 7th to December 31st, for the years 1990 to 2014, ADM produced an average gain of 12.3% and was positive 81% of the time.

12.3% gain & positive 81% of the time positive

The business of "growing" really takes place in the last part of the year. This is the harvest season for the northern hemisphere and the time when cash flows in the agriculture business. As a result, investors are much more interested in committing money to the agriculture sector.

ADM - Avg. Year 1990 to 2015

ADM / S&P 500 Relative Strength - Avg Yr. 1990 - 2015

ADM* vs. S&P 500
1990 to 2015

Aug 7 to Dec 31	S&P 500	ADM	Diff
		Positive	
1990	-1.3%	0.1%	1.4%
1991	6.8	40.5	33.7
1992	3.6	3.1	-0.5
1993	4.0	2.2	-1.8
1994	0.5	31.9	31.4
1995	10.2	17.3	7.1
1996	11.8	27.5	15.7
1997	1.1	1.8	0.8
1998	12.8	8.6	-4.2
1999	13.0	-10.3	-23.3
2000	-9.8	58.7	68.4
2001	-4.4	14.6	19.0
2002	2.4	13.6	11.2
2003	15.0	16.7	1.7
2004	13.9	42.9	29.0
2005	1.8	18.7	16.9
2006	10.9	-21.9	-32.7
2007	0.1	34.5	34.5
2008	-29.9	5.4	35.3
2009	11.8	9.3	-2.6
2010	12.1	-0.3	-12.5
2011	4.9	-0.1	-5.0
2012	2.3	6.9	4.6
2013	8.9	14.5	5.7
2014	7.2	6.9	-0.3
2015	-1.9	-23.5	-21.6
Avg	4.1%	12.3%	8.1%
Fq > 0	81%	81%	62%

On the other hand, the first seven months leading up to the favorable season (January 1st to August 6th) has produced an average loss of 2.6% and has only been positive 42% of the time.

Investors should avoid investing in ADM for the first seven months of the year. In fact, shorting ADM during the first seven months of the year and then switching to a long position for the last five months has proven to be a profitable strategy.

Seasonal investors can take advantage of the growing interest in the agriculture sector in the second half of the year by investing at the beginning of August. The idea is to get in before everyone else and get out when interest in the sector is at a maximum, towards the end of the year.

Investing in ADM for the last five months of the year has produced very strong results over the long-term.

(i) *ADM - stock symbol for Archer-Daniels-Midland which trades on the NYSE. Archer-Daniels-Midland Company engages in the manufacture and sale of protein meal, vegetable oil, corn sweeteners, flour, biodiesel, ethanol, and other value-added food and feed ingredients. Data adjusted for stock splits.*

ADM Performance

ADM Monthly Performance (1990-2015)

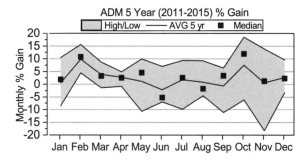

Legend: Avg % Gain | Med % Gain

	Jan	Feb	Mar	Apr	May	Jun	Jul	Aug	Sep	Oct	Nov	Dec
Avg. % Gain	-1.2	1.4	-0.8	-1.2	2.6	-1.8	-0.7	0.6	-0.4	5.5	2.1	3.2
Med. % Gain	-2.8	0.9	-1.3	0.7	3.3	-1.9	0.1	0.6	1.2	5.2	0.8	1.9
Fq %>0	35	58	38	54	62	38	50	58	54	73	54	62
Fq %>S&P 500	35	54	31	38	62	23	46	58	54	77	46	54

ADM 5 Year (2011-2015) % Gain

Legend: High/Low — AVG 5 yr ■ Median

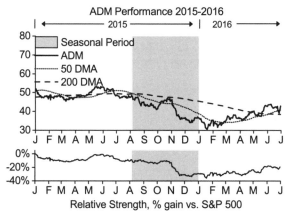

Jan Feb Mar Apr May Jun Jul Aug Sep Oct Nov Dec

ADM Performance 2015-2016

Legend: Seasonal Period, ADM, 50 DMA, 200 DMA

Relative Strength, % gain vs. S&P 500

WEEK 31

Market Indices & Rates
Weekly Values**

Stock Markets	2014	2015
Dow	16,766	17,652
S&P500	1,955	2,096
Nasdaq	4,415	5,100
TSX	15,393	14,246
FTSE	6,756	6,611
DAX	9,493	11,202
Nikkei	15,588	20,418
Hang Seng	24,618	24,522

Commodities	2014	2015
Oil	99.79	47.96
Gold	1295.0	1094.5

Bond Yields	2014	2015
USA 5 Yr Treasury	1.73	1.59
USA 10 Yr T	2.53	2.25
USA 20 Yr T	3.03	2.65
Moody's Aaa	4.13	4.06
Moody's Baa	4.72	5.16
CAN 5 Yr T	1.49	0.80
CAN 10 Yr T	2.13	1.48

Money Market	2014	2015
USA Fed Funds	0.25	0.25
USA 3 Mo T-B	0.03	0.06
CAN tgt overnight rate	1.00	0.50
CAN 3 Mo T-B	0.95	0.41

Foreign Exchange	2014	2015
EUR/USD	1.34	1.10
GBP/USD	1.69	1.56
USD/CAD	1.09	1.30
USD/JPY	102.44	123.76

AUGUST

M	T	W	T	F	S	S
	1	2	3	4	5	6
7	8	9	10	11	12	13
14	15	16	17	18	19	20
21	22	23	24	25	26	27
28	29	30	31			

SEPTEMBER

M	T	W	T	F	S	S
					1	2	3
4	5	6	7	8	9	10
11	12	13	14	15	16	17
18	19	20	21	22	23	24
25	26	27	28	29	30	

OCTOBER

M	T	W	T	F	S	S
						1
2	3	4	5	6	7	8
9	10	11	12	13	14	15
16	17	18	19	20	21	22
23	24	25	26	27	28	29
30	31					

Although ADM's period of seasonal strength starts in August, the sweet spot of the trade starts in October, which is its strongest month of the year on an average, median and frequency basis. On an average and median basis, November and December are also strong months.

Over the last five years, the dispersion between the maximum and minimum monthly returns has been large, but the overall seasonal strategy has been positive.

In 2015, the seasonal strategy for ADM was negative, as agriculture stocks corrected sharply.

TRANSPORTATION— ON A ROLL

①LONG (Jan23-Apr16) ②SELL SHORT (Aug1-Oct9) ③LONG (Oct10-Nov13)

The transportation sector can provide a "hilly" ride as the seasonal trends rise and fall throughout the year.

Activity in the transportation sub-sectors in rails, airlines and freight, tends to bottom in February.

15.8% gain & positive 88% of the time

Increased transportation activity in the spring, coupled with a typically positive economic outlook in the first part of the year, creates a positive seasonal trend, starting January 23rd and lasting until April 16th.

The next seasonal period is a weak period, giving investors an opportunity to sell short the sector and profit from its decline. This negative seasonal period lasts from August 1st to October 9th and is largely the result of investors questioning economic growth at this time of the year.

The third seasonal period is positive and occurs from October 10th to November 13th. This trend is the result of a generally improved economic outlook at this time of the year and investors wanting to get into the sector ahead of earnings announcements.

ⓘ *The SP GICS Transportation Sector encompasses a wide range transportation based companies. For more information, see www.standardandpoors.com*

Transportation Sector* vs. S&P 500 1990 to 2015

Negative Short ☐   Positive Long ▢

Year	Jan 23 to Apr 16		Aug 1 to Oct 9		Oct 10 to Nov 13		Compound Growth	
	S&P 500	Trans port	S&P 500	Trans port	S&P 500	Trans port	S&P 500	Trans port
1990	4.4 %	4.1 %	-14.3 %	-19.2 %	4.1	3.3 %	-6.9 %	28.1 %
1991	18.1	11.4	-2.8	0.5	5.5	9.6	21.0	21.5
1992	-0.5	3.7	-5.1	-9.1	4.9	14.1	-0.9	29.1
1993	2.9	9.1	2.7	-0.3	1.1	6.4	6.9	16.5
1994	-6.0	-10.7	-0.7	-9.3	1.6	0.8	-5.2	-1.6
1995	9.6	10.5	2.9	-1.3	2.4	5.0	15.5	17.6
1996	5.2	9.4	8.9	4.9	4.9	6.1	20.1	10.4
1997	-2.9	-2.0	1.7	0.9	-5.6	-5.4	-6.7	-8.2
1998	15.1	12.2	-12.2	-16.5	14.4	12.5	15.6	47.0
1999	7.7	17.7	0.6	-11.0	4.5	4.0	13.1	35.8
2000	-5.9	-2.7	-2.0	-6.0	-3.6	13.0	-11.1	16.6
2001	12.2	0.1	-12.8	-20.0	7.8	14.1	-17.4	37.0
2002	0.8	6.9	-14.8	-11.2	13.6	8.2	-2.4	28.6
2003	0.2	0.6	4.9	4.9	1.9	8.0	7.1	3.3
2004	-0.8	-2.9	1.9	6.6	5.5	11.1	6.6	0.7
2005	-2.2	-5.1	-3.1	-0.5	3.3	9.0	-2.1	3.9
2006	2.2	13.2	5.8	6.4	2.5	3.8	10.8	9.9
2007	3.2	4.8	7.6	-0.2	-5.4	-2.9	5.0	1.9
2008	4.1	19.1	-28.2	-23.5	0.2	4.0	-25.1	52.9
2009	4.6	7.2	8.5	6.7	2.1	5.9	15.8	5.9
2010	9.2	17.4	5.8	7.9	2.9	2.5	18.9	10.9
2011	2.8	2.2	-10.6	-11.8	9.4	11.4	0.6	26.9
2012	4.1	-2.0	4.5	-3.5	-4.6	-1.1	3.8	0.3
2013	5.5	3.5	-1.7	1.8	7.6	10.9	11.5	12.7
2014	1.0	1.7	-0.1	2.6	5.8	14.9	6.6	13.8
2015	2.0	-10.0	-4.2	-0.7	0.4	-2.0	-1.9	-11.2
Avg.	2.8 %	4.6 %	-2.2 %	-3.9 %	3.3 %	6.4 %	3.8 %	15.8 %
Fq>0	73 %	73 %	46	38 %	85 %	85 %	62 %	88 %

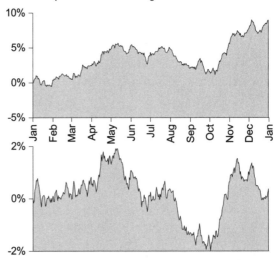

Transportation Sector - Avg. Year 1990 to 2015

Transportation / S&P 500 Rel. Strength- Avg. Yr. 1990-2015

Transportation Performance

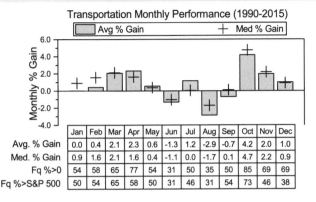

Transportation Monthly Performance (1990-2015)

	Jan	Feb	Mar	Apr	May	Jun	Jul	Aug	Sep	Oct	Nov	Dec
Avg. % Gain	0.0	0.4	2.1	2.3	0.6	-1.3	1.2	-2.9	-0.7	4.2	2.0	1.0
Med. % Gain	0.9	1.6	2.1	1.6	0.4	-1.1	0.0	-1.7	0.1	4.7	2.2	0.9
Fq %>0	54	58	65	77	54	31	50	35	50	85	69	69
Fq %>S&P 500	50	54	65	58	50	31	46	31	54	73	46	38

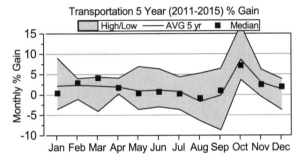

Transportation 5 Year (2011-2015) % Gain

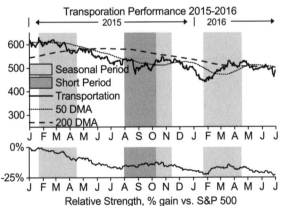

Transportation Performance 2015-2016

Relative Strength, % gain vs. S&P 500

Market Indices & Rates
Weekly Values**

Stock Markets	2014	2015
Dow	16,473	17,496
S&P500	1,924	2,090
Nasdaq	4,360	5,092
TSX	15,176	14,426
FTSE	6,632	6,719
DAX	9,104	11,522
Nikkei	15,193	20,614
Hang Seng	24,510	24,452

Commodities	2014	2015
Oil	97.50	44.92
Gold	1296.8	1090.2

Bond Yields	2014	2015
USA 5 Yr Treasury	1.65	1.60
USA 10 Yr T	2.48	2.22
USA 20 Yr T	3.00	2.58
Moody's Aaa	4.15	4.02
Moody's Baa	4.73	5.12
CAN 5 Yr T	1.48	0.78
CAN 10 Yr T	2.09	1.44

Money Market	2014	2015
USA Fed Funds	0.25	0.25
USA 3 Mo T-B	0.03	0.07
CAN tgt overnight rate	1.00	0.50
CAN 3 Mo T-B	0.96	0.39

Foreign Exchange	2014	2015
EUR/USD	1.34	1.09
GBP/USD	1.68	1.56
USD/CAD	1.09	1.32
USD/JPY	102.28	124.45

The transportation sector has a roller coaster seasonal trend. In the early part of the year it typically outperforms, and then underperforms in the summer, and then outperforms at the end of the year. From 1990 to 2015, October has been the best month for the transportation sector on an average, median and frequency basis. Over the last five years, on average, generally the transportation sector has followed its seasonal pattern throughout the year. In 2015, the transportation sector underperformed the S&P 500 during its seasonal periods. In 2016, the transportation sector was positive and outperformed the S&P 500 in its seasonal period.

AUGUST

M	T	W	T	F	S	S
	1	2	3	4	5	6
7	8	9	10	11	12	13
14	15	16	17	18	19	20
21	22	23	24	25	26	27
28	29	30	31			

SEPTEMBER

M	T	W	T	F	S	S
					1	2	3
4	5	6	7	8	9	10
11	12	13	14	15	16	17
18	19	20	21	22	23	24
25	26	27	28	29	30	

OCTOBER

M	T	W	T	F	S	S
						1
2	3	4	5	6	7	8
9	10	11	12	13	14	15
16	17	18	19	20	21	22
23	24	25	26	27	28	29
30	31					

AGRICULTURE MOOOVES
LAST 5 MONTHS OF THE YEAR – Aug to Dec

The agriculture sector has typically performed well during the last five months of the year (August to December).

This is the result of the major summer growing season in the northern hemisphere producing cash for the growers and subsequently, increasing sales for the farming suppliers.

68% of the time
better than the S&P 500

Although this sector can represent a good opportunity, investors should be wary of the wide performance swings. Out of the twenty-two cycles from 1994 to 2015, during August to December, there have been six years with absolute returns greater than +25% or less than -25%, and twelve years of returns greater than +10% or less than -10%. In other words, this sector is very volatile.

Agriculture* vs. S&P 500 1994 to 2015

Aug 1 to Dec 31	S&P 500	Positive	
		Agri	Diff
1994	0.2 %	8.0 %	7.8 %
1995	9.6	31.7	22.1
1996	15.8	30.2	14.5
1997	1.7	14.7	13.0
1998	9.7	-3.4	-13.1
1999	10.6	-2.6	-13.2
2000	-7.7	68.0	75.7
2001	-5.2	12.5	17.7
2002	-3.5	6.0	9.5
2003	12.3	15.8	3.6
2004	10.0	44.6	34.6
2005	1.1	7.5	6.4
2006	11.1	-27.4	-38.5
2007	0.9	38.2	37.3
2008	-28.7	0.7	29.4
2009	12.9	4.0	-9.0
2010	14.2	9.9	-4.2
2011	-2.7	-5.9	-3.2
2012	3.4	5.0	1.6
2013	9.7	19.0	9.4
2014	6.6	12.1	5.4
2015	-2.9	-22.5	-19.8
Avg.	3.6 %	12.1 %	8.5 %
Fq > 0	73 %	77 %	68 %

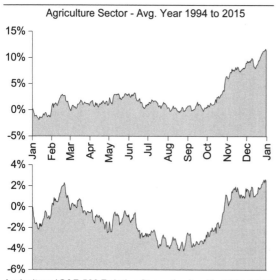

Agriculture Sector - Avg. Year 1994 to 2015

Agriculture / S&P 500 Relative Strength - Avg Yr. 1994-2015

On a year by year basis, the agriculture sector produced its biggest gain during its seasonally strong period in 2000, producing a gain of 68%. It is interesting to note that this is the same year that the technology sector's bubble burst.

After realizing that technology stocks were not going to grow to the sky, investors started to have an epiphany– that the world might be running out of food and

as a result, interest in the agriculture sector started to pick up.

In the second half of 2006, the agriculture sector corrected after a strong run in the first half of the year. In 2007 and the first half of 2008, the agriculture sector once again rocketed upwards due to the increase in prices of agricultural products.

Although food prices have had a reprieve with the global slowdown, the world population is still increasing and imbalances in food supply and demand will continue to exist in the future.

Investors should consider "mooov-ing" into the agriculture sector for the last five months of the year.

 The SP GICS Agriculture Sector # 30202010
For more information on the agriculture sector, see www.standardandpoors.com

Agriculture Performance

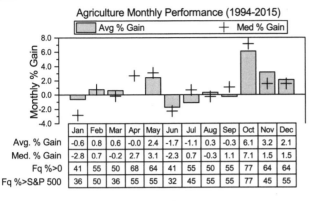

Agriculture Monthly Performance (1994-2015)

	Jan	Feb	Mar	Apr	May	Jun	Jul	Aug	Sep	Oct	Nov	Dec
Avg. % Gain	-0.6	0.8	0.6	-0.0	2.4	-1.7	-1.1	0.3	-0.3	6.1	3.2	2.1
Med. % Gain	-2.8	0.7	-0.2	2.7	3.1	-2.3	0.7	-0.3	1.1	7.1	1.5	1.5
Fq %>0	41	55	50	68	64	41	55	50	55	77	64	64
Fq %>S&P 500	36	50	36	55	55	32	45	55	55	77	45	55

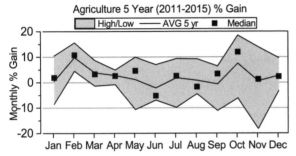

Agriculture 5 Year (2011-2015) % Gain

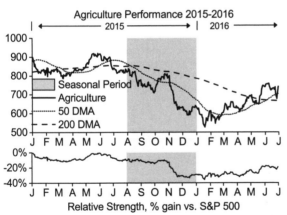

Agriculture Performance 2015-2016

Relative Strength, % gain vs. S&P 500

Market Indices & Rates Weekly Values**

Stock Markets	2014	2015
Dow	16,632	17,461
S&P500	1,946	2,090
Nasdaq	4,429	5,053
TSX	15,279	14,347
FTSE	6,653	6,618
DAX	9,142	11,165
Nikkei	15,228	20,607
Hang Seng	24,796	24,189

Commodities	2014	2015
Oil	97.15	43.21
Gold	1308.9	1111.9

Bond Yields	2014	2015
USA 5 Yr Treasury	1.59	1.57
USA 10 Yr T	2.41	2.18
USA 20 Yr T	2.95	2.54
Moody's Aaa	4.08	4.02
Moody's Baa	4.71	5.14
CAN 5 Yr T	1.52	0.75
CAN 10 Yr T	2.07	1.41

Money Market	2014	2015
USA Fed Funds	0.25	0.25
USA 3 Mo T-B	0.04	0.10
CAN tgt overnight rate	1.00	0.50
CAN 3 Mo T-B	0.96	0.39

Foreign Exchange	2014	2015
EUR/USD	1.34	1.11
GBP/USD	1.67	1.56
USD/CAD	1.09	1.30
USD/JPY	102.34	124.54

AUGUST

M	T	W	T	F	S	S
	1	2	3	4	5	6
7	8	9	10	11	12	13
14	15	16	17	18	19	20
21	22	23	24	25	26	27
28	29	30	31			

SEPTEMBER

M	T	W	T	F	S	S
					1	2	3
4	5	6	7	8	9	10
11	12	13	14	15	16	17
18	19	20	21	22	23	24
25	26	27	28	29	30	

OCTOBER

M	T	W	T	F	S	S
						1
2	3	4	5	6	7	8
9	10	11	12	13	14	15
16	17	18	19	20	21	22
23	24	25	26	27	28	29
30	31					

From 1994 to 2015, October has been the sweet spot for the agriculture seasonal trade. On an average, median and frequency basis, October has also been the best month of the year over the same yearly period.

Over the last five years, on average, the general trend provided nominal seasonal benefits. The big anomaly was the sector's strong performance in February on an average and median basis.

In 2015, the agriculture sector produced a negative performance and underperformed the S&P 500.

AMGEN
June 23rd to September 13th

Biotech has a period of seasonal strength from June 23rd to September 13th (see *Biotech Summer Solstice* strategy). Amgen is considered one of the major biotech companies and has a similar seasonal trend. Amgen has an additional benefit during the biotech seasonal period, as it typically releases its second quarter earnings towards the end of July. This gives Amgen a seasonal boost as investors buy Amgen ahead of their earnings in anticipation of any possible good news.

Strong earnings are particularly welcome in the second quarter, as the first quarter tends to be the weakest quarter of the year for Amgen. The first quarter of the year tends to be weak due to slower sales and the effects of wholesale inventory over-stocking at the end of the previous year.

14.8% gain & positive 81% of the time

From 1990 to 2015, in its seasonal period, Amgen has produced an average gain of 14.8% and has been positive 81% of the time. During this same time period, it has beaten the S&P 500 by an average 14.6% and has outperformed it 85% of the time. This is a strong track record of outperformance, especially the percentage of times that Amgen has beaten the S&P 500.

AMGN* vs. S&P 500 - 1990 to 2015

Jun 23 to Sep 13	S&P 500	AGMN	Positive Diff
1990	-10.4%	29.5%	39.8%
1991	1.6	42.4	40.9
1992	4.0	17.9	13.9
1993	3.6	3.4	-0.2
1994	3.2	24.3	21.1
1995	5.0	31.4	26.4
1996	2.1	7.0	4.9
1997	2.8	-19.0	-21.8
1998	-8.5	20.6	29.1
1999	0.6	64.3	63.7
2000	2.3	7.9	5.6
2001	-10.8	-1.6	9.3
2002	-10.0	12.9	23.0
2003	2.3	5.5	3.2
2004	-0.8	9.1	9.8
2005	1.4	36.0	34.5
2006	5.8	6.4	0.6
2007	-1.2	2.1	3.3
2008	-5.0	39.2	44.2
2009	16.8	14.8	-2.0
2010	2.4	-3.1	-5.5
2011	-8.9	-5.6	3.3
2012	9.4	15.0	5.6
2013	6.0	17.1	11.1
2014	1.2	14.0	12.8
2015	-7.6	-5.6	2.1
Avg	0.3%	14.8%	14.6%
Fq > 0	65%	81%	85%

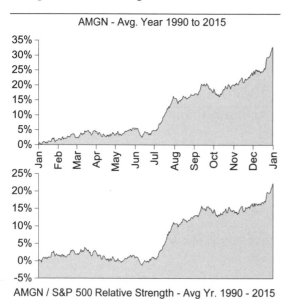

AMGN - Avg. Year 1990 to 2015

AMGN / S&P 500 Relative Strength - Avg Yr. 1990 - 2015

place in the summer months when the stock market typically does not have strong results and the selection of seasonal long trades are limited.

The seasonal trade for Amgen focuses on the sweet spot of its best performance, but like the biotech sector, on average the second half of the year for Amgen is much stronger than the first half of the year. From July 1st to December 31st, for the yearly period 1990 to 2015, Amgen has produced an average gain of 22.6% and has been positive 81% of the time. This compares to the weaker first half of the year, where the average gain over the same yearly period is 4.9% and the frequency of positive performance is 50%.

The Amgen seasonal trade is a valued trade not just because of its strong results, but also because of the time of year when the trade occurs. The trade takes

 * Amgen is a biotech company. Amgen trades on the Nasdaq Exchange. Data adjusted for stock splits.

Amgen Performance

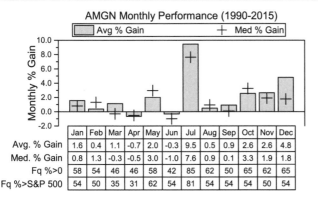

AMGN Monthly Performance (1990-2015)

	Jan	Feb	Mar	Apr	May	Jun	Jul	Aug	Sep	Oct	Nov	Dec
Avg. % Gain	1.6	0.4	1.1	-0.7	2.0	-0.3	9.5	0.5	0.9	2.6	2.6	4.8
Med. % Gain	0.8	1.3	-0.3	-0.5	3.0	-1.0	7.6	0.9	0.1	3.3	1.9	1.8
Fq %>0	58	54	46	46	58	42	85	62	50	65	62	65
Fq %>S&P 500	54	50	35	31	62	54	81	54	54	54	50	54

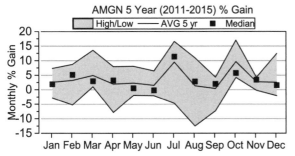

AMGN 5 Year (2011-2015) % Gain

Market Indices & Rates
Weekly Values**

Stock Markets	2014	2015
Dow	16,956	17,171
S&P500	1,984	2,057
Nasdaq	4,527	4,951
TSX	15,494	13,939
FTSE	6,766	6,407
DAX	9,327	10,619
Nikkei	15,470	20,173
Hang Seng	25,069	23,125

Commodities	2014	2015
Oil	95.86	41.33
Gold	1288.2	1126.0

Bond Yields	2014	2015
USA 5 Yr Treasury	1.63	1.53
USA 10 Yr T	2.41	2.13
USA 20 Yr T	2.93	2.49
Moody's Aaa	4.08	3.99
Moody's Baa	4.70	5.16
CAN 5 Yr T	1.54	0.67
CAN 10 Yr T	2.08	1.33

Money Market	2014	2015
USA Fed Funds	0.25	0.25
USA 3 Mo T-B	0.03	0.05
CAN tgt overnight rate	1.00	0.50
CAN 3 Mo T-B	0.94	0.38

Foreign Exchange	2014	2015
EUR/USD	1.33	1.12
GBP/USD	1.66	1.57
USD/CAD	1.09	1.31
USD/JPY	103.41	123.61

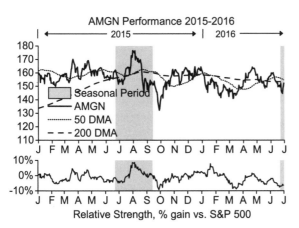

AMGN Performance 2015-2016

Relative Strength, % gain vs. S&P 500

From 1990 to 2015, the best month of the year for Amgen was July on an average, median and frequency basis. The gains in July were substantially above the other months of the year.

Over the last five years, the seasonal trade has worked well, mainly with the strong support from July's results.

In 2015, Amgen was performing at market coming into its seasonal period. Shortly after its seasonal period started, Amgen started to perform well, outperforming the S&P 500 in its seasonal period, despite faltering at the end of the trade.

AUGUST

M	T	W	T	F	S	S
	1	2	3	4	5	6
7	8	9	10	11	12	13
14	15	16	17	18	19	20
21	22	23	24	25	26	27
28	29	30	31			

SEPTEMBER

M	T	W	T	F	S	S
				1	2	3
4	5	6	7	8	9	10
11	12	13	14	15	16	17
18	19	20	21	22	23	24
25	26	27	28	29	30	

OCTOBER

M	T	W	T	F	S	S
						1
2	3	4	5	6	7	8
9	10	11	12	13	14	15
16	17	18	19	20	21	22
23	24	25	26	27	28	29
30	31					

HEALTH CARE
AUGUST PRESCRIPTION RENEWAL
August 15th to October 18th

Health care stocks have traditionally been classified as defensive stocks because of their stable earnings. Pharmaceutical and other health care companies typically still perform relatively well in an economic downturn.

Even in tough times, people still need to take their medication. As a result, investors have typically found comfort in this sector starting in the late summer and riding the momentum into mid-October.

2.4% extra & 17 out of 26 times better than the S&P 500

Health Care* vs. S&P 500
Performance 1990 to 2015

Aug 15 to Oct 18	S&P 500	Positive Health Care	Diff
1990	-9.9 %	-1.3 %	8.6 %
1991	0.7	1.3	0.6
1992	-1.9	-9.0	-7.1
1993	4.1	13.5	9.5
1994	1.2	7.2	6.0
1995	4.9	11.7	6.7
1996	7.4	9.4	2.1
1997	2.1	5.8	3.7
1998	-0.6	3.0	3.6
1999	-5.5	-0.5	5.0
2000	-10.0	6.9	16.9
2001	-10.0	-0.4	9.6
2002	-3.8	2.4	6.2
2003	4.9	-0.5	-5.4
2004	4.6	-0.8	-5.4
2005	-4.2	-3.1	1.2
2006	7.7	6.4	-1.3
2007	8.0	6.0	-2.0
2008	-27.3	-20.4	6.8
2009	8.3	5.1	-3.3
2010	9.8	8.2	-1.6
2011	4.0	3.2	-0.8
2012	3.8	6.9	3.1
2013	3.5	4.3	0.8
2014	-3.5	-1.1	2.5
2015	-2.8	-7.4	-4.6
Avg	-0.2 %	2.2 %	2.4 %
Fq > 0	58 %	62 %	65 %

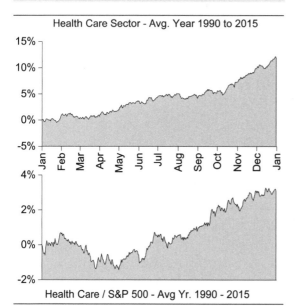

Health Care Sector - Avg. Year 1990 to 2015

Health Care / S&P 500 - Avg Yr. 1990 - 2015

From 1990 to 2015, the health care sector has typically outperformed the S&P 500 during the period from August 15th to October 18th.

During this time period, the broad market (S&P 500) produced an average loss of 0.2%, compared with the health care sector's gain of 2.2%.

Despite competing with a runaway market in 2003 and legal problems which required drugs to be withdrawn from the market in 2004, the sector has beaten the S&P 500 seventeen out of twenty-six times from 1990 to 2015 in its seasonal period.

The real benefit of investing in the health care sector has been the positive returns that have been generated when the market has typically been negative.

Since 1950, August and September have been the worst two-month combination for gains in the broad stock market.

Having an alternative sector to invest in during the summer and early autumn is a valuable asset.

Alternate Strategy—As the health care sector has had a tendency to perform at par with the broad market from late October to early December, an alternative strategy is to continue holding the health care sector during this time period if the fundamentals or technicals are favorable.

*Health Care SP GIC Sector# 35: An index designed to represent a cross section of health care companies. For more information on the health care sector, see www.standardandpoors.com.

Health Care Performance

Health Care Monthly Performance (1990-2015)

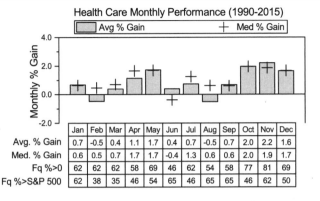

	Jan	Feb	Mar	Apr	May	Jun	Jul	Aug	Sep	Oct	Nov	Dec
Avg. % Gain	0.7	-0.5	0.4	1.1	1.7	0.4	0.7	-0.5	0.7	2.0	2.2	1.6
Med. % Gain	0.6	0.5	0.7	1.7	1.7	-0.4	1.3	0.6	0.6	2.0	1.9	1.7
Fq %>0	62	62	62	58	69	46	62	54	58	77	81	69
Fq %>S&P 500	62	38	35	46	54	65	46	65	65	46	62	50

Health Care 5 Year (2011-2015) % Gain

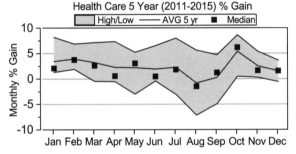

Health Care Performance 2015-2016

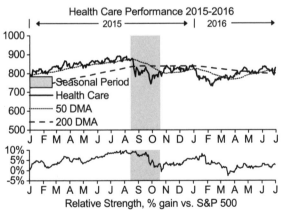

Relative Strength, % gain vs. S&P 500

Market Indices & Rates
Weekly Values**

Stock Markets	2014	2015
Dow	17,097	16,224
S&P500	2,000	1,936
Nasdaq	4,567	4,674
TSX	15,601	13,443
FTSE	6,820	6,080
DAX	9,520	10,098
Nikkei	15,511	18,487
Hang Seng	24,929	21,438

Commodities	2014	2015
Oil	94.67	41.38
Gold	1286.6	1135.8

Bond Yields	2014	2015
USA 5 Yr Treasury	1.66	1.47
USA 10 Yr T	2.37	2.14
USA 20 Yr T	2.85	2.56
Moody's Aaa	3.98	4.09
Moody's Baa	4.61	5.29
CAN 5 Yr T	1.53	0.68
CAN 10 Yr T	2.02	1.39

Money Market	2014	2015
USA Fed Funds	0.25	0.25
USA 3 Mo T-B	0.03	0.06
CAN tgt overnight rate	1.00	0.50
CAN 3 Mo T-B	0.94	0.37

Foreign Exchange	2014	2015
EUR/USD	1.32	1.14
GBP/USD	1.66	1.55
USD/CAD	1.09	1.33
USD/JPY	103.96	119.98

AUGUST

M	T	W	T	F	S	S
	1	2	3	4	5	6
7	8	9	10	11	12	13
14	15	16	17	18	19	20
21	22	23	24	25	26	27
28	29	30	31			

SEPTEMBER

M	T	W	T	F	S	S
				1	2	3
4	5	6	7	8	9	10
11	12	13	14	15	16	17
18	19	20	21	22	23	24
25	26	27	28	29	30	

OCTOBER

M	T	W	T	F	S	S
						1
2	3	4	5	6	7	8
9	10	11	12	13	14	15
16	17	18	19	20	21	22
23	24	25	26	27	28	29
30	31					

Over the long-term, on average, August is one of the worst performing months for the health care sector and yet the middle of the month starts off the sector's seasonal period. In this case, averages can be deceiving. Since 1990, not only is the median positive in August, but also the frequency of outperformance relative to the S&P 500 is high, at 65%. Nevertheless, the second half of August is the better performing half. Over the last five years, the health care sector's average performance throughout the year has placed August as the weakest month of the year and the best two performing months as September and October. In 2015, the health care sector produced a loss in its seasonal period, and underperformed the S&P 500.

SEPTEMBER

	MONDAY	TUESDAY	WEDNESDAY
WEEK 35	28	29	30
WEEK 36	**4** 26 USA Market Closed- Labor Day CAN Market Closed- Labor Day	**5** 25	**6** 24
WEEK 37	**11** 19	**12** 18	**11** 17
WEEK 38	**18** 12	**19** 11	**20** 10
WEEK 39	**25** 5	**26** 4	**27** 3

THURSDAY		FRIDAY	
31		1	29
7	23	8	22
14	16	15	15
21	9	22	8
28	2	29	1

OCTOBER

M	T	W	T	F	S	S
						1
2	3	4	5	6	7	8
9	10	11	12	13	14	15
16	17	18	19	20	21	22
23	24	25	26	27	28	29
30	31					

NOVEMBER

M	T	W	T	F	S	S
		1	2	3	4	5
6	7	8	9	10	11	12
13	14	15	16	17	18	19
20	21	22	23	24	25	26
27	28	29	30			

DECEMBER

M	T	W	T	F	S	S
				1	2	3
4	5	6	7	8	9	10
11	12	13	14	15	16	17
18	19	20	21	22	23	24
25	26	27	28	29	30	31

JANUARY

M	T	W	T	F	S	S
1	2	3	4	5	6	7
8	9	10	11	12	13	14
15	16	17	18	19	20	21
22	23	24	25	26	27	28
29	30	31				

SEPTEMBER
S U M M A R Y

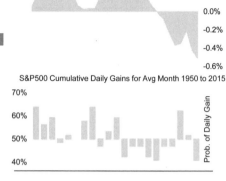

0.4%
0.2%
0.0%
-0.2%
-0.4%
-0.6%

S&P500 Cumulative Daily Gains for Avg Month 1950 to 2015

70%
60%
50%
40%

Prob. of Daily Gain

	Dow Jones	S&P 500	Nasdaq	TSX Comp
Month Rank	12	12	12	12
# Up	26	29	23	12
# Down	40	37	21	19
% Pos	39	44	52	39
% Avg. Gain	-0.8	-0.5	-0.6	-1.7

Dow & S&P 1950-2015, Nasdaq 1972-2015, TSX 1985-2015

♦ September has the reputation of being the worst month of the year for the S&P 500. From 1950 to 2015, September has produced an average loss of 0.5% and was only positive 44% of the time. ♦ In particular, the last part of September tends to be negative. ♦ In September 2015, the stock market corrected for most of the month and then in the final days, started to rally. ♦ The materials sector tends to perform poorly in September and has outperformed the S&P 500 only 25% of the time since 1990.

BEST / WORST SEPTEMBER BROAD MKTS. 2006-2015

BEST SEPTEMBER MARKETS
♦ Russell 2000 (2010) 12.3%
♦ Nasdaq (2010) 12.0%
♦ Russell 1000 (2010) 9.0%

WORST SEPTEMBER MARKETS
♦ TSX Comp. (2008) -14.7%
♦ Nikkei 225 (2008) -13.9%
♦ FTSE 100 (2008) -13.0%

Index Values End of Month

	2006	2007	2008	2009	2010	2011	2012	2013	2014	2015
Dow	11,679	13,896	10,851	9,712	10,788	10,913	13,437	15,130	17,043	16,285
S&P 500	1,336	1,527	1,166	1,057	1,141	1,131	1,441	1,682	1,972	1,920
Nasdaq	2,258	2,702	2,092	2,122	2,369	2,415	3,116	3,771	4,493	4,620
TSX Comp.	11,761	14,099	11,753	11,395	12,369	11,624	12,317	12,787	14,961	13,307
Russell 1000	1,391	1,597	1,219	1,115	1,211	1,198	1,526	1,806	2,108	2,054
Russell 2000	1,803	2,002	1,689	1,502	1,680	1,601	2,081	2,669	2,738	2,735
FTSE 100	5,961	6,467	4,903	5,134	5,549	5,129	5,742	6,462	6,623	6,062
Nikkei 225	16,128	16,786	11,260	10,133	9,369	8,700	8,870	14,456	16,174	17,388

Percent Gain for September

	2006	2007	2008	2009	2010	2011	2012	2013	2014	2015
Dow	2.6	4.0	-6.0	2.3	7.7	-6.0	2.6	2.2	-0.3	-1.5
S&P 500	2.5	3.6	-9.1	3.6	8.8	-7.2	2.4	3.0	-1.6	-2.6
Nasdaq	3.4	4.0	-11.6	5.6	12.0	-6.4	1.6	5.1	-1.9	-3.3
TSX Comp.	-2.6	3.2	-14.7	4.8	3.8	-9.0	3.1	1.1	-4.3	-4.0
Russell 1000	2.3	3.7	-9.7	3.9	9.0	-7.6	2.4	3.3	-1.9	-2.9
Russell 2000	0.7	1.6	-8.1	5.6	12.3	-11.4	3.1	6.2	-6.2	-5.1
FTSE 100	0.9	2.6	-13.0	4.6	6.2	-4.9	0.5	0.8	-2.9	-3.0
Nikkei 225	-0.1	1.3	-13.9	-3.4	6.2	-2.8	0.3	8.0	4.9	-8.0

September Market Avg. Performance 2006 to 2015[1]

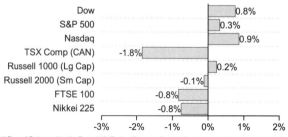

Dow 0.8%
S&P 500 0.3%
Nasdaq 0.9%
TSX Comp (CAN) -1.8%
Russell 1000 (Lg Cap) 0.2%
Russell 2000 (Sm Cap) -0.1%
FTSE 100 -0.8%
Nikkei 225 -0.8%

-3% -2% -1% 0% 1% 2%

Interest Corner Sep[2]

	Fed Funds %[3]	3 Mo. T-Bill %[4]	10 Yr %[5]	20 Yr %[6]
2015	0.25	0.00	2.06	2.51
2014	0.25	0.02	2.52	2.98
2013	0.25	0.02	2.64	3.41
2012	0.25	0.10	1.65	2.42
2011	0.25	0.02	1.92	2.66

(1) Russell Data provided by Russell (2) Federal Reserve Bank of St. Louis- end of month values (3) Target rate set by FOMC (4)(5)(6) Constant yield maturities.

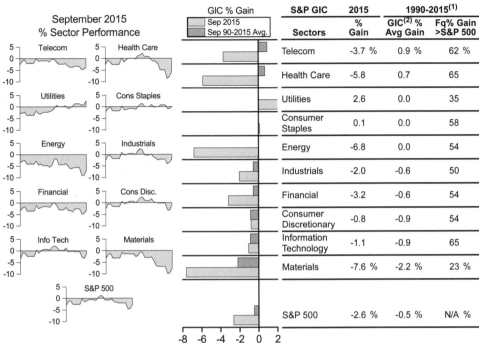

September 2015
% Sector Performance

GIC % Gain
Sep 2015
Sep 90-2015 Avg.

S&P GIC Sectors	2015 % Gain	1990-2015[1] GIC[2] % Avg Gain	Fq% Gain >S&P 500
Telecom	-3.7 %	0.9 %	62 %
Health Care	-5.8	0.7	65
Utilities	2.6	0.0	35
Consumer Staples	0.1	0.0	58
Energy	-6.8	0.0	54
Industrials	-2.0	-0.6	50
Financial	-3.2	-0.6	54
Consumer Discretionary	-0.8	-0.9	54
Information Technology	-1.1	-0.9	65
Materials	-7.6 %	-2.2 %	23 %
S&P 500	-2.6 %	-0.5 %	N/A %

Sector Commentary

♦ In September 2015, the energy sector, typically a stronger sector in the month, produced a large loss of 6.8% as a glut of oil hurt prices. ♦ The materials sector also lost a lot of ground, producing a loss of 7.6%. ♦ The materials sector was impacted by slowing global growth. ♦ The defensive sectors, consumer staples and utilities lived up to their seasonal track record of better performing sectors, being the only positive performing sectors in September.

Sub-Sector Commentary

♦ September is typically the month when precious metals tend to perform well. In September 2015, gold produced a loss of 1.9% as investors were concerned about the possibility of the U.S. Federal Reserve raising interest rates. ♦ The metals and mining sector continued its August slide with a 6.7% loss in September. ♦ The railroads, usually a weak performing sub-sector, produced a gain of 0.9%. ♦ The steel sub-sector, typically weak in September, lived up to its reputation and produced a large loss of 13.3%.

SELECTED SUB-SECTORS[3]			
Gold	-1.9 %	2.5 %	65 %
Silver	1.5	1.7	69
Biotech (1993-2015)	-8.1	1.5	65
Pharma	-4.7	0.8	62
Agriculture (1994-2015)	-7.9	-0.3	55
Retail	-1.5	-0.6	46
Transportation	-0.1	-0.7	54
Homebuilders	-5.5	-0.7	61
Railroads	0.9	-0.7	38
Banks	-4.5	-0.9	54
Chemicals	-7.5	-1.9	31
Metals & Mining	-6.7	-2.0	42
Automotive & Components	-0.5	-2.5	38
SOX (1995-2015)	-1.4	-2.9	43
Steel	-13.3	-3.8	42

(1) Sector data provided by Standard and Poors (2) GIC is short form for Global Industry Classification (3) Sub Sector data provided by Standard and Poors, except where marked by symbol.

PROCTER AND GAMBLE
SOMETHING FOR EVERYONE – Aug 7 to Nov 19

In the investors' eyes, Procter and Gamble is a relatively defensive investment, as the company is in the consumer packaged goods business and its revenues are generated in over 180 countries. Defensive stocks have a reputation of producing sub-par performance compared with the broad market. This is not the case with PG, as on average, it has outperformed the S&P 500 over the last twenty-five years during its seasonally strong period.

9.7% gain & positive 88% of the time

Interestingly, on average, the gains have been produced largely in the second half of the year. In the first half of the year, PG has been relatively flat and has underperformed the S&P 500.

PG - Avg. Year 1990 to 2015

PG / S&P 500 Relative Strength - Avg Yr. 1990 - 2015

PG* vs. S&P 500 - 1990 to 2015

Aug 7 to Nov 19	S&P 500	PG	Positive Diff
1990	-4.5%	8.3%	12.8%
1991	-2.9	-2.2	0.7
1992	0.7	10.1	9.4
1993	3.1	17.7	14.6
1994	1.0	19.3	18.3
1995	7.4	27.8	20.4
1996	12.0	18.6	6.5
1997	-1.6	0.2	1.9
1998	5.8	14.0	8.2
1999	9.4	18.7	9.3
2000	-6.5	31.8	38.3
2001	-4.1	11.2	15.3
2002	4.3	-0.7	-5.0
2003	7.8	8.2	0.4
2004	10.0	2.5	-7.5
2005	1.8	6.2	4.4
2006	9.5	7.4	-2.1
2007	-2.3	12.0	14.4
2008	-37.4	-8.1	29.3
2009	9.8	20.8	11.0
2010	7.0	6.7	-0.3
2011	1.4	4.4	3.0
2012	-0.5	3.2	3.7
2013	5.3	3.2	-2.2
2014	6.7	9.4	2.7
2015	-0.1	0.6	0.8
Avg	1.7%	9.7%	8.0%
Fq > 0	65%	88%	81%

From a seasonal perspective, the best time to invest in PG has been from August 7th to November 19th. During this period, from 1990 to 2015, PG on average produced a gain of 9.7% and was positive 88% of the time. In addition, it substantially outperformed the S&P 500, generating an extra profit of 8.0% and beating its performance 81% of the time.

Investors will often seek sanctuary in defensive stocks in late summer and early autumn. Although August is not typically the worst month of the year, it does have a weak risk-reward profile. With the dreaded month of September falling right after August, investors become "gun shy" and start to become more conservative in August.

This trend benefits PG as more investors switch over to defensive companies. PG's outperformance, on average, starts to occur just after it releases its fourth quarter earnings at the beginning of August.

PG continues to outperform the S&P 500 through September and October. For the S&P 500, September on average is the worst month of the year and October is the most volatile month. The outperformance of PG continues into mid-November.

PG's seasonally strong period extends past the seasonal period for the consumer staples sector. It is possible that investors wait until after PG's first quarter results are released in the beginning of November before adjusting their portfolios.

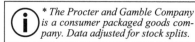
The Procter and Gamble Company is a consumer packaged goods company. Data adjusted for stock splits.

Procter & Gamble Performance

PG Monthly Performance (1990-2015)

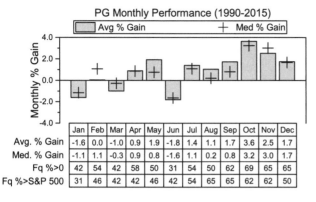

	Jan	Feb	Mar	Apr	May	Jun	Jul	Aug	Sep	Oct	Nov	Dec
Avg. % Gain	-1.6	0.0	-1.0	0.9	1.9	-1.8	1.4	1.1	1.7	3.6	2.5	1.7
Med. % Gain	-1.1	1.1	-0.3	0.9	0.8	-1.6	1.1	0.2	0.8	3.2	3.0	1.7
Fq %>0	42	54	42	58	50	31	54	50	62	69	65	65
Fq %>S&P 500	31	46	42	42	46	42	54	65	65	62	62	50

PG 5 Year (2011-2015) % Gain

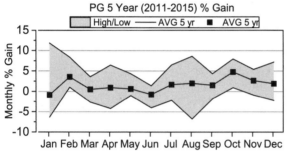

PG Performance 2015-2016

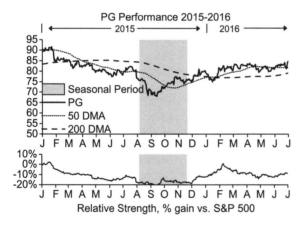

Relative Strength, % gain vs. S&P 500

Market Indices & Rates
Weekly Values**

Stock Markets	2014	2015
Dow	17,088	16,283
S&P500	2,002	1,941
Nasdaq	4,579	4,716
TSX	15,606	13,592
FTSE	6,852	6,095
DAX	9,617	10,136
Nikkei	15,644	18,225
Hang Seng	25,071	21,158
Commodities	**2014**	**2015**
Oil	94.04	46.73
Gold	1271.3	1131.6
Bond Yields	**2014**	**2015**
USA 5 Yr Treasury	1.70	1.50
USA 10 Yr T	2.44	2.18
USA 20 Yr T	2.93	2.63
Moody's Aaa	4.03	4.12
Moody's Baa	4.69	5.34
CAN 5 Yr T	1.57	0.75
CAN 10 Yr T	2.08	1.46
Money Market	**2014**	**2015**
USA Fed Funds	0.25	0.25
USA 3 Mo T-B	0.03	0.04
CAN tgt overnight rate	1.00	0.50
CAN 3 Mo T-B	0.93	0.37
Foreign Exchange	**2014**	**2015**
EUR/USD	1.31	1.12
GBP/USD	1.64	1.53
USD/CAD	1.09	1.32
USD/JPY	104.92	120.00

SEPTEMBER

M	T	W	T	F	S	S
				1	2	3
4	5	6	7	8	9	10
11	12	13	14	15	16	17
18	19	20	21	22	23	24
25	26	27	28	29	30	

OCTOBER

M	T	W	T	F	S	S
						1
2	3	4	5	6	7	8
9	10	11	12	13	14	15
16	17	18	19	20	21	22
23	24	25	26	27	28	29
30	31					

From 1990 to 2015, October was the strongest month for Procter & Gamble on an average and frequency basis. Over the same time period, June was the weakest month.

Over the last five years, Procter & Gamble has generally followed its average seasonal trend. The exception is February's relatively strong performance.

In 2015, Proctor and Gamble started the year with negative performance and bottomed shortly after its seasonal period started. In the end, it nominally outperformed the S&P 500 during its seasonal period.

NOVEMBER

M	T	W	T	F	S	S
	1	2	3	4	5	
6	7	8	9	10	11	12
13	14	15	16	17	18	19
20	21	22	23	24	25	26
27	28	29	30			

CARNIVAL CRUISE LINES
CRUISING FOR RETURNS– Sep 8 to Dec 31

The cruise industry is a seasonal business. The first quarter has the highest number of bookings and the third quarter has the highest number of voyages.

Investors look to be invested in Carnival Cruise Lines (Carnival) ahead of its booking season, increasing the relative performance of the stock price from September 8th until December 31st. In this time period, from 1990 to 2015, Carnival has produced an average return of 13.5% and has been positive 77% of the time.

13.5% gain & positive 77% of the time

The cruise industry has a large number of variables affecting its performance which can be fairly volatile. In the last decade, demand for cruise trips have been adversely affected by news stories of outbreaks of sickness, on-board fires immobilizing ships and general ship breakdowns at sea. Although these problems have adversely affected the stock prices of cruise companies in the short-term, the cruise companies have worked hard at preventing future problems and the stock prices have responded positively.

CCL* vs. S&P 500 - 1990 to 2015

Sep 8 to Dec 31	S&P 500	CCL	Diff
		Positive	
1990	2.1%	-20.5%	-22.6%
1991	7.2	26.4	19.2
1992	4.5	23.0	18.5
1993	1.7	15.5	13.8
1994	-2.5	-2.9	-0.4
1995	8.0	12.8	4.8
1996	13.0	20.0	7.0
1997	4.5	20.6	16.1
1998	26.2	83.8	57.6
1999	8.8	8.7	-0.1
2000	-12.1	56.5	68.6
2001	5.7	-3.3	-9.1
2002	-1.6	3.1	4.7
2003	8.9	15.2	6.3
2004	8.1	22.7	14.6
2005	1.0	7.2	6.3
2006	9.6	16.5	6.9
2007	1.0	-0.5	-1.5
2008	-27.3	-37.6	-10.3
2009	9.7	8.0	-1.7
2010	15.2	36.1	21.0
2011	4.9	2.5	-2.4
2012	-0.8	-0.8	0.1
2013	11.7	12.0	0.4
2014	2.6	15.3	12.7
2015	6.4	11.3	5.0
Avg	4.5%	13.5%	9.0%
Fq > 0	81%	77%	69%

August tends to be a weaker month of the year for Carnival and given that its seasonal period starts the following month, investors should be cautious on timing the entry into the seasonal trade. This is particularly true as September tends to be a negative month for the S&P 500 and any large corrections would have a high likelihood of having a negative influence on Carnival.

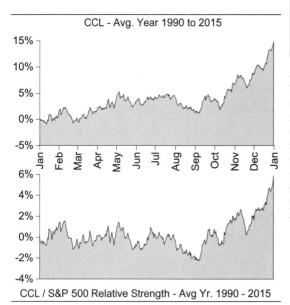

CCL - Avg. Year 1990 to 2015

CCL / S&P 500 Relative Strength - Avg Yr. 1990 - 2015

In its seasonal period, Carnival has on average outperformed the S&P 500 by 9.0% since 1990. Although the 83.8% return in 1998 helps to skew the average higher, Carnival has had returns 10% or greater, fifteen times since 1990. This compares to losses of 10% or greater, which have occurred twice in the same time period.

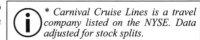

* Carnival Cruise Lines is a travel company listed on the NYSE. Data adjusted for stock splits.

CCL Performance

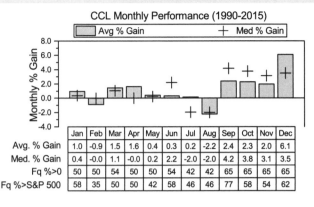

CCL Monthly Performance (1990-2015)

Avg % Gain   + Med % Gain

	Jan	Feb	Mar	Apr	May	Jun	Jul	Aug	Sep	Oct	Nov	Dec
Avg. % Gain	1.0	-0.9	1.5	1.6	0.4	0.3	0.2	-2.2	2.4	2.3	2.0	6.1
Med. % Gain	0.4	-0.0	1.1	-0.0	0.2	2.2	-2.0	-2.0	4.2	3.8	3.1	3.5
Fq %>0	50	50	54	50	50	54	42	42	65	65	65	65
Fq %>S&P 500	58	35	50	50	42	58	46	46	77	58	54	62

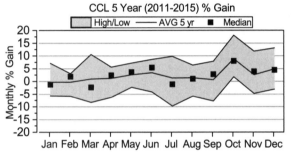

CCL 5 Year (2011-2015) % Gain

High/Low   —— AVG 5 yr   ■ Median

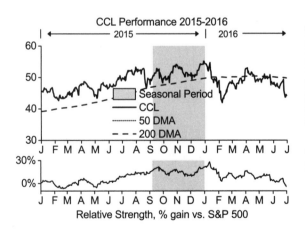

CCL Performance 2015-2016

2015 ◄———► 2016

Seasonal Period
— CCL
······· 50 DMA
- - - 200 DMA

J F M A M J J A S O N D J F M A M J J

30%
0%

J F M A M J J A S O N D J F M A M J J

Relative Strength, % gain vs. S&P 500

WEEK 37

Market Indices & Rates
Weekly Values**

Stock Markets	2014	2015
Dow	17,046	16,377
S&P500	1,994	1,956
Nasdaq	4,578	4,797
TSX	15,517	13,548
FTSE	6,820	6,145
DAX	9,702	10,203
Nikkei	15,820	18,124
Hang Seng	24,788	21,408

Commodities	2014	2015
Oil	92.44	45.16
Gold	1247.7	1112.1

Bond Yields	2014	2015
USA 5 Yr Treasury	1.78	1.53
USA 10 Yr T	2.54	2.21
USA 20 Yr T	3.01	2.65
Moody's Aaa	4.13	4.09
Moody's Baa	4.79	5.33
CAN 5 Yr T	1.66	0.77
CAN 10 Yr T	2.19	1.47

Money Market	2014	2015
USA Fed Funds	0.25	0.25
USA 3 Mo T-B	0.02	0.04
CAN tgt overnight rate	1.00	0.50
CAN 3 Mo T-B	0.93	0.38

Foreign Exchange	2014	2015
EUR/USD	1.29	1.12
GBP/USD	1.62	1.54
USD/CAD	1.10	1.33
USD/JPY	106.71	120.16

From 1990 to 2015, the best four contiguous months of the year for Carnival on an average, median and frequency basis was September through December.

From 2011 to 2015, Carnival has followed its general seasonal pattern with the last four months of the year being strong and July and August being weak. An anomaly existed in this time period, as April, May and June were on average strong.

Leading into its seasonal period in 2015, Carnival started to outperform the S&P 500 in May, and continued its outperformance in its seasonal period.

SEPTEMBER

M	T	W	T	F	S	S
				1	2	3
4	5	6	7	8	9	10
11	12	13	14	15	16	17
18	19	20	21	22	23	24
25	26	27	28	29	30	

OCTOBER

M	T	W	T	F	S	S
						1
2	3	4	5	6	7	8
9	10	11	12	13	14	15
16	17	18	19	20	21	22
23	24	25	26	27	28	29
30	31					

NOVEMBER

M	T	W	T	F	S	S
	1	2	3	4	5	
6	7	8	9	10	11	12
13	14	15	16	17	18	19
20	21	22	23	24	25	26
27	28	29	30			

Info Tech Seasonal Per. Adjustment

The interim seasonal period (Dec 6th, to Dec 14th) has been taken out of the information technology sector as it has produced an average loss of 2.2% and has only been positive 22% of the time from 1989 to 2015.

From 1989 to 2015, during its seasonal period of October 9th to December 5th, the information technology sector has produced an average gain of 7.8% and has been positive 74% of the time. From 1990 to 2016, during the second seasonal period of December 15th to January 17th, the information technology sector has produced an average gain of 3.3% and has been positive 70%. The combined seasonal gains have been 11.6% and has been positive 70% of the time.

11.6% gain

Technology stocks get bid up at the end of the year for three reasons.

First, a lot of companies operate with year end budgets and if they do not spend the money in their budget, they lose it. In the last few months of the year, whatever money they have, they spend. The number one purchase item for this budget flush is technology equipment. Second, consumers indirectly help push up technology stocks by purchasing electronic items during the holiday season.

Third, the "Conference Effect" helps maintain the momentum in January. This phenomenon is the result of investors increasing positions ahead of major conferences in order to benefit from positive announcements. In the case of the information technology sector, investors increase their holdings ahead of the Las Vegas Consumer Electronics Conference that typically occurs in the second week of January.

Info Tech* vs. S&P 500 1989/90 to 2015/16   Positive ☐

Year	Oct 9 to Dec 5 S&P 500	IT	Dec 15 to Jan 17 S&P 500	IT	Compound Growth S&P 500	IT
1989/90	-2.6%	-5.7%	-3.9%	3.8%	-6.3%	-2.1%
1990/91	5.2	11.2	0.4	5.5	5.6	17.3
1991/92	-0.9	-1.4	8.9	17.6	8.0	16.0
1992/93	6.0	6.8	1.0	7.4	7.0	14.7
1993/94	1.0	6.9	2.2	8.8	3.2	16.3
1994/95	-0.4	8.5	3.3	9.6	2.9	18.9
1995/96	6.0	3.2	-1.7	-8.0	4.2	-5.1
1996/97	6.2	14.4	6.5	7.3	13.2	22.8
1997/98	1.0	-8.1	0.9	4.0	1.9	-4.4
1998/99	22.7	46.8	8.9	18.7	33.6	74.2
1999/00	7.3	18.7	4.4	9.7	12.0	30.3
2000/01	-2.3	-12.8	-0.9	-3.3	-3.1	-15.7
2001/02	10.2	31.9	1.4	2.3	11.7	34.8
2002/03	13.5	37.2	1.4	-0.6	15.1	36.4
2003/04	2.7	2.3	6.1	11.1	9.0	13.6
2004/05	6.2	11.7	-1.6	-4.1	4.5	7.1
2005/06	5.5	8.4	0.8	1.5	6.4	10.0
2006/07	4.8	6.5	0.4	0.8	5.2	7.4
2007/08	-4.4	-14.2	-9.2	-12.7	-13.1	-14.9
2008/09	-11.1	-14.2	-3.4	-1.9	-14.0	-15.8
2009/10	3.8	6.3	2.0	2.7	5.8	9.2
2010/11	5.1	7.0	4.2	4.9	9.5	12.3
2011/12	8.8	7.6	6.8	4.9	16.1	12.8
2012/13	-3.2	-6.4	4.8	4.0	1.4	-2.6
2013/14	7.8	10.2	3.6	5.5	11.7	16.3
2014/15	5.4	6.8	0.9	-0.7	6.3	6.1
2015/16	3.9	8.2	-7.0	-9.4	-3.4	-1.9
Avg.	4.0%	7.8%	1.5%	3.3%	5.7%	11.6%
Fq > 0	74%	74%	74%	70%	81%	70%

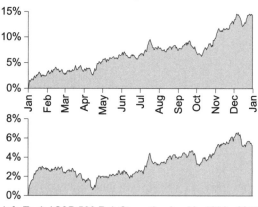

Info Tech Sector - Avg. Year 1990 to 2015

Info Tech / S&P 500 Rel. Strength - Avg Yr. 1990 - 2015

 Alternate Strategy— Investors can bridge the gap between the two positive seasonal trends for the information technology sector by holding from October 9th to January 17th. Longer term investors may prefer this strategy, shorter term investors can use technical tools to determine the appropriate strategy.

ⓘ *The SP GICS Information Technology Sector. For more information on the information technology sector, see www.standardandpoors.com*

Information Technology Performance

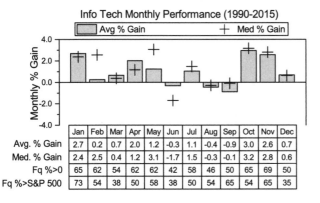

Info Tech Monthly Performance (1990-2015)

	Jan	Feb	Mar	Apr	May	Jun	Jul	Aug	Sep	Oct	Nov	Dec
Avg. % Gain	2.7	0.2	0.7	2.0	1.2	-0.3	1.1	-0.4	-0.9	3.0	2.6	0.7
Med. % Gain	2.4	2.5	0.4	1.2	3.1	-1.7	1.5	-0.3	-0.1	3.2	2.8	0.6
Fq %>0	65	62	54	62	62	42	58	46	50	65	69	50
Fq %>S&P 500	73	54	38	50	58	38	50	54	65	54	65	35

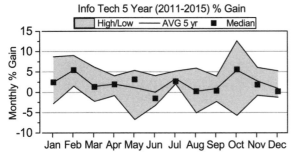

Info Tech 5 Year (2011-2015) % Gain

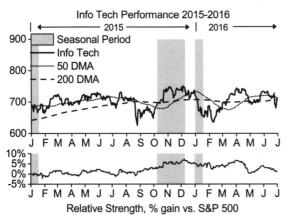

Info Tech Performance 2015-2016

Relative Strength, % gain vs. S&P 500

Market Indices & Rates
Weekly Values**

Stock Markets	2014	2015
Dow	17,173	16,554
S&P500	2,001	1,975
Nasdaq	4,561	4,855
TSX	15,437	13,603
FTSE	6,807	6,149
DAX	9,710	10,139
Nikkei	16,047	18,133
Hang Seng	24,269	21,752

Commodities	2014	2015
Oil	93.54	45.46
Gold	1228.6	1117.5

Bond Yields	2014	2015
USA 5 Yr Treasury	1.82	1.54
USA 10 Yr T	2.61	2.22
USA 20 Yr T	3.10	2.67
Moody's Aaa	4.21	4.10
Moody's Baa	4.89	5.37
CAN 5 Yr T	1.71	0.82
CAN 10 Yr T	2.26	1.53

Money Market	2014	2015
USA Fed Funds	0.25	0.25
USA 3 Mo T-B	0.02	0.04
CAN tgt overnight rate	1.00	0.50
CAN 3 Mo T-B	0.92	0.39

Foreign Exchange	2014	2015
EUR/USD	1.29	1.13
GBP/USD	1.63	1.55
USD/CAD	1.10	1.32
USD/JPY	108.08	120.24

SEPTEMBER

M	T	W	T	F	S	S
				1	2	3
4	5	6	7	8	9	10
11	12	13	14	15	16	17
18	19	20	21	22	23	24
25	26	27	28	29	30	

OCTOBER

M	T	W	T	F	S	S
						1
2	3	4	5	6	7	8
9	10	11	12	13	14	15
16	17	18	19	20	21	22
23	24	25	26	27	28	29
30	31					

From 1990 to 2015, on average, the technology sector performed well from October to January, except for the month of December.

Over the last five years, the technology sector has on average followed its seasonal trend. The largest anomaly has been the strong performance in February. October has been the strongest month and also had the widest dispersion in returns. In 2015, the technology sector was positive and outperformed the S&P 500 in its seasonal period. In 2016, the technology sector performed poorly in its seasonal period as the S&P 500 corrected sharply.

NOVEMBER

M	T	W	T	F	S	S
	1	2	3	4	5	
6	7	8	9	10	11	12
13	14	15	16	17	18	19
20	21	22	23	24	25	26
27	28	29	30			

CANADIAN BANKS
①Oct10-Dec 31   ②Jan23-Apr13

Canadian banks have their year-end on October 31st. Why does this matter? In the past Canadian banks have announced most of their dividend increases and stock splits when they announce their typically optimistic full year fiscal reports at the end of November and beginning of December. This helps to push up the sector at this time.

11.2% gain & positive 90% of the time

The Canadian bank sector, from October 10th to December 31st for the years 1989/1990 to 2015/2016, has been positive 78% of the time and has produced an average gain of 5.1%. From January 23rd to April 13th, the sector has been positive 74% of the time and has produced an average gain of 5.8%. On a compound basis, the strategy has been positive 90% of the time and produced an average gain of 11.2%.

In the table above, Canadian bank returns in December have been separated out to show the impact of bank earnings on returns. In December, Canadian banks on average have provided gains 77% of the time, but they have underperformed the TSX Composite. If Canadian banks have performed well leading into their earnings, they often pause in December.

(i) *Banks SP GIC Canadian Sector Level 2 Represents a cross section of Canadian banking companies.*

Canadian Banks* vs. S&P 500 1989 to 2016
Positive [ ]

Year	Oct 10 to Dec 31 TSX- Comp	Cdn. Banks	Jan 23 to Apr 13 TSX- Comp	Cdn. Banks	Compound Growth TSX- Comp	Cdn. Banks	Dec 1 Dec 31 TSX- Comp	Cdn. Banks
89/90	-1.7 %	-1.8 %	-6.3 %	-9.1 %	-7.9	-10.8 %	0.7 %	-1.4 %
90/91	3.7	8.9	9.8	14.6	13.9	24.8	3.4	5.5
91/92	5.2	10.2	-6.8	-11.6	-2.0	-2.6	1.9	4.6
92/93	4.1	2.5	10.7	14.4	15.2	17.3	2.1	1.8
93/94	6.3	6.8	-5.6	-13.3	0.3	-7.4	3.4	5.1
94/95	-1.8	3.4	5.0	10.0	3.1	13.8	2.9	0.9
95/96	4.9	3.5	3.6	-3.2	8.6	0.1	1.1	1.5
96/97	9.0	15.1	-6.2	0.7	2.3	15.9	-1.5	-1.9
97/98	-6.1	7.6	19.9	38.8	12.6	49.4	2.9	4.2
98/99	18.3	28.0	4.8	13.0	24.0	44.6	2.2	3.0
99/00	18.2	5.1	3.8	22.1	22.8	28.3	11.8	0.7
00/01	-14.4	1.7	-14.1	-6.7	-26.4	-5.1	1.3	9.6
01/02	11.9	6.5	2.3	8.2	14.5	15.1	3.5	3.4
02/03	16.1	21.3	-4.3	2.6	11.1	24.4	0.7	2.6
03/04	8.1	5.1	2.0	2.1	10.3	7.4	4.6	2.0
04/05	4.9	6.2	4.5	6.9	9.6	13.5	2.4	4.7
05/06	6.2	8.4	5.5	2.7	12.1	11.3	4.1	2.1
06/07	10.4	8.4	6.9	3.2	18.0	11.8	1.2	3.7
07/08	-3.0	-10.4	8.2	-3.5	5.0	-13.5	1.1	-7.7
08/09	-6.4	-14.8	9.4	24.4	2.4	6.1	-3.1	-11.2
09/10	2.7	2.4	6.7	15.2	9.6	18.0	2.6	0.1
10/11	7.2	-0.2	4.3	9.1	11.9	8.9	3.8	-0.5
11/12	3.2	3.1	-2.9	1.1	0.2	4.2	-2.0	2.7
12/13	1.3	4.4	-3.8	-2.0	-2.5	2.3	1.6	1.5
13/14	7.0	9.0	1.9	1.6	9.1	10.7	1.7	0.9
14/15	1.2	-0.9	4.2	4.4	5.4	3.5	-0.8	-4.3
15/16	-6.8	-1.5	10.4	11.0	2.8	9.4	-3.4	-3.6
Avg.	4.1 %	5.1 %	2.7 %	5.8 %	6.9 %	11.2 %	1.9 %	1.2 %
Fq>0	74 %	78 %	70	74 %	80 %	90 %	81 %	77 %

Canadian Banking Sector - Avg. Year 1990 to 2015

Cdn. Banking / TSX Comp Rel. Strength- Avg Yr. 1990-2015

Canadian Banks Performance

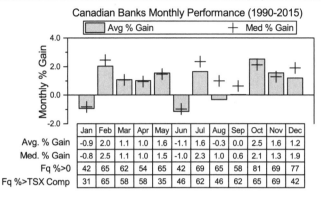

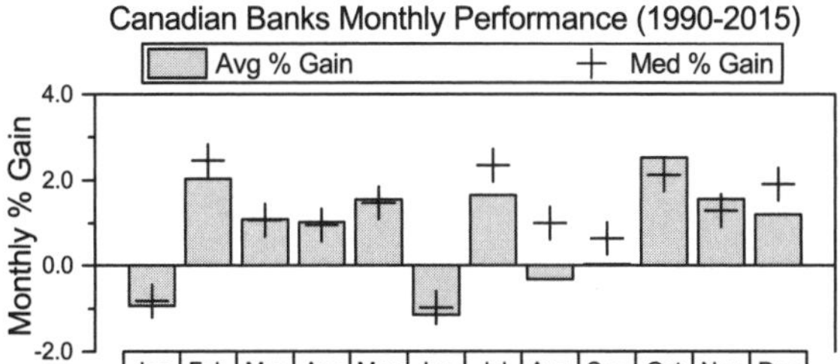
Canadian Banks Monthly Performance (1990-2015)
Avg % Gain
Med % Gain
Monthly % Gain
4.0
2.0
0.0
-2.0

	Jan	Feb	Mar	Apr	May	Jun	Jul	Aug	Sep	Oct	Nov	Dec
Avg. % Gain	-0.9	2.0	1.1	1.0	1.6	-1.1	1.6	-0.3	0.0	2.5	1.6	1.2
Med. % Gain	-0.8	2.5	1.1	1.0	1.5	-1.0	2.3	1.0	0.6	2.1	1.3	1.9
Fq %>0	42	65	62	54	65	42	69	65	58	81	69	77
Fq %>TSX Comp	31	65	58	58	35	46	62	46	62	65	69	42

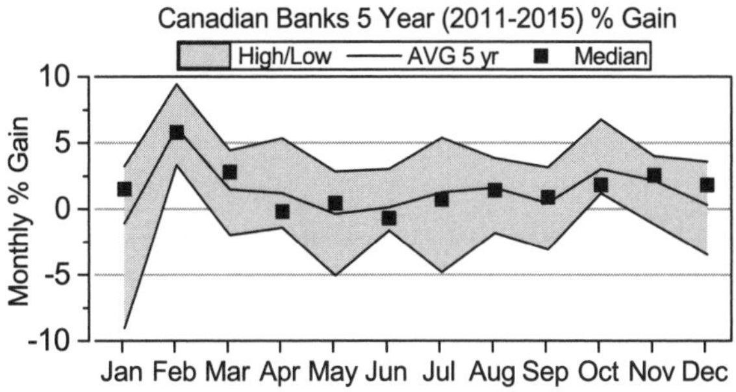
Canadian Banks 5 Year (2011-2015) % Gain
High/Low
AVG 5 yr
Median
Monthly % Gain
10
5
0
-5
-10
Jan Feb Mar Apr May Jun Jul Aug Sep Oct Nov Dec

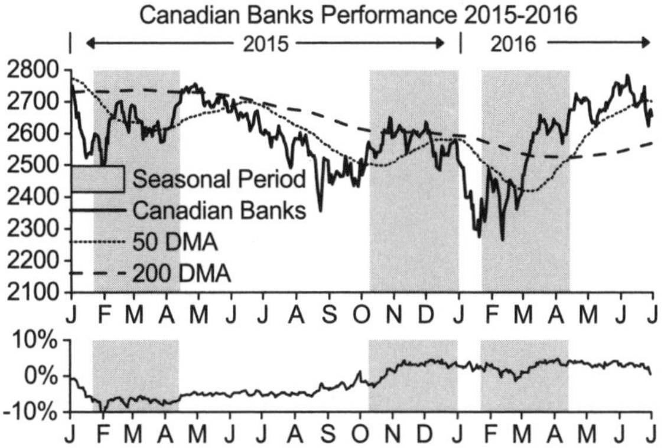
Canadian Banks Performance 2015-2016
2015
2016
2800
2700
2600
2500
2400
2300
2200
2100
Seasonal Period
Canadian Banks
50 DMA
200 DMA
J F M A M J J A S O N D J F M A M J J
10%
0%
-10%
J F M A M J J A S O N D J F M A M J J

Relative Strength, % gain vs. TSX Comp.

From 1990 to 2015, October has been the best month for Canadian banks on an average and frequency basis. One of the weaker months of the year is September. This juxtaposition makes the timing of the transition into the seasonal period that starts in October important. The second seasonal leg starts in late January. On average, January is a weak month making the timing of the transition critical.

Over the last five years, February has been the best month of the year for Canadian banks. In the late 2015 seasonal leg, Canadian banks outperformed the TSX Composite. It also outperformed the TSX Composite in its first 2016 leg.

WEEK 39

Market Indices & Rates Weekly Values**

Stock Markets	2014	2015
Dow	17,100	16,327
S&P500	1,985	1,942
Nasdaq	4,514	4,752
TSX	15,059	13,474
FTSE	6,689	6,029
DAX	9,601	9,650
Nikkei	16,244	17,726
Hang Seng	23,832	21,428
Commodities	**2014**	**2015**
Oil	93.19	45.47
Gold	1216.1	1137.7
Bond Yields	**2014**	**2015**
USA 5 Yr Treasury	1.79	1.47
USA 10 Yr T	2.55	2.16
USA 20 Yr T	3.01	2.60
Moody's Aaa	4.10	4.03
Moody's Baa	4.82	5.33
CAN 5 Yr T	1.65	0.82
CAN 10 Yr T	2.18	1.50
Money Market	**2014**	**2015**
USA Fed Funds	0.25	0.25
USA 3 Mo T-B	0.01	0.01
CAN tgt overnight rate	1.00	0.50
CAN 3 Mo T-B	0.92	0.42
Foreign Exchange	**2014**	**2015**
EUR/USD	1.28	1.12
GBP/USD	1.63	1.53
USD/CAD	1.11	1.33
USD/JPY	108.96	120.33

SEPTEMBER

M	T	W	T	F	S	S
				1	2	3
4	5	6	7	8	9	10
11	12	13	14	15	16	17
18	19	20	21	22	23	24
25	26	27	28	29	30	

OCTOBER

M	T	W	T	F	S	S
						1
2	3	4	5	6	7	8
9	10	11	12	13	14	15
16	17	18	19	20	21	22
23	24	25	26	27	28	29
30	31					

NOVEMBER

M	T	W	T	F	S	S
		1	2	3	4	5
6	7	8	9	10	11	12
13	14	15	16	17	18	19
20	21	22	23	24	25	26
27	28	29	30			

OCTOBER

	MONDAY	TUESDAY	WEDNESDAY
WEEK 40	**2** 29	**3** 28	**4** 27
WEEK 41	**9** 22 USA Bond Market Closed- Columbus Day CAN Market Closed- Thanksgiving Day	**10** 21	**11** 20
WEEK 42	**16** 15	**17** 14	**18** 13
WEEK 43	**23** 8	**24** 7	**25** 6
WEEK 44	**30** 1	**31**	1

THURSDAY		FRIDAY	
5	26	**6**	25
12	19	**13**	18
19	12	**20**	11
26	5	**27**	4
2		3	

NOVEMBER

M	T	W	T	F	S	S
		1	2	3	4	5
6	7	8	9	10	11	12
13	14	15	16	17	18	19
20	21	22	23	24	25	26
27	28	29	30			

DECEMBER

M	T	W	T	F	S	S
				1	2	3
4	5	6	7	8	9	10
11	12	13	14	15	16	17
18	19	20	21	22	23	24
25	26	27	28	29	30	31

JANUARY

M	T	W	T	F	S	S
1	2	3	4	5	6	7
8	9	10	11	12	13	14
15	16	17	18	19	20	21
22	23	24	25	26	27	28
29	30	31				

FEBRUARY

M	T	W	T	F	S	S
			1	2	3	4
5	6	7	8	9	10	11
12	13	14	15	16	17	18
19	20	21	22	23	24	25
26	27	28				

OCTOBER
S U M M A R Y

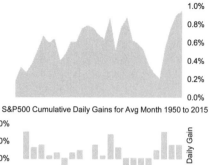

1.0%
0.8%
0.6%
0.4%
0.2%
0.0%

S&P500 Cumulative Daily Gains for Avg Month 1950 to 2015

	Dow Jones	S&P 500	Nasdaq	TSX Comp
Month Rank	7	7	6	9
# Up	40	40	25	20
# Down	26	26	19	11
% Pos	61	61	57	65
% Avg. Gain	0.7	0.9	0.9	0.1

Dow & S&P 1950-2015, Nasdaq 1972-2015, TSX 1985-2015

70%
60%
50%
40%
30%

Prob. of Daily Gain

♦ October, on average, is the most volatile month of the year for the stock market and often provides opportunities for short-term traders. The first half of October tends to be positive. ♦ The second half of the month, leading up to the last four days, tends to be negative, and prone to large drops. ♦ Seasonal opportunities in mid-October include Canadian banks, technology and transportation. ♦ In late October, a lot of sectors start their seasonal period, including the materials, industrials, consumer discretionary and retail sectors.

BEST / WORST OCTOBER BROAD MKTS. 2006-2015

BEST OCTOBER MARKETS
♦ Russell 2000 (2011) 15.0%
♦ Nasdaq (2011) 11.1%
♦ Russell 1000 (2011) 11.1%

WORST OCTOBER MARKETS
♦ Nikkei 225 (2008) -23.8%
♦ Russell 2000 (2008) -20.9%
♦ Nasdaq (2008) -17.7%

Index Values End of Month

	2006	2007	2008	2009	2010	2011	2012	2013	2014	2015
Dow	12,081	13,930	9,325	9,713	11,118	11,955	13,096	15,546	17,391	17,664
S&P 500	1,378	1,549	969	1,036	1,183	1,253	1,412	1,757	2,018	2,079
Nasdaq	2,367	2,859	1,721	2,045	2,507	2,684	2,977	3,920	4,631	5,054
TSX Comp.	12,345	14,625	9,763	10,911	12,676	12,252	12,423	13,361	14,613	13,529
Russell 1000	1,437	1,623	1,004	1,089	1,256	1,331	1,498	1,883	2,157	2,217
Russell 2000	1,906	2,058	1,336	1,399	1,748	1,842	2,035	2,734	2,916	2,888
FTSE 100	6,129	6,722	4,377	5,045	5,675	5,544	5,783	6,731	6,547	6,361
Nikkei 225	16,399	16,738	8,577	10,035	9,202	8,988	8,928	14,328	16,414	19,083

Percent Gain for October

	2006	2007	2008	2009	2010	2011	2012	2013	2014	2015
Dow	3.4	0.2	-14.1	0.0	3.1	9.5	-2.5	2.8	2.0	8.5
S&P 500	3.2	1.5	-16.9	-2.0	3.7	10.8	-2.0	4.5	2.3	8.3
Nasdaq	4.8	5.8	-17.7	-3.6	5.9	11.1	-4.5	3.9	3.1	9.4
TSX Comp.	5.0	3.7	-16.9	-4.2	2.5	5.4	0.9	4.5	-2.3	1.7
Russell 1000	3.3	1.6	-17.6	-2.3	3.8	11.1	-1.8	4.3	2.3	8.0
Russell 2000	5.7	2.8	-20.9	-6.9	4.0	15.0	-2.2	2.5	6.5	5.6
FTSE 100	2.8	3.9	-10.7	-1.7	2.3	8.1	0.7	4.2	-1.2	4.9
Nikkei 225	1.7	-0.3	-23.8	-1.0	-1.8	3.3	0.7	-0.9	1.5	9.7

October Market Avg. Performance 2006 to 2015[1]

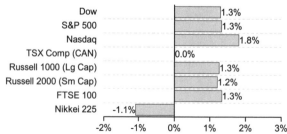

Dow	1.3%
S&P 500	1.3%
Nasdaq	1.8%
TSX Comp (CAN)	0.0%
Russell 1000 (Lg Cap)	1.3%
Russell 2000 (Sm Cap)	1.2%
FTSE 100	1.3%
Nikkei 225	-1.1%

-2% -1% 0% 1% 2% 3%

Interest Corner Oct[2]

	Fed Funds % [3]	3 Mo. T-Bill % [4]	10 Yr % [5]	20 Yr % [6]
2015	0.25	0.08	2.16	2.57
2014	0.25	0.01	2.35	2.81
2013	0.25	0.04	2.57	3.33
2012	0.25	0.11	1.72	2.46
2011	0.25	0.01	2.17	2.89

(1) Russell Data provided by Russell (2) Federal Reserve Bank of St. Louis- end of month values (3) Target rate set by FOMC (4)(5)(6) Constant yield maturities.

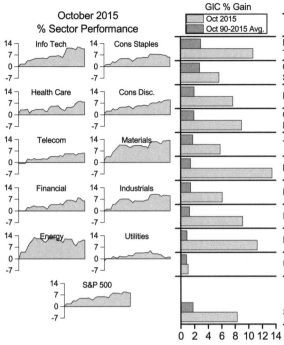

S&P GIC Sectors	2015 % Gain	1990-2015[1] GIC[2] % Avg Gain	Fq% Gain >S&P 500
Information Technology	10.7 %	3.0 %	54 %
Consumer Staples	5.6	2.8	58
Health Care	7.7	2.0	46
Consumer Discretionary	9.0	1.9	54
Telecom	5.8	1.8	38
Materials	13.4	1.4	46
Financial	6.1	1.4	42
Industrials	9.1	1.3	42
Energy	11.3	0.9	42
Utilities	1.1 %	0.8 %	38 %
S&P 500	8.3 %	1.8 %	N/A %

SELECTED SUB-SECTORS[3]			
Agriculture (1994-2015)	10.2 %	6.1 %	77 %
Railroads	0.8	4.2	69
Transportation	6.9	4.2	73
Steel	12.7	2.5	42
Pharma	7.9	2.4	58
Chemicals	15.0	2.3	54
SOX (1995-2015)	9.9	2.2	43
Biotech (1993-2015)	11.1	2.1	48
Retail	9.5	2.1	58
Banks	5.3	1.0	35
Homebuilders	0.8	0.8	34
Automotive & Components	9.5	0.7	42
Metals & Mining	10.7	0.4	38
Gold	2.5	-1.0	23
Silver	6.7	-1.2	31

Sector Commentary

♦ The consumer staples sector, on average, is one of the top performing sectors of the stock market in October. In 2015, the consumer staples sector performed well in October with a 5.6% gain, but it underperformed the S&P 500 which had produced a strong gain of 8.3%. ♦ The cyclical sectors performed well in October and in particular the materials sector which produced a gain of 13.4%. ♦ After performing poorly in September, the energy sector bounced in the month of October and produced a gain of 11.3%.

Sub-Sector Commentary

♦ With a strongly advancing S&P 500 in October 2015, the cyclical sub-sectors performed well. ♦ The chemical sub-sector produced a gain of 15.0% and steel produced a gain of 12.7%. ♦ Typically, the homebuilders sub-sector starts its seasonally period in October, but the sub-sector got off to a weak start only producing a small gain of 0.8%.

MCDONALD'S
① Oct 28-Nov 24 ② Jan 30-Apr 8

McDonald's is part of the consumer discretionary sector, but it has a slightly different seasonal pattern. Investors tend to push up the price of McDonald's stock price in autumn, but then lose interest once the holiday shopping season starts in November.

10.8% gain & 85% of the time positive

From 1989 to 2015, in the period from October 28th to November 24th, McDonald's has produced an average gain of 4.9% and has been positive 85% of the time.

McDonald's tends to underperform the S&P 500 in December and January, but once the holiday season ends and the worst month of the year for retail comes close to finishing (January), investors warm up to the idea of McDonald's once again.

McDonald's tends to perform well from January 30th to April 8th. In this period from 1990 to 2016, McDonald's has produced an average gain of 5.6% and has been positive 67% of the time.

In the summer months, investors lose interest in McDonald's and it tends to underperform the S&P 500.

The time period between July 19th to August 31st tends to be very weak for McDonald's. In this time period from 1990 to 2016, McDonald's has produced an average loss of 2.7% and has only been positive 35% of the time.

MCD* vs. S&P 500 - 1989/90 to 2015/16   Positive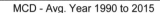

Year	Oct 28 to Nov 24 S&P 500	MCD	Jan 30 to Apr 8 S&P 500	MCD	Compound Growth S&P 500	MCD
1989/90	2.7 %	6.5 %	4.6 %	0.0 %	7.4 %	6.5 %
1990/91	3.4	13.4	12.8	32.7	16.6	50.5
1991/92	-2.1	-1.4	-3.9	-1.7	-5.9	-3.1
1992/93	2.2	6.8	0.7	3.8	2.9	10.9
1993/94	-0.5	2.8	-6.6	-5.8	-7.0	-3.1
1994/95	-3.4	0.9	7.7	8.6	4.0	9.6
1995/96	3.5	4.5	3.2	-5.0	6.8	-0.7
1996/97	6.8	7.3	-0.8	9.0	5.9	17.0
1997/98	8.0	11.2	11.8	27.2	20.7	41.5
1998/99	11.0	10.1	5.0	19.0	16.6	31.0
1999/00	9.3	14.9	11.5	0.7	21.8	15.7
2000/01	-2.7	14.2	-17.3	-11.1	-19.5	1.5
2001/02	4.1	-4.9	2.2	8.5	6.5	3.1
2002/03	3.7	0.8	1.6	10.2	5.3	11.0
2003/04	2.0	5.7	0.5	12.4	2.5	18.9
2004/05	5.0	4.2	0.8	-2.7	5.9	1.3
2005/06	7.4	6.9	0.9	-0.5	8.3	6.3
2006/07	1.7	1.0	1.6	5.9	3.4	6.9
2007/08	-6.2	-1.3	0.2	10.1	-5.9	8.7
2008/09	0.3	7.2	-2.4	-4.4	-2.0	2.5
2009/10	4.0	8.8	10.5	10.1	14.9	19.8
2010/11	1.3	2.6	4.1	3.8	5.5	6.4
2011/12	-9.6	-1.8	6.2	-0.1	-3.9	-1.8
2012/13	-0.2	0.4	3.7	6.9	3.5	7.3
2013/14	2.6	3.7	4.4	5.3	7.1	9.2
2014/15	5.5	5.6	3.0	3.8	8.7	9.7
2015/16	1.1	2.4	5.5	3.4	6.7	5.8
Avg.	2.3 %	4.9 %	2.6 %	5.6 %	5.1 %	10.8 %
Fq>0	74 %	85 %	81 %	67 %	78 %	85 %

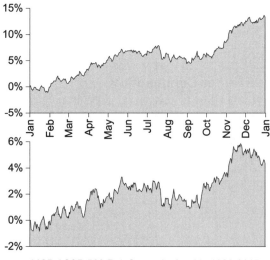

MCD - Avg. Year 1990 to 2015

MCD / S&P 500 Rel. Strength- Avg Yr. 1990-2015

ⓘ *McDonald's Corporation is in the restaurant sector. For more information, see McDonalds.com*

McDonald's Performance

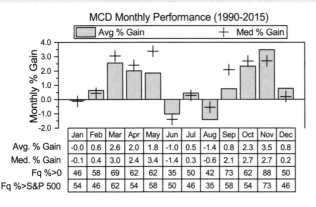

MCD Monthly Performance (1990-2015)

□ Avg % Gain   + Med % Gain

	Jan	Feb	Mar	Apr	May	Jun	Jul	Aug	Sep	Oct	Nov	Dec
Avg. % Gain	-0.0	0.6	2.6	2.0	1.8	-1.0	0.5	-1.4	0.8	2.3	3.5	0.8
Med. % Gain	-0.1	0.4	3.0	2.4	3.4	-1.4	0.3	-0.6	2.1	2.7	2.7	0.2
Fq %>0	46	58	69	62	62	35	50	42	73	62	88	50
Fq %>S&P 500	54	46	62	54	58	50	46	35	58	54	73	46

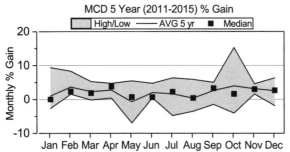

MCD 5 Year (2011-2015) % Gain

□ High/Low — AVG 5 yr ■ Median

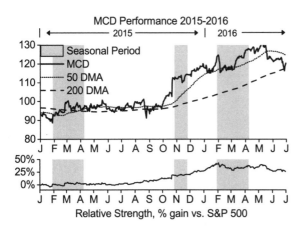

MCD Performance 2015-2016

Seasonal Period
MCD
50 DMA
200 DMA

Relative Strength, % gain vs. S&P 500

Market Indices & Rates
Weekly Values**

Stock Markets	2014	2015
Dow	16,946	16,216
S&P500	1,962	1,912
Nasdaq	4,465	4,603
TSX	14,859	13,186
FTSE	6,560	6,026
DAX	9,369	9,531
Nikkei	15,987	17,482
Hang Seng	23,076	20,970

Commodities	2014	2015
Oil	91.44	45.01
Gold	1211.9	1127.4

Bond Yields	2014	2015
USA 5 Yr Treasury	1.73	1.36
USA 10 Yr T	2.47	2.05
USA 20 Yr T	2.92	2.49
Moody's Aaa	4.00	3.98
Moody's Baa	4.76	5.33
CAN 5 Yr T	1.60	0.79
CAN 10 Yr T	2.11	1.43

Money Market	2014	2015
USA Fed Funds	0.25	0.25
USA 3 Mo T-B	0.02	0.00
CAN tgt overnight rate	1.00	0.50
CAN 3 Mo T-B	0.92	0.44

Foreign Exchange	2014	2015
EUR/USD	1.26	1.12
GBP/USD	1.62	1.52
USD/CAD	1.12	1.33
USD/JPY	109.24	119.88

OCTOBER

M	T	W	T	F	S	S
						1
2	3	4	5	6	7	8
9	10	11	12	13	14	15
16	17	18	19	20	21	22
23	24	25	26	27	28	29
30	31					

NOVEMBER

M	T	W	T	F	S	S
		1	2	3	4	5
6	7	8	9	10	11	12
13	14	15	16	17	18	19
20	21	22	23	24	25	26
27	28	29	30			

DECEMBER

M	T	W	T	F	S	S
			1	2	3	
4	5	6	7	8	9	10
11	12	13	14	15	16	17
18	19	20	21	22	23	24
25	26	27	28	29	30	31

From 1990 to 2015, McDonald's has had two periods of seasonal strength, one in the spring and one in the autumn. The trend has been weaker performance around year-end and in the summer months.

Over the last five years, from 2011 to 2015, the average and median performance has oscillated in a tight range and has not shown strong relative seasonal trends. In its autumn 2015 seasonal period, McDonald's slightly outperformed the S&P 500 in a very positive year for McDonald's. In its 2016 seasonal period, McDonald's slightly underperformed the S&P 500.

HOMEBUILDERS—
TIME TO BREAK & TIME TO BUILD
①SELL SHORT (Apr27-Jun13) ②LONG (Oct28-Feb3)

The homebuilders sector has been in the spotlight for the last few years: first when the mortgage meltdown occurred in 2007 and 2008, and more recently, as the housing market has bounced back giving the homebuilders sector a boost.

21.0% gain & positive 20 times out of 26

Historically, the best time to be in the homebuilders sector has been from October 28th to February 3rd. In this time period, during the years 1990/91 to 2015/16, the homebuilders sector has produced an average gain of 16.7% and have been positive 88% of the time.

In the 2015/16 seasonal period, investors became very concerned about the possible impact of the U.S. Federal Reserve raising its discount rate on the U.S. economy and the housing market. As a result, the homebuilders sector produced a loss.

Generally the time period outside of the strong seasonal period for homebuilders, should be avoided by investors, as not only has the average performance relative to the S&P 500 been negative, but the sector has produced both large gains and losses. In other words, the risk is substantially higher that a large drawdown will occur.

This is particularly true for the time period from April 27th to June 13th. In this time period from 1990 to 2015, the homebuilders sector produced an average loss of 3.5% and was only positive 31% of the time.

ⓘ *Homebuilders: SP GIC Sector: An index designed to represent a cross section of homebuilding companies.*
For more information, see www.standardandpoors.com.

Homebuilders (HB)* vs. S&P 500 1990/91 to 2015/16
Negative Short □   Positive Long ▢

	SHORT Apr 27 to Jun 13		LONG Oct 28 to Feb 3		Compound Growth	
	S&P		S&P		S&P	
Year	500	HB	500	HB	500	HB
1990/91	9.6 %	7.9 %	12.6 %	58.0 %	1.8 %	45.5 %
1991/92	-0.4	-4.8	6.6	41.2	7.0	48.0
1992/93	0.2	-11.5	6.9	26.7	6.7	41.2
1993/94	3.2	12.6	3.5	8.6	0.2	-5.1
1994/95	1.6	-4.0	2.8	-4.0	1.1	-0.2
1995/96	4.6	11.1	9.7	16.7	4.7	3.7
1996/97	2.2	10.6	12.2	6.3	9.8	-4.9
1997/98	16.7	22.6	14.7	24.8	-4.5	-3.4
1998/99	-0.8	-10.6	19.4	12.4	20.4	24.2
1999/00	-4.9	-7.1	9.9	-3.9	15.3	2.9
2000/01	0.6	-3.8	-2.2	18.6	-2.7	23.1
2001/02	0.6	-17.5	1.6	43.1	1.0	68.1
2002/03	-6.2	-5.3	-4.2	6.7	1.8	12.3
2003/04	10.0	31.5	10.2	7.6	-0.8	-26.3
2004/05	0.1	-2.6	5.7	23.7	5.6	26.9
2005/06	4.3	11.9	7.2	14.8	2.7	1.1
2006/07	-6.3	-27.1	5.2	16.8	11.7	48.4
2007/08	1.4	-7.9	-9.1	8.8	-10.4	17.4
2008/09	-2.7	-25.3	-1.2	27.7	1.4	60.0
2009/10	9.2	-25.1	3.2	15.5	-6.3	44.4
2010/11	-9.9	-22.9	10.5	12.9	21.5	38.7
2011/12	-5.6	-11.2	4.7	35.0	10.6	50.1
2012/13	-6.1	-9.3	7.2	13.7	13.7	24.3
2013/14	3.4	-7.2	-1.0	10.1	-4.4	18.1
2014/15	3.9	4.5	4.5	7.8	0.4	3.0
2015/16	-1.1	-0.8	-7.4	-15.3	-6.4	-14.6
Avg.	1.1 %	-3.5 %	5.1 %	16.7 %	3.9 %	21.0 %
Fq>0	62 %	31 %	77 %	88 %	73 %	77 %

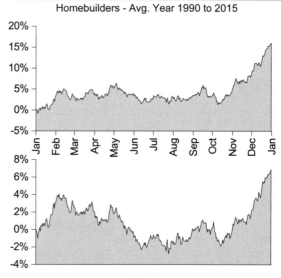

Homebuilders - Avg. Year 1990 to 2015

Homebuilders / S&P 500 Rel. Strength- Avg Yr. 1990-2015

Homebuilders Performance

Homebuilders Monthly Performance (1990-2015)

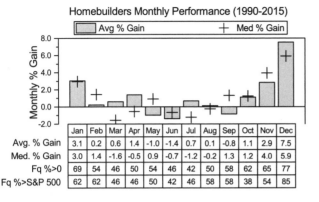

	Jan	Feb	Mar	Apr	May	Jun	Jul	Aug	Sep	Oct	Nov	Dec
Avg. % Gain	3.1	0.2	0.6	1.4	-1.0	-1.4	0.7	0.1	-0.8	1.1	2.9	7.5
Med. % Gain	3.0	1.4	-1.6	-0.5	0.9	-0.7	-1.2	-0.2	1.3	1.2	4.0	5.9
Fq %>0	69	54	46	50	54	46	42	50	58	62	65	77
Fq %>S&P 500	62	62	46	46	50	42	46	58	58	38	54	85

Homebuilders 5 Year (2011-2015) % Gain

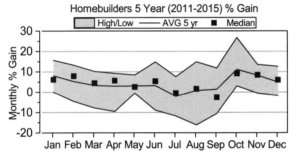

Homebuilders Performance 2015-2016

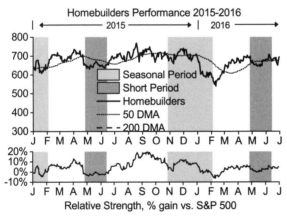

Relative Strength, % gain vs. S&P 500

Market Indices & Rates
Weekly Values**

Stock Markets	2014	2015
Dow	16,782	16,923
S&P500	1,941	1,998
Nasdaq	4,393	4,792
TSX	14,535	13,802
FTSE	6,463	6,350
DAX	9,017	9,956
Nikkei	15,610	18,219
Hang Seng	23,325	22,203
Commodities	**2014**	**2015**
Oil	87.62	48.33
Gold	1213.8	1144.7
Bond Yields	**2014**	**2015**
USA 5 Yr Treasury	1.61	1.37
USA 10 Yr T	2.36	2.09
USA 20 Yr T	2.82	2.53
Moody's Aaa	3.92	4.01
Moody's Baa	4.68	5.38
CAN 5 Yr T	1.52	0.82
CAN 10 Yr T	2.04	1.47
Money Market	**2014**	**2015**
USA Fed Funds	0.25	0.25
USA 3 Mo T-B	0.01	0.00
CAN tgt overnight rate	1.00	0.50
CAN 3 Mo T-B	0.90	0.41
Foreign Exchange	**2014**	**2015**
EUR/USD	1.27	1.13
GBP/USD	1.61	1.53
USD/CAD	1.12	1.30
USD/JPY	108.08	120.18

OCTOBER

M	T	W	T	F	S	S
						1
2	3	4	5	6	7	8
9	10	11	12	13	14	15
16	17	18	19	20	21	22
23	24	25	26	27	28	29
30	31					

NOVEMBER

M	T	W	T	F	S	S
		1	2	3	4	5
6	7	8	9	10	11	12
13	14	15	16	17	18	19
20	21	22	23	24	25	26
27	28	29	30			

DECEMBER

M	T	W	T	F	S	S
				1	2	3
4	5	6	7	8	9	10
11	12	13	14	15	16	17
18	19	20	21	22	23	24
25	26	27	28	29	30	31

From 1990/91 to 2015/16, the best month of the year for the homebuilders sector has been December on an average, median and frequency basis. On average, it has been best to enter the sector in late October and exit in early February. The months immediately after February do not perform particularly well for the sector. In particular, May and June on average have produced a loss. Over the last five years, on average, the homebuilders sector has followed its general seasonal trend. In 2015/16, the seasonal long position was negative and substantially underperformed the S&P 500. Shortly after its seasonal period the sector started to outperform the S&P 500.

UNITED TECHNOLOGIES
UTX ①Jan23-May5 ②Oct10-Dec31

United Technologies is a conglomerate industrial company and as such has similar seasonal periods to the industrial sector. The difference is that United Technologies starts one of its seasonal periods earlier in October. The industrial sector starts its seasonal period on October 28th, whereas United Technologies starts its seasonal period on October 10th.

During the time period from October 10th to October 27th, in the years 1990 to 2015, United Technologies has produced an average gain of 3.1% and has been positive 65% of the time. As a result, it is worthwhile to consider entering a position in United Technologies before the start of the industrial sector's seasonal period. When United Technologies outperforms in early October, it is often a precursor of what to expect for the broad market.

The combined trade of January 23rd to May 5th and October 10th to December 31st has produced a 19.3% gain and has been successful 96% of the time since 1990.

Investors should note that being positive 96% of the time in the past does not guarantee the success of the trade in the future. Nevertheless, it does indicate the strength of the seasonal trade.

8.9% extra & positive 25 times out of 26

Given that United Technologies produces 6% of its revenues from China (Reuters), investors should be looking to the strength of the Chinese economy in order to help determine the possible strength of the United Technologies seasonal trade.

(i) *United Technologies Corporation is a multinational conglomerate in the industrial sector. For more information, see UTC.com*

UTX* vs. S&P 500 - 1990 to 2015   Positive ☐

Year	Jan 23 to May 5 S&P 500	UTX	Oct 10 to Dec 31 S&P 500	UTX	Compound Growth S&P 500	UTX
1990	2.4 %	10.2 %	8.2 %	5.2 %	10.8 %	15.9 %
1991	16.0	4.0	10.7	27.3	28.4	32.4
1992	-0.3	-0.9	8.2	4.1	7.9	3.1
1993	1.9	4.7	1.3	8.5	3.3	13.7
1994	-4.9	-0.4	0.9	1.2	-4.0	0.8
1995	11.9	15.0	6.5	12.0	19.2	28.8
1996	4.6	14.1	6.3	7.8	11.2	23.0
1997	5.6	15.9	0.0	-7.5	5.6	7.3
1998	15.8	31.5	24.9	41.7	44.6	86.3
1999	10.0	27.2	10.0	9.7	20.9	39.6
2000	-0.6	7.7	-5.8	12.2	-6.4	20.9
2001	-5.7	9.9	8.6	26.7	2.5	39.2
2002	-4.1	7.6	13.3	25.9	8.6	35.5
2003	5.5	-2.6	7.1	14.7	12.9	11.8
2004	-2.0	-9.6	8.0	11.8	5.9	1.1
2005	0.4	2.3	4.4	11.5	4.8	14.1
2006	5.1	18.0	5.0	-4.1	10.4	13.2
2007	5.8	6.1	-6.2	-5.7	-0.7	0.0
2008	7.4	11.0	-0.7	15.7	6.6	28.4
2009	9.2	5.9	4.1	11.7	13.7	18.2
2010	6.8	6.5	7.9	8.0	15.3	15.0
2011	4.0	10.4	8.8	2.3	13.2	12.9
2012	4.1	3.6	-1.1	6.1	3.0	9.9
2013	8.2	6.5	11.6	10.7	20.7	17.8
2014	2.2	0.6	6.8	15.1	9.1	15.8
2015	1.3	-4.5	1.4	0.7	2.7	-3.8
Avg.	4.3 %	7.7 %	5.8 %	10.5 %	10.4 %	19.3 %
Fq>0	77 %	81 %	81 %	88 %	88 %	96 %

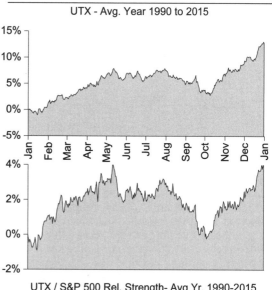

UTX - Avg. Year 1990 to 2015

UTX / S&P 500 Rel. Strength- Avg Yr. 1990-2015

UTX Performance

UTX Monthly Performance (1990-2015)

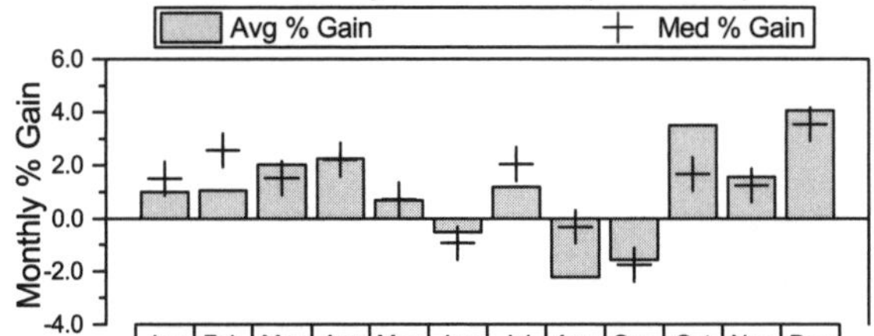

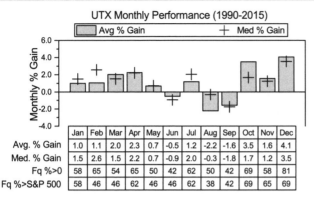

	Jan	Feb	Mar	Apr	May	Jun	Jul	Aug	Sep	Oct	Nov	Dec
Avg. % Gain	1.0	1.1	2.0	2.3	0.7	-0.5	1.2	-2.2	-1.6	3.5	1.6	4.1
Med. % Gain	1.5	2.6	1.5	2.2	0.7	-0.9	2.0	-0.3	-1.8	1.7	1.2	3.5
Fq %>0	58	65	54	65	50	42	62	50	42	69	58	81
Fq %>S&P 500	58	46	46	62	46	46	62	38	42	69	65	69

UTX 5 Year (2011-2015) % Gain

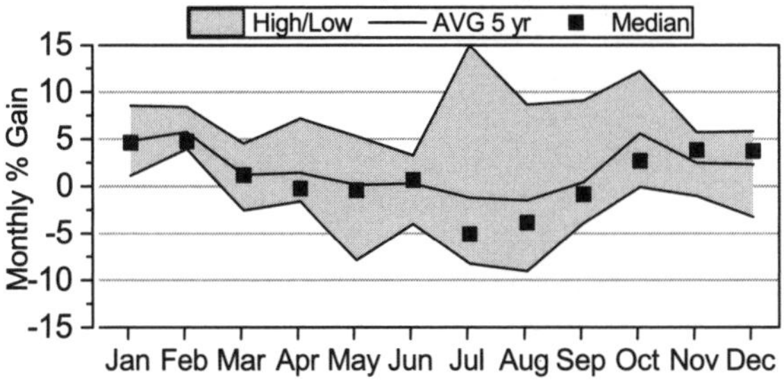

UTX Performance 2015-2016

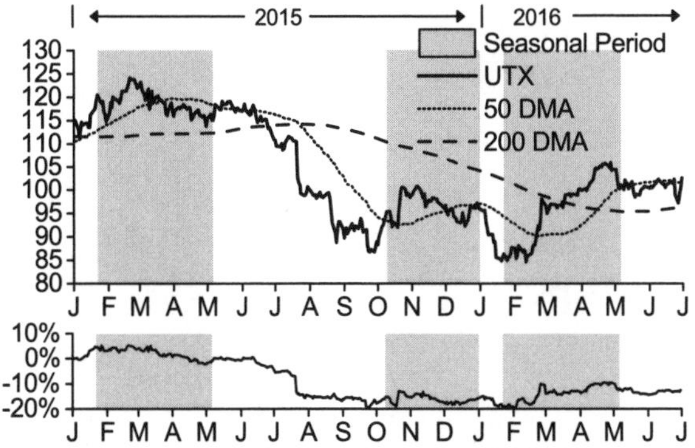

Relative Strength, % gain vs. S&P 500

From 1990 to 2015, the best month for United Technologies is December on an average, median and frequency basis. December is the last month of the autumn seasonal period and as such, investors should give the stock some leeway to demonstrate its strength at this time. Over the last five years, United Technologies has generally followed its seasonal trend with weaker summer months. The dispersion of returns in the summer months was much larger than at other times, despite the average poor performance at this time. In the 2015/16 seasonal trade, United Technologies underperformed in its first two legs of its seasonal trade, but managed to outperform in its 2016 seasonal period.

WEEK 42

Market Indices & Rates
Weekly Values**

Stock Markets	**2014**	**2015**
Dow	16,255	17,099
S&P500	1,873	2,014
Nasdaq	4,226	4,835
TSX	14,047	13,847
FTSE	6,295	6,340
DAX	8,729	10,048
Nikkei	14,820	18,129
Hang Seng	23,051	22,745
Commodities	**2014**	**2015**
Oil	82.96	46.81
Gold	1234.7	1173.8
Bond Yields	**2014**	**2015**
USA 5 Yr Treasury	1.41	1.34
USA 10 Yr T	2.19	2.03
USA 20 Yr T	2.67	2.46
Moody's Aaa	3.83	3.92
Moody's Baa	4.62	5.32
CAN 5 Yr T	1.43	0.82
CAN 10 Yr T	1.95	1.45
Money Market	**2014**	**2015**
USA Fed Funds	0.25	0.25
USA 3 Mo T-B	0.02	0.01
CAN tgt overnight rate	1.00	0.50
CAN 3 Mo T-B	0.88	0.40
Foreign Exchange	**2014**	**2015**
EUR/USD	1.28	1.14
GBP/USD	1.60	1.54
USD/CAD	1.13	1.30
USD/JPY	106.61	119.39

OCTOBER

M	T	W	T	F	S	S
						1
2	3	4	5	6	7	8
9	10	11	12	13	14	15
16	17	18	19	20	21	22
23	24	25	26	27	28	29
30	31					

NOVEMBER

M	T	W	T	F	S	S
		1	2	3	4	5
6	7	8	9	10	11	12
13	14	15	16	17	18	19
20	21	22	23	24	25	26
27	28	29	30			

DECEMBER

M	T	W	T	F	S	S
				1	2	3
4	5	6	7	8	9	10
11	12	13	14	15	16	17
18	19	20	21	22	23	24
25	26	27	28	29	30	31

RETAIL – SHOP EARLY
October 28th to November 29th

The *Retail – Shop Early* strategy is the second retail sector strategy of the year and it occurs before the biggest shopping season of the year – the Christmas holiday season.

3.0% extra & 81% of the time better than S&P 500

The time to go shopping for retail stocks is at the end of October, which is about one month before Thanksgiving. It is the time when two favorable influences happen at the same time.

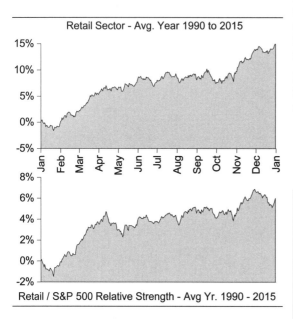

Retail Sector - Avg. Year 1990 to 2015

Retail / S&P 500 Relative Strength - Avg Yr. 1990 - 2015

prefer not to invest in this sector until it comes back into favor towards the end of October.

The trick to investing is not to be too early, but early. If an investor gets into a sector too early, they can suffer from the frustration of having dead money– an investment that goes nowhere, while the rest of the market increases.

If an investor moves into a sector too late, there is very little upside potential. In fact, this can be a dangerous strategy because if the sales or earnings numbers disappoint the analysts, the sector can severely correct.

For the *Retail – Shop Early* strategy, the time to enter is approximately one month before Black Friday.

First, historically, the three best months in a row for the stock market have been November, December and January. The end of October usually represents an excellent buying opportunity, not only for the next three months, but the next six months.

Second, investors tend to buy retail stocks in anticipation of a strong holiday sales season. At the same time that the market tends to increase, investors are attracted back into the retail sector.

Retail sales tend to be lower in the summer and a lot of investors view investing in retail stocks at this time as dead money. During the summertime, investors

Retail Sector vs. S&P 500 1990 to 2015

Oct 28 to Nov 29	Positive		
	S&P 500	Retail	Diff
1990	3.8 %	9.9 %	6.0 %
1991	-2.3	2.7	5.0
1992	2.8	5.5	2.8
1993	-0.6	6.3	6.9
1994	-2.3	0.4	2.7
1995	4.8	9.5	4.7
1996	8.0	0.4	-7.6
1997	8.9	16.9	7.9
1998	11.9	20.4	8.4
1999	8.6	14.1	5.5
2000	-2.7	9.9	12.6
2001	3.2	7.9	4.7
2002	4.3	-1.7	-6.0
2003	2.6	2.5	-0.1
2004	4.7	7.0	2.3
2005	6.7	9.9	3.2
2006	1.6	0.2	-1.4
2007	-4.3	-7.5	-3.2
2008	5.6	7.5	1.9
2009	2.6	3.6	1.0
2010	0.5	5.2	4.7
2011	-7.0	-4.5	2.5
2012	0.3	5.1	4.8
2013	2.6	5.0	2.4
2014	5.4	8.9	3.5
2015	1.2	3.9	2.7
Avg.	2.7 %	5.7 %	3.0 %
Fq > 0	77 %	88 %	81 %

Retail Performance

Retail Monthly Performance (1990-2015)

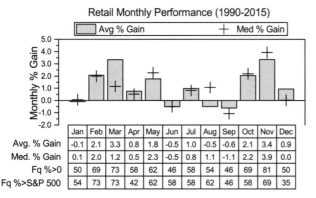

	Jan	Feb	Mar	Apr	May	Jun	Jul	Aug	Sep	Oct	Nov	Dec
Avg. % Gain	-0.1	2.1	3.3	0.8	1.8	-0.5	1.0	-0.5	-0.6	2.1	3.4	0.9
Med. % Gain	0.1	2.0	1.2	0.5	2.3	-0.5	0.8	1.1	-1.1	2.2	3.9	0.0
Fq %>0	50	69	73	58	62	46	58	54	46	69	81	50
Fq %>S&P 500	54	73	73	42	62	58	58	62	46	58	69	35

Retail 5 Year (2011-2015) % Gain

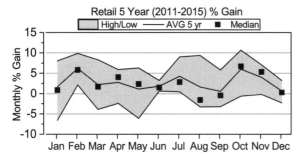

Retail Performance 2015-2016

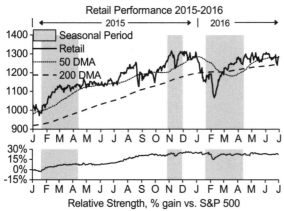

Relative Strength, % gain vs. S&P 500

Market Indices & Rates
Weekly Values**

Stock Markets	2014	2015
Dow	16,592	17,350
S&P500	1,938	2,042
Nasdaq	4,411	4,916
TSX	14,446	13,827
FTSE	6,369	6,373
DAX	8,916	10,367
Nikkei	15,108	18,431
Hang Seng	23,240	23,016

Commodities	2014	2015
Oil	82.11	44.91
Gold	1240.8	1169.7

Bond Yields	2014	2015
USA 5 Yr Treasury	1.47	1.38
USA 10 Yr T	2.25	2.06
USA 20 Yr T	2.73	2.50
Moody's Aaa	3.93	3.92
Moody's Baa	4.68	5.33
CAN 5 Yr T	1.45	0.84
CAN 10 Yr T	1.98	1.48

Money Market	2014	2015
USA Fed Funds	0.25	0.25
USA 3 Mo T-B	0.02	0.01
CAN tgt overnight rate	1.00	0.50
CAN 3 Mo T-B	0.89	0.40

Foreign Exchange	2014	2015
EUR/USD	1.27	1.12
GBP/USD	1.61	1.54
USD/CAD	1.12	1.31
USD/JPY	107.50	120.29

OCTOBER

M	T	W	T	F	S	S
						1
2	3	4	5	6	7	8
9	10	11	12	13	14	15
16	17	18	19	20	21	22
23	24	25	26	27	28	29
30	31					

NOVEMBER

M	T	W	T	F	S	S
		1	2	3	4	5
6	7	8	9	10	11	12
13	14	15	16	17	18	19
20	21	22	23	24	25	26
27	28	29	30			

DECEMBER

M	T	W	T	F	S	S
				1	2	3
4	5	6	7	8	9	10
11	12	13	14	15	16	17
18	19	20	21	22	23	24
25	26	27	28	29	30	31

From 1990 to 2015, the two best months for the retail sector were March and November, on an average basis. November is the core part of the autumn retail seasonal trade and has the highest monthly median performance. Over the last five years, on average, the retail sector has followed its general seasonal pattern, with the strongest months being February, April, October and November. These months are part of either the spring seasonal trade or the autumn seasonal trade. In 2015, the retail sector outperformed the S&P 500 in its autumn seasonal period and in 2016, it underperformed in its spring seasonal period.

INDUSTRIAL STRENGTH
①Oct28-Dec31 ②Jan23-May5

The industrial sector's seasonal trends are largely the same as the broad market, such as the S&P 500. Although the trends are similar, there still exists an opportunity to take advantage of the time period when the industrial sector tends to outperform.

11.6% gain & positive 93% of the time

Industrials tend to outperform in the favorable six months, but there is an opportunity to temporarily get out of the sector to avoid a time period when the sector has, on average, decreased before turning positive again.

The overall strategy is to be invested in the industrial sector from October 28th to December 31st, sell at the end of the day on the 31st, and re-enter the sector to be invested from January 23rd to May 5th.

Using the complete *Industrial Strength* strategy from 1989/90 to 2015/16, the industrial sector has produced a total compound average annual gain of 11.6%.

In addition, the industrial sector has been positive 93% of the time and has outperformed the S&P 500, 74% of the time.

During the time period from January 1st to January 22nd, in the yearly period from 1990 to 2015, the industrial sector has on average lost 0.7% and has only been positive 48% of the time.

It should be noted that longer term investors may decide to be invested during the whole time period from October 28th to May 5th. Shorter term investors may decide to use technical analysis to determine, if and when, they should temporarily sell the industrials sector during its weak period from January 1st to January 22nd.

Industrials* vs. S&P 500 1989/90 to 2015/16   Positive ▢

Year	Oct 28 to Dec 31 S&P 500	Ind.	Jan 23 to May 5 S&P 500	Ind.	Compound Growth S&P 500	Ind.
1989/90	5.5 %	6.9 %	2.4 %	5.5 %	8.0 %	12.7 %
1990/91	8.4	10.7	16.0	15.2	25.7	27.5
1991/92	8.6	7.2	-0.3	-1.0	8.2	6.1
1992/93	4.1	6.3	1.9	5.4	6.1	12.0
1993/94	0.4	5.1	-4.9	-6.7	-4.5	-2.0
1994/95	-1.4	-0.5	11.9	12.4	10.3	11.8
1995/96	6.3	10.7	4.6	7.6	11.1	19.1
1996/97	5.7	4.5	5.6	5.2	11.6	9.9
1997/98	10.7	10.5	15.8	11.5	28.2	23.2
1998/99	15.4	10.5	10.0	19.5	26.9	32.1
1999/00	13.3	10.8	-0.6	4.5	12.6	15.8
2000/01	-4.3	1.8	-5.7	4.7	-9.7	6.6
2001/02	3.9	8.1	-4.1	-5.3	-0.3	2.4
2002/03	-2.0	-1.3	5.5	8.6	3.4	7.1
2003/04	7.8	11.6	-2.0	-3.3	5.7	7.9
2004/05	7.7	8.7	0.4	0.2	8.1	8.9
2005/06	5.9	7.6	5.1	14.3	11.3	23.0
2006/07	3.0	3.1	5.8	6.8	9.0	10.1
2007/08	-4.4	-3.4	7.4	9.7	2.7	6.0
2008/09	6.4	7.1	9.2	6.1	16.2	13.7
2009/10	4.9	6.4	6.8	13.4	12.0	20.6
2010/11	6.4	8.1	4.0	4.9	10.6	13.5
2011/12	-2.1	-1.0	4.1	0.3	1.9	-0.7
2012/13	1.0	4.1	8.2	4.9	9.3	9.2
2013/14	5.0	7.3	2.2	1.6	7.3	9.0
2014/15	5.0	5.2	1.3	-1.0	6.3	4.1
2015/16	-1.1	-1.2	4.3	5.6	3.1	4.3
Avg.	4.4 %	5.7 %	4.3 %	5.6 %	8.9 %	11.6 %
Fq > 0	78 %	81 %	77 %	81 %	89 %	93 %

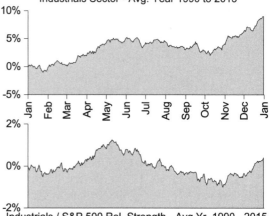

Industrials Sector - Avg. Year 1990 to 2015

Industrials / S&P 500 Rel. Strength - Avg Yr. 1990 - 2015

> **(Y)** *Alternate Strategy—*
> *Investors can bridge the gap between the two positive seasonal trends for the industrials sector by holding from October 28th to May 5th. Longer term investors may prefer this strategy, shorter term investors can use technical tools to determine the appropriate strategy.*

> **(i)** **The SP GICS Industrial Sector. For more information on the industrials sector, see www.standardandpoors.com*

Industrials Performance

Industrials Monthly Performance (1990-2015)

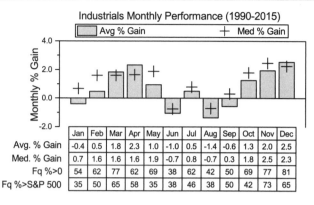

	Jan	Feb	Mar	Apr	May	Jun	Jul	Aug	Sep	Oct	Nov	Dec
Avg. % Gain	-0.4	0.5	1.8	2.3	1.0	-1.0	0.5	-1.4	-0.6	1.3	2.0	2.5
Med. % Gain	0.7	1.6	1.6	1.6	1.9	-0.7	0.8	-0.7	0.3	1.8	2.5	2.3
Fq %>0	54	62	77	62	69	38	62	42	50	69	77	81
Fq %>S&P 500	35	50	65	58	35	38	46	38	50	42	73	65

Industrials 5 Year (2011-2015) % Gain

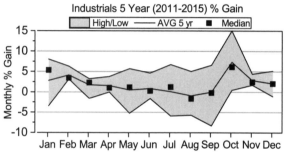

Industrials Performance 2015-2016

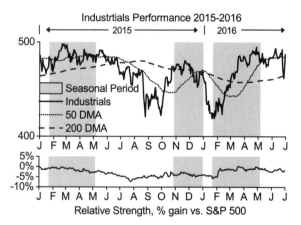

Relative Strength, % gain vs. S&P 500

Market Indices & Rates
Weekly Values**

Stock Markets	2014	2015
Dow	17,077	17,681
S&P500	1,988	2,079
Nasdaq	4,559	5,058
TSX	14,539	13,735
FTSE	6,446	6,395
DAX	9,099	10,795
Nikkei	15,669	18,929
Hang Seng	23,637	22,935

Commodities	2014	2015
Oil	81.26	45.15
Gold	1209.6	1160.5

Bond Yields	2014	2015
USA 5 Yr Treasury	1.57	1.46
USA 10 Yr T	2.32	2.11
USA 20 Yr T	2.78	2.53
Moody's Aaa	3.92	3.94
Moody's Baa	4.72	5.33
CAN 5 Yr T	1.53	0.83
CAN 10 Yr T	2.04	1.49

Money Market	2014	2015
USA Fed Funds	0.25	0.25
USA 3 Mo T-B	0.02	0.05
CAN tgt overnight rate	1.00	0.50
CAN 3 Mo T-B	0.89	0.41

Foreign Exchange	2014	2015
EUR/USD	1.26	1.10
GBP/USD	1.61	1.53
USD/CAD	1.12	1.32
USD/JPY	109.28	120.88

OCTOBER

M	T	W	T	F	S	S
						1
2	3	4	5	6	7	8
9	10	11	12	13	14	15
16	17	18	19	20	21	22
23	24	25	26	27	28	29
30	31					

NOVEMBER

M	T	W	T	F	S	S
	1	2	3	4	5
6	7	8	9	10	11	12
13	14	15	16	17	18	19
20	21	22	23	24	25	26
27	28	29	30			

DECEMBER

M	T	W	T	F	S	S
				1	2	3
4	5	6	7	8	9	10
11	12	13	14	15	16	17
18	19	20	21	22	23	24
25	26	27	28	29	30	31

From 1990 to 2015, the sweet spot for the industrial sector trade, on average, has been November and December. The worst two months have been June and August.

Over the last five years, on average, the industrial sector has somewhat followed its seasonal trend, with its poorest performance in the summer months and its better performance in the autumn months.

In 2015, the industrial sector nominally underperformed in its autumn seasonal leg and then outperformed in its 2016 spring seasonal period.

NOVEMBER

	MONDAY	TUESDAY	WEDNESDAY
WEEK 44	30	31	1 29
WEEK 45	6 24	7 23	8 22
WEEK 46	13 17	14 16	15 15
WEEK 47	20 10	21 9	22 8
WEEK 48	27 3	28 2	29 1

THURSDAY		FRIDAY	
2	28	**3**	27
9	21	**10**	20
		USA Bond Market Closed-Veterans Day	
		CAD Bond Market Closed-Remembrance Day	
16	14	**17**	13
23	7	**24**	6
USA Market Closed-Thanksgiving Day		USA Early Market Close Thanksgiving	
30		1	

DECEMBER

M	T	W	T	F	S	S
				1	2	3
4	5	6	7	8	9	10
11	12	13	14	15	16	17
18	19	20	21	22	23	24
25	26	27	28	29	30	31

JANUARY

M	T	W	T	F	S	S
1	2	3	4	5	6	7
8	9	10	11	12	13	14
15	16	17	18	19	20	21
22	23	24	25	26	27	28
29	30	31				

FEBRUARY

M	T	W	T	F	S	S
			1	2	3	4
5	6	7	8	9	10	11
12	13	14	15	16	17	18
19	20	21	22	23	24	25
26	27	28				

MARCH

M	T	W	T	F	S	S
			1	2	3	4
5	6	7	8	9	10	11
12	13	14	15	16	17	18
19	20	21	22	23	24	25
26	27	28	29	30	31	

NOVEMBER
S U M M A R Y

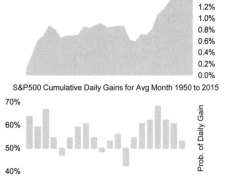

	Dow Jones	S&P 500	Nasdaq	TSX Comp
Month Rank	3	2	3	8
# Up	45	44	30	18
# Down	21	22	14	13
% Pos	68	67	68	58
% Avg. Gain	1.5	1.5	1.7	0.6

Dow & S&P 1950-2015, Nasdaq 1972-2015, TSX 1985-2015

S&P500 Cumulative Daily Gains for Avg Month 1950 to 2015

♦ November, on average, is one of the better months of the year for the S&P 500. From 1950 to 2015, it has produced an average gain of 1.5% and has been positive 67% of the time. ♦ In November, the cyclical sectors start to increase their relative performance to the S&P 500, with the metals and mining sector starting its period of seasonal strength on November 16th. ♦ For investors looking for a short-term investment, the day before and the day after Thanksgiving are on average the two strongest days of the year.

BEST / WORST NOVEMBER BROAD MKTS. 2006-2015

BEST NOVEMBER MARKETS
- Nikkei 225 (2013) 9.3%
- Nikkei 225 (2010) 8.0%
- Dow Jones (2009) 6.5%

WORST NOVEMBER MARKETS
- Russell 2000 (2008) -12.0%
- Nasdaq (2008) -10.8%
- Russell 1000 (2008) -7.9%

Index Values End of Month

	2006	2007	2008	2009	2010	2011	2012	2013	2014	2015
Dow	12,222	13,372	8,829	10,345	11,006	12,046	13,026	16,086	17,828	17,720
S&P 500	1,401	1,481	896	1,096	1,181	1,247	1,416	1,806	2,068	2,080
Nasdaq	2,432	2,661	1,536	2,145	2,498	2,620	3,010	4,060	4,792	5,109
TSX Comp.	12,752	13,689	9,271	11,447	12,953	12,204	12,239	13,395	14,745	13,470
Russell 1000	1,464	1,550	925	1,150	1,258	1,324	1,506	1,932	2,209	2,220
Russell 2000	1,954	1,908	1,176	1,441	1,807	1,833	2,043	2,840	2,916	2,978
FTSE 100	6,049	6,433	4,288	5,191	5,528	5,505	5,867	6,651	6,723	6,356
Nikkei 225	16,274	15,681	8,512	9,346	9,937	8,435	9,446	15,662	17,460	19,747

Percent Gain for November

	2006	2007	2008	2009	2010	2011	2012	2013	2014	2015
Dow	1.2	-4.0	-5.3	6.5	-1.0	0.8	-0.5	3.5	2.5	0.3
S&P 500	1.6	-4.4	-7.5	5.7	-0.2	-0.5	0.3	2.8	2.5	0.1
Nasdaq	2.7	-6.9	-10.8	4.9	-0.4	-2.4	1.1	3.6	3.5	1.1
TSX Comp.	3.3	-6.4	-5.0	4.9	2.2	-0.4	-1.5	0.3	0.9	-0.4
Russell 1000	1.9	-4.5	-7.9	5.6	0.1	-0.5	0.5	2.6	2.4	0.1
Russell 2000	2.5	-7.3	-12.0	3.0	3.4	-0.5	0.4	3.9	0.0	3.1
FTSE 100	-1.3	-4.3	-2.0	2.9	-2.6	-0.7	1.5	-1.2	2.7	-0.1
Nikkei 225	-0.8	-6.3	-0.8	-6.9	8.0	-6.2	5.8	9.3	6.4	3.5

November Market Avg. Performance 2006 to 2015[1]

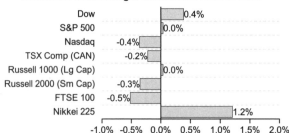

	Dow	0.4%
	S&P 500	0.0%
	Nasdaq	-0.4%
	TSX Comp (CAN)	-0.2%
	Russell 1000 (Lg Cap)	0.0%
	Russell 2000 (Sm Cap)	-0.3%
	FTSE 100	-0.5%
	Nikkei 225	1.2%

Interest Corner Nov[2]

	Fed Funds %[3]	3 Mo. T-Bill %[4]	10 Yr %[5]	20 Yr %[6]
2015	0.25	0.22	2.21	2.63
2014	0.25	0.02	2.18	2.62
2013	0.25	0.06	2.75	3.54
2012	0.25	0.08	1.62	2.37
2011	0.25	0.01	2.08	2.77

(1) Russell Data provided by Russell (2) Federal Reserve Bank of St. Louis- end of month values (3) Target rate set by FOMC (4)(5)(6) Constant yield maturities.

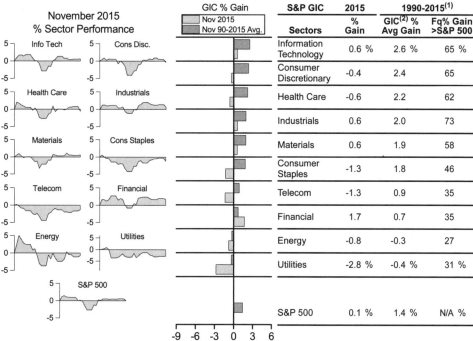

November 2015 % Sector Performance	GIC % Gain	S&P GIC	2015	1990-2015[1]	
	Nov 2015 / Nov 90-2015 Avg.	Sectors	% Gain	GIC[2] % Avg Gain	Fq% Gain >S&P 500
Info Tech / Cons Disc.		Information Technology	0.6 %	2.6 %	65 %
Health Care / Industrials		Consumer Discretionary	-0.4	2.4	65
Materials / Cons Staples		Health Care	-0.6	2.2	62
Telecom / Financial		Industrials	0.6	2.0	73
Energy / Utilities		Materials	0.6	1.9	58
S&P 500		Consumer Staples	-1.3	1.8	46
		Telecom	-1.3	0.9	35
		Financial	1.7	0.7	35
		Energy	-0.8	-0.3	27
		Utilities	-2.8 %	-0.4 %	31 %
		S&P 500	0.1 %	1.4 %	N/A %

Sector Commentary

♦ In November 2015, the S&P 500 produced a nominal gain of 0.1%. The financial sector was the top performing sector as investors started to perceive that an increase in the probability of the U.S. Federal Reserve raising its target interest rate. The financial sector tends to benefit from rising rates as the net interest margins increase. The worst performing sector was the utilities sector. The sector performed poorly as investors were concerned the impact of rising interest rates. Likewise, the consumer staples and telecom sectors performed poorly as the value of their dividends were lowered.

Sub-Sector Commentary

♦ The agriculture sub-sector has only outperformed the S&P 500 45% of the time since 1994, but on average has strongly outperformed on a percentage gain basis. The sector is very volatile in November. In November 2015, the agriculture sub-sector lost 20.1%. ♦ The homebuilders sub-sector produced a gain of 6.2%. November is typically a strong month for the homebuilders sub-sector and it has outperformed the S&P 500 63% of the time since 1990.

SELECTED SUB-SECTORS[3]			
Homebuilders	6.2 %	3.7 %	63 %
Retail	0.7	3.4	69
SOX (1994-2015)	2.2	3.3	57
Agriculture (1994-2015)	-20.1	3.2	45
Steel	-2.0	2.7	50
Pharma	-0.2	2.1	58
Transportation	-1.6	2.0	46
Chemicals	2.1	1.8	50
Biotech (1993-2015)	-2.1	1.7	43
Automotive & Components	1.2	1.6	54
Gold	-7.0	1.4	54
Metals & Mining	-8.9	1.1	50
Railroads	1.6	1.0	54
Silver	-9.9	0.9	50
Banks	3.3	0.8	46

(1) Sector data provided by Standard and Poors (2) GIC is short form for Global Industry Classification (3) Sub Sector data provided by Standard and Poors, except where marked by symbol.

MATERIAL STOCKS — MATERIAL GAINS
①Oct28-Jan6 ②Jan23-May5

The materials sector (U.S.) generally does well during the favorable six months of the year, from the end of October to the beginning of May. The sector is economically sensitive and is leveraged to economic forecasts. Generally, if the economy is expected to slow, the materials sector tends to decline and vice versa.

Positive 96% of the time

The materials sector has two seasonal periods. The first period is from October 28th to January 6th and second period is from January 23rd to May 5th.

In the first seasonal period, the materials sector has produced an average gain of 6.5% in the years from 1990 to 2015 and has been positive 81% of the time.

The second seasonal period from January 23rd to May 5th, has produced an average gain of 7.7% (almost double the S&P 500) and has been positive 78% of the time.

The time period in between the two seasonal periods, from January 7th to January 22nd, has had an average loss of 2.6% and only been positive 37% of the time (1989/90 to 2015/16). Investors may decide to bridge the gap between the two seasonal periods if the materials sector has strong momentum at the beginning of January.

The complete materials strategy is to be invested from October 28th to January 6th, out of the sector from January 7th to the 22nd, and back in from January 23rd to May 5th. This strategy has produced an average gain of 14.6% and has been positive 96% of the time.

Materials* vs. S&P 500 1989/90 to 2015/16   Positive ☐

Year	Oct 28 to Jan 6 S&P 500	Mat.	Jan 23 to May 5 S&P 500	Mat.	Compound Growth S&P 500	Mat.
1989/90	5.1%	9.1%	2.4%	-3.1%	7.7%	5.7%
1990/91	5.4	9.2	16.0	15.3	22.2	26.0
1991/92	8.8	1.5	-0.3	5.5	8.5	7.1
1992/93	3.8	5.6	1.9	4.3	5.8	10.2
1993/94	0.5	9.4	-4.9	-5.3	-4.4	3.6
1994/95	-1.1	-3.5	11.9	6.1	10.7	2.4
1995/96	6.4	7.6	4.6	11.1	11.3	19.5
1996/97	6.7	2.3	5.6	2.3	12.6	4.6
1997/98	10.2	1.4	15.8	20.9	27.7	22.6
1998/99	19.4	6.1	10.0	31.5	31.3	39.6
1999/00	8.2	15.7	-0.6	-7.1	7.6	7.5
2000/01	-5.9	19.2	-5.7	15.1	-11.2	37.2
2001/02	6.2	8.5	-4.1	14.9	1.8	24.7
2002/03	3.5	9.2	5.5	2.7	9.2	12.1
2003/04	9.0	16.6	-2.0	-3.0	6.8	13.1
2004/05	5.6	5.4	0.4	0.3	6.0	5.8
2005/06	9.0	16.3	5.1	14.7	14.6	33.5
2006/07	2.4	3.1	5.8	10.7	8.3	14.2
2007/08	-8.1	-5.1	7.4	16.7	-1.2	10.8
2008/09	10.1	12.0	9.2	23.3	20.3	38.1
2009/10	6.9	13.8	6.8	3.0	14.2	17.2
2010/11	7.7	11.7	4.0	4.2	12.1	16.4
2011/12	-0.5	-2.3	4.1	-2.7	3.5	-4.9
2012/13	3.9	7.2	8.2	0.0	12.3	7.2
2013/14	3.8	3.1	2.2	4.3	6.1	7.5
2014/15	2.1	-0.7	1.3	2.9	3.4	2.2
2015/16	-3.7	-6.2	7.5	18.3	3.6	11.0
Avg.	4.6%	6.5%	4.4%	7.7%	9.3%	14.6%
Fq > 0	81%	81%	78%	78%	89%	96%

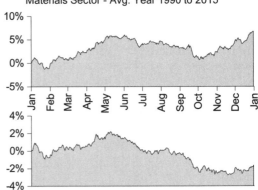

Materials Sector - Avg. Year 1990 to 2015

Materials / S&P 500 Rel. Strength - Avg Yr. 1990 - 2015

Alternate Strategy—
Investors can bridge the gap between the two positive seasonal trends for the materials sector by holding from October 28th to May 5th. Longer term investors may prefer this strategy. Shorter term investors can use technical tools to determine the appropriate strategy.

The SP GICS Materials Sector encompasses a wide range of materials based companies.
For more information on the materials sector, see www.standardandpoors.com

Materials Performance

Materials Monthly Performance (1990-2015)

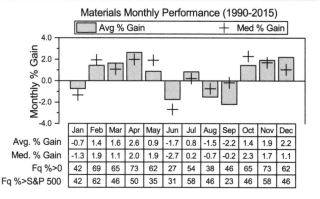

	Jan	Feb	Mar	Apr	May	Jun	Jul	Aug	Sep	Oct	Nov	Dec
Avg. % Gain	-0.7	1.4	1.6	2.6	0.9	-1.7	0.8	-1.5	-2.2	1.4	1.9	2.2
Med. % Gain	-1.3	1.9	1.1	2.0	1.9	-2.7	0.2	-0.7	-0.2	2.3	1.7	1.1
Fq %>0	42	69	65	73	62	27	54	38	46	65	73	62
Fq %>S&P 500	42	62	46	50	35	31	58	46	23	46	58	46

Materials 5 Year (2011-2015) % Gain

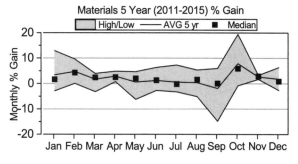

Materials Performance 2015-2016

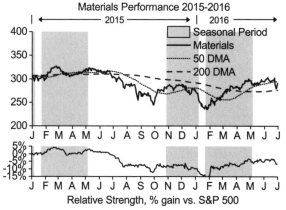

Relative Strength, % gain vs. S&P 500

WEEK 45

Market Indices & Rates
Weekly Values**

Stock Markets	2014	2015
Dow	17,473	17,878
S&P500	2,023	2,103
Nasdaq	4,631	5,138
TSX	14,546	13,621
FTSE	6,520	6,375
DAX	9,281	10,925
Nikkei	16,868	18,998
Hang Seng	23,731	22,782

Commodities	2014	2015
Oil	78.24	45.97
Gold	1155.2	1113.4

Bond Yields	2014	2015
USA 5 Yr Treasury	1.63	1.64
USA 10 Yr T	2.36	2.26
USA 20 Yr T	2.79	2.67
Moody's Aaa	3.90	4.05
Moody's Baa	4.76	5.43
CAN 5 Yr T	1.53	0.96
CAN 10 Yr T	2.05	1.64

Money Market	2014	2015
USA Fed Funds	0.25	0.25
USA 3 Mo T-B	0.03	0.06
CAN tgt overnight rate	1.00	0.50
CAN 3 Mo T-B	0.90	0.42

Foreign Exchange	2014	2015
EUR/USD	1.25	1.09
GBP/USD	1.59	1.53
USD/CAD	1.14	1.32
USD/JPY	114.42	121.66

NOVEMBER

M	T	W	T	F	S	S
		1	2	3	4	5
6	7	8	9	10	11	12
13	14	15	16	17	18	19
20	21	22	23	24	25	26
27	28	29	30			

DECEMBER

M	T	W	T	F	S	S
				1	2	3
4	5	6	7	8	9	10
11	12	13	14	15	16	17
18	19	20	21	22	23	24
25	26	27	28	29	30	31

JANUARY

M	T	W	T	F	S	S
1	2	3	4	5	6	7
8	9	10	11	12	13	14
15	16	17	18	19	20	21
22	23	24	25	26	27	28
29	30	31				

From 1990 to 2015, on average, the six best months for the materials sector were February, March, April, October, November and December. February, March and April make up the core part of the spring seasonal trade and October, November and December make up the core part of the winter seasonal trade. Over the last five years, the materials sector has on average, generally followed its seasonal trend with weaker performance in the summer months.

In 2015, the materials sector underperformed the S&P 500 in its winter seasonal period, and then outperformed in its 2016 spring seasonal period as cyclical sectors rallied at this time.

SOX (SEMICONDUCTOR) TIME TO PUT ON YOUR SOX TRADE
①Oct28-Nov6 ②Jan1-Feb15

Many investors think of the semiconductor sector as the technology sector on steroids, but there are some differences.

The seasonal trends in the semiconductor sector are largely driven by the ordering cycle of semiconductors and economic expectations.

13.4% gain & positive 82% of the time

Demand for semiconductors tends to reach a low in the second quarter and the beginning of the third quarter. It tends to reach a peak towards the end of the third quarter and into the fourth quarter. Most of the major semiconductor companies report their third quarter earnings in mid-October. Although this quarter realizes some of the seasonal earnings peak, the market is often volatile in this month and investors tend to defer their entry into the sector until the market shows consistent strength, typically towards the end of October.

The first quarter of the year tends to be positive for semiconductor companies as the sector tends to perform well into mid-February.

As a result of the cyclical demand for semiconductors, the semiconductor sector has two periods of seasonal strength, with a short period of market performance in between.

The first period of seasonal strength is very short, starting on October 28th and finishing on November 6th. In this time period, from 1994 to 2015 the semiconductor sector has produced an average gain of 5.8% and has been positive 91% of the time. The second period of seasonal strength is from January 1st to February 15th. In this time period, from 1995 to 2015, the semiconductor sector has produced an average gain of 6.8% and has been positive 77% of the time.

SOX Semiconductor* vs. S&P 500   Positive ☐
1994/95 to 2015/16

Year	Oct 28 to Nov 6 S&P 500	SOX	Jan 1 to Feb 15 S&P 500	SOX	Compound Growth S&P 500	SOX
1994/95	-0.8 %	1.4 %	5.5 %	13.9 %	4.7 %	15.5 %
1995/96	1.5	1.5	5.8	-4.5	7.3	-3.1
1996/97	3.4	7.6	9.1	19.5	12.8	28.6
1997/98	7.0	9.9	5.1	16.4	12.4	27.9
1998/99	7.1	11.1	0.1	11.8	7.2	24.2
1999/00	5.7	25.9	-4.6	35.4	0.8	70.5
2000/01	3.8	8.8	0.5	23.4	4.3	34.2
2001/02	1.3	8.2	-3.8	6.2	-2.6	14.9
2002/03	2.9	12.8	-5.1	-3.1	-2.3	9.2
2003/04	2.6	13.8	3.1	0.5	5.7	14.3
2004/05	3.6	1.7	-0.2	1.4	3.5	3.1
2005/06	3.5	5.7	2.5	12.3	6.1	18.6
2006/07	0.2	1.1	2.7	1.3	2.9	2.4
2007/08	-1.0	0.8	-8.1	-14.8	-9.0	-14.2
2008/09	6.6	3.2	-8.5	4.0	-2.4	7.3
2009/10	0.6	-2.5	-3.6	-7.5	-3.0	-9.8
2010/11	3.7	5.8	5.6	12.0	9.5	18.6
2011/12	-2.4	-1.1	6.8	16.8	4.2	15.5
2012/13	1.2	4.5	6.6	11.6	7.8	16.5
2013/14	0.6	1.7	-0.5	4.5	0.1	6.3
2014/15	3.6	4.7	1.9	2.7	5.5	7.5
2015/16	1.6	1.6	-8.8	-13.8	-7.3	-12.4
Avg.	2.6 %	5.8 %	0.6 %	6.8 %	3.1 %	13.4 %
Fq > 0	86 %	91 %	59 %	77 %	73 %	82 %

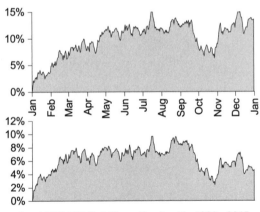

SOX PHLX Semiconductor - Avg. Year 1995 to 2015

Sox / S&P 500 Rel. Strength - Avg. Yr. 1990 - 2015

> Ⓨ *Alternate Strategy—*
> *Investors can bridge the gap between the two positive seasonal trends for the semiconductor sector by holding from October 28th to March 1st. Longer term investors may prefer this strategy, shorter term investors can use technical tools to determine the appropriate strategy.*

> ⓘ **PHLX Semiconductor Index (SOX):*
> *For more information on the PHLX Semiconductor Index (SOX), see www.nasdaq.com.*

SOX Performance

SOX Monthly Performance (1995-2015)

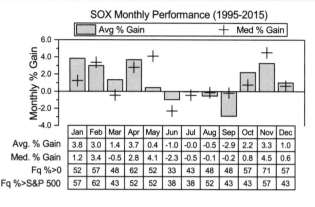

	Avg % Gain	+ Med % Gain

	Jan	Feb	Mar	Apr	May	Jun	Jul	Aug	Sep	Oct	Nov	Dec
Avg. % Gain	3.8	3.0	1.4	3.7	0.4	-1.0	-0.0	-0.5	-2.9	2.2	3.3	1.0
Med. % Gain	1.2	3.4	-0.5	2.8	4.1	-2.3	-0.5	-0.1	-0.2	0.8	4.5	0.6
Fq %>0	52	57	48	62	52	33	43	48	48	57	71	57
Fq %>S&P 500	57	62	43	52	52	38	38	52	43	43	57	43

SOX 5 Year (2011-2015) % Gain

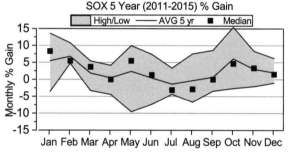

	High/Low	AVG 5 yr	■ Median

SOX Performance 2015-2016

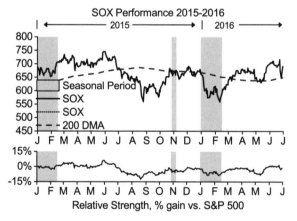

Relative Strength, % gain vs. S&P 500

NOVEMBER

M	T	W	T	F	S	S
		1	2	3	4	5
6	7	8	9	10	11	12
13	14	15	16	17	18	19
20	21	22	23	24	25	26
27	28	29	30			

DECEMBER

M	T	W	T	F	S	S
				1	2	3
4	5	6	7	8	9	10
11	12	13	14	15	16	17
18	19	20	21	22	23	24
25	26	27	28	29	30	31

JANUARY

M	T	W	T	F	S	S
1	2	3	4	5	6	7
8	9	10	11	12	13	14
15	16	17	18	19	20	21
22	23	24	25	26	27	28
29	30	31				

From 1995 to 2015, on average, the semiconductor sector produced gains in the months from October to April. The end of October and the beginning of November make up most of the gains for both months in the autumn seasonal trade. January and the first part of February tend to be strong and make up the second, longer winter seasonal period for the semiconductor sector. Over the last five years, the semiconductor sector has on average followed its general seasonal trend by performing well in January, poorly in the summer months and then performing well in October and November. In 2016, the winter seasonal trade performed poorly as the stock market corrected sharply.

At the macro level, the metals and mining (M&M) sector is driven by future economic growth expectations. When worldwide growth expectations are increasing, there is a greater need for raw materials, and vice versa.

Within the macro trend, the M&M sector has traditionally followed the overall market cycle of performing well from autumn until spring. This is the time of year that investors have a positive outlook on the economy and as a result, the cyclical sectors tend to outperform, including the metals and mining sector.

14.4% gain and positive 81% of the time

The metals and mining sector has two seasonal "sweet spots" – the first from November 19th to January 5th and the second from January 23rd to May 5th.

Investors have the option to hold and "bridge the gap" across the two sweet spots, but over the long-term, nimble traders have been able to capture extra value by being out of the sector from January 6th to the 22nd. During this period, from 1990 to 2015, the metals and mining sector has produced an average loss of 3.3% and has only been positive 48% of the time.

From a portfolio perspective, it is important to consider reducing exposure at the beginning of May. The danger of holding on too long is that the sector tends not to perform well in the late summer, particularly in September.

For more information on the metals and mining sector, see www.standardandpoors.com

Metals & Mining* vs. S&P 500
1989/90 to 2015/16   Positive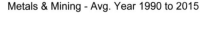

Year	Nov 19 to Jan 5		Jan 23 to May 5		Compound Growth	
	S&P 500	M&M	S&P 500	M&M	S&P 500	M&M
1989/90	3.1 %	6.3 %	2.4 %	-4.6 %	5.6 %	1.4 %
1990/91	1.2	6.4	16.0	7.1	17.4	13.9
1991/92	8.9	1.0	-0.3	-1.7	8.5	-0.7
1992/93	2.7	12.5	1.9	3.2	4.7	16.1
1993/94	0.9	9.0	-4.9	-11.1	-4.1	-3.1
1994/95	-0.2	-1.2	11.9	-3.0	11.6	-4.1
1995/96	2.8	8.3	4.6	5.8	7.5	14.6
1996/97	1.5	-1.9	5.6	-1.2	7.2	-3.0
1997/98	4.1	-4.5	15.8	19.3	20.6	13.9
1998/99	8.8	-7.9	10.0	31.0	19.6	20.6
1999/00	-1.6	17.0	-0.6	-10.4	-2.2	9.1
2000/01	-5.1	17.0	-5.7	19.6	-10.5	40.0
2001/02	3.0	5.5	-4.1	12.8	-1.3	19.0
2002/03	0.9	9.3	5.5	3.2	6.4	12.8
2003/04	8.5	18.2	-2.0	-12.1	6.4	3.9
2004/05	0.0	-8.4	0.4	-4.0	0.4	-12.0
2005/06	2.0	17.3	5.1	27.3	7.2	49.4
2006/07	0.6	3.0	5.8	17.2	6.5	20.8
2007/08	-3.2	0.9	7.4	27.4	3.9	28.5
2008/09	8.0	43.8	9.2	30.6	17.9	87.8
2009/10	2.4	6.3	6.8	4.8	9.4	11.3
2010/11	6.7	15.0	4.0	-1.6	11.0	13.1
2011/12	5.4	1.2	4.1	-16.0	9.7	-15.0
2012/13	7.8	3.9	8.2	-16.8	16.6	-13.6
2013/14	2.2	1.2	2.2	2.6	4.4	3.8
2014/15	-1.5	-14.2	1.3	5.3	-0.3	-9.7
2015/16	-3.2	-3.4	7.5	76.3	4.1	70.2
Avg.	2.5 %	6.2 %	4.4 %	7.8 %	7.0 %	14.4 %
Fq > 0	78 %	74 %	78 %	59 %	70 %	81 %

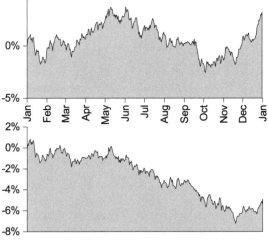

Metals & Mining - Avg. Year 1990 to 2015

Metals & Mining / S&P 500 Rel. Strength- Avg Yr. 1990-2015

Metals & Mining Performance

Metals and Mining Monthly Performance (1990-2015)

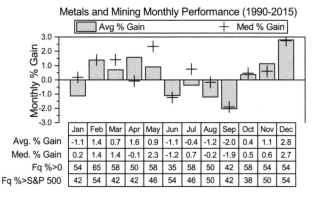

	Jan	Feb	Mar	Apr	May	Jun	Jul	Aug	Sep	Oct	Nov	Dec
Avg. % Gain	-1.1	1.4	0.7	1.6	0.9	-1.1	-0.4	-1.2	-2.0	0.4	1.1	2.8
Med. % Gain	0.2	1.4	1.4	-0.1	2.3	-1.2	0.7	-0.2	-1.9	0.5	0.6	2.7
Fq %>0	54	65	58	50	58	35	58	50	42	58	54	54
Fq %>S&P 500	42	54	42	42	46	54	46	50	42	38	50	54

Metals and Mining 5 Year (2011-2015) % Gain

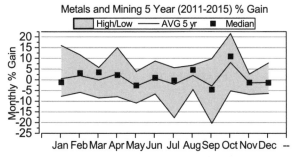

Metals and Mining Performance 2015-2016

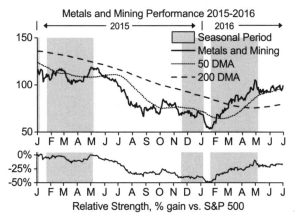

Relative Strength, % gain vs. S&P 500

From 1990 to 2015, the strongest month for the metals and mining sector was December on an average and median basis. Overall, the metals and mining sector does not have a strong track record of positive performance and outperforming the S&P 500 in any month. Nevertheless, the seasonal trend provides value, particularly in a strong commodity cycle.

Over the last five years, on average, the metals and mining sector's monthly performance has somewhat followed its seasonal trend with the first few months of the year performing well. The seasonal period starting in January 2016 performed very well as the sector had just come off a substantial correction.

WEEK 47

Market Indices & Rates
Weekly Values**

Stock Markets	2014	2015
Dow	17,710	17,653
S&P500	2,052	2,072
Nasdaq	4,693	5,045
TSX	15,004	13,381
FTSE	6,701	6,272
DAX	9,490	10,970
Nikkei	17,253	19,683
Hang Seng	23,497	22,344

Commodities	2014	2015
Oil	75.36	40.82
Gold	1193.0	1079.2

Bond Yields	2014	2015
USA 5 Yr Treasury	1.64	1.68
USA 10 Yr T	2.33	2.26
USA 20 Yr T	2.78	2.69
Moody's Aaa	3.96	4.07
Moody's Baa	4.84	5.47
CAN 5 Yr T	1.52	0.95
CAN 10 Yr T	2.02	1.64

Money Market	2014	2015
USA Fed Funds	0.25	0.25
USA 3 Mo T-B	0.02	0.13
CAN tgt overnight rate	1.00	0.50
CAN 3 Mo T-B	0.90	0.45

Foreign Exchange	2014	2015
EUR/USD	1.25	1.07
GBP/USD	1.57	1.52
USD/CAD	1.13	1.33
USD/JPY	117.50	123.19

NOVEMBER

M	T	W	T	F	S	S
	1	2	3	4	5	
6	7	8	9	10	11	12
13	14	15	16	17	18	19
20	21	22	23	24	25	26
27	28	29	30			

DECEMBER

M	T	W	T	F	S	S
				1	2	3
4	5	6	7	8	9	10
11	12	13	14	15	16	17
18	19	20	21	22	23	24
25	26	27	28	29	30	31

JANUARY

M	T	W	T	F	S	S
1	2	3	4	5	6	7
8	9	10	11	12	13	14
15	16	17	18	19	20	21
22	23	24	25	26	27	28
29	30	31				

THANKSGIVING
GIVE THANKS & TAKE RETURNS
Day Before and After – Two of the Best Days

We have a lot to be thankful for on Thanksgiving Day. As a bonus, the market day before and the market day after Thanksgiving, on average, have been two of the best days of the year in the stock market.

Each day, by itself, has produced spectacular results. From 1950 to 2015, the S&P 500 has had an average gain of 0.4% on the day before Thanksgiving and 0.3% on the day after Thanksgiving.

The day before Thanksgiving and the day after have had an average cumulative return of 0.7% and together have been positive 85% of the time

To put the performance of these two days in perspective, the average daily return of the S&P 500 over the same time period is 0.03%.

The gains the day before Thanksgiving and the day after are almost ten times better than the average market and have a much greater positive frequency.

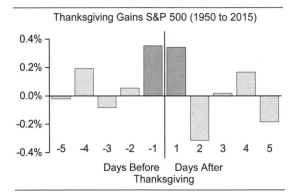

Thanksgiving Gains S&P 500 (1950 to 2015)

Days Before   Days After
Thanksgiving

Ⓨ *Alternate Strategy — Although the focus has been on the performance of two specific days, the day before and the day after Thanksgiving, the holiday occurs at the end of November which tends to be a strong month. December, the next month is also strong. Investors have an option of expanding their trade to include the "Santa Arrives Early & Stays Late" Strategy.*

ⓘ *History of Thanksgiving:*
It was originally a "thanksgiving feast" by the pilgrims for surviving their first winter. Initially it was celebrated sporadically and the holiday, when it was granted, had its date changed several times. It was not until 1941 that it was proclaimed to be the 4th Thursday in November.

S&P500	Day Before	Day After
		Positive
1950	1.4	0.8
1951	-0.2	-1.1
1952	0.6	0.5
1953	0.1	0.6
1954	0.6	1.0
1955	0.1	-0.1
1956	-0.5	1.1
1957	2.9	1.1
1958	1.7	1.1
1959	0.2	0.5
1960	0.1	0.6
1961	-0.1	0.2
1962	0.6	1.2
1963	-0.2	1.4
1964	-0.3	-0.3
1965	0.2	0.1
1966	0.7	0.8
1967	0.6	0.3
1968	0.5	0.6
1969	0.4	0.6
1970	0.4	1.0
1971	0.2	1.8
1972	0.6	0.3
1973	1.1	-0.3
1974	0.7	0.0
1975	0.3	0.3
1976	0.4	0.7
1977	0.4	0.2
1978	0.5	0.3
1979	0.2	0.8
1980	0.6	0.2
1981	0.4	0.8
1982	0.7	0.7
1983	0.1	0.1
1984	0.2	1.5
1985	0.9	-0.2
1986	0.2	0.2
1987	-0.9	-1.5
1988	0.7	-0.7
1989	0.7	0.6
1990	0.2	-0.3
1991	-0.4	-0.4
1992	0.4	0.2
1993	0.3	0.2
1994	0.0	0.5
1995	-0.3	0.3
1996	-0.1	0.3
1997	0.1	0.4
1998	0.3	0.5
1999	0.9	0.0
2000	-1.9	1.5
2001	-0.5	1.2
2002	2.8	-0.3
2003	0.4	0.0
2004	0.4	0.1
2005	0.3	0.2
2006	0.2	-0.4
2007	-1.6	1.7
2008	3.5	1.0
2009	0.5	-1.7
2010	1.5	-0.7
2011	-2.2	-0.3
2012	0.2	1.3
2013	0.2	-0.1
2014	0.3	-0.3
2015	0.0	0.1
Total Avg %	0.4%	0.3%
Fq > 0	77%	73%

(THANKSGIVING DAY printed vertically alongside the table)

Thanksgiving Strategy Performance

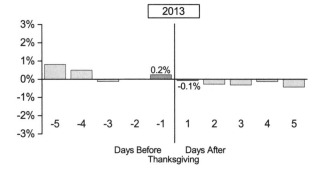

2013

Days Before   Days After
Thanksgiving

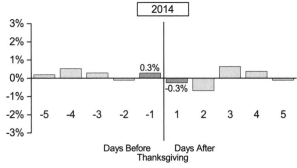

2014

Days Before   Days After
Thanksgiving

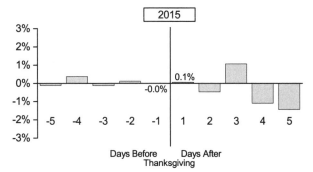

2015

Days Before   Days After
Thanksgiving

Market Indices & Rates
Weekly Values**

Stock Markets	2014	2015
Dow	17,822	17,804
S&P500	2,069	2,089
Nasdaq	4,773	5,112
TSX	14,959	13,397
FTSE	6,727	6,338
DAX	9,904	11,162
Nikkei	17,375	19,900
Hang Seng	23,968	22,462

Commodities	2014	2015
Oil	72.44	41.21
Gold	1194.3	1068.7

Bond Yields	2014	2015
USA 5 Yr Treasury	1.56	1.67
USA 10 Yr T	2.25	2.24
USA 20 Yr T	2.68	2.65
Moody's Aaa	3.88	4.01
Moody's Baa	4.74	5.44
CAN 5 Yr T	1.45	0.92
CAN 10 Yr T	1.92	1.59

Money Market	2014	2015
USA Fed Funds	0.25	0.25
USA 3 Mo T-B	0.02	0.17
CAN tgt overnight rate	1.00	0.50
CAN 3 Mo T-B	0.91	0.47

Foreign Exchange	2014	2015
EUR/USD	1.25	1.06
GBP/USD	1.57	1.51
USD/CAD	1.13	1.33
USD/JPY	118.06	122.70

In 2013, the net returns from the day before and the day after Thanksgiving were small. In fact, the days surrounding Thanksgiving were unusually quiet, producing either small gains or losses.

In 2014, the S&P 500 had a solid run starting in mid-October. The S&P 500 paused slightly around Thanksgiving, and did not produce a gain.

In 2015, the S&P 500 rallied strongly in October and then corrected at the beginning of November, after an initial bounce mid-month, the S&P 500 flat lined heading into November. The end result was a nominal positive gain for the *Thanksgiving Give Thanks & Take Returns* trade.

NOVEMBER

M	T	W	T	F	S	S
		1	2	3	4	5
6	7	8	9	10	11	12
13	14	15	16	17	18	19
20	21	22	23	24	25	26
27	28	29	30			

DECEMBER

M	T	W	T	F	S	S
				1	2	3
4	5	6	7	8	9	10
11	12	13	14	15	16	17
18	19	20	21	22	23	24
25	26	27	28	29	30	31

JANUARY

M	T	W	T	F	S	S
1	2	3	4	5	6	7
8	9	10	11	12	13	14
15	16	17	18	19	20	21
22	23	24	25	26	27	28
29	30	31				

DECEMBER

	MONDAY	TUESDAY	WEDNESDAY
WEEK 48	27	28	29
WEEK 49	**4** 27	**5** 26	**6** 25
WEEK 50	**11** 20	**12** 19	**13** 18
WEEK 51	**18** 13	**19** 12	**20** 11
WEEK 52	**25** 6 CAN Market Closed-Christmas Day USA Market Closed-Christmas Day	**26** 5 CAN Market Closed-Boxing Day	**27** 4

THURSDAY	FRIDAY
30	**1** 30
7 24	**8** 23
14 17	**15** 16
21 10	**22** 9
28 3	**29** 2

JANUARY

M	T	W	T	F	S	S
1	2	3	4	5	6	7
8	9	10	11	12	13	14
15	16	17	18	19	20	21
22	23	24	25	26	27	28
29	30	31				

FEBRUARY

M	T	W	T	F	S	S
			1	2	3	4
5	6	7	8	9	10	11
12	13	14	15	16	17	18
19	20	21	22	23	24	25
26	27	28				

MARCH

M	T	W	T	F	S	S
			1	2	3	4
5	6	7	8	9	10	11
12	13	14	15	16	17	18
19	20	21	22	23	24	25
26	27	28	29	30	31	

APRIL

M	T	W	T	F	S	S
						1
2	3	4	5	6	7	8
9	10	11	12	13	14	15
16	17	18	19	20	21	22
23	24	25	26	27	28	29

DECEMBER
S U M M A R Y

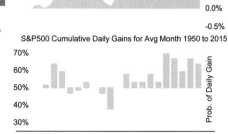

	Dow Jones	S&P 500	Nasdaq	TSX Comp
Month Rank	2	1	2	1
# Up	46	49	25	26
# Down	20	17	19	5
% Pos	70	74	57	84
% Avg. Gain	1.6	1.6	1.7	2.0

Dow & S&P 1950-2015, Nasdaq 1972-2015, TSX 1985-2015

S&P500 Cumulative Daily Gains for Avg Month 1950 to 2015

♦ December is typically one of the strongest months of the year for the S&P 500. From 1950 to 2015, the S&P 500 produced an average gain of 1.7% and was positive 74% of the time. ♦ Most of the gains for the S&P 500 tend to occur in the second half of the month. ♦ The Nasdaq tends to outperform the S&P 500 starting mid-December. ♦ The small cap sector also starts to outperform mid-month.

BEST / WORST DECEMBER BROAD MKTS. 2006-2015

BEST DECEMBER MARKETS
- ♦ Nikkei 225 (2009) 12.8%
- ♦ Nikkei 225 (2012) 10.0%
- ♦ Russell 2000 (2009) 7.9%

WORST DECEMBER MARKETS
- ♦ Russell 2000 (2015) -5.2%
- ♦ Nikkei 225 (2015) -3.6%
- ♦ TSX Comp (2015) - 3.4%

Index Values End of Month

	2006	2007	2008	2009	2010	2011	2012	2013	2014	2015
Dow	12,463	13,265	8,776	10,428	11,578	12,218	13,104	16,577	17,823	17,425
S&P 500	1,418	1,468	903	1,115	1,258	1,258	1,426	1,848	2,059	2,044
Nasdaq	2,415	2,652	1,577	2,269	2,653	2,605	3,020	4,177	4,736	5,007
TSX Comp.	12,908	13,833	8,988	11,746	13,443	11,955	12,434	13,622	14,632	13,010
Russell 1000	1,480	1,538	938	1,176	1,340	1,333	1,518	1,981	2,200	2,176
Russell 2000	1,958	1,904	1,241	1,554	1,948	1,841	2,111	2,892	2,994	2,823
FTSE 100	6,221	6,457	4,434	5,413	5,900	5,572	5,898	6,749	6,566	6,242
Nikkei 225	17,226	15,308	8,860	10,546	10,229	8,455	10,395	16,291	17,451	19,034

Percent Gain for December

	2006	2007	2008	2009	2010	2011	2012	2013	2014	2015
Dow	2.0	-0.8	-0.6	0.8	5.2	1.4	0.6	3.0	0.0	-1.7
S&P 500	1.3	-0.9	0.8	1.8	6.5	0.9	0.7	2.4	-0.4	-1.8
Nasdaq	-0.7	-0.3	2.7	5.8	6.2	-0.6	0.3	2.9	-1.2	-2.0
TSX Comp.	1.2	1.1	-3.1	2.6	3.8	-2.0	1.6	1.7	-0.8	-3.4
Russell 1000	1.1	-0.8	1.3	2.3	6.5	0.7	0.8	2.5	-0.4	-2.0
Russell 2000	0.2	-0.2	5.6	7.9	7.8	0.5	3.3	1.8	2.7	-5.2
FTSE 100	2.8	0.4	3.4	4.3	6.7	1.2	0.5	1.5	-2.3	-1.8
Nikkei 225	5.8	-2.4	4.1	12.8	2.9	0.2	10.0	4.0	-0.1	-3.6

December Market Avg. Performance 2006 to 2015[1]

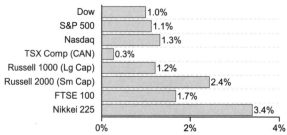

Dow	1.0%
S&P 500	1.1%
Nasdaq	1.3%
TSX Comp (CAN)	0.3%
Russell 1000 (Lg Cap)	1.2%
Russell 2000 (Sm Cap)	2.4%
FTSE 100	1.7%
Nikkei 225	3.4%

Interest Corner Dec[2]

	Fed Funds %[3]	3 Mo. T-Bill %[4]	10 Yr %[5]	20 Yr %[6]
2015	0.50	0.16	2.27	2.67
2014	0.25	0.04	2.17	2.47
2013	0.25	0.07	3.04	3.72
2012	0.25	0.05	1.78	2.54
2011	0.25	0.02	1.89	2.57

(1) Russell Data provided by Russell (2) Federal Reserve Bank of St. Louis- end of month values (3) Target rate set by FOMC (4)(5)(6) Constant yield maturities.

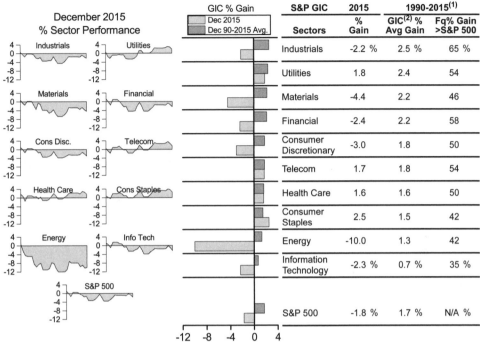

S&P GIC Sectors	2015 % Gain	1990-2015[1]	
		GIC[2] % Avg Gain	Fq% Gain >S&P 500
Industrials	-2.2 %	2.5 %	65 %
Utilities	1.8	2.4	54
Materials	-4.4	2.2	46
Financial	-2.4	2.2	58
Consumer Discretionary	-3.0	1.8	50
Telecom	1.7	1.8	54
Health Care	1.6	1.6	50
Consumer Staples	2.5	1.5	42
Energy	-10.0	1.3	42
Information Technology	-2.3 %	0.7 %	35 %
S&P 500	-1.8 %	1.7 %	N/A %

Sector Commentary

♦ In December 2015, the S&P 500 produced a loss of 1.8% as the stock market reacted to the U.S. Federal Reserve increasing its target interest rate ♦ As the stock market corrected, the defensive sectors bucked the trend and increased in value. The consumer staples sector produced a gain of 2.5%, telecom 1.7% and utilities 1.8%. The energy sector, after performing well in October and having a nominal loss in November, continued its previous downward trend and lost 10%.

Sub-Sector Commentary

♦ The homebuilders sub-sector typically performs well in December, but in December 2015, the sub-sector suffered a loss of 4.0%. ♦ The automotive sub-sector produced a loss of 5.3% as investors expressed their concern that higher interest rates would slow the economy. Likewise, the transportation sub-sector lost 4.8%.

SELECTED SUB-SECTORS[3]			
Home builders	-4.0 %	9.9 %	89 %
Steel	-2.8	4.9	65
Biotech (1993-2015)	1.9	4.2	52
Metals & Mining	-3.4	2.8	54
Agriculture (1994-2015)	0.5	2.1	55
Banks	-2.3	1.9	58
Chemicals	-4.0	1.9	58
Railroads	-8.9	1.4	50
Automotive & Components	-5.3	1.3	38
Pharma	0.7	1.2	42
Silver	-1.8	1.1	46
SOX (1994-2015)	-2.0	1.0	43
Transportation	-4.8	1.0	38
Retail	-1.0	0.9	35
Gold	-0.2	-0.1	35

EMERGING MARKETS(USD)– TRUNCATED SIX MONTH SEASONAL
November 24th to April 18th

Emerging markets become popular periodically, mainly after they have had a strong run, or if they have suffered a major correction and investors perceive them as having a lot of value.

Markets around the world tend to have the same broad seasonal trends, including the emerging markets. Typically, emerging markets will outperform when the U.S. market is increasing and underperform when it is decreasing.

The exceptions to this usually occur if there is a global economic contraction underway, or economic growth is in question, and investors seek the "safety" of the U.S. market. In this case, the emerging markets can underperform the U.S. market.

10.1% gain & positive 85% of the time positive

Seasonal investors have benefited from concentrating their emerging market exposure in a truncated, or shorter version, of the favorable six month seasonal period.

Emerging Markets (USD)* vs. S&P 500 1989/90 to 2015/16			
		Positive	
Nov 24 to Apr 18	S&P 500	Em. Mkts.	Diff
1989/90	-0.4%	4.5	4.9%
1990/91	23.8	33.8%	10.5
1991/92	10.6	37.5	26.8
1992/93	5.6	11.8	6.2
1993/94	-4.0	3.7	7.8
1994/95	12.3	-16.4	-28.7
1995/96	7.6	14.7	7.1
1996/97	2.4	7.1	4.7
1997/98	16.6	6.7	-9.9
1998/99	11.0	18.1	7.1
1999/00	2.6	3.5	0.8
2000/01	-6.4	-4.6	1.8
2001/02	-2.3	22.3	24.5
2002/03	-4.0	0.0	4.0
2003/04	9.6	19.5	9.9
2004/05	-2.6	4.3	7.0
2005/06	3.3	24.7	21.4
2006/07	4.7	13.2	8.5
2007/08	-3.5	-0.9	2.6
2008/09	8.7	37.6	28.9
2009/10	7.8	5.6	-2.2
2010/11	10.5	6.6	-3.9
2011/12	19.2	15.6	-3.6
2012/13	9.4	0.1	-9.3
2013/14	3.3	0.3	-3.1
2014/15	0.9	3.8	3.0
2015/16	0.4	0.3	-0.1
Avg	5.4%	10.1%	4.7%
Fq > 0	74%	85%	70%

Emerging Mkts. (USD)- Avg. Year 1990 to 2015

Emerg. Mkts. (USD)/S&P 500 Rel. Str. - Avg Yr. 1990-2015

ing markets sector (USD) produced an average rate of return of 10.1% and has been positive 85% of the time.

As the world has grappled with the sub-prime crisis and then the EU crisis in the last few years, investors have sought the safety of the U.S. markets and as a result, emerging markets have underperformed.

As worldwide economic growth gains traction in the future, seasonal investors should consider adding emerging markets to their portfolio from November 24th to April 18th.

The seasonally strong period for the emerging markets sector is from November 24th to April 18th. In this time period, from 1990/91 to 2015/16, the emerg-

(i) ** Emerging Markets (USD)- For more information on the emerging markets, see www.standardandpoors.com*

Emerging Markets Performance

Emerging Markets Monthly Performance (1990-2015)

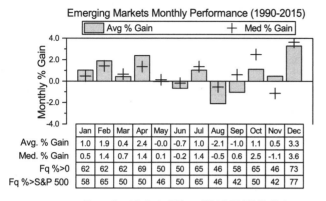

	Jan	Feb	Mar	Apr	May	Jun	Jul	Aug	Sep	Oct	Nov	Dec
Avg. % Gain	1.0	1.9	0.4	2.4	-0.0	-0.7	1.0	-2.1	-1.0	1.1	0.5	3.3
Med. % Gain	0.5	1.4	0.7	1.4	0.1	-0.2	1.4	-0.5	0.6	2.5	-1.1	3.6
Fq %>0	62	62	62	69	50	50	65	46	58	65	46	73
Fq %>S&P 500	58	65	50	50	46	50	65	46	42	50	42	77

Emerging Markets 5 Year (2011-2015) % Gain

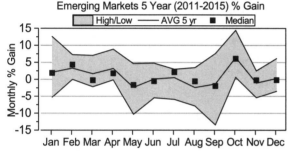

Emerging Markets Performance 2015-2016

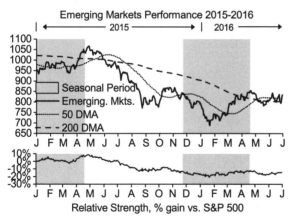

Relative Strength, % gain vs. S&P 500

WEEK 49

Market Indices & Rates
Weekly Values**

Stock Markets	2014	2015
Dow	17,886	17,733
S&P500	2,068	2,081
Nasdaq	4,762	5,114
TSX	14,589	13,451
FTSE	6,707	6,337
DAX	9,962	11,075
Nikkei	17,756	19,828
Hang Seng	23,657	22,302

Commodities	2014	2015
Oil	67.18	40.90
Gold	1199.4	1063.5

Bond Yields	2014	2015
USA 5 Yr Treasury	1.60	1.66
USA 10 Yr T	2.27	2.23
USA 20 Yr T	2.69	2.62
Moody's Aaa	3.90	3.97
Moody's Baa	4.79	5.41
CAN 5 Yr T	1.44	0.91
CAN 10 Yr T	1.93	1.56

Money Market	2014	2015
USA Fed Funds	0.25	0.25
USA 3 Mo T-B	0.03	0.22
CAN tgt overnight rate	1.00	0.50
CAN 3 Mo T-B	0.90	0.48

Foreign Exchange	2014	2015
EUR/USD	1.24	1.07
GBP/USD	1.57	1.51
USD/CAD	1.14	1.34
USD/JPY	119.73	122.99

DECEMBER

M	T	W	T	F	S	S
				1	2	3
4	5	6	7	8	9	10
11	12	13	14	15	16	17
18	19	20	21	22	23	24
25	26	27	28	29	30	31

JANUARY

M	T	W	T	F	S	S
1	2	3	4	5	6	7
8	9	10	11	12	13	14
15	16	17	18	19	20	21
22	23	24	25	26	27	28
29	30	31				

FEBRUARY

M	T	W	T	F	S	S
		1	2	3	4	
5	6	7	8	9	10	11
12	13	14	15	16	17	18
19	20	21	22	23	24	25
26	27	28				

From 1990 to 2015, December has been the strongest month of the year for emerging markets on an average, median and frequency basis. Although November tends to have a negative median, the last part of the month tends to be a good launching point into the seasonal period for emerging markets.

Over the last five years, October has been the strongest month, mainly the result of the S&P 500's strong rallies in October.

In its 2015/2016 seasonal period, the emerging markets sector was positive but nominally underperformed the S&P 500.

Aerospace & Defense Sector Flying High
December 12th to May 5th

The aerospace and defense sector is highly dependent on government purchases and as a result is subject not only to economic cycles, but also the political environment. Despite the fact that outside variables have a large impact on aerospace and defense orders, the sector has a seasonal trend.

The aerospace and defense sector has a seasonal trend that is similar to the overall broad market's seasonal trend. The big difference is that aerospace and defense has a track record of strongly outperforming the S&P 500 up until the beginning of May.

9.7% gain & positive 89% of the time

The difference in the sector's seasonal trend compared with the S&P 500's trend is largely the result of the U.S. governments procurement cycle, which has a year-end of September 30th. The first quarter of the government's fiscal year (October, November and December) tends to be the weakest for orders, as typically, major purchases are made towards the end of the last fiscal quarter and the new fiscal quarter is slow to get off the ground. Government procurement tends to pick up at the start of the new calendar year, helping to boost aerospace and defense stocks up until the beginning of May.

Aerospace & Defense* vs. S&P 500
1989/90 to 2015/16

Dec 12 to May 5	S&P 500	Aero & Def.	Positive Diff
1989/90	-2.9%	6.1%	9.0%
1990/91	16.7	11.6	-5.1
1991/92	10.4	10.1	-0.3
1992/93	2.5	14.3	11.9
1993/94	-2.7	2.7	5.4
1994/95	16.4	26.0	9.7
1995/96	3.6	11.6	8.0
1996/97	12.1	8.0	-4.1
1997/98	16.8	11.5	-5.3
1998/99	15.5	29.1	13.6
1999/00	1.1	3.6	2.5
2000/01	-8.2	-0.9	7.4
2001/02	-5.6	23.3	28.9
2002/03	2.4	-7.4	-9.8
2003/04	4.7	5.6	0.9
2004/05	-1.3	4.1	5.4
2005/06	5.3	21.0	15.8
2006/07	6.6	9.0	2.5
2007/08	-4.8	-2.5	2.3
2008/09	3.5	8.5	5.1
2009/10	5.4	12.8	7.4
2010/11	7.6	13.0	5.4
2011/12	9.1	7.4	-1.7
2012/13	13.1	14.7	1.7
2013/14	5.8	8.9	3.1
2014/15	2.7	3.0	0.3
2015/16	1.9	5.5	3.6
Avg	5.1%	9.7%	4.6%
Fq > 0	78%	89%	78%

been positive 89% of the time. Compared to the S&P 500, it has produced an extra 4.6% and outperformed it 78% of the time.

In the other seven months of the year, from May 6th to December 11th, the aerospace and defense sector has only had a gain of 2.2% and has outperformed the S&P 500, 42% of the time. In this time period, there have been eight years of gains greater than 10% and five years of losses greater than 10%. In other words, the results in the unfavorable period for the sector tend to be volatile.

Aerospace and Defense- Avg. Year 1990 to 2015

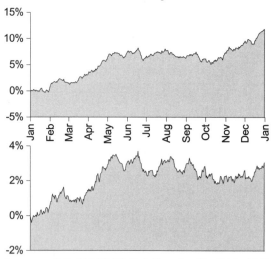

Aerospace & Def./ S&P 500 Rel. Str. - Avg Yr. 1990 - 2015

From 1989/90 to 2015/16, during its seasonal period, December 12th to May 5th, the aerospace and defense sector has produced an average gain of 9.7% and has

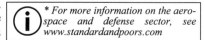
For more information on the aerospace and defense sector, see www.standardandpoors.com

Aerospace & Defense Performance

Aerospace Monthly Performance (1990-2015)

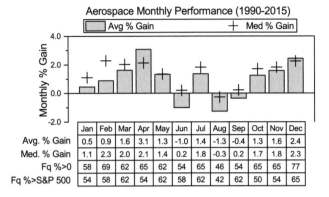

	Jan	Feb	Mar	Apr	May	Jun	Jul	Aug	Sep	Oct	Nov	Dec
Avg. % Gain	0.5	0.9	1.6	3.1	1.3	-1.0	1.4	-1.3	-0.4	1.3	1.6	2.4
Med. % Gain	1.1	2.3	2.0	2.1	1.4	0.2	1.8	-0.3	0.2	1.7	1.8	2.3
Fq %>0	58	69	62	65	62	54	65	46	54	65	65	77
Fq %>S&P 500	54	58	62	54	62	58	62	42	62	50	54	65

Aerospace 5 Year (2011-2015) % Gain

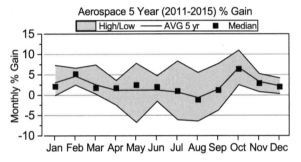

Aerospace Performance 2015-2016

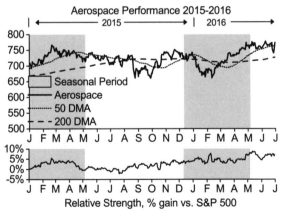

Relative Strength, % gain vs. S&P 500

Market Indices & Rates
Weekly Values**

Stock Markets	2014	2015
Dow	17,613	17,526
S&P500	2,037	2,051
Nasdaq	4,711	5,040
TSX	13,966	12,942
FTSE	6,493	6,105
DAX	9,813	10,618
Nikkei	17,558	19,354
Hang Seng	23,524	21,816

Commodities	2014	2015
Oil	61.11	36.94
Gold	1216.5	1074.5

Bond Yields	2014	2015
USA 5 Yr Treasury	1.61	1.65
USA 10 Yr T	2.19	2.21
USA 20 Yr T	2.55	2.58
Moody's Aaa	3.75	3.95
Moody's Baa	4.72	5.40
CAN 5 Yr T	1.39	0.82
CAN 10 Yr T	1.84	1.48

Money Market	2014	2015
USA Fed Funds	0.25	0.25
USA 3 Mo T-B	0.03	0.26
CAN tgt overnight rate	1.00	0.50
CAN 3 Mo T-B	0.89	0.46

Foreign Exchange	2014	2015
EUR/USD	1.24	1.09
GBP/USD	1.57	1.51
USD/CAD	1.15	1.36
USD/JPY	119.12	122.06

DECEMBER

M	T	W	T	F	S	S
				1	2	3
4	5	6	7	8	9	10
11	12	13	14	15	16	17
18	19	20	21	22	23	24
25	26	27	28	29	30	31

JANUARY

M	T	W	T	F	S	S
1	2	3	4	5	6	7
8	9	10	11	12	13	14
15	16	17	18	19	20	21
22	23	24	25	26	27	28
29	30	31				

FEBRUARY

M	T	W	T	F	S	S
		1	2	3	4
5	6	7	8	9	10	11
12	13	14	15	16	17	18
19	20	21	22	23	24	25
26	27	28				

From 1990 to 2015, on a monthly average basis, the aerospace and defense sector has increased its gains from January to May, with April being the best month. The summer months have tended to be the weaker months, with August being the weakest.

Over the last five years, on average, the first few months of the year have been stronger than the average month for the rest of the year. The outlier has been October, with an average gain of over 5%. In the December 2015 to May 2016 seasonal period, the aerospace and defense sector was positive and outperformed the S&P 500.

DO THE "NAZ" WITH SANTA
Nasdaq Gives More at Christmas – Dec 15th to Jan 23rd

One of the best times to invest in the major stock markets is the period around Christmas. The markets are generally positive at this time of the year as investors reposition their portfolios for the start of the new year. A lot of investors are familiar with the *Small Cap Effect* opportunity that starts approximately at this time of the year, where small caps tend to outperform from mid-December to the beginning of March (*see Small Cap Effect*), but few investors know that the last half of December and the first half of January is also a seasonally strong period for the Nasdaq.

80% of time better than S&P 500

The Nasdaq tends to perform well in the last two weeks of December, as investors typically increase their investment allocation to higher beta investments, including the Nasdaq, to finish the year.

In addition, the major sector drivers of the Nasdaq (biotech and technology), tend to perform well in the second half of December and the first half of January. Biotech tends to perform well in the last half of December and technology tends to perform well in the first half of January. The end result is a Nasdaq Christmas trade that lasts from December 15th to January 23rd. In this time period, for the years 1971/72 to 2015/16, the Nasdaq has outperformed the S&P 500 by an average 2.1% per year. This rate of return is considered to be very high given that the length of the favorable period is just over one month. Even more impressive is the 80% frequency that the Nasdaq outperforms the S&P 500.

Nasdaq vs. S&P 500 Dec 15th to Jan 23rd 1971/72 To 2015/16

Dec 15 to Jan 23	S&P 500	Positive	
		Nasdaq	Diff
1971/72	6.1 %	7.5 %	1.3 %
1972/73	0.0	-0.7	-0.7
1973/74	4.1	6.8	2.8
1974/75	7.5	8.9	1.4
1975/76	13.0	13.8	0.9
1976/77	-1.7	2.8	4.5
1977/78	-5.1	-3.5	1.6
1978/79	4.7	6.2	1.4
1979/80	4.1	5.6	1.5
1980/81	0.8	3.3	2.5
1981/82	-6.0	-5.0	1.0
1982/83	4.7	5.5	0.8
1983/84	0.9	1.4	0.4
1984/85	9.0	13.3	4.3
1985/86	-2.7	0.8	3.5
1986/87	9.2	10.2	1.0
1987/88	1.8	9.1	7.3
1988/89	3.3	4.6	1.3
1989/90	-5.5	-3.8	1.7
1990/91	1.0	4.1	3.1
1991/92	7.9	15.2	7.2
1992/93	0.8	7.2	6.4
1993/94	2.5	5.7	3.2
1994/95	2.4	4.7	2.3
1995/96	-0.7	-1.0	-0.3
1996/97	6.7	7.3	0.6
1997/98	0.4	2.6	2.1
1998/99	7.4	18.9	11.6
1999/00	2.7	18.6	15.9
2000/01	1.5	4.1	2.6
2001/02	0.5	-1.6	-2.0
2002/03	-0.2	1.9	2.1
2003/04	6.3	9.0	2.7
2004/05	-3.0	-5.8	-2.9
2005/06	-0.7	-0.6	0.1
2006/07	0.2	-0.9	-1.1
2007/08	-8.8	-12.1	-3.3
2008/09	-5.4	-4.1	1.3
2009/10	-2.0	-0.3	1.7
2010/11	3.4	2.4	-1.0
2011/12	8.6	9.6	1.1
2012/13	5.8	6.1	0.4
2013/14	3.0	5.5	2.5
2014/15	2.5	2.2	-0.2
2015/16	-5.7	-7.3	-1.6
Avg	1.9 %	4.0 %	2.1 %
Fq > 0	69 %	71 %	80 %

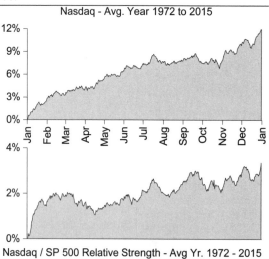

Nasdaq - Avg. Year 1972 to 2015

Nasdaq / SP 500 Relative Strength - Avg Yr. 1972 - 2015

Alternate Strategy — For those investors who favor the Nasdaq, an alternative strategy is to invest in the Nasdaq at an earlier date: October 28th. Historically, on average the Nasdaq has started its outperformance at this time. The "Do the Naz with Santa" strategy focuses on the sweet spot of the Nasdaq's outper-

Nasdaq is a market that has a focused on biotech and technology and is typically more volatile than the S&P 500.

Nasdaq Performance

Nasdaq Monthly Performance (1972-2015)

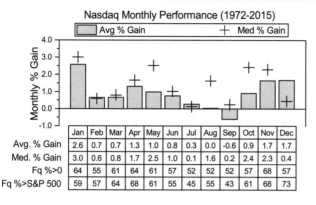

	Jan	Feb	Mar	Apr	May	Jun	Jul	Aug	Sep	Oct	Nov	Dec
Avg. % Gain	2.6	0.7	0.7	1.3	1.0	0.8	0.3	0.0	-0.6	0.9	1.7	1.7
Med. % Gain	3.0	0.6	0.8	1.7	2.5	1.0	0.1	1.6	0.2	2.4	2.3	0.4
Fq %>0	64	55	61	64	61	57	52	52	52	57	68	57
Fq %>S&P 500	59	57	64	68	61	55	45	55	43	61	68	73

Nasdaq 5 Year (2011-2015) % Gain

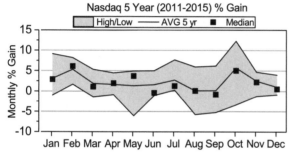

Nasdaq Performance 2015-2016

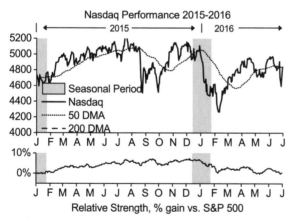

Relative Strength, % gain vs. S&P 500

Market Indices & Rates
Weekly Values**

Stock Markets	2014	2015
Dow	17,438	17,453
S&P500	2,021	2,037
Nasdaq	4,662	4,989
TSX	14,119	12,963
FTSE	6,372	6,022
DAX	9,608	10,481
Nikkei	17,101	18,968
Hang Seng	22,847	21,583

Commodities	2014	2015
Oil	55.79	35.77
Gold	1200.4	1063.6

Bond Yields	2014	2015
USA 5 Yr Treasury	1.61	1.70
USA 10 Yr T	2.14	2.25
USA 20 Yr T	2.47	2.59
Moody's Aaa	3.74	3.97
Moody's Baa	4.72	5.47
CAN 5 Yr T	1.35	0.79
CAN 10 Yr T	1.80	1.46

Money Market	2014	2015
USA Fed Funds	0.25	0.50
USA 3 Mo T-B	0.04	0.23
CAN tgt overnight rate	1.00	0.50
CAN 3 Mo T-B	0.90	0.46

Foreign Exchange	2014	2015
EUR/USD	1.24	1.09
GBP/USD	1.57	1.50
USD/CAD	1.16	1.38
USD/JPY	118.24	121.73

DECEMBER

M	T	W	T	F	S	S
				1	2	3
4	5	6	7	8	9	10
11	12	13	14	15	16	17
18	19	20	21	22	23	24
25	26	27	28	29	30	31

JANUARY

M	T	W	T	F	S	S
1	2	3	4	5	6	7
8	9	10	11	12	13	14
15	16	17	18	19	20	21
22	23	24	25	26	27	28
29	30	31				

FEBRUARY

M	T	W	T	F	S	S
		1	2	3	4
5	6	7	8	9	10	11
12	13	14	15	16	17	18
19	20	21	22	23	24	25
26	27	28				

From 1972 to 2015, the best month of the year for the Nasdaq has been January on an average and median basis. January is the core part of the Nasdaq trade. December is also a positive month, but on a median basis, it is weaker than most other months. It is the first part of December that tends to be weaker for the Nasdaq, leading to a mid-month entry into the Nasdaq trade. Over the last five years, the strongest months of the year for the Nasdaq have been February and October. January was positive in the same time frame, but just not as strong. The 2015/16 Nasdaq trade was negative as it corrected sharply in its seasonal period.

ESTÉE LAUDER— LOOKING GOOD
①Feb1-May5 ②Oct28-Dec31

Everyone likes to look good: especially around the Christmas holiday season. Estee Lauder benefits from this trend as stores stock up in the second half of the year, (1st half of the fiscal year for Estee Lauder as Estée Lauder's year end is June 30th).

Investors take advantage of the higher demand for beauty products by pushing up the price of Estée Lauder from October 28th to December 31st. In this time period, from 1996 to 2015, Estée Lauder has produced an average gain of 7.7% and has been positive 70% of the time. This compares to the S&P 500 which has produced an average gain of 4.4% and has been positive 75% of the time.

18.8% Gain & Positive 85% of the time

In the same time period, Estée Lauder has a higher average gain but is not as positive as often as the S&P 500. Although the frequency of positive occurrences is lower for Estée Lauder and it has only outperformed the S&P 500 approximately 50% of the time, its returns are significantly larger and it has small draw-downs.

In the period from February 1st to May 5th, from 1996 to 2015, Estée Lauder has produced an average gain of 10.0% and has been positive 85% of the time, which is better than the S&P 500 on both counts.

Although, on average, Estée Lauder has slightly outperformed the S&P 500 in January, the returns have been volatile. As a result, January has not been included in the seasonal period. Investors can always opt to carry the trade through the month of January, particularly if the trade has strong momentum.

Estée Lauder* vs. S&P 500 1996 to 2015   Positive

Year	Feb 1 to May 5 S&P 500	Feb 1 to May 5 EL	Oct 28 to Dec 31 S&P 500	Oct 28 to Dec 31 EL	Compound Growth S&P 500	Compound Growth EL
1996	0.9 %	-1.1 %	5.7 %	15.0 %	6.6 %	13.8 %
1997	5.6	0.8	10.7	29.0	16.9	30.0
1998	13.8	23.4	15.4	31.6	31.3	62.3
1999	5.3	18.1	13.3	7.7	19.3	27.2
2000	2.7	-15.8	-4.3	-0.5	-1.7	-16.2
2001	-7.3	7.2	3.9	-4.9	-3.6	2.0
2002	-5.0	15.5	-2.0	-2.6	-6.9	12.5
2003	8.3	10.7	7.8	6.8	16.8	18.3
2004	-0.9	14.7	7.7	5.1	6.8	20.5
2005	-0.7	-16.0	5.9	8.7	5.1	-8.7
2006	3.6	9.3	3.0	2.1	6.6	11.6
2007	4.7	0.9	-4.4	-3.4	0.1	-2.5
2008	2.1	7.5	6.4	-5.0	8.6	2.1
2009	9.4	31.7	4.9	17.3	14.7	54.5
2010	8.6	19.6	6.4	24.6	15.5	49.0
2011	3.8	20.5	-2.1	10.7	1.6	33.4
2012	4.3	4.8	1.0	-1.5	5.4	3.2
2013	7.8	16.9	5.0	5.3	13.2	23.1
2014	5.7	7.7	5.0	2.3	11.0	10.2
2015	4.7	23.1	-1.1	5.3	3.6	29.6
Avg.	3.9 %	10.0 %	4.4 %	7.7 %	8.5 %	18.8 %
Fq > 0	80 %	85 %	75 %	70 %	85 %	85 %

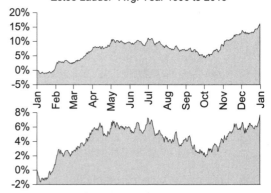

Estée Lauder- Avg. Year 1996 to 2015

Estée Lauder/S&P 500 Rel Strength - Avg Yr. 1996 - 2015

> *Alternate Strategy—*
> *Investors can bridge the gap between the two positive seasonal trends for Estée Lauder by holding from October 28th to May 5th. Longer term investors may prefer this strategy. Shorter term investors can use technical tools to determine the appropriate strategy.*

> **Estée Lauder is a beauty care products company. It trades on the NYSE, under the symbol EL. For more information, please see www.elcompanies.com*

Estée Lauder Performance

EL Monthly Performance (1996-2015)

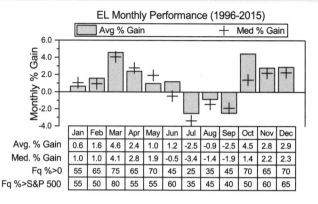

	Jan	Feb	Mar	Apr	May	Jun	Jul	Aug	Sep	Oct	Nov	Dec
Avg. % Gain	0.6	1.6	4.6	2.4	1.0	1.2	-2.5	-0.9	-2.5	4.5	2.8	2.9
Med. % Gain	1.0	1.0	4.1	2.8	1.9	-0.5	-3.4	-1.4	-1.9	1.4	2.2	2.3
Fq %>0	55	65	75	65	70	45	25	35	45	70	65	70
Fq %>S&P 500	55	50	80	55	55	60	35	45	40	50	60	65

EL 5 Year (2011-2015) % Gain

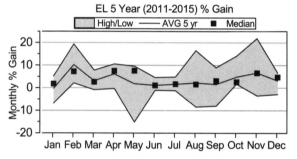

EL Performance 2015-2016

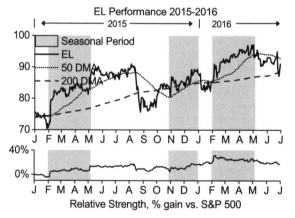

Relative Strength, % gain vs. S&P 500

Market Indices & Rates
Weekly Values**

Stock Markets	2014	2015
Dow	18,017	17,456
S&P500	2,083	2,046
Nasdaq	4,782	5,016
TSX	14,545	13,178
FTSE	6,595	6,177
DAX	9,894	10,613
Nikkei	17,779	18,840
Hang Seng	23,364	21,950

Commodities	2014	2015
Oil	55.56	36.38
Gold	1185.5	1074.0

Bond Yields	2014	2015
USA 5 Yr Treasury	1.74	1.71
USA 10 Yr T	2.24	2.24
USA 20 Yr T	2.54	2.60
Moody's Aaa	3.79	3.97
Moody's Baa	4.75	5.49
CAN 5 Yr T	1.43	0.73
CAN 10 Yr T	1.89	1.39

Money Market	2014	2015
USA Fed Funds	0.25	0.50
USA 3 Mo T-B	0.03	0.21
CAN tgt overnight rate	1.00	0.50
CAN 3 Mo T-B	0.90	0.47

Foreign Exchange	2014	2015
EUR/USD	1.22	1.09
GBP/USD	1.56	1.49
USD/CAD	1.16	1.39
USD/JPY	120.33	120.79

DECEMBER

M	T	W	T	F	S	S
				1	2	3
4	5	6	7	8	9	10
11	12	13	14	15	16	17
18	19	20	21	22	23	24
25	26	27	28	29	30	31

JANUARY

M	T	W	T	F	S	S
1	2	3	4	5	6	7
8	9	10	11	12	13	14
15	16	17	18	19	20	21
22	23	24	25	26	27	28
29	30	31				

FEBRUARY

M	T	W	T	F	S	S
		1	2	3	4	
5	6	7	8	9	10	11
12	13	14	15	16	17	18
19	20	21	22	23	24	25
26	27	28				

From 1996 to 2015, there has been a large difference in the performance of Estée Lauder in its strong seasonal period versus its three weakest months of July, August and September.

Over the last five years, from 2011 to 2015, Estée Lauder has generally followed its seasonal trend with the summer months performing poorly.

In 2015, Estée Lauder benefited from better than expected earnings, helping it to outperform in its seasonal period. In 2016, Estée Lauder performed well due to an earnings bump at the beginning of its seasonal period.

FINANCIALS (U.S.) YEAR END CLEAN UP
December 15th to April 13th

The U.S. financial sector often starts its strong performance in October, steps up its performance in mid-December and then strongly outperforms the S&P 500 starting in mid-January.

Extra 1.9% &
63% of the time better than the S&P 500

In the 1990s and early 2000s, financial stocks benefited from the tailwind of falling interest rates. During this period, with a few exceptions, this sector has participated in both the rallies and the declines.

Dec 15 to Apr 13	S&P 500	Positive Financials	Diff
1989/90	-1.9 %	-9.9 %	-8.0 %
1990/91	16.4	29.2	12.8
1991/92	5.6	9.2	3.5
1992/93	3.8	17.9	14.1
1993/94	-3.6	-0.4	3.2
1994/95	11.9	14.0	2.1
1995/96	3.2	5.5	2.3
1996/97	1.2	4.7	3.4
19/9798	16.4	19.7	3.3
1998/99	18.3	24.9	6.6
1999/00	2.7	4.0	1.3
2000/01	-11.7	-4.8	6.9
2001/02	-1.1	6.5	7.6
2002/03	-2.4	-1.8	0.6
2003/04	5.2	6.7	1.5
2004/05	-2.5	-6.2	-3.7
2005/06	1.3	1.1	-0.2
2006/07	1.9	-2.2	-4.1
2007/08	-9.2	-14.1	-4.9
2008/09	-2.4	-7.0	-4.6
2009/10	7.5	15.2	7.8
2010/11	5.9	4.6	-1.3
2011/12	13.1	20.7	7.7
2012/13	12.4	16.0	3.6
2013/14	2.3	1.0	-1.3
2014/15	4.5	1.1	-3.4
2015/16	3.0	-2.0	-5.0
Avg.	3.8 %	5.7 %	1.9 %
Fq > 0	70 %	67 %	63 %

Financials* vs. S&P 500
1989/90 to 2015/16

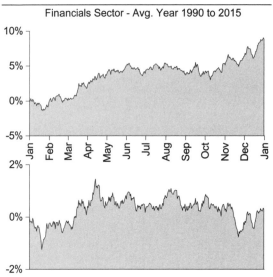

Financials Sector - Avg. Year 1990 to 2015

Financials / S&P 500 Relative Strength - Avg Yr. 1990-2015

The main driver for the strong seasonal performance of the financial sector has been the year-end earnings of the banks that start to report in mid-January. A strong performance from mid-December has been the result of investors getting into the market early to take advantage of positive year-end earnings.

Interest rates, after the U.S. Federal Reserve's quarter point increase in its target interest rate in December of 2015, continue to be at historic lows. If the Federal Reserve continues to increase its target interest rate, banks should benefit in the short-term as their net interest margin will increase. A large portion of their loans are tied to the Federal Reserve's target rate and with an increase in the target rate, the banks will earn more money. Although the interest that they will have to pay out will also increase, the rate of increase will be much slower.

On the other hand, a tighter monetary policy will slow the economy and reduce bank profits. Given this volatile situation, investors should concentrate their financial investments during the sector's strong seasonal period.

It should be noted that Canadian banks have their year-ends at the end of October (reporting in November) and as such, their seasonally strong period starts in October.

Financial SP GIC Sector # 40: For more information on the financial sector, see www.standardandpoors.com

Financials Performance

Financials Monthly Performance (1990-2015)

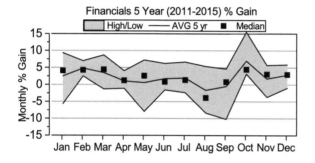

	Jan	Feb	Mar	Apr	May	Jun	Jul	Aug	Sep	Oct	Nov	Dec
Avg. % Gain	-0.3	0.1	2.0	2.1	1.5	-1.2	1.4	-1.5	-0.6	1.4	0.7	2.2
Med. % Gain	0.1	1.9	0.1	1.2	1.8	-0.3	2.0	-0.2	1.2	1.6	1.9	1.8
Fq %>0	50	65	54	62	65	46	62	50	58	65	58	73
Fq %>S&P 500	62	65	62	50	46	42	50	38	54	42	35	58

Financials 5 Year (2011-2015) % Gain

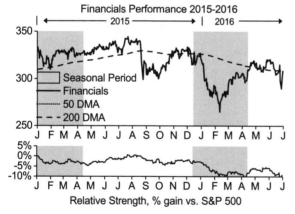

Financials Performance 2015-2016

Relative Strength, % gain vs. S&P 500

From 1990 to 2015, December through to April, the core of the seasonal time period for the financial sector, have been the only months (other than September) that have outperformed the S&P 500 at least half of the time. Over the same yearly time period, there has been a large dispersion between the monthly averages and the medians, indicating inconsistent performance of the financial sector. These results have been largely skewed by the 2008-2009 financial crisis. Over the last five years, the summer months have been the weaker months for the financial sector, consistent with its seasonal trend. In its 2015/16 seasonal period, the financial sector underperformed the S&P 500.

JANUARY

M	T	W	T	F	S	S
1	2	3	4	5	6	7
8	9	10	11	12	13	14
15	16	17	18	19	20	21
22	23	24	25	26	27	28
29	30	31				

FEBRUARY

M	T	W	T	F	S	S
			1	2	3	4
5	6	7	8	9	10	11
12	13	14	15	16	17	18
19	20	21	22	23	24	25
26	27	28				

MARCH

M	T	W	T	F	S	S
			1	2	3	4
5	6	7	8	9	10	11
12	13	14	15	16	17	18
19	20	21	22	23	24	25
26	27	28	29	30	31	

APRIL

M	T	W	T	F	S	S
						1
2	3	4	5	6	7	8
9	10	11	12	13	14	15
16	17	18	19	20	21	22
23	24	25	26	27	28	29
30						

MAY

M	T	W	T	F	S	S
	1	2	3	4	5	6
7	8	9	10	11	12	13
14	15	16	17	18	19	20
21	22	23	24	25	26	27
28	29	30	31			

JUNE

M	T	W	T	F	S	S
			1	2	3
4	5	6	7	8	9	10
11	12	13	14	15	16	17
18	19	20	21	22	23	24
25	26	27	28	29	30	

APPENDIX

STOCK MARKET RETURNS

S&P 500
PERCENT CHANGES

	JAN	FEB	MAR	APR	MAY	JUN
1950	1.5 %	1.0 %	0.4 %	4.5 %	3.9 %	— 5.8 %
1951	6.1	0.6	— 1.8	4.8	— 4.1	— 2.6
1952	1.6	— 3.6	4.8	— 4.3	2.3	4.6
1953	— 0.7	— 1.8	— 2.4	— 2.6	— 0.3	— 1.6
1954	5.1	0.3	3.0	4.9	3.3	0.1
1955	1.8	0.4	— 0.5	3.8	— 0.1	8.2
1956	— 3.6	3.5	6.9	— 0.2	— 6.6	3.9
1957	— 4.2	— 3.3	2.0	3.7	3.7	— 0.1
1958	4.3	2.1	3.1	3.2	1.5	2.6
1959	0.4	— 0.1	0.1	3.9	1.9	— 0.4
1960	— 7.1	0.9	— 1.4	— 1.8	2.7	2.0
1961	6.3	2.7	2.6	0.4	1.9	— 2.9
1962	— 3.8	1.6	— 0.6	— 6.2	— 8.6	— 8.2
1963	4.9	— 2.9	3.5	4.9	1.4	— 2.0
1964	2.7	1.0	1.5	0.6	1.1	1.6
1965	3.3	— 0.1	— 1.5	3.4	— 0.8	— 4.9
1966	0.5	— 1.8	— 2.2	2.1	— 5.4	— 1.6
1967	7.8	0.2	3.9	4.2	— 5.2	1.8
1968	— 4.4	— 3.1	0.9	8.0	1.3	0.9
1969	— 0.8	— 4.7	3.4	2.1	— 0.2	— 5.6
1970	— 7.6	5.3	0.1	— 9.0	— 6.1	— 5.0
1971	4.0	0.9	3.7	3.6	— 4.2	— 0.9
1972	1.8	2.5	0.6	0.4	1.7	— 2.2
1973	— 1.7	— 3.7	— 0.1	— 4.1	— 1.9	— 0.7
1974	— 1.0	— 0.4	— 2.3	— 3.9	— 3.4	— 1.5
1975	12.3	6.0	2.2	4.7	4.4	4.4
1976	11.8	— 1.1	3.1	— 1.1	— 1.4	4.1
1977	— 5.1	— 2.2	— 1.4	0.0	— 2.4	4.5
1978	— 6.2	— 2.5	2.5	8.5	0.4	— 1.8
1979	4.0	— 3.7	5.5	0.2	— 2.6	3.9
1980	5.8	— 0.4	— 10.2	4.1	4.7	2.7
1981	— 4.6	1.3	3.6	— 2.3	— 0.2	— 1.0
1982	— 1.8	— 6.1	— 1.0	4.0	— 3.9	— 2.0
1983	3.3	1.9	3.3	7.5	— 1.2	3.2
1984	— 0.9	— 3.9	1.3	0.5	— 5.9	1.7
1985	7.4	0.9	— 0.3	— 0.5	5.4	1.2
1986	0.2	7.1	5.3	— 1.4	5.0	1.4
1987	13.2	3.7	2.6	— 1.1	0.6	4.8
1988	4.0	4.2	— 3.3	0.9	0.3	4.3
1989	7.1	— 2.9	2.1	5.0	3.5	— 0.8
1990	— 6.9	0.9	2.4	— 2.7	9.2	— 0.9
1991	4.2	6.7	2.2	0.0	3.9	— 4.8
1992	— 2.0	1.0	— 2.2	2.8	0.1	— 1.7
1993	0.7	1.0	1.9	— 2.5	2.3	0.1
1994	3.3	— 3.0	— 4.6	1.2	1.2	— 2.7
1995	2.4	3.6	2.7	2.8	3.6	2.1
1996	3.3	0.7	0.8	1.3	2.3	0.2
1997	6.1	0.6	— 4.3	5.8	5.9	4.3
1998	1.0	7.0	5.0	0.9	— 1.9	3.9
1999	4.1	— 3.2	3.9	3.8	— 2.5	5.4
2000	— 5.1	— 2.0	9.7	— 3.1	— 2.2	2.4
2001	3.5	— 9.2	— 6.4	7.7	0.5	— 2.5
2002	— 1.6	— 2.1	3.7	— 6.1	— 0.9	— 7.2
2003	— 2.7	— 1.7	0.8	8.1	5.1	1.1
2004	1.7	1.2	— 1.6	— 1.7	1.2	1.8
2005	— 2.5	1.9	— 1.9	— 2.0	3.0	0.0
2006	2.5	0.0	1.1	1.2	— 3.1	0.0
2007	1.4	— 2.2	1.0	4.3	3.3	— 1.8
2008	— 6.1	— 3.5	— 0.6	4.8	1.1	— 8.6
2009	— 8.6	— 11.0	8.5	9.4	5.3	0.0
2010	— 3.7	2.9	5.9	1.5	— 8.2	— 5.4
2011	2.3	3.2	— 0.1	2.8	— 1.4	— 1.8
2012	4.4	4.1	3.1	— 0.7	— 6.3	4.0
2013	5.0	1.1	3.6	1.8	2.1	— 1.5
2014	— 3.6	4.3	0.7	0.6	2.1	1.9
2015	— 3.1	5.5	— 1.7	0.9	1.0	— 2.1
FQ POS*	40/ 66	37 / 66	43 / 66	45 / 66	38 / 66	34 / 66
% FQ POS*	61 %	56 %	65 %	68 %	58 %	52 %
AVG GAIN*	1.0 %	0.1 %	1.2 %	1.5 %	0.2 %	0.0 %
RANK GAIN*	5	9	4	3	8	10

S&P 500 PERCENT CHANGES · STOCK MKT

JUL	AUG	SEP	OCT	NOV	DEC		YEAR
0.8 %	3.3 %	5.6 %	0.4 %	— 0.1 %	4.6 %	**1950**	21.7 %
6.9	3.9	— 0.1	— 1.4	— 0.3	3.9	**1951**	16.5
1.8	— 1.5	— 2.0	— 0.1	4.6	3.5	**1952**	11.8
2.5	— 5.8	0.1	5.1	0.9	0.2	**1953**	— 6.6
5.7	— 3.4	8.3	— 1.9	8.1	5.1	**1954**	45.0
6.1	— 0.8	1.1	— 3.0	7.5	— 0.1	**1955**	26.4
5.2	— 3.8	— 4.5	0.5	— 1.1	3.5	**1956**	2.6
1.1	— 5.6	— 6.2	— 3.2	1.6	— 4.1	**1957**	— 14.3
4.3	1.2	4.8	2.5	2.2	5.2	**1958**	38.1
3.5	— 1.5	— 4.6	1.1	1.3	2.8	**1959**	8.5
— 2.5	2.6	— 6.0	— 0.2	4.0	4.6	**1960**	— 3.0
3.3	2.0	— 2.0	2.8	3.9	0.3	**1961**	23.1
6.4	1.5	— 4.8	0.4	10.2	1.3	**1962**	— 11.8
— 0.3	4.9	— 1.1	3.2	— 1.1	2.4	**1963**	18.9
1.8	— 1.6	2.9	0.8	— 0.5	0.4	**1964**	13.0
1.3	2.3	3.2	2.7	— 0.9	0.9	**1965**	9.1
— 1.3	— 7.8	— 0.7	4.8	0.3	— 0.1	**1966**	— 13.1
4.5	— 1.2	3.3	— 3.5	0.8	2.6	**1967**	20.1
— 1.8	1.1	3.9	0.7	4.8	— 4.2	**1968**	7.7
— 6.0	4.0	— 2.5	4.3	— 3.4	— 1.9	**1969**	— 11.4
7.3	4.4	3.4	— 1.2	4.7	5.7	**1970**	0.1
— 3.2	3.6	— 0.7	— 4.2	— 0.3	8.6	**1971**	10.8
0.2	3.4	— 0.5	0.9	4.6	1.2	**1972**	15.6
3.8	— 3.7	4.0	— 0.1	— 11.4	1.7	**1973**	— 17.4
— 7.8	— 9.0	— 11.9	16.3	— 5.3	— 2.0	**1974**	— 29.7
6.8	— 2.1	— 3.5	6.2	2.5	— 1.2	**1975**	31.5
— 0.8	— 0.5	2.3	— 2.2	— 0.8	5.2	**1976**	19.1
— 1.6	— 2.1	— 0.2	— 4.3	2.7	0.3	**1977**	— 11.5
5.4	2.6	— 0.7	— 9.2	1.7	1.5	**1978**	1.1
0.9	5.3	0.0	— 6.9	4.3	1.7	**1979**	12.3
6.5	0.6	2.5	1.6	10.2	— 3.4	**1980**	25.8
— 0.2	— 6.2	— 5.4	4.9	3.7	— 3.0	**1981**	— 9.7
— 2.3	11.6	0.8	11.0	3.6	1.5	**1982**	14.8
— 3.0	1.1	1.0	— 1.5	1.7	— 0.9	**1983**	17.3
— 1.6	10.6	— 0.3	0.0	— 1.5	2.2	**1984**	1.4
— 0.5	— 1.2	— 3.5	4.3	6.5	4.5	**1985**	26.3
— 5.9	7.1	— 8.5	5.5	2.1	— 2.8	**1986**	14.6
4.8	3.5	— 2.4	— 21.8	— 8.5	7.3	**1987**	2.0
— 0.5	— 3.9	4.0	2.6	— 1.9	1.5	**1988**	12.4
8.8	1.6	— 0.7	— 2.5	1.7	2.1	**1989**	27.3
— 0.5	— 9.4	— 5.1	— 0.7	6.0	2.5	**1990**	— 6.6
4.5	2.0	— 1.9	1.2	— 4.4	11.2	**1991**	26.3
3.9	— 2.4	0.9	0.2	3.0	1.0	**1992**	4.5
— 0.5	3.4	— 1.0	1.9	— 1.3	1.0	**1993**	7.1
3.1	3.8	— 2.7	2.1	— 4.0	1.2	**1994**	— 1.5
3.2	0.0	4.0	— 0.5	4.1	1.7	**1995**	34.1
— 4.6	1.9	5.4	2.6	7.3	— 2.2	**1996**	20.3
7.8	— 5.7	5.3	— 3.4	4.5	1.6	**1997**	31.0
— 1.2	— 14.6	6.2	8.0	5.9	5.6	**1998**	26.7
— 3.2	— 0.6	— 2.9	6.3	1.9	5.8	**1999**	19.5
— 1.6	6.1	— 5.3	— 0.5	— 8.0	0.4	**2000**	— 10.1
— 1.1	— 6.4	— 8.2	1.8	7.5	0.8	**2001**	— 13.0
— 7.9	0.5	— 11.0	8.6	5.7	— 6.0	**2002**	— 23.4
1.6	1.8	— 1.2	5.5	0.7	5.1	**2003**	26.4
-3.4	0.2	0.9	1.4	3.9	3.2	**2004**	9.0
3.6	— 1.1	0.7	— 1.8	3.5	— 0.1	**2005**	3.0
0.5	2.1	2.5	3.2	1.6	1.3	**2006**	13.6
— 3.2	1.3	3.6	1.5	— 4.4	— 0.9	**2007**	3.5
— 1.0	1.2	— 9.1	— 16.9	— 7.5	0.8	**2008**	-38.5
7.4	3.4	3.6	— 2.0	5.7	1.8	**2009**	23.5
6.9	— 4.7	8.8	3.7	— 0.2	6.5	**2010**	12.8
— 2.1	— 5.7	— 7.2	10.8	— 0.5	0.9	**2011**	0.0
1.3	2.0	2.4	— 2.0	0.3	0.7	**2012**	13.4
4.9	— 3.1	3.0	4.5	2.8	2.4	**2013**	29.6
— 1.5	3.8	— 1.6	2.3	2.5	— 0.4	**2014**	11.4
2.0	— 6.3	— 2.6	8.3	0.1	— 1.8	**2015**	— 0.7
36 / 66	36 / 66	29 / 66	40 / 66	44/ 66	49 / 66		48 / 66
55 %	55 %	44 %	61 %	67 %	74 %		73 %
1.0 %	— 0.1 %	— 0.5 %	0.9 %	1.5 %	1.6 %		8.9 %
6	11	12	7	2	1		

S&P 500 MONTH
CLOSING VALUES

	JAN	FEB	MAR	APR	MAY	JUN
1950	17	17	17	18	19	18
1951	22	22	21	22	22	21
1952	24	23	24	23	24	25
1953	26	26	25	25	25	24
1954	26	26	27	28	29	29
1955	37	37	37	38	38	41
1956	44	45	48	48	45	47
1957	45	43	44	46	47	47
1958	42	41	42	43	44	45
1959	55	55	55	58	59	58
1960	56	56	55	54	56	57
1961	62	63	65	65	67	65
1962	69	70	70	65	60	55
1963	66	64	67	70	71	69
1964	77	78	79	79	80	82
1965	88	87	86	89	88	84
1966	93	91	89	91	86	85
1967	87	87	90	94	89	91
1968	92	89	90	97	99	100
1969	103	98	102	104	103	98
1970	85	90	90	82	77	73
1971	96	97	100	104	100	99
1972	104	107	107	108	110	107
1973	116	112	112	107	105	104
1974	97	96	94	90	87	86
1975	77	82	83	87	91	95
1976	101	100	103	102	100	104
1977	102	100	98	98	96	100
1978	89	87	89	97	97	96
1979	100	96	102	102	99	103
1980	114	114	102	106	111	114
1981	130	131	136	133	133	131
1982	120	113	112	116	112	110
1983	145	148	153	164	162	168
1984	163	157	159	160	151	153
1985	180	181	181	180	190	192
1986	212	227	239	236	247	251
1987	274	284	292	288	290	304
1988	257	268	259	261	262	274
1989	297	289	295	310	321	318
1990	329	332	340	331	361	358
1991	344	367	375	375	390	371
1992	409	413	404	415	415	408
1993	439	443	452	440	450	451
1994	482	467	446	451	457	444
1995	470	487	501	515	533	545
1996	636	640	646	654	669	671
1997	786	791	757	801	848	885
1998	980	1049	1102	1112	1091	1134
1999	1280	1238	1286	1335	1302	1373
2000	1394	1366	1499	1452	1421	1455
2001	1366	1240	1160	1249	1256	1224
2002	1130	1107	1147	1077	1067	990
2003	856	841	848	917	964	975
2004	1131	1145	1126	1107	1121	1141
2005	1181	1204	1181	1157	1192	1191
2006	1280	1281	1295	1311	1270	1270
2007	1438	1407	1421	1482	1531	1503
2008	1379	1331	1323	1386	1400	1280
2009	826	735	798	873	919	919
2010	1074	1104	1169	1187	1089	1031
2011	1286	1327	1326	1364	1345	1321
2012	1312	1366	1408	1398	1310	1362
2013	1498	1515	1569	1598	1631	1606
2014	1783	1869	1872	1884	1924	1960
2015	1995	2105	2068	2086	2107	2063

S&P 500 MONTH CLOSING VALUES

JUL	AUG	SEP	OCT	NOV	DEC	
18	18	19	20	20	20	1950
22	23	23	23	23	24	1951
25	25	25	25	26	27	1952
25	23	23	25	25	25	1953
31	30	32	32	34	36	1954
44	43	44	42	46	45	1955
49	48	45	46	45	47	1956
48	45	42	41	42	40	1957
47	48	50	51	52	55	1958
61	60	57	58	58	60	1959
56	57	54	53	56	58	1960
67	68	67	69	71	72	1961
58	59	56	57	62	63	1962
69	73	72	74	73	75	1963
83	82	84	85	84	85	1964
85	87	90	92	92	92	1965
84	77	77	80	80	80	1966
95	94	97	93	94	96	1967
98	99	103	103	108	104	1968
92	96	93	97	94	92	1969
78	82	84	83	87	92	1970
96	99	98	94	94	102	1971
107	111	111	112	117	118	1972
108	104	108	108	96	98	1973
79	72	64	74	70	69	1974
89	87	84	89	91	90	1975
103	103	105	103	102	107	1976
99	97	97	92	95	95	1977
101	103	103	93	95	96	1978
104	109	109	102	106	108	1979
122	122	125	127	141	136	1980
131	123	116	122	126	123	1981
107	120	120	134	139	141	1982
163	164	166	164	166	165	1983
151	167	166	166	164	167	1984
191	189	182	190	202	211	1985
236	253	231	244	249	242	1986
319	330	322	252	230	247	1987
272	262	272	279	274	278	1988
346	351	349	340	346	353	1989
356	323	306	304	322	330	1990
388	395	388	392	375	417	1991
424	414	418	419	431	436	1992
448	464	459	468	462	466	1993
458	475	463	472	454	459	1994
562	562	584	582	605	616	1995
640	652	687	705	757	741	1996
954	899	947	915	955	970	1997
1121	957	1017	1099	1164	1229	1998
1329	1320	1283	1363	1389	1469	1999
1431	1518	1437	1429	1315	1320	2000
1211	1134	1041	1060	1139	1148	2001
912	916	815	886	936	880	2002
990	1008	996	1051	1058	1112	2003
1102	1104	1115	1130	1174	1212	2004
1234	1220	1229	1207	1249	1248	2005
1277	1304	1336	1378	1401	1418	2006
1455	1474	1527	1549	1481	1468	2007
1267	1283	1165	969	896	903	2008
987	1021	1057	1036	1096	1115	2009
1102	1049	1141	1183	1181	1258	2010
1292	1219	1131	1253	1247	1258	2011
1379	1407	1441	1412	1416	1426	2012
1686	1633	1682	1757	1806	1848	2013
1931	2003	1972	2018	2068	2059	2014
2104	1972	1920	2079	2080	2044	2015

DOW JONES PERCENT MONTH CHANGES

	JAN	FEB	MAR	APR	MAY	JUN
1950	0.8 %	0.8 %	1.3 %	4.0 %	4.2 %	— 6.4 %
1951	5.7	1.3	— 1.7	4.5	— 3.6	— 2.8
1952	0.6	— 3.9	3.6	— 4.4	2.1	4.3
1953	— 0.7	— 2.0	— 1.5	— 1.8	— 0.9	— 1.5
1954	4.1	0.7	3.1	5.2	2.6	1.8
1955	1.1	0.8	— 0.5	3.9	— 0.2	6.2
1956	— 3.6	2.8	5.8	0.8	— 7.4	3.1
1957	— 4.1	— 3.0	2.2	4.1	2.1	— 0.3
1958	3.3	— 2.2	1.6	2.0	1.5	3.3
1959	1.8	1.6	— 0.3	3.7	3.2	0.0
1960	— 8.4	1.2	— 2.1	— 2.4	4.0	2.4
1961	5.2	2.1	2.2	0.3	2.7	— 1.8
1962	— 4.3	1.2	— 0.2	— 5.9	— 7.8	— 8.5
1963	4.7	— 2.9	3.0	5.2	1.3	— 2.8
1964	2.9	1.9	1.6	— 0.3	1.2	1.3
1965	3.3	0.1	— 1.6	3.7	— 0.5	— 5.4
1966	1.5	— 3.2	— 2.8	1.0	— 5.3	— 1.6
1967	8.2	— 1.2	3.2	3.6	— 5.0	0.9
1968	— 5.5	— 1.8	0.0	8.5	— 1.4	— 0.1
1969	0.2	— 4.3	3.3	1.6	— 1.3	— 6.9
1970	— 7.0	4.5	1.0	— 6.3	— 4.8	— 2.4
1971	3.5	1.2	2.9	4.1	— 3.6	— 1.8
1972	1.3	2.9	1.4	1.4	0.7	— 3.3
1973	— 2.1	— 4.4	— 0.4	— 3.1	— 2.2	— 1.1
1974	0.6	0.6	— 1.6	— 1.2	— 4.1	0.0
1975	14.2	5.0	3.9	6.9	1.3	5.6
1976	14.4	— 0.3	2.8	— 0.3	— 2.2	2.8
1977	— 5.0	— 1.9	— 1.8	0.8	— 3.0	2.0
1978	— 7.4	— 3.6	2.1	10.5	0.4	— 2.6
1979	4.2	— 3.6	6.6	— 0.8	— 3.8	2.4
1980	4.4	— 1.5	— 9.0	4.0	4.1	2.0
1981	— 1.7	2.9	3.0	— 0.6	— 0.6	— 1.5
1982	— 0.4	— 5.4	— 0.2	3.1	— 3.4	— 0.9
1983	2.8	3.4	1.6	8.5	— 2.1	1.8
1984	— 3.0	— 5.4	0.9	0.5	— 5.6	2.5
1985	6.2	— 0.2	— 1.3	— 0.7	4.6	1.5
1986	1.6	8.8	6.4	— 1.9	5.2	0.9
1987	13.8	3.1	3.6	— 0.8	0.2	5.5
1988	1.0	5.8	— 4.0	2.2	— 0.1	5.4
1989	8.0	— 3.6	1.6	5.5	2.5	— 1.6
1990	— 5.9	1.4	3.0	— 1.9	8.3	0.1
1991	3.9	5.3	1.1	— 0.9	4.8	— 4.0
1992	1.7	1.4	— 1.0	3.8	1.1	— 2.3
1993	0.3	1.8	1.9	— 0.2	2.9	— 0.3
1994	6.0	— 3.7	— 5.1	1.3	2.1	— 3.5
1995	0.2	4.3	3.7	3.9	3.3	2.0
1996	5.4	1.7	1.9	— 0.3	1.3	0.2
1997	5.7	0.9	— 4.3	6.5	4.6	4.7
1998	0.0	8.1	3.0	3.0	— 1.8	0.6
1999	1.9	— 0.6	5.2	10.2	— 2.1	3.9
2000	— 4.5	— 7.4	7.8	— 1.7	— 2.0	— 0.7
2001	0.9	— 3.6	— 5.9	8.7	1.6	— 3.8
2002	— 1.0	1.9	2.9	— 4.4	— 0.2	— 6.9
2003	— 3.5	— 2.0	1.3	6.1	4.4	1.5
2004	0.3	0.9	— 2.1	— 1.3	— 0.4	2.4
2005	— 2.7	2.6	— 2.4	— 3.0	2.7	— 1.8
2006	1.4	1.2	1.1	2.3	— 1.7	— 0.2
2007	1.3	— 2.8	0.7	5.7	4.3	— 1.6
2008	— 4.6	— 3.0	0.0	4.5	— 1.4	— 10.2
2009	— 8.8	— 11.7	7.7	7.3	4.1	— 0.6
2010	— 3.5	2.6	5.1	1.4	— 7.9	— 3.6
2011	2.7	2.8	0.8	4.0	— 1.9	— 1.2
2012	3.4	3.8	2.0	0.0	— 6.2	3.9
2013	5.8	4.8	3.7	1.8	1.9	— 1.4
2014	— 5.3	5.8	0.8	0.7	0.8	0.7
2015	— 3.7	6.8	— 2.0	0.4	1.0	— 2.2
FQ POS	42 / 66	38 / 66	43 / 66	44 / 66	34 / 66	30 / 66
% FQ POS	64 %	58 %	65 %	67 %	52 %	45 %
AVG GAIN	1.0 %	0.3 %	1.1 %	1.9 %	0.0 %	— 0.3 %
RANK GAIN	6	8	5	1	9	11

JUL	AUG	SEP	OCT	NOV	DEC		YEAR
0.1 %	3.6 %	4.4 %	− 0.6 %	1.2 %	3.4 %	**1950**	17.6 %
6.3	4.8	0.3	− 3.2	− 0.4	3.0	**1951**	14.4
1.9	− 1.6	− 1.6	− 0.5	5.4	2.9	**1952**	8.4
2.6	− 5.2	1.1	4.5	2.0	− 0.2	**1953**	− 3.8
4.3	− 3.5	7.4	− 2.3	9.9	4.6	**1954**	44.0
3.2	0.5	− 0.3	− 2.5	6.2	1.1	**1955**	20.8
5.1	− 3.1	− 5.3	1.0	− 1.5	5.6	**1956**	2.3
1.0	− 4.7	− 5.8	− 3.4	2.0	− 3.2	**1957**	− 12.8
5.2	1.1	4.6	2.1	2.6	4.7	**1958**	34.0
4.9	− 1.6	− 4.9	2.4	1.9	3.1	**1959**	16.4
− 3.7	1.5	− 7.3	0.1	2.9	3.1	**1960**	− 9.3
3.1	2.1	− 2.6	0.4	2.5	1.3	**1961**	18.7
6.5	1.9	− 5.0	1.9	10.1	0.4	**1962**	− 10.8
− 1.6	4.9	0.5	3.1	− 0.6	1.7	**1963**	17.0
1.2	− 0.3	4.4	− 0.3	0.3	− 0.1	**1964**	14.6
1.6	1.3	4.2	3.2	− 1.5	2.4	**1965**	10.9
− 2.6	− 7.0	− 1.8	4.2	− 1.9	− 0.7	**1966**	− 18.9
5.1	− 0.3	2.8	− 5.1	− 0.4	3.3	**1967**	15.2
− 1.6	1.5	4.4	1.8	3.4	− 4.2	**1968**	4.3
− 6.6	2.6	− 2.8	5.3	− 5.1	− 1.5	**1969**	− 15.2
7.4	4.2	− 0.5	− 0.7	5.1	5.6	**1970**	4.8
− 3.7	4.6	− 1.2	− 5.4	− 0.9	7.1	**1971**	6.1
0.5	4.2	− 1.1	0.2	6.6	0.2	**1972**	14.6
3.9	− 4.2	6.7	1.0	− 14.0	3.5	**1973**	− 16.6
− 5.6	− 10.4	− 10.4	9.5	− 7.0	− 0.4	**1974**	− 27.6
− 5.4	0.5	− 5.0	5.3	3.0	− 1.0	**1975**	38.3
− 1.8	− 1.1	1.7	− 2.6	− 1.8	6.1	**1976**	17.9
− 2.9	− 3.2	− 1.7	− 3.4	1.4	0.2	**1977**	− 17.3
5.3	1.7	− 1.3	− 8.5	0.8	0.8	**1978**	− 3.2
0.5	4.9	− 1.0	− 7.2	0.8	2.0	**1979**	4.2
7.8	− 0.3	0.0	− 0.8	7.4	− 2.9	**1980**	14.9
− 2.5	− 7.4	− 3.6	0.3	4.3	− 1.6	**1981**	− 9.2
− 0.4	11.5	− 0.6	10.6	4.8	0.7	**1982**	19.6
− 1.9	1.4	1.4	− 0.6	4.1	− 1.4	**1983**	20.3
− 1.5	9.8	− 1.4	0.1	− 1.5	1.9	**1984**	− 3.7
0.9	− 1.0	− 0.4	3.4	7.1	5.1	**1985**	27.7
− 6.2	6.9	− 6.9	6.2	1.9	− 1.0	**1986**	22.6
6.4	3.5	− 2.5	− 23.2	− 8.0	5.7	**1987**	2.3
− 0.6	− 4.6	4.0	1.7	− 1.6	2.6	**1988**	11.9
9.0	2.9	− 1.6	− 1.8	2.3	1.7	**1989**	27.0
0.9	− 10.0	− 6.2	− 0.4	4.8	2.9	**1990**	− 4.3
4.1	0.6	− 0.9	1.7	− 5.7	9.5	**1991**	20.3
2.3	− 4.0	0.4	− 1.4	2.4	− 0.1	**1992**	4.2
0.7	3.2	− 2.6	3.5	0.1	1.9	**1993**	13.7
3.8	4.0	− 1.8	1.7	− 4.3	2.5	**1994**	2.1
3.3	− 2.1	3.9	− 0.7	6.7	0.8	**1995**	33.5
− 2.2	1.6	4.7	2.5	8.2	− 1.1	**1996**	26.0
7.2	− 7.3	4.2	− 6.3	5.1	1.1	**1997**	22.6
− 0.8	− 15.1	4.0	9.6	6.1	0.7	**1998**	16.1
− 2.9	1.6	− 4.5	3.8	1.4	5.3	**1999**	24.7
0.7	6.6	− 5.0	3.0	− 5.1	3.6	**2000**	− 5.8
0.2	− 5.4	− 11.1	2.6	8.6	1.7	**2001**	− 7.1
5.5	− 0.8	− 12.4	10.6	5.9	− 6.2	**2002**	− 16.8
2.8	2.0	− 1.5	5.7	− 0.2	6.9	**2003**	25.3
− 2.8	0.3	− 0.9	− 0.5	4.0	3.4	**2004**	3.1
3.6	− 1.5	0.8	− 1.2	3.5	− 0.8	**2005**	− 0.6
0.3	1.7	2.6	3.4	1.2	2.0	**2006**	16.3
− 1.5	1.1	4.0	0.2	− 4.0	− 0.8	**2007**	6.4
0.2	1.5	− 6.0	− 14.1	− 5.3	− 0.6	**2008**	− 33.8
8.6	3.5	2.3	0.0	6.5	0.8	**2009**	18.8
7.1	− 4.3	7.7	3.1	− 1.0	5.2	**2010**	11.0
− 2.2	− 4.4	− 6.0	9.5	0.8	1.4	**2011**	5.5
1.0	0.6	2.6	− 2.5	− 0.5	0.6	**2012**	7.3
4.0	− 4.4	2.2	2.8	3.5	3.0	**2013**	26.5
− 1.6	3.2	− 0.3	2.0	2.5	0.0	**2014**	7.5
0.4	− 6.6	− 1.5	8.5	0.3	− 2.2	**2015**	− 2.2
41 / 66	37 / 66	26 / 66	40/ 66	45/ 66	46 / 66		47 / 66
62 %	56 %	39 %	61 %	68 %	70 %		71 %
1.1 %	− 0.2 %	− 0.8 %	0.7 %	1.5 %	1.6 %		8.2 %
4	10	12	7	3	2		

DOW JONES
MONTH CLOSING VALUES

	JAN	FEB	MAR	APR	MAY	JUN
1950	202	203	206	214	223	209
1951	249	252	248	259	250	243
1952	271	260	270	258	263	274
1953	290	284	280	275	272	268
1954	292	295	304	319	328	334
1955	409	412	410	426	425	451
1956	471	484	512	516	478	493
1957	479	465	475	494	505	503
1958	450	440	447	456	463	478
1959	594	604	602	624	644	644
1960	623	630	617	602	626	641
1961	648	662	677	679	697	684
1962	700	708	707	665	613	561
1963	683	663	683	718	727	707
1964	785	800	813	811	821	832
1965	903	904	889	922	918	868
1966	984	952	925	934	884	870
1967	850	839	866	897	853	860
1968	856	841	841	912	899	898
1969	946	905	936	950	938	873
1970	744	778	786	736	700	684
1971	869	879	904	942	908	891
1972	902	928	941	954	961	929
1973	999	955	951	921	901	892
1974	856	861	847	837	802	802
1975	704	739	768	821	832	879
1976	975	973	1000	997	975	1003
1977	954	936	919	927	899	916
1978	770	742	757	837	841	819
1979	839	809	862	855	822	842
1980	876	863	786	817	851	868
1981	947	975	1004	998	992	977
1982	871	824	823	848	820	812
1983	1076	1113	1130	1226	1200	1222
1984	1221	1155	1165	1171	1105	1132
1985	1287	1284	1267	1258	1315	1336
1986	1571	1709	1819	1784	1877	1893
1987	2158	2224	2305	2286	2292	2419
1988	1958	2072	1988	2032	2031	2142
1989	2342	2258	2294	2419	2480	2440
1990	2591	2627	2707	2657	2877	2881
1991	2736	2882	2914	2888	3028	2907
1992	3223	3268	3236	3359	3397	3319
1993	3310	3371	3435	3428	3527	3516
1994	3978	3832	3636	3682	3758	3625
1995	3844	4011	4158	4321	4465	4556
1996	5395	5486	5587	5569	5643	5655
1997	6813	6878	6584	7009	7331	7673
1998	7907	8546	8800	9063	8900	8952
1999	9359	9307	9786	10789	10560	10971
2000	10941	10128	10922	10734	10522	10448
2001	10887	10495	9879	10735	10912	10502
2002	9920	10106	10404	9946	9925	9243
2003	8054	7891	7992	8480	8850	8985
2004	10488	10584	10358	10226	10188	10435
2005	10490	10766	10504	10193	10467	10275
2006	10865	10993	11109	11367	11168	11150
2007	12622	12269	12354	13063	13628	13409
2008	12650	12266	12263	12820	12638	11350
2009	8001	7063	7609	8168	8500	8447
2010	10067	10325	10857	11009	10137	9774
2011	11892	12226	12320	12811	12570	12414
2012	12633	12952	13212	13214	12393	12880
2013	13861	14054	14579	14840	15116	14910
2014	15699	16322	16458	16581	16717	16827
2015	17165	18133	17776	17841	18011	17620

DOW JONES
MONTH CLOSING VALUES

STOCK MKT

JUL	AUG	SEP	OCT	NOV	DEC	
209	217	226	225	228	235	1950
258	270	271	262	261	269	1951
280	275	271	269	284	292	1952
275	261	264	276	281	281	1953
348	336	361	352	387	404	1954
466	468	467	455	483	488	1955
518	502	475	480	473	500	1956
509	484	456	441	450	436	1957
503	509	532	543	558	584	1958
675	664	632	647	659	679	1959
617	626	580	580	597	616	1960
705	720	701	704	722	731	1961
598	609	579	590	649	652	1962
695	729	733	755	751	763	1963
841	839	875	873	875	874	1964
882	893	931	961	947	969	1965
847	788	774	807	792	786	1966
904	901	927	880	876	905	1967
883	896	936	952	985	944	1968
816	837	813	856	812	800	1969
734	765	761	756	794	839	1970
858	898	887	839	831	890	1971
925	964	953	956	1018	1020	1972
926	888	947	957	822	851	1973
757	679	608	666	619	616	1974
832	835	794	836	861	852	1975
985	974	990	965	947	1005	1976
890	862	847	818	830	831	1977
862	877	866	793	799	805	1978
846	888	879	816	822	839	1979
935	933	932	925	993	964	1980
952	882	850	853	889	875	1981
809	901	896	992	1039	1047	1982
1199	1216	1233	1225	1276	1259	1983
1115	1224	1207	1207	1189	1212	1984
1348	1334	1329	1374	1472	1547	1985
1775	1898	1768	1878	1914	1896	1986
2572	2663	2596	1994	1834	1939	1987
2129	2032	2113	2149	2115	2169	1988
2661	2737	2693	2645	2706	2753	1989
2905	2614	2453	2442	2560	2634	1990
3025	3044	3017	3069	2895	3169	1991
3394	3257	3272	3226	3305	3301	1992
3540	3651	3555	3681	3684	3754	1993
3765	3913	3843	3908	3739	3834	1994
4709	4611	4789	4756	5075	5117	1995
5529	5616	5882	6029	6522	6448	1996
8223	7622	7945	7442	7823	7908	1997
8883	7539	7843	8592	9117	9181	1998
10655	10829	10337	10730	10878	11453	1999
10522	11215	10651	10971	10415	10788	2000
10523	9950	8848	9075	9852	10022	2001
8737	8664	7592	8397	8896	8342	2002
9234	9416	9275	9801	9782	10454	2003
10140	10174	10080	10027	10428	10783	2004
10641	10482	10569	10440	10806	10718	2005
11186	11381	11679	12801	12222	12463	2006
13212	13358	13896	13930	13372	13265	2007
11378	11544	10851	9325	8829	8776	2008
9172	9496	9712	9713	10345	10428	2009
10466	10015	10788	11118	11006	11578	2010
12143	11614	10913	11955	12046	12218	2011
13009	13091	13437	13096	13026	13104	2012
15500	14810	15130	15546	16086	16577	2013
16563	17098	17043	17391	17828	17823	2014
17690	16528	16285	17664	17720	17425	2015

NASDAQ PERCENT MONTH CHANGES

	JAN	FEB	MAR	APR	MAY	JUN
1972	4.2	5.5	2.2	2.5	0.9	— 1.8
1973	— 4.0	— 6.2	— 2.4	— 8.2	— 4.8	— 1.6
1974	3.0	— 0.6	— 2.2	— 5.9	— 7.7	— 5.3
1975	16.6	4.6	3.6	3.8	5.8	4.7
1976	12.1	3.7	0.4	— 0.6	— 2.3	2.6
1977	— 2.4	— 1.0	— 0.5	1.4	0.1	4.3
1978	— 4.0	0.6	4.7	8.5	4.4	0.0
1979	6.6	— 2.6	7.5	1.6	— 1.8	5.1
1980	7.0	— 2.3	— 17.1	6.9	7.5	4.9
1981	— 2.2	0.1	6.1	3.1	3.1	— 3.5
1982	— 3.8	— 4.8	— 2.1	5.2	— 3.3	— 4.1
1983	6.9	5.0	3.9	8.2	5.3	3.2
1984	— 3.7	— 5.9	— 0.7	— 1.3	— 5.9	2.9
1985	12.8	2.0	— 1.8	0.5	3.6	1.9
1986	3.4	7.1	4.2	2.3	4.4	1.3
1987	12.4	8.4	1.2	— 2.9	— 0.3	2.0
1988	4.3	6.5	2.1	1.2	— 2.3	6.6
1989	5.2	— 0.4	1.8	5.1	4.3	— 2.4
1990	— 8.6	2.4	2.3	— 3.5	9.3	0.7
1991	10.8	9.4	6.4	0.5	4.4	— 6.0
1992	5.8	2.1	— 4.7	— 4.2	1.1	— 3.7
1993	2.9	— 3.7	2.9	— 4.2	5.9	0.5
1994	3.0	— 1.0	— 6.2	— 1.3	0.2	— 4.0
1995	0.4	5.1	3.0	3.3	2.4	8.0
1996	0.7	3.8	0.1	8.1	4.4	— 4.7
1997	6.9	— 5.1	— 6.7	3.2	11.1	3.0
1998	3.1	9.3	3.7	1.8	— 4.8	6.5
1999	14.3	— 8.7	7.6	3.3	— 2.8	8.7
2000	— 3.2	19.2	— 2.6	— 15.6	— 11.9	16.6
2001	12.2	— 22.4	— 14.5	15.0	— 0.3	2.4
2002	— 0.8	— 10.5	6.6	— 8.5	— 4.3	— 9.4
2003	— 1.1	1.3	0.3	9.2	9.0	1.7
2004	3.1	— 1.8	— 1.8	— 3.7	3.5	3.1
2005	— 5.2	— 0.5	— 2.6	— 3.9	7.6	— 0.5
2006	4.6	— 1.1	2.6	— 0.7	— 6.2	— 0.3
2007	2.0	— 1.9	0.2	4.3	3.1	0.0
2008	— 9.9	— 5.0	0.3	5.9	4.6	— 9.1
2009	— 6.4	— 6.7	10.9	12.3	3.3	3.4
2010	— 5.4	4.2	7.1	2.6	— 8.3	— 6.5
2011	1.8	3.0	0.0	3.3	— 1.3	— 2.2
2012	8.0	5.4	4.2	— 1.5	— 7.2	3.8
2013	4.1	0.6	3.4	1.9	3.8	— 1.5
2014	— 1.7	5.0	— 2.5	— 2.0	3.1	3.9
2015	— 2.1	7.1	— 1.3	0.8	2.6	— 1.6
FQ POS	28/44	24/44	27/44	28/44	27/44	25/44
% FQ POS	64 %	55 %	61 %	64 %	61 %	57 %
AVG GAIN	2.6 %	0.7 %	0.7 %	1.3 %	1.0 %	0.8 %
RANK GAIN	1	9	8	4	5	7

NASDAQ PERCENT MONTH CHANGES 🇺🇸 STOCK MKT

JUL	AUG	SEP	OCT	NOV	DEC		YEAR
— 1.8	1.7	— 0.3	0.5	2.1	0.6	**1972**	17.2
7.6	— 3.5	6.0	— 0.9	— 15.1	— 1.4	**1973**	— 31.1
— 7.9	— 10.9	— 10.7	17.2	— 3.5	— 5.0	**1974**	— 35.1
— 4.4	— 5.0	— 5.9	3.6	2.4	— 1.5	**1975**	29.8
1.1	— 1.7	1.7	— 1.0	0.9	7.4	**1976**	26.1
0.9	— 0.5	0.7	— 3.3	5.8	1.8	**1977**	7.3
5.0	6.9	— 1.6	— 16.4	3.2	2.9	**1978**	12.3
2.3	6.4	— 0.3	— 9.6	6.4	4.8	**1979**	28.1
8.9	5.7	3.4	2.7	8.0	— 2.8	**1980**	33.9
— 1.9	— 7.5	— 8.0	8.4	3.1	— 2.7	**1981**	— 3.2
— 2.3	6.2	5.6	13.3	9.3	0.0	**1982**	18.7
— 4.6	— 3.8	1.4	— 7.4	4.1	— 2.5	**1983**	19.9
— 4.2	10.9	— 1.8	— 1.2	— 1.9	1.9	**1984**	— 11.3
1.7	— 1.2	— 5.8	4.4	7.4	3.5	**1985**	31.5
— 8.4	3.1	— 8.4	2.9	— 0.3	— 3.0	**1986**	7.4
2.4	4.6	— 2.4	— 27.2	— 5.6	8.3	**1987**	— 5.2
— 1.9	— 2.8	2.9	— 1.3	— 2.9	2.7	**1988**	15.4
4.2	3.4	0.8	— 3.7	0.1	— 0.3	**1989**	19.2
— 5.2	— 13.0	— 9.6	— 4.3	8.9	4.1	**1990**	— 17.8
5.5	4.7	0.2	3.1	— 3.5	11.9	**1991**	56.9
3.1	— 3.0	3.6	3.8	7.9	3.7	**1992**	15.5
0.1	5.4	2.7	2.2	— 3.2	3.0	**1993**	14.7
2.3	6.0	— 0.2	1.7	— 3.5	0.2	**1994**	— 3.2
7.3	1.9	2.3	— 0.7	2.2	— 0.7	**1995**	39.9
— 8.8	5.6	7.5	— 0.4	5.8	— 0.1	**1996**	22.7
10.5	— 0.4	6.2	— -5.5	0.4	— 1.9	**1997**	21.6
— 1.2	— 19.9	13.0	4.6	10.1	12.5	**1998**	39.6
— 1.8	3.8	0.2	8.0	12.5	22.0	**1999**	85.6
— 5.0	11.7	— 12.7	— 8.3	— 22.9	— 4.9	**2000**	— 39.3
— 6.2	— 10.9	— 17.0	12.8	14.2	1.0	**2001**	— 21.1
— 9.2	— 1.0	— 10.9	13.5	11.2	— 9.7	**2002**	— 31.5
6.9	4.3	— 1.3	8.1	1.5	2.2	**2003**	50.0
— 7.8	— 2.6	3.2	4.1	6.2	3.7	**2004**	8.6
6.2	— 1.5	0.0	— 1.5	5.3	— 1.2	**2005**	1.4
— 3.7	4.4	3.4	4.8	2.7	— 0.7	**2006**	9.5
— 2.2	2.0	4.0	5.8	— 6.9	— 0.3	**2007**	9.8
1.4	1.8	— 11.6	— 17.7	— 10.8	2.7	**2008**	— 40.5
7.8	1.5	5.6	— 3.6	4.9	5.8	**2009**	43.9
6.9	— 6.2	12.0	5.9	— 0.4	6.2	**2010**	16.9
— 0.6	— 6.4	— 6.4	11.1	— 2.4	— 0.6	**2011**	— 1.8
0.2	4.3	1.6	— 4.5	1.1	0.3	**2012**	15.9
6.6	— 1.0	5.1	3.9	3.6	2.9	**2013**	38.3
— 0.9	4.8	— 1.9	3.1	3.5	— 1.2	**2014**	13.4
2.8	— 6.9	— 3.3	9.4	1.1	— 2.0	**2015**	5.7
23/44	23/44	23/44	25/44	30/44	25/44		32/44
52 %	52 %	52 %	57 %	68 %	57 %		73 %
0.3 %	0.0 %	— 0.6 %	0.9 %	1.7 %	1.7 %		12.2 %
10	11	12	6	3	2		

NASDAQ MONTH CLOSING VALUES

	JAN	FEB	MAR	APR	MAY	JUN
1972	119	125	128	131	133	130
1973	128	120	117	108	103	101
1974	95	94	92	87	80	76
1975	70	73	76	79	83	87
1976	87	90	91	90	88	90
1977	96	95	94	95	96	100
1978	101	101	106	115	120	120
1979	126	123	132	134	131	138
1980	162	158	131	140	150	158
1981	198	198	210	217	223	216
1982	188	179	176	185	179	171
1983	248	261	271	293	309	319
1984	268	253	251	247	233	240
1985	279	284	279	281	291	296
1986	336	360	375	383	400	406
1987	392	425	430	418	417	425
1988	345	367	375	379	370	395
1989	401	400	407	428	446	435
1990	416	426	436	420	459	462
1991	414	453	482	485	506	476
1992	620	633	604	579	585	564
1993	696	671	690	661	701	704
1994	800	793	743	734	735	706
1995	755	794	817	844	865	933
1996	1060	1100	1101	1191	1243	1185
1997	1380	1309	1222	1261	1400	1442
1998	1619	1771	1836	1868	1779	1895
1999	2506	2288	2461	2543	2471	2686
2000	3940	4697	4573	3861	3401	3966
2001	2773	2152	1840	2116	2110	2161
2002	1934	1731	1845	1688	1616	1463
2003	1321	1338	1341	1464	1596	1623
2004	2066	2030	1994	1920	1987	2048
2005	2062	2052	1999	1922	2068	2057
2006	2306	2281	2340	2323	2179	2172
2007	2464	2416	2422	2525	2605	2603
2008	2390	2271	2279	2413	2523	2293
2009	1476	1378	1529	1717	1774	1835
2010	2147	2238	2398	2461	2257	2109
2011	2700	2782	2781	2874	2835	2774
2012	2814	2967	3092	3046	2827	2935
2013	3142	3160	3268	3329	3456	3403
2014	4104	4308	4199	4115	4243	4408
2015	4635	4964	4901	4941	5070	4987

JUL	AUG	SEP	OCT	NOV	DEC	
128	130	130	130	133	134	**1972**
109	105	111	110	94	92	**1973**
70	62	56	65	63	60	**1974**
83	79	74	77	79	78	**1975**
91	90	91	90	91	98	**1976**
101	100	101	98	103	105	**1977**
126	135	133	111	115	118	**1978**
141	150	150	136	144	151	**1979**
172	182	188	193	208	202	**1980**
212	196	180	195	201	196	**1981**
167	178	188	213	232	232	**1982**
304	292	297	275	286	279	**1983**
230	255	250	247	242	247	**1984**
301	298	280	293	314	325	**1985**
371	383	351	361	360	349	**1986**
435	455	444	323	305	331	**1987**
387	377	388	383	372	381	**1988**
454	469	473	456	456	455	**1989**
438	381	345	330	359	374	**1990**
502	526	527	543	524	586	**1991**
581	563	583	605	653	677	**1992**
705	743	763	779	754	777	**1993**
722	766	764	777	750	752	**1994**
1001	1020	1044	1036	1059	1052	**1995**
1081	1142	1227	1222	1293	1291	**1996**
1594	1587	1686	1594	1601	1570	**1997**
1872	1499	1694	1771	1950	2193	**1998**
2638	2739	2746	2966	3336	4069	**1999**
3767	4206	3673	3370	2598	2471	**2000**
2027	1805	1499	1690	1931	1950	**2001**
1328	1315	1172	1330	1479	1336	**2002**
1735	1810	1787	1932	1960	2003	**2003**
1887	1838	1897	1975	2097	2175	**2004**
2185	2152	2152	2120	2233	2205	**2005**
2091	2184	2258	2367	2432	2415	**2006**
2546	2596	2702	2859	2661	2652	**2007**
2326	2368	2092	1721	1536	1577	**2008**
1979	2009	2122	2045	2145	2269	**2009**
2255	2114	2369	2507	2498	2653	**2010**
2756	2579	2415	2684	2620	2605	**2011**
2940	3067	3116	2977	3010	3020	**2012**
3626	3590	3771	3920	4060	4177	**2013**
4370	4580	4493	4631	4792	4736	**2014**
5128	4777	4620	5054	5109	5007	**2015**

S&P/TSX MONTH PERCENT CHANGES

	JAN	FEB	MAR	APR	MAY	JUN
1985	8.1	0.0	0.7	0.8	3.8	— 0.8
1986	— 1.7	0.5	6.7	1.1	1.4	— 1.2
1987	9.2	4.5	6.9	— 0.6	— 0.9	1.5
1988	— 3.3	4.8	3.4	0.8	— 2.7	5.9
1989	6.7	— 1.2	0.2	1.4	2.2	1.5
1990	— 6.7	— 0.5	— 1.3	— 8.2	6.7	— 0.6
1991	0.5	5.8	1.0	-0.8	2.2	— 2.3
1992	2.4	— 0.4	— 4.7	— 1.7	1.0	0.0
1993	— 1.3	4.4	4.4	5.2	2.5	2.2
1994	5.4	— 2.9	— 2.1	— 1.4	1.4	— 7.0
1995	— 4.7	2.7	4.6	— -0.8	4.0	1.8
1996	5.4	— 0.7	0.8	3.5	1.9	— 3.9
1997	3.1	0.8	— 5.0	2.2	6.8	0.9
1998	0.0	5.9	6.6	1.4	— 1.0	— 2.9
1999	3.8	— 6.2	4.5	6.3	— 2.5	2.5
2000	0.8	7.6	3.7	— 1.2	— 1.0	10.2
2001	4.3	— 13.3	— 5.8	4.5	2.7	— 5.2
2002	— 0.5	— 0.1	2.8	— 2.4	— 0.1	— 6.7
2003	— 0.7	— 0.2	— 3.2	3.8	4.2	1.8
2004	3.7	3.1	— 2.3	— 4.0	2.1	1.5
2005	— 0.5	5.0	— 0.6	— 3.5	3.6	3.1
2006	6.0	— 2.2	3.6	0.8	— 3.8	— 1.1
2007	1.0	0.1	0.9	1.9	4.8	— 1.1
2008	— 4.9	3.3	— 1.7	4.4	5.6	— 1.7
2009	— 3.3	— 6.6	7.4	6.9	11.2	0.0
2010	— 5.5	4.8	3.5	1.4	— 3.7	— 4.0
2011	0.8	4.3	— 0.1	— 1.2	— 1.0	— 3.6
2012	4.2	1.5	— 2.0	— 0.8	— 6.3	0.7
2013	2.0	1.1	— 0.6	— 2.3	1.6	— 4.1
2014	0.5	3.8	0.9	2.2	— 0.3	3.7
2015	0.3	3.8	— 2.2	2.2	— 1.4	— 3.1
FQ POS	20/31	19/31	18/31	18/31	19/31	14/31
% FQ POS	65 %	61 %	58 %	58 %	61 %	45 %
AVG GAIN	1.1 %	1.1 %	1.0 %	0.7 %	1.4 %	-0.4 %
RANK GAIN	3	4	5	7	2	11

JUL	AUG	SEP	OCT	NOV	DEC		YEAR
2.4	1.5	− 6.7	1.6	6.8	1.3	1985	20.5
− 4.9	3.2	− 1.6	1.6	0.7	0.6	1986	6.0
7.8	− 0.9	− 2.3	− 22.6	− 1.4	6.1	1987	3.1
− 1.9	− 2.7	− 0.1	3.4	− 3.0	2.9	1988	7.3
5.6	1.0	− 1.7	− 0.6	0.6	0.7	1989	17.1
0.5	− 6.0	− 5.6	− 2.5	2.3	3.4	1990	− 18.0
2.1	− 0.6	− 3.7	3.8	− 1.9	1.9	1991	7.8
1.6	− 1.2	− 3.1	1.2	− 1.6	2.1	1992	− 4.6
0.0	4.3	− 3.6	6.6	− 1.8	3.4	1993	29.0
3.8	4.1	0.1	− 1.4	− 4.6	2.9	1994	− 2.5
1.9	− 2.1	0.3	− 1.6	4.5	1.1	1995	11.9
− 2.3	4.3	2.9	5.8	7.5	− 1.5	1996	25.7
6.8	− 3.9	6.5	− 2.8	− 4.8	2.9	1997	13.0
− 5.9	− 20.2	1.5	10.6	2.2	2.2	1998	− 3.2
1.0	− 1.6	− 0.2	4.3	3.6	11.9	1999	29.7
2.1	8.1	− 7.7	− 7.1	− 8.5	1.3	2000	6.2
− 0.6	− 3.8	− 7.6	0.7	7.8	3.5	2001	− 13.9
− 7.6	0.1	− 6.5	1.1	5.1	0.7	2002	− 14.0
3.9	3.6	− 1.3	4.7	1.1	4.6	2003	24.3
− 1.0	− 1.0	3.5	2.3	1.8	2.4	2004	12.5
5.3	2.4	3.2	− 5.7	4.2	4.1	2005	21.9
1.9	2.1	− 2.6	5.0	3.3	1.2	2006	14.5
− 0.3	− 1.5	3.2	3.7	− 6.4	1.1	2007	7.2
− 6.0	1.3	− 14.7	− 16.9	− 5.0	− 3.1	2008	− 35.0
4.0	0.8	4.8	− 4.2	4.9	2.6	2009	30.7
3.7	1.7	3.8	2.5	2.2	3.8	2010	14.4
− 2.7	− 1.4	− 9.0	5.4	− 0.4	− 2.0	2011	− 11.1
0.6	2.4	3.1	0.9	− 1.5	1.6	2012	4.0
2.9	1.3	1.1	4.5	0.3	1.7	2013	9.6
1.2	1.9	− 4.3	− 2.3	0.9	− 0.8	2014	7.4
− 0.6	− 4.2	− 4.0	1.7	− 0.4	− 3.4	2015	− 11.1
20/31	17/31	12/31	20/31	18/31	26/31		22/31
65 %	55 %	39 %	65 %	58 %	84 %		71 %
0.8 %	− 0.2 %	− 1.7 %	0.1 %	0.6 %	2.0 %		6.8 %
6	10	12	9	8	1		

S&P/TSX MONTH CLOSING VALUES

	JAN	FEB	MAR	APR	MAY	JUN
1985	2595	2595	2613	2635	2736	2713
1986	2843	2856	3047	3079	3122	3086
1987	3349	3499	3739	3717	3685	3740
1988	3057	3205	3314	3340	3249	3441
1989	3617	3572	3578	3628	3707	3761
1990	3704	3687	3640	3341	3565	3544
1991	3273	3462	3496	3469	3546	3466
1992	3596	3582	3412	3356	3388	3388
1993	3305	3452	3602	3789	3883	3966
1994	4555	4424	4330	4267	4327	4025
1995	4018	4125	4314	4280	4449	4527
1996	4968	4934	4971	5147	5246	5044
1997	6110	6158	5850	5977	6382	6438
1998	6700	7093	7559	7665	7590	7367
1999	6730	6313	6598	7015	6842	7010
2000	8481	9129	9462	9348	9252	10196
2001	9322	8079	7608	7947	8162	7736
2002	7649	7638	7852	7663	7656	7146
2003	6570	6555	6343	6586	6860	6983
2004	8521	8789	8586	8244	8417	8546
2005	9204	9668	9612	9275	9607	9903
2006	11946	11688	12111	12204	11745	11613
2007	13034	13045	13166	13417	14057	13907
2008	13155	13583	13350	13937	14715	14467
2009	8695	8123	8720	9325	10370	10375
2010	11094	11630	12038	12211	11763	11294
2011	13552	14137	14116	13945	13803	13301
2012	12452	12644	12392	12293	11513	11597
2013	12685	12822	12750	12457	12650	12129
2014	13695	14210	14335	14652	14604	15146
2015	14674	15234	14902	15225	15014	14553

S&P/TSX PERCENT CLOSING VALUES

STOCK MKT

JUL	AUG	SEP	OCT	NOV	DEC	
2779	2820	2632	2675	2857	2893	**1985**
2935	3028	2979	3027	3047	3066	**1986**
4030	3994	3902	3019	2978	3160	**1987**
3377	3286	3284	3396	3295	3390	**1988**
3971	4010	3943	3919	3943	3970	**1989**
3561	3346	3159	3081	3151	3257	**1990**
3540	3518	3388	3516	3449	3512	**1991**
3443	3403	3298	3336	3283	3350	**1992**
3967	4138	3991	4256	4180	4321	**1993**
4179	4350	4354	4292	4093	4214	**1994**
4615	4517	4530	4459	4661	4714	**1995**
4929	5143	5291	5599	6017	5927	**1996**
6878	6612	7040	6842	6513	6699	**1997**
6931	5531	5614	6208	6344	6486	**1998**
7081	6971	6958	7256	7520	8414	**1999**
10406	11248	10378	9640	8820	8934	**2000**
7690	7399	6839	6886	7426	7688	**2001**
6605	6612	6180	6249	6570	6615	**2002**
7258	7517	7421	7773	7859	8221	**2003**
8458	8377	8668	8871	9030	9247	**2004**
10423	10669	11012	10383	10824	11272	**2005**
11831	12074	11761	12345	12752	12908	**2006**
13869	13660	14099	14625	13689	13833	**2007**
13593	13771	11753	9763	9271	8988	**2008**
10787	10868	11935	10911	11447	11746	**2009**
11713	11914	12369	12676	12953	13443	**2010**
12946	12769	11624	12252	12204	11955	**2011**
11665	11949	12317	12423	12239	12434	**2012**
12487	12654	12787	13361	13395	13622	**2013**
15331	15626	14961	14613	14745	14632	**2014**
14468	13859	13307	13529	13470	13010	**2015**

S&P 500 1950 - 2015
BEST - WORST

10 BEST

10 WORST

YEARS

	Close	Change	Change
1954	36	11 pt	45.0 %
1958	55	15	38.1
1995	616	157	34.1
1975	90	22	31.5
1997	970	230	31.0
2013	1848	422	29.6
1989	353	76	27.3
1998	1229	259	26.7
1955	45	10	26.4
2003	1112	232	26.4

YEARS

	Close	Change	Change
2008	903	− 566 pt	− 38.5 %
1974	69	− 29	− 29.7
2002	880	− 268	− 23.4
1973	98	− 21	− 17.4
1957	40	− 7	− 14.3
1966	80	− 12	− 13.1
2001	1148	− 172	− 13.0
1962	63	− 8	− 11.8
1977	95	− 12	− 11.5
1969	92	− 12	− 11.4

MONTHS

	Close	Change	Change
Oct 1974	74	10 pt	16.3 %
Aug 1982	120	12	11.6
Dec 1991	417	42	11.2
Oct 1982	134	13	11.0
Oct 2011	1253	122	10.8
Aug 1984	167	16	10.6
Nov 1980	141	13	10.2
Nov 1962	62	6	10.2
Mar 2000	1499	132	9.7
Apr 2009	798	75	9.4

MONTHS

	Close	Change	Change
Oct 1987	252	− 70 pt	− 21.8 %
Oct 2008	969	− 196	− 16.8
Aug 1998	957	− 163	− 14.6
Sep 1974	64	− 9	− 11.9
Nov 1973	96	− 12	− 11.4
Sep 2002	815	− 101	− 11.0
Feb 2009	735	− 91	− 11.0
Mar 1980	102	− 12	− 10.2
Aug 1990	323	− 34	− 9.4
Feb 2001	1240	− 126	− 9.2

DAYS

		Close	Change	Change
Mon	2008 Oct 13	1003	104 pt	11.6 %
Tue	2008 Oct 28	941	92	10.8
Wed	1987 Oct 21	258	22	9.1
Mon	2009 Mar 23	883	54	7.1
Thu	2008 Nov 13	911	59	6.9
Mon	2008 Nov 24	852	52	6.5
Tues	2009 Mar 10	720	43	6.4
Fri	2008 Nov 21	800	48	6.3
Wed	2002 Jul 24	843	46	5.7
Tue	2008 Sep 30	1166	60	5.4

DAYS

		Close	Change	Change
Mon	1987 Oct 19	225	− 58 pt	− 20.5 %
Wed	2008 Oct 15	908	− 90	− 9.0
Mon	2008 Dec 01	816	− 80	− 8.9
Mon	2008 Sep 29	1106	− 107	− 8.8
Mon	1987 Oct 26	228	− 21	− 8.3
Thu	2008 Oct 09	910	− 75	− 7.6
Mon	1997 Oct 27	877	− 65	− 6.9
Mon	1998 Aug 31	957	− 70	− 6.8
Fri	1988 Jan 8	243	− 18	− 6.8
Thu	2008 Nov 20	752	− 54	− 6.7

10 BEST

10 WORST

YEARS

	Close	Change	Change
1954	404	124 pt	44.0 %
1975	852	236	38.3
1958	584	148	34.0
1995	5117	1283	33.5
1985	1547	335	27.7
1989	2753	585	27.0
2013	16577	3473	26.5
1996	6448	1331	26.0
2003	10454	2112	25.3
1999	11453	2272	25.2

YEARS

	Close	Change	Change
2008	8776	− 4488 pt	− 33.8 %
1974	616	− 235	− 27.6
1966	786	− 184	− 18.9
1977	831	− 174	− 17.3
2002	8342	− 1680	− 16.8
1973	851	− 169	− 16.6
1969	800	− 143	− 15.2
1957	436	− 64	− 12.8
1962	652	− 79	− 10.8
1960	616	− 64	− 9.3

MONTHS

	Close	Change	Change
Aug 1982	901	93 pt	11.5 %
Oct 1982	992	95	10.6
Oct 2002	8397	805	10.6
Apr 1978	837	80	10.5
Apr 1999	10789	1003	10.2
Nov 1962	649	60	10.1
Nov 1954	387	35	9.9
Aug 1984	1224	109	9.8
Oct 1998	8592	750	9.6
Oct 2011	11955	1042	9.5

MONTHS

	Close	Change	Change
Oct 1987	1994	− 603 pt	− 23.2 %
Aug 1998	7539	− 1344	− 15.1
Oct 2008	9325	− 1526	− 14.1
Nov 1973	822	− 134	− 14.0
Sep 2002	7592	− 1072	− 12.4
Feb 2009	7063	− 938	− 11.7
Sep 2001	8848	− 1102	− 11.1
Sep 1974	608	− 71	− 10.4
Aug 1974	679	− 79	− 10.4
Jun 2008	11350	− 1288	− 10.2

DAYS

		Close	Change	Change
Mon	2008 Oct 13	9388	936 pt	11.1 %
Tue	2008 Oct 28	9065	889	10.9
Wed	1987 Oct 21	2028	187	10.2
Mon	2009 Mar 23	7776	497	6.8
Thu	2008 Nov 13	8835	553	6.7
Fri	2008 Nov 21	8046	494	6.5
Wed	2002 Jul 24	8191	489	6.3
Tue	1987 Oct 20	1841	102	5.9
Tue	2009 Mar 10	6926	379	5.8
Mon	2002 Jul 29	8712	448	5.4

DAYS

		Close	Change	Change
Mon	1987 Oct 19	1739	− 508 pt	− 22.6 %
Mon	1987 Oct 26	1794	− 157	− 8.0
Wed	2008 Oct 15	8578	− 733	− 7.9
Mon	2008 Dec 01	8149	− 680	− 7.7
Thu	2008 Oct 09	8579	− 679	− 7.3
Mon	1997 Oct 27	8366	− 554	− 7.2
Mon	2001 Sep 17	8921	− 685	− 7.1
Mon	2008 Sep 29	10365	− 778	− 7.0
Fri	1989 Oct 13	2569	− 191	− 6.9
Fri	1988 Jan 8	1911	− 141	− 6.9

10 BEST

YEARS

	Close	Change	Change
1999	4069	1877 pt	85.6 %
1991	586	213	56.9
2003	2003	668	50.0
2009	2269	692	43.9
1995	1052	300	39.9
1998	2193	622	39.6
2013	4161	1157	38.3
1980	202	51	33.9
1985	325	78	31.5
1975	78	18	29.8

MONTHS

	Close	Change	Change
Dec 1999	4069	733 pt	22.0 %
Feb 2000	4697	756	19.2
Oct 1974	65	10	17.2
Jun 2000	3966	565	16.6
Apr 2001	2116	276	15.0
Nov 2001	1931	240	14.2
Oct 2002	1330	158	13.5
Oct 1982	1771	25	13.3
Sep 1998	1694	195	13.0
Oct 2001	1690	191	12.8

DAYS

		Close	Change	Change
Wed	2001 Jan 3	2617	325 pt	14.2 %
Mon	2008 Oct 13	1844	195	11.8
Tue	2000 Dec 5	2890	274	10.5
Tue	2008 Oct 28	1649	144	9.5
Thu	2001 Apr 5	1785	146	8.9
Wed	2001 Apr 18	2079	156	8.1
Tue	2000 May 30	3459	254	7.9
Fri	2000 Oct 13	3317	242	7.9
Thu	2000 Oct 19	3419	247	7.8
Wed	2002 May 8	1696	122	7.8

10 WORST

YEARS

	Close	Change	Change
2008	1577	− 1075 pt	− 40.5 %
2000	2471	− 1599	− 39.3
1974	60	− 32	− 35.1
2002	1336	− 615	− 31.5
1973	92	− 42	− 31.1
2001	1950	− 520	− 21.1
1990	374	− 81	− 17.8
1984	247	− 32	− 11.3
1987	331	− 18	− 5.2
1981	196	− 7	− 3.2

MONTHS

	Close	Change	Change
Oct 1987	323	− 121 pt	− 27.2 %
Nov 2000	2598	− 772	− 22.9
Feb 2001	2152	− 621	− 22.4
Aug 1998	1499	− 373	− 19.9
Oct 2008	1721	− 371	− 17.7
Mar 1980	131	− 27	− 17.1
Sep 2001	1499	− 307	− 17.0
Oct 1978	111	− 22	− 16.4
Apr 2000	3861	− 712	− 15.6
Nov 1973	94	− 17	− 15.1

DAYS

		Close	Change	Change
Mon	1987 Oct 19	360	− 46 pt	− 11.3 %
Fri	2000 Apr 14	3321	− 355	− 9.7
Mon	2008 Sep 29	1984	− 200	− 9.1
Mon	1987 Oct 26	299	− 30	− 9.0
Tue	1987 Oct 20	328	− 32	− 9.0
Mon	2008 Dec 01	1398	− 138	− 9.0
Mon	1998 Aug 31	1499	− 140	− 8.6
Wed	2008 Oct 15	1628	− 151	− 8.5
Mon	2000 Apr 03	4224	− 349	− 7.6
Tue	2001 Jan 02	2292	− 179	− 7.2

10 BEST

YEARS

	Close	Change	Change
2009	8414	2758 pt	30.7 %
1999	4321	1928	29.7
1993	5927	971	29.0
1996	8221	1213	25.7
2003	11272	1606	24.3
2005	2893	2026	21.9
1985	3970	500	20.8
1989	12908	580	17.1
2006	6699	1636	14.5
2010	13433	1697	14.4

MONTHS

	Close	Change	Change
Dec 1999	8414	891 pt	11.8 %
May 2009	8500	1045	11.2
Oct 1998	6208	594	10.6
Jun 2000	10196	943	10.2
Jan 1985	2595	195	8.1
Aug 2000	11248	842	8.1
Nov 2001	7426	540	7.8
Jul 1987	4030	290	7.8
Feb 2000	9129	648	7.6
Nov 1996	6017	418	7.5

DAYS

		Close	Change	Change
Tue	2008 Oct 14	9956	891 pt	9.8 %
Wed	1987 Oct 21	3246	269	9.0
Mon	2008 Oct 20	10251	689	7.2
Tue	2008 Oct 28	9152	614	7.2
Fri	2008 Sep 19	12913	848	7.0
Fri	2008 Nov 28	9271	517	5.9
Fri	2008 Nov 21	8155	431	5.6
Mon	2008 Dec 08	8567	450	5.5
Mon	2009 Mar 23	8959	452	5.3
Fri	1987 Oct 30	3019	147	5.1

10 WORST

YEARS

	Close	Change	Change
2008	8988	− 4845 pt	− 35.0 %
1990	3257	− 713	− 18.0
2002	6615	− 1074	− 14.0
2001	7688	− 1245	− 13.9
2015	13010	− 1622	− 11.9
2011	11955	− 1488	− 11.7
1992	3350	− 162	− 4.6
1998	6486	− 214	− 3.2
1994	4214	− 108	− 2.5
1987	3160	94	3.1

MONTHS

	Close	Change	Change
Oct 1987	3019	− 883 pt	− 22.6 %
Aug 1998	5531	− 1401	− 20.2
Oct 2008	9763	− 1990	− 16.9
Sep 2008	11753	− 2018	− 14.7
Feb 2001	8079	− 1243	− 13.3
Sep 2011	11624	− 1145	− 9.0
Nov 2000	8820	− 820	− 8.5
Apr 1990	3341	− 299	− 8.2
Sep 2000	10378	− 870	− 7.7
Sep 2001	6839	− 561	− 7.6

DAYS

		Close	Change	Change
Mon	1987 Oct 19	3192	− 407 pt	− 11.3 %
Mon	2008 Dec 01	8406	− 864	− 9.3
Thu	2008 Nov 20	7725	− 766	− 9.0
Mon	2008 Oct 27	8537	− 757	− 8.1
Wed	2000 Oct 25	9512	− 840	− 8.1
Mon	1987 Oct 26	2846	− 233	− 7.6
Thu	2008 Oct 02	10901	− 814	− 6.9
Mon	2008 Sep 29	11285	− 841	− 6.9
Tue	1987 Oct 20	2977	− 215	− 6.7
Fri	2001 Feb 16	8393	− 574	− 6.4

BOND YIELDS

	JAN	FEB	MAR	APR	MAY	JUN
1954	2.48	2.47	2.37	2.29	2.37	2.38
1955	2.61	2.65	2.68	2.75	2.76	2.78
1956	2.9	2.84	2.96	3.18	3.07	3
1957	3.46	3.34	3.41	3.48	3.6	3.8
1958	3.09	3.05	2.98	2.88	2.92	2.97
1959	4.02	3.96	3.99	4.12	4.31	4.34
1960	4.72	4.49	4.25	4.28	4.35	4.15
1961	3.84	3.78	3.74	3.78	3.71	3.88
1962	4.08	4.04	3.93	3.84	3.87	3.91
1963	3.83	3.92	3.93	3.97	3.93	3.99
1964	4.17	4.15	4.22	4.23	4.2	4.17
1965	4.19	4.21	4.21	4.2	4.21	4.21
1966	4.61	4.83	4.87	4.75	4.78	4.81
1967	4.58	4.63	4.54	4.59	4.85	5.02
1968	5.53	5.56	5.74	5.64	5.87	5.72
1969	6.04	6.19	6.3	6.17	6.32	6.57
1970	7.79	7.24	7.07	7.39	7.91	7.84
1971	6.24	6.11	5.7	5.83	6.39	6.52
1972	5.95	6.08	6.07	6.19	6.13	6.11
1973	6.46	6.64	6.71	6.67	6.85	6.9
1974	6.99	6.96	7.21	7.51	7.58	7.54
1975	7.5	7.39	7.73	8.23	8.06	7.86
1976	7.74	7.79	7.73	7.56	7.9	7.86
1977	7.21	7.39	7.46	7.37	7.46	7.28
1978	7.96	8.03	8.04	8.15	8.35	8.46
1979	9.1	9.1	9.12	9.18	9.25	8.91
1980	10.8	12.41	12.75	11.47	10.18	9.78
1981	12.57	13.19	13.12	13.68	14.1	13.47
1982	14.59	14.43	13.86	13.87	13.62	14.3
1983	10.46	10.72	10.51	10.4	10.38	10.85
1984	11.67	11.84	12.32	12.63	13.41	13.56
1985	11.38	11.51	11.86	11.43	10.85	10.16
1986	9.19	8.7	7.78	7.3	7.71	7.8
1987	7.08	7.25	7.25	8.02	8.61	8.4
1988	8.67	8.21	8.37	8.72	9.09	8.92
1989	9.09	9.17	9.36	9.18	8.86	8.28
1990	8.21	8.47	8.59	8.79	8.76	8.48
1991	8.09	7.85	8.11	8.04	8.07	8.28
1992	7.03	7.34	7.54	7.48	7.39	7.26
1993	6.6	6.26	5.98	5.97	6.04	5.96
1994	5.75	5.97	6.48	6.97	7.18	7.1
1995	7.78	7.47	7.2	7.06	6.63	6.17
1996	5.65	5.81	6.27	6.51	6.74	6.91
1997	6.58	6.42	6.69	6.89	6.71	6.49
1998	5.54	5.57	5.65	5.64	5.65	5.5
1999	4.72	5	5.23	5.18	5.54	5.9
2000	6.66	6.52	6.26	5.99	6.44	6.1
2001	5.16	5.1	4.89	5.14	5.39	5.28
2002	5.04	4.91	5.28	5.21	5.16	4.93
2003	4.05	3.9	3.81	3.96	3.57	3.33
2004	4.15	4.08	3.83	4.35	4.72	4.73
2005	4.22	4.17	4.5	4.34	4.14	4.00
2006	4.42	4.57	4.72	4.99	5.11	5.11
2007	4.76	4.72	4.56	4.69	4.75	5.10
2008	3.74	3.74	3.51	3.68	3.88	4.10
2009	2.52	2.87	2.82	2.93	3.29	3.72
2010	3.73	3.69	3.73	3.85	3.42	3.20
2011	3.39	3.58	3.41	3.46	3.17	3.00
2012	1.97	1.97	2.17	2.05	1.80	1.62
2013	1.91	1.98	1.96	1.76	1.93	2.30
2014	2.86	2.71	2.72	2.71	2.56	2.60
2015	1.88	1.98	2.04	1.94	2.20	2.36

* Source: Federal Reserve Bank of St. Louis, monthly data calculated as average of business days

JUL	AUG	SEP	OCT	NOV	DEC	
2.3	2.36	2.38	2.43	2.48	2.51	**1954**
2.9	2.97	2.97	2.88	2.89	2.96	**1955**
3.11	3.33	3.38	3.34	3.49	3.59	**1956**
3.93	3.93	3.92	3.97	3.72	3.21	**1957**
3.2	3.54	3.76	3.8	3.74	3.86	**1958**
4.4	4.43	4.68	4.53	4.53	4.69	**1959**
3.9	3.8	3.8	3.89	3.93	3.84	**1960**
3.92	4.04	3.98	3.92	3.94	4.06	**1961**
4.01	3.98	3.98	3.93	3.92	3.86	**1962**
4.02	4	4.08	4.11	4.12	4.13	**1963**
4.19	4.19	4.2	4.19	4.15	4.18	**1964**
4.2	4.25	4.29	4.35	4.45	4.62	**1965**
5.02	5.22	5.18	5.01	5.16	4.84	**1966**
5.16	5.28	5.3	5.48	5.75	5.7	**1967**
5.5	5.42	5.46	5.58	5.7	6.03	**1968**
6.72	6.69	7.16	7.1	7.14	7.65	**1969**
7.46	7.53	7.39	7.33	6.84	6.39	**1970**
6.73	6.58	6.14	5.93	5.81	5.93	**1971**
6.11	6.21	6.55	6.48	6.28	6.36	**1972**
7.13	7.4	7.09	6.79	6.73	6.74	**1973**
7.81	8.04	8.04	7.9	7.68	7.43	**1974**
8.06	8.4	8.43	8.14	8.05	8	**1975**
7.83	7.77	7.59	7.41	7.29	6.87	**1976**
7.33	7.4	7.34	7.52	7.58	7.69	**1977**
8.64	8.41	8.42	8.64	8.81	9.01	**1978**
8.95	9.03	9.33	10.3	10.65	10.39	**1979**
10.25	11.1	11.51	11.75	12.68	12.84	**1980**
14.28	14.94	15.32	15.15	13.39	13.72	**1981**
13.95	13.06	12.34	10.91	10.55	10.54	**1982**
11.38	11.85	11.65	11.54	11.69	11.83	**1983**
13.36	12.72	12.52	12.16	11.57	11.5	**1984**
10.31	10.33	10.37	10.24	9.78	9.26	**1985**
7.3	7.17	7.45	7.43	7.25	7.11	**1986**
8.45	8.76	9.42	9.52	8.86	8.99	**1987**
9.06	9.26	8.98	8.8	8.96	9.11	**1988**
8.02	8.11	8.19	8.01	7.87	7.84	**1989**
8.47	8.75	8.89	8.72	8.39	8.08	**1990**
8.27	7.9	7.65	7.53	7.42	7.09	**1991**
6.84	6.59	6.42	6.59	6.87	6.77	**1992**
5.81	5.68	5.36	5.33	5.72	5.77	**1993**
7.3	7.24	7.46	7.74	7.96	7.81	**1994**
6.28	6.49	6.2	6.04	5.93	5.71	**1995**
6.87	6.64	6.83	6.53	6.2	6.3	**1996**
6.22	6.3	6.21	6.03	5.88	5.81	**1997**
5.46	5.34	4.81	4.53	4.83	4.65	**1998**
5.79	5.94	5.92	6.11	6.03	6.28	**1999**
6.05	5.83	5.8	5.74	5.72	5.24	**2000**
5.24	4.97	4.73	4.57	4.65	5.09	**2001**
4.65	4.26	3.87	3.94	4.05	4.03	**2002**
3.98	4.45	4.27	4.29	4.3	4.27	**2003**
4.5	4.28	4.13	4.1	4.19	4.23	**2004**
4.18	4.26	4.20	4.46	4.54	4.47	**2005**
5.09	4.88	4.72	4.73	4.60	4.56	**2006**
5.00	4.67	4.52	4.53	4.15	4.10	**2007**
4.01	3.89	3.69	3.81	3.53	2.42	**2008**
3.56	3.59	3.40	3.39	3.40	3.59	**2009**
3.01	2.70	2.65	2.54	2.76	3.29	**2010**
3.00	2.30	1.98	2.15	2.01	1.98	**2011**
1.53	1.68	1.72	1.75	1.65	1.72	**2012**
2.58	2.74	2.81	2.62	2.72	2.90	**2013**
2.54	2.42	2.53	2.30	2.33	2.21	**2014**
2.32	2.17	2.17	2.07	2.26	2.24	**2015**

BOND YIELDS ▤ 5 YEAR TREASURY*

	JAN	FEB	MAR	APR	MAY	JUN
1954	2.17	2.04	1.93	1.87	1.92	1.92
1955	2.32	2.38	2.48	2.55	2.56	2.59
1956	2.84	2.74	2.93	3.20	3.08	2.97
1957	3.47	3.39	3.46	3.53	3.64	3.83
1958	2.88	2.78	2.64	2.46	2.41	2.46
1959	4.01	3.96	3.99	4.12	4.35	4.50
1960	4.92	4.69	4.31	4.29	4.49	4.12
1961	3.67	3.66	3.60	3.57	3.47	3.81
1962	3.94	3.89	3.68	3.60	3.66	3.64
1963	3.58	3.66	3.68	3.74	3.72	3.81
1964	4.07	4.03	4.14	4.15	4.05	4.02
1965	4.10	4.15	4.15	4.15	4.15	4.15
1966	4.86	4.98	4.92	4.83	4.89	4.97
1967	4.70	4.74	4.54	4.51	4.75	5.01
1968	5.54	5.59	5.76	5.69	6.04	5.85
1969	6.25	6.34	6.41	6.30	6.54	6.75
1970	8.17	7.82	7.21	7.50	7.97	7.85
1971	5.89	5.56	5.00	5.65	6.28	6.53
1972	5.59	5.69	5.87	6.17	5.85	5.91
1973	6.34	6.60	6.80	6.67	6.80	6.69
1974	6.95	6.82	7.31	7.92	8.18	8.10
1975	7.41	7.11	7.30	7.99	7.72	7.51
1976	7.46	7.45	7.49	7.25	7.59	7.61
1977	6.58	6.83	6.93	6.79	6.94	6.76
1978	7.77	7.83	7.86	7.98	8.18	8.36
1979	9.20	9.13	9.20	9.25	9.24	8.85
1980	10.74	12.60	13.47	11.84	9.95	9.21
1981	12.77	13.41	13.41	13.99	14.63	13.95
1982	14.65	14.54	13.98	14.00	13.75	14.43
1983	10.03	10.26	10.08	10.02	10.03	10.63
1984	11.37	11.54	12.02	12.37	13.17	13.48
1985	10.93	11.13	11.52	11.01	10.34	9.60
1986	8.68	8.34	7.46	7.05	7.52	7.64
1987	6.64	6.79	6.79	7.57	8.26	8.02
1988	8.18	7.71	7.83	8.19	8.58	8.49
1989	9.15	9.27	9.51	9.30	8.91	8.29
1990	8.12	8.42	8.60	8.77	8.74	8.43
1991	7.70	7.47	7.77	7.70	7.70	7.94
1992	6.24	6.58	6.95	6.78	6.69	6.48
1993	5.83	5.43	5.19	5.13	5.20	5.22
1994	5.09	5.40	5.94	6.52	6.78	6.70
1995	7.76	7.37	7.05	6.86	6.41	5.93
1996	5.36	5.38	5.97	6.30	6.48	6.69
1997	6.33	6.20	6.54	6.76	6.57	6.38
1998	5.42	5.49	5.61	5.61	5.63	5.52
1999	4.60	4.91	5.14	5.08	5.44	5.81
2000	6.58	6.68	6.50	6.26	6.69	6.30
2001	4.86	4.89	4.64	4.76	4.93	4.81
2002	4.34	4.30	4.74	4.65	4.49	4.19
2003	3.05	2.90	2.78	2.93	2.52	2.27
2004	3.12	3.07	2.79	3.39	3.85	3.93
2005	3.71	3.77	4.17	4.00	3.85	3.77
2006	4.35	4.57	4.72	4.90	5.00	5.07
2007	4.75	4.71	4.48	4.59	4.67	5.03
2008	2.98	2.78	2.48	2.84	3.15	3.49
2009	1.60	1.87	1.82	1.86	2.13	2.71
2010	2.48	2.36	2.43	2.58	2.18	2.00
2011	1.99	2.26	2.11	2.17	1.84	1.58
2012	0.84	0.83	1.02	0.89	0.76	0.71
2013	0.81	0.85	0.82	0.71	0.84	1.20
2014	1.65	1.52	1.64	1.70	1.59	1.68
2015	1.37	1.47	1.52	1.35	1.54	1.68

* Source: Federal Reserve Bank of St. Louis, monthly data calculated as average of business days

5 YEAR TREASURY BOND YIELDS

JUL	AUG	SEP	OCT	NOV	DEC	
1.85	1.90	1.96	2.02	2.09	2.16	1954
2.72	2.86	2.85	2.76	2.81	2.93	1955
3.12	3.41	3.47	3.40	3.56	3.70	1956
4.00	4.00	4.03	4.08	3.72	3.08	1957
2.77	3.29	3.69	3.78	3.70	3.82	1958
4.58	4.57	4.90	4.72	4.75	5.01	1959
3.79	3.62	3.61	3.76	3.81	3.67	1960
3.84	3.96	3.90	3.80	3.82	3.91	1961
3.80	3.71	3.70	3.64	3.60	3.56	1962
3.89	3.89	3.96	3.97	4.01	4.04	1963
4.03	4.05	4.08	4.07	4.04	4.09	1964
4.15	4.20	4.25	4.34	4.46	4.72	1965
5.17	5.50	5.50	5.27	5.36	5.00	1966
5.23	5.31	5.40	5.57	5.78	5.75	1967
5.60	5.50	5.48	5.55	5.66	6.12	1968
7.01	7.03	7.57	7.51	7.53	7.96	1969
7.59	7.57	7.29	7.12	6.47	5.95	1970
6.85	6.55	6.14	5.93	5.78	5.69	1971
5.97	6.02	6.25	6.18	6.12	6.16	1972
7.33	7.63	7.05	6.77	6.92	6.80	1973
8.38	8.63	8.37	7.97	7.68	7.31	1974
7.92	8.33	8.37	7.97	7.80	7.76	1975
7.49	7.31	7.13	6.75	6.52	6.10	1976
6.84	7.03	7.04	7.32	7.34	7.48	1977
8.54	8.33	8.43	8.61	8.84	9.08	1978
8.90	9.06	9.41	10.63	10.93	10.42	1979
9.53	10.84	11.62	11.86	12.83	13.25	1980
14.79	15.56	15.93	15.41	13.38	13.60	1981
14.07	13.00	12.25	10.80	10.38	10.22	1982
11.21	11.63	11.43	11.28	11.41	11.54	1983
13.27	12.68	12.53	12.06	11.33	11.07	1984
9.70	9.81	9.81	9.69	9.28	8.73	1985
7.06	6.80	6.92	6.83	6.76	6.67	1986
8.01	8.32	8.94	9.08	8.35	8.45	1987
8.66	8.94	8.69	8.51	8.79	9.09	1988
7.83	8.09	8.17	7.97	7.81	7.75	1989
8.33	8.44	8.51	8.33	8.02	7.73	1990
7.91	7.43	7.14	6.87	6.62	6.19	1991
5.84	5.60	5.38	5.60	6.04	6.08	1992
5.09	5.03	4.73	4.71	5.06	5.15	1993
6.91	6.88	7.08	7.40	7.72	7.78	1994
6.01	6.24	6.00	5.86	5.69	5.51	1995
6.64	6.39	6.60	6.27	5.97	6.07	1996
6.12	6.16	6.11	5.93	5.80	5.77	1997
5.46	5.27	4.62	4.18	4.54	4.45	1998
5.68	5.84	5.80	6.03	5.97	6.19	1999
6.18	6.06	5.93	5.78	5.70	5.17	2000
4.76	4.57	4.12	3.91	3.97	4.39	2001
3.81	3.29	2.94	2.95	3.05	3.03	2002
2.87	3.37	3.18	3.19	3.29	3.27	2003
3.69	3.47	3.36	3.35	3.53	3.60	2004
3.98	4.12	4.01	4.33	4.45	4.39	2005
5.04	4.82	4.67	4.69	4.58	4.53	2006
4.88	4.43	4.20	4.20	3.67	3.49	2007
3.30	3.14	2.88	2.73	2.29	1.52	2008
2.46	2.57	2.37	2.33	2.23	2.34	2009
1.76	1.47	1.41	1.18	1.35	1.93	2010
1.54	1.02	0.90	1.06	0.91	0.89	2011
0.62	0.71	0.67	0.71	0.67	0.70	2012
1.40	1.52	1.60	1.37	1.37	1.58	2013
1.70	1.63	1.77	1.55	1.62	1.64	2014
1.63	1.54	1.49	1.39	1.67	1.70	2015

BOND YIELDS 🇺🇸 3 MONTH TREASURY

	JAN	FEB	MAR	APR	MAY	JUN
1982	12.92	14.28	13.31	13.34	12.71	13.08
1983	8.12	8.39	8.66	8.51	8.50	9.14
1984	9.26	9.46	9.89	10.07	10.22	10.26
1985	8.02	8.56	8.83	8.22	7.73	7.18
1986	7.30	7.29	6.76	6.24	6.33	6.40
1987	5.58	5.75	5.77	5.82	5.85	5.85
1988	6.00	5.84	5.87	6.08	6.45	6.66
1999	8.56	8.84	9.14	8.96	8.74	8.43
1990	7.90	8.00	8.17	8.04	8.01	7.99
1991	6.41	6.12	6.09	5.83	5.63	5.75
1992	3.91	3.95	4.14	3.84	3.72	3.75
1993	3.07	2.99	3.01	2.93	3.03	3.14
1994	3.04	3.33	3.59	3.78	4.27	4.25
1995	5.90	5.94	5.91	5.84	5.85	5.64
1996	5.15	4.96	5.10	5.09	5.15	5.23
1997	5.17	5.14	5.28	5.30	5.20	5.07
1998	5.18	5.23	5.16	5.08	5.14	5.12
1999	4.45	4.56	4.57	4.41	4.63	4.72
2000	5.50	5.73	5.86	5.82	5.99	5.86
2001	5.29	5.01	4.54	3.97	3.70	3.57
2002	1.68	1.76	1.83	1.75	1.76	1.73
2003	1.19	1.19	1.15	1.15	1.09	0.94
2004	0.90	0.94	0.95	0.96	1.04	1.29
2005	2.37	2.58	2.80	2.84	2.90	3.04
2006	4.34	4.54	4.63	4.72	4.84	4.92
2007	5.11	5.16	5.08	5.01	4.87	4.74
2008	2.82	2.17	1.28	1.31	1.76	1.89
2009	0.13	0.30	0.22	0.16	0.18	0.18
2010	0.06	0.11	0.15	0.16	0.16	0.12
2011	0.15	0.13	0.10	0.06	0.04	0.04
2012	0.03	0.09	0.08	0.08	0.09	0.09
2013	0.07	0.10	0.09	0.06	0.04	0.05
2014	0.04	0.05	0.05	0.03	0.03	0.04
2015	0.03	0.02	0.03	0.02	0.02	0.02

* Source: Federal Reserve Bank of St. Louis, monthly data calculated as average of business days

3 MONTH TREASURY ≣ BOND YIELDS

JUL	AUG	SEP	OCT	NOV	DEC	
11.86	9.00	8.19	7.97	8.35	8.20	**1982**
9.45	9.74	9.36	8.99	9.11	9.36	**1983**
10.53	10.90	10.80	10.12	8.92	8.34	**1984**
7.32	7.37	7.33	7.40	7.48	7.33	**1985**
6.00	5.69	5.35	5.32	5.50	5.68	**1986**
5.88	6.23	6.62	6.35	5.89	5.96	**1987**
6.95	7.30	7.48	7.60	8.03	8.35	**1988**
8.15	8.17	8.01	7.90	7.94	7.88	**1999**
7.87	7.69	7.60	7.40	7.29	6.95	**1990**
5.75	5.50	5.37	5.14	4.69	4.18	**1991**
3.28	3.20	2.97	2.93	3.21	3.29	**1992**
3.11	3.09	3.01	3.09	3.18	3.13	**1993**
4.46	4.61	4.75	5.10	5.45	5.76	**1994**
5.59	5.57	5.43	5.44	5.52	5.29	**1995**
5.30	5.19	5.24	5.12	5.17	5.04	**1996**
5.19	5.28	5.08	5.11	5.28	5.30	**1997**
5.09	5.04	4.74	4.07	4.53	4.50	**1998**
4.69	4.87	4.82	5.02	5.23	5.36	**1999**
6.14	6.28	6.18	6.29	6.36	5.94	**2000**
3.59	3.44	2.69	2.20	1.91	1.72	**2001**
1.71	1.65	1.66	1.61	1.25	1.21	**2002**
0.92	0.97	0.96	0.94	0.95	0.91	**2003**
1.36	1.50	1.68	1.79	2.11	2.22	**2004**
3.29	3.52	3.49	3.79	3.97	3.97	**2005**
5.08	5.09	4.93	5.05	5.07	4.97	**2006**
4.96	4.32	3.99	4.00	3.35	3.07	**2007**
1.66	1.75	1.15	0.69	0.19	0.03	**2008**
0.18	0.17	0.12	0.07	0.05	0.05	**2009**
0.16	0.16	0.15	0.13	0.14	0.14	**2010**
0.04	0.02	0.01	0.02	0.01	0.01	**2011**
0.10	0.10	0.11	0.10	0.09	0.07	**2012**
0.04	0.04	0.02	0.05	0.07	0.07	**2013**
0.03	0.03	0.02	0.02	0.02	0.03	**2014**
0.03	0.07	0.02	0.02	0.13	0.23	**2015**

MOODY'S SEASONED
CORPORATE Aaa*

	JAN	FEB	MAR	APR	MAY	JUN
1950	2.57	2.58	2.58	2.60	2.61	2.62
1951	2.66	2.66	2.78	2.87	2.89	2.94
1952	2.98	2.93	2.96	2.93	2.93	2.94
1953	3.02	3.07	3.12	3.23	3.34	3.40
1954	3.06	2.95	2.86	2.85	2.88	2.90
1955	2.93	2.93	3.02	3.01	3.04	3.05
1956	3.11	3.08	3.10	3.24	3.28	3.26
1957	3.77	3.67	3.66	3.67	3.74	3.91
1958	3.60	3.59	3.63	3.60	3.57	3.57
1959	4.12	4.14	4.13	4.23	4.37	4.46
1960	4.61	4.56	4.49	4.45	4.46	4.45
1961	4.32	4.27	4.22	4.25	4.27	4.33
1962	4.42	4.42	4.39	4.33	4.28	4.28
1963	4.21	4.19	4.19	4.21	4.22	4.23
1964	4.39	4.36	4.38	4.40	4.41	4.41
1965	4.43	4.41	4.42	4.43	4.44	4.46
1966	4.74	4.78	4.92	4.96	4.98	5.07
1967	5.20	5.03	5.13	5.11	5.24	5.44
1968	6.17	6.10	6.11	6.21	6.27	6.28
1969	6.59	6.66	6.85	6.89	6.79	6.98
1970	7.91	7.93	7.84	7.83	8.11	8.48
1971	7.36	7.08	7.21	7.25	7.53	7.64
1972	7.19	7.27	7.24	7.30	7.30	7.23
1973	7.15	7.22	7.29	7.26	7.29	7.37
1974	7.83	7.85	8.01	8.25	8.37	8.47
1975	8.83	8.62	8.67	8.95	8.90	8.77
1976	8.60	8.55	8.52	8.40	8.58	8.62
1977	7.96	8.04	8.10	8.04	8.05	7.95
1978	8.41	8.47	8.47	8.56	8.69	8.76
1979	9.25	9.26	9.37	9.38	9.50	9.29
1980	11.09	12.38	12.96	12.04	10.99	10.58
1981	12.81	13.35	13.33	13.88	14.32	13.75
1982	15.18	15.27	14.58	14.46	14.26	14.81
1983	11.79	12.01	11.73	11.51	11.46	11.74
1984	12.20	12.08	12.57	12.81	13.28	13.55
1985	12.08	12.13	12.56	12.23	11.72	10.94
1986	10.05	9.67	9.00	8.79	9.09	9.13
1987	8.36	8.38	8.36	8.85	9.33	9.32
1988	9.88	9.40	9.39	9.67	9.90	9.86
1989	9.62	9.64	9.80	9.79	9.57	9.10
1990	8.99	9.22	9.37	9.46	9.47	9.26
1991	9.04	8.83	8.93	8.86	8.86	9.01
1992	8.20	8.29	8.35	8.33	8.28	8.22
1993	7.91	7.71	7.58	7.46	7.43	7.33
1994	6.92	7.08	7.48	7.88	7.99	7.97
1995	8.46	8.26	8.12	8.03	7.65	7.30
1996	6.81	6.99	7.35	7.50	7.62	7.71
1997	7.42	7.31	7.55	7.73	7.58	7.41
1998	6.61	6.67	6.72	6.69	6.69	6.53
1999	6.24	6.40	6.62	6.64	6.93	7.23
2000	7.78	7.68	7.68	7.64	7.99	7.67
2001	7.15	7.10	6.98	7.20	7.29	7.18
2002	6.55	6.51	6.81	6.76	6.75	6.63
2003	6.17	5.95	5.89	5.74	5.22	4.97
2004	5.54	5.50	5.33	5.73	6.04	6.01
2005	5.36	5.20	5.40	5.33	5.15	4.96
2006	5.29	5.35	5.53	5.84	5.95	5.89
2007	5.40	5.39	5.30	5.47	5.47	5.79
2008	5.33	5.53	5.51	5.55	5.57	5.68
2009	5.05	5.27	5.50	5.39	5.54	5.61
2010	5.26	5.35	5.27	5.29	4.96	4.88
2011	5.04	5.22	5.13	5.16	4.96	4.99
2012	3.85	3.85	3.99	3.96	3.80	3.64
2013	3.80	3.90	3.93	3.73	3.89	4.27
2014	4.49	4.45	4.38	4.24	4.16	4.25
2015	3.98	3.61	3.64	3.52	3.98	4.19

* Source: Federal Reserve Bank of St. Louis, monthly data calculated as average of business days

MOODY'S SEASONED CORPORATE Aaa BOND YIELDS

JUL	AUG	SEP	OCT	NOV	DEC	
2.65	2.61	2.64	2.67	2.67	2.67	1950
2.94	2.88	2.84	2.89	2.96	3.01	1951
2.95	2.94	2.95	3.01	2.98	2.97	1952
3.28	3.24	3.29	3.16	3.11	3.13	1953
2.89	2.87	2.89	2.87	2.89	2.90	1954
3.06	3.11	3.13	3.10	3.10	3.15	1955
3.28	3.43	3.56	3.59	3.69	3.75	1956
3.99	4.10	4.12	4.10	4.08	3.81	1957
3.67	3.85	4.09	4.11	4.09	4.08	1958
4.47	4.43	4.52	4.57	4.56	4.58	1959
4.41	4.28	4.25	4.30	4.31	4.35	1960
4.41	4.45	4.45	4.42	4.39	4.42	1961
4.34	4.35	4.32	4.28	4.25	4.24	1962
4.26	4.29	4.31	4.32	4.33	4.35	1963
4.40	4.41	4.42	4.42	4.43	4.44	1964
4.48	4.49	4.52	4.56	4.60	4.68	1965
5.16	5.31	5.49	5.41	5.35	5.39	1966
5.58	5.62	5.65	5.82	6.07	6.19	1967
6.24	6.02	5.97	6.09	6.19	6.45	1968
7.08	6.97	7.14	7.33	7.35	7.72	1969
8.44	8.13	8.09	8.03	8.05	7.64	1970
7.64	7.59	7.44	7.39	7.26	7.25	1971
7.21	7.19	7.22	7.21	7.12	7.08	1972
7.45	7.68	7.63	7.60	7.67	7.68	1973
8.72	9.00	9.24	9.27	8.89	8.89	1974
8.84	8.95	8.95	8.86	8.78	8.79	1975
8.56	8.45	8.38	8.32	8.25	7.98	1976
7.94	7.98	7.92	8.04	8.08	8.19	1977
8.88	8.69	8.69	8.89	9.03	9.16	1978
9.20	9.23	9.44	10.13	10.76	10.74	1979
11.07	11.64	12.02	12.31	12.97	13.21	1980
14.38	14.89	15.49	15.40	14.22	14.23	1981
14.61	13.71	12.94	12.12	11.68	11.83	1982
12.15	12.51	12.37	12.25	12.41	12.57	1983
13.44	12.87	12.66	12.63	12.29	12.13	1984
10.97	11.05	11.07	11.02	10.55	10.16	1985
8.88	8.72	8.89	8.86	8.68	8.49	1986
9.42	9.67	10.18	10.52	10.01	10.11	1987
9.96	10.11	9.82	9.51	9.45	9.57	1988
8.93	8.96	9.01	8.92	8.89	8.86	1989
9.24	9.41	9.56	9.53	9.30	9.05	1990
9.00	8.75	8.61	8.55	8.48	8.31	1991
8.07	7.95	7.92	7.99	8.10	7.98	1992
7.17	6.85	6.66	6.67	6.93	6.93	1993
8.11	8.07	8.34	8.57	8.68	8.46	1994
7.41	7.57	7.32	7.12	7.02	6.82	1995
7.65	7.46	7.66	7.39	7.10	7.20	1996
7.14	7.22	7.15	7.00	6.87	6.76	1997
6.55	6.52	6.40	6.37	6.41	6.22	1998
7.19	7.40	7.39	7.55	7.36	7.55	1999
7.65	7.55	7.62	7.55	7.45	7.21	2000
7.13	7.02	7.17	7.03	6.97	6.77	2001
6.53	6.37	6.15	6.32	6.31	6.21	2002
5.49	5.88	5.72	5.70	5.65	5.62	2003
5.82	5.65	5.46	5.47	5.52	5.47	2004
5.06	5.09	5.13	5.35	5.42	5.37	2005
5.85	5.68	5.51	5.51	5.33	5.32	2006
5.73	5.79	5.74	5.66	5.44	5.49	2007
5.67	5.64	5.65	6.28	6.12	5.05	2008
5.41	5.26	5.13	5.15	5.19	5.26	2009
4.72	4.49	4.53	4.68	4.87	5.02	2010
4.93	4.37	4.09	3.98	3.87	3.93	2011
3.40	3.48	3.49	3.47	3.50	3.65	2012
4.34	4.54	4.64	4.53	4.63	4.62	2013
4.16	4.08	4.11	3.92	3.92	3.79	2014
4.15	4.04	4.07	3.95	4.06	3.97	2015

MOODY'S SEASONED CORPORATE Baa*

	JAN	FEB	MAR	APR	MAY	JUN
1950	3.24	3.24	3.24	3.23	3.25	3.28
1951	3.17	3.16	3.23	3.35	3.40	3.49
1952	3.59	3.53	3.51	3.50	3.49	3.50
1953	3.51	3.53	3.57	3.65	3.78	3.86
1954	3.71	3.61	3.51	3.47	3.47	3.49
1955	3.45	3.47	3.48	3.49	3.50	3.51
1956	3.60	3.58	3.60	3.68	3.73	3.76
1957	4.49	4.47	4.43	4.44	4.52	4.63
1958	4.83	4.66	4.68	4.67	4.62	4.55
1959	4.87	4.89	4.85	4.86	4.96	5.04
1960	5.34	5.34	5.25	5.20	5.28	5.26
1961	5.10	5.07	5.02	5.01	5.01	5.03
1962	5.08	5.07	5.04	5.02	5.00	5.02
1963	4.91	4.89	4.88	4.87	4.85	4.84
1964	4.83	4.83	4.83	4.85	4.85	4.85
1965	4.80	4.78	4.78	4.80	4.81	4.85
1966	5.06	5.12	5.32	5.41	5.48	5.58
1967	5.97	5.82	5.85	5.83	5.96	6.15
1968	6.84	6.80	6.85	6.97	7.03	7.07
1969	7.32	7.30	7.51	7.54	7.52	7.70
1970	8.86	8.78	8.63	8.70	8.98	9.25
1971	8.74	8.39	8.46	8.45	8.62	8.75
1972	8.23	8.23	8.24	8.24	8.23	8.20
1973	7.90	7.97	8.03	8.09	8.06	8.13
1974	8.48	8.53	8.62	8.87	9.05	9.27
1975	10.81	10.65	10.48	10.58	10.69	10.62
1976	10.41	10.24	10.12	9.94	9.86	9.89
1977	9.08	9.12	9.12	9.07	9.01	8.91
1978	9.17	9.20	9.22	9.32	9.49	9.60
1979	10.13	10.08	10.26	10.33	10.47	10.38
1980	12.42	13.57	14.45	14.19	13.17	12.71
1981	15.03	15.37	15.34	15.56	15.95	15.80
1982	17.10	17.18	16.82	16.78	16.64	16.92
1983	13.94	13.95	13.61	13.29	13.09	13.37
1984	13.65	13.59	13.99	14.31	14.74	15.05
1985	13.26	13.23	13.69	13.51	13.15	12.40
1986	11.44	11.11	10.50	10.19	10.29	10.34
1987	9.72	9.65	9.61	10.04	10.51	10.52
1988	11.07	10.62	10.57	10.90	11.04	11.00
1989	10.65	10.61	10.67	10.61	10.46	10.03
1990	9.94	10.14	10.21	10.30	10.41	10.22
1991	10.45	10.07	10.09	9.94	9.86	9.96
1992	9.13	9.23	9.25	9.21	9.13	9.05
1993	8.67	8.39	8.15	8.14	8.21	8.07
1994	7.65	7.76	8.13	8.52	8.62	8.65
1995	9.08	8.85	8.70	8.60	8.20	7.90
1996	7.47	7.63	8.03	8.19	8.30	8.40
1997	8.09	7.94	8.18	8.34	8.20	8.02
1998	7.19	7.25	7.32	7.33	7.30	7.13
1999	7.29	7.39	7.53	7.48	7.72	8.02
2000	8.33	8.29	8.37	8.40	8.90	8.48
2001	7.93	7.87	7.84	8.07	8.07	7.97
2002	7.87	7.89	8.11	8.03	8.09	7.95
2003	7.35	7.06	6.95	6.85	6.38	6.19
2004	6.44	6.27	6.11	6.46	6.75	6.78
2005	6.02	5.82	6.06	6.05	6.01	5.86
2006	6.24	6.27	6.41	6.68	6.75	6.78
2007	6.34	6.28	6.27	6.39	6.39	6.70
2008	6.54	6.82	6.89	6.97	6.93	7.07
2009	8.14	8.08	8.42	8.39	8.06	7.50
2010	6.25	6.34	6.27	6.25	6.05	6.23
2011	6.09	6.15	6.03	6.02	5.78	5.75
2012	5.23	5.14	5.23	5.19	5.07	5.02
2013	4.73	4.85	4.85	4.59	4.73	5.19
2014	5.19	5.10	5.06	4.90	4.76	4.80
2015	4.45	4.51	4.54	4.48	4.89	5.13

* Source: Federal Reserve Bank of St. Louis, monthly data calculated as average of business days

MOODY'S SEASONED CORPORATE Baa* BOND YIELDS

JUL	AUG	SEP	OCT	NOV	DEC	
3.32	3.23	3.21	3.22	3.22	3.20	**1950**
3.53	3.50	3.46	3.50	3.56	3.61	**1951**
3.50	3.51	3.52	3.54	3.53	3.51	**1952**
3.86	3.85	3.88	3.82	3.75	3.74	**1953**
3.50	3.49	3.47	3.46	3.45	3.45	**1954**
3.52	3.56	3.59	3.59	3.58	3.62	**1955**
3.80	3.93	4.07	4.17	4.24	4.37	**1956**
4.73	4.82	4.93	4.99	5.09	5.03	**1957**
4.53	4.67	4.87	4.92	4.87	4.85	**1958**
5.08	5.09	5.18	5.28	5.26	5.28	**1959**
5.22	5.08	5.01	5.11	5.08	5.10	**1960**
5.09	5.11	5.12	5.13	5.11	5.10	**1961**
5.05	5.06	5.03	4.99	4.96	4.92	**1962**
4.84	4.83	4.84	4.83	4.84	4.85	**1963**
4.83	4.82	4.82	4.81	4.81	4.81	**1964**
4.88	4.88	4.91	4.93	4.95	5.02	**1965**
5.68	5.83	6.09	6.10	6.13	6.18	**1966**
6.26	6.33	6.40	6.52	6.72	6.93	**1967**
6.98	6.82	6.79	6.84	7.01	7.23	**1968**
7.84	7.86	8.05	8.22	8.25	8.65	**1969**
9.40	9.44	9.39	9.33	9.38	9.12	**1970**
8.76	8.76	8.59	8.48	8.38	8.38	**1971**
8.23	8.19	8.09	8.06	7.99	7.93	**1972**
8.24	8.53	8.63	8.41	8.42	8.48	**1973**
9.48	9.77	10.18	10.48	10.60	10.63	**1974**
10.55	10.59	10.61	10.62	10.56	10.56	**1975**
9.82	9.64	9.40	9.29	9.23	9.12	**1976**
8.87	8.82	8.80	8.89	8.95	8.99	**1977**
9.60	9.48	9.42	9.59	9.83	9.94	**1978**
10.29	10.35	10.54	11.40	11.99	12.06	**1979**
12.65	13.15	13.70	14.23	14.64	15.14	**1980**
16.17	16.34	16.92	17.11	16.39	16.55	**1981**
16.80	16.32	15.63	14.73	14.30	14.14	**1982**
13.39	13.64	13.55	13.46	13.61	13.75	**1983**
15.15	14.63	14.35	13.94	13.48	13.40	**1984**
12.43	12.50	12.48	12.36	11.99	11.58	**1985**
10.16	10.18	10.20	10.24	10.07	9.97	**1986**
10.61	10.80	11.31	11.62	11.23	11.29	**1987**
11.11	11.21	10.90	10.41	10.48	10.65	**1988**
9.87	9.88	9.91	9.81	9.81	9.82	**1989**
10.20	10.41	10.64	10.74	10.62	10.43	**1990**
9.89	9.65	9.51	9.49	9.45	9.26	**1991**
8.84	8.65	8.62	8.84	8.96	8.81	**1992**
7.93	7.60	7.34	7.31	7.66	7.69	**1993**
8.80	8.74	8.98	9.20	9.32	9.10	**1994**
8.04	8.19	7.93	7.75	7.68	7.49	**1995**
8.35	8.18	8.35	8.07	7.79	7.89	**1996**
7.75	7.82	7.70	7.57	7.42	7.32	**1997**
7.15	7.14	7.09	7.18	7.34	7.23	**1998**
7.95	8.15	8.20	8.38	8.15	8.19	**1999**
8.35	8.26	8.35	8.34	8.28	8.02	**2000**
7.97	7.85	8.03	7.91	7.81	8.05	**2001**
7.90	7.58	7.40	7.73	7.62	7.45	**2002**
6.62	7.01	6.79	6.73	6.66	6.60	**2003**
6.62	6.46	6.27	6.21	6.20	6.15	**2004**
5.95	5.96	6.03	6.30	6.39	6.32	**2005**
6.76	6.59	6.43	6.42	6.20	6.22	**2006**
6.65	6.65	6.59	6.48	6.40	6.65	**2007**
7.16	7.15	7.31	8.88	9.21	8.43	**2008**
7.09	6.58	6.31	6.29	6.32	6.37	**2009**
6.01	5.66	5.66	5.72	5.92	6.10	**2010**
5.76	5.36	5.27	5.37	5.14	5.25	**2011**
4.87	4.91	4.84	4.58	4.51	4.63	**2012**
5.32	5.42	5.47	5.31	5.38	5.38	**2013**
4.73	4.69	4.80	4.69	4.79	4.74	**2014**
5.20	5.19	5.34	5.34	5.46	5.46	**2015**

COMMODITIES

OIL - WEST TEXAS INTERMEDIATE
CLOSING VALUES $ / bbl

	JAN	FEB	MAR	APR	MAY	JUN
1950	2.6	2.6	2.6	2.6	2.6	2.6
1951	2.6	2.6	2.6	2.6	2.6	2.6
1952	2.6	2.6	2.6	2.6	2.6	2.6
1953	2.6	2.6	2.6	2.6	2.6	2.8
1954	2.8	2.8	2.8	2.8	2.8	2.8
1955	2.8	2.8	2.8	2.8	2.8	2.8
1956	2.8	2.8	2.8	2.8	2.8	2.8
1957	2.8	3.1	3.1	3.1	3.1	3.1
1958	3.1	3.1	3.1	3.1	3.1	3.1
1959	3.0	3.0	3.0	3.0	3.0	3.0
1960	3.0	3.0	3.0	3.0	3.0	3.0
1961	3.0	3.0	3.0	3.0	3.0	3.0
1962	3.0	3.0	3.0	3.0	3.0	3.0
1963	3.0	3.0	3.0	3.0	3.0	3.0
1964	3.0	3.0	3.0	3.0	3.0	3.0
1965	2.9	2.9	2.9	2.9	2.9	2.9
1966	2.9	2.9	2.9	2.9	2.9	2.9
1967	3.0	3.0	3.0	3.0	3.0	3.0
1968	3.1	3.1	3.1	3.1	3.1	3.1
1969	3.1	3.1	3.3	3.4	3.4	3.4
1970	3.4	3.4	3.4	3.4	3.4	3.4
1971	3.6	3.6	3.6	3.6	3.6	3.6
1972	3.6	3.6	3.6	3.6	3.6	3.6
1973	3.6	3.6	3.6	3.6	3.6	3.6
1974	10.1	10.1	10.1	10.1	10.1	10.1
1975	11.2	11.2	11.2	11.2	11.2	11.2
1976	11.2	12.0	12.1	12.2	12.2	12.2
1977	13.9	13.9	13.9	13.9	13.9	13.9
1978	14.9	14.9	14.9	14.9	14.9	14.9
1979	14.9	15.9	15.9	15.9	18.1	19.1
1980	32.5	37.0	38.0	39.5	39.5	39.5
1981	38.0	38.0	38.0	38.0	38.0	36.0
1982	33.9	31.6	28.5	33.5	35.9	35.1
1983	31.2	29.0	28.8	30.6	30.0	31.0
1984	29.7	30.1	30.8	30.6	30.5	30.0
1985	25.6	27.3	28.2	28.8	27.6	27.1
1986	22.9	15.4	12.6	12.8	15.4	13.5
1987	18.7	17.7	18.3	18.6	19.4	20.0
1988	17.2	16.8	16.2	17.9	17.4	16.5
1989	18.0	17.8	19.4	21.0	20.0	20.0
1990	22.6	22.1	20.4	18.6	18.2	16.9
1991	25.0	20.5	19.9	20.8	21.2	20.2
1992	18.8	19.0	18.9	20.2	20.9	22.4
1993	19.1	20.1	20.3	20.3	19.9	19.1
1994	15.0	14.8	14.7	16.4	17.9	19.1
1995	18.0	18.5	18.6	19.9	19.7	18.4
1996	18.9	19.1	21.4	23.6	21.3	20.5
1997	25.2	22.2	21.0	19.7	20.8	19.2
1998	16.7	16.1	15.0	15.4	14.9	13.7
1999	12.5	12.0	14.7	17.3	17.8	17.9
2000	27.2	29.4	29.9	25.7	28.8	31.8
2001	29.6	29.6	27.2	27.4	28.6	27.6
2002	19.7	20.7	24.4	26.3	27.0	25.5
2003	32.9	35.9	33.6	28.3	28.1	30.7
2004	34.3	34.7	36.8	36.7	40.3	38.0
2005	46.8	48.0	54.3	53.0	49.8	56.3
2006	65.5	61.6	62.9	69.7	70.9	71.0
2007	54.6	59.3	60.6	64.0	63.5	67.5
2008	93.0	95.4	105.6	112.6	125.4	133.9
2009	41.7	39.2	48.0	49.8	59.2	69.7
2010	78.2	76.4	81.2	84.5	73.8	75.4
2011	89.4	89.6	102.9	110.0	101.3	96.3
2012	100.3	102.3	106.2	103.3	94.7	82.3
2013	94.8	95.3	92.9	92.0	94.5	95.8
2014	94.6	100.8	100.8	102.1	102.2	105.8
2015	47.2	50.6	47.8	54.5	59.3	59.8

* Source: Federal Reserve

OIL - WEST TEXAS INTERMEDIATE
CLOSING VALUES $ / bbl

JUL	AUG	SEP	OCT	NOV	DEC	
2.6	2.6	2.6	2.6	2.6	2.6	1950
2.6	2.6	2.6	2.6	2.6	2.6	1951
2.6	2.6	2.6	2.6	2.6	2.6	1952
2.8	2.8	2.8	2.8	2.8	2.8	1953
2.8	2.8	2.8	2.8	2.8	2.8	1954
2.8	2.8	2.8	2.8	2.8	2.8	1955
2.8	2.8	2.8	2.8	2.8	2.8	1956
3.1	3.1	3.1	3.1	3.1	3.0	1957
3.1	3.1	3.1	3.1	3.0	3.0	1958
3.0	3.0	3.0	3.0	3.0	3.0	1959
3.0	3.0	3.0	3.0	3.0	3.0	1960
3.0	3.0	3.0	3.0	3.0	3.0	1961
3.0	3.0	3.0	3.0	3.0	3.0	1962
3.0	3.0	3.0	3.0	3.0	3.0	1963
2.9	2.9	2.9	2.9	2.9	2.9	1964
2.9	2.9	2.9	2.9	2.9	2.9	1965
2.9	2.9	3.0	3.0	3.0	3.0	1966
3.0	3.1	3.1	3.1	3.1	3.1	1967
3.1	3.1	3.1	3.1	3.1	3.1	1968
3.4	3.4	3.4	3.4	3.4	3.4	1969
3.3	3.3	3.3	3.3	3.3	3.6	1970
3.6	3.6	3.6	3.6	3.6	3.6	1971
3.6	3.6	3.6	3.6	3.6	3.6	1972
3.6	4.3	4.3	4.3	4.3	4.3	1973
10.1	10.1	10.1	11.2	11.2	11.2	1974
11.2	11.2	11.2	11.2	11.2	11.2	1975
12.2	12.2	13.9	13.9	13.9	13.9	1976
13.9	14.9	14.9	14.9	14.9	14.9	1977
14.9	14.9	14.9	14.9	14.9	14.9	1978
21.8	26.5	28.5	29.0	31.0	32.5	1979
39.5	38.0	36.0	36.0	36.0	37.0	1980
36.0	36.0	36.0	35.0	36.0	35.0	1981
34.2	34.0	35.6	35.7	34.2	31.7	1982
31.7	31.9	31.1	30.4	29.8	29.2	1983
28.8	29.3	29.3	28.8	28.1	25.4	1984
27.3	27.8	28.3	29.5	30.8	27.2	1985
11.6	15.1	14.9	14.9	15.2	16.1	1986
21.4	20.3	19.5	19.8	18.9	17.2	1987
15.5	15.5	14.5	13.8	14.0	16.3	1988
19.6	18.5	19.6	20.1	19.8	21.1	1989
18.6	27.2	33.7	35.9	32.3	27.3	1990
21.4	21.7	21.9	23.2	22.5	19.5	1991
21.8	21.4	21.9	21.7	20.3	19.4	1992
17.9	18.0	17.5	18.1	16.7	14.5	1993
19.7	18.4	17.5	17.7	18.1	17.2	1994
17.3	18.0	18.2	17.4	18.0	19.0	1995
21.3	22.0	24.0	24.9	23.7	25.4	1996
19.6	19.9	19.8	21.3	20.2	18.3	1997
14.1	13.4	15.0	14.4	12.9	11.3	1998
20.1	21.3	23.9	22.6	25.0	26.1	1999
29.8	31.2	33.9	33.1	34.4	28.5	2000
26.5	27.5	25.9	22.2	19.7	19.3	2001
26.9	28.4	29.7	28.9	26.3	29.4	2002
30.8	31.6	28.3	30.3	31.1	32.2	2003
40.7	44.9	46.0	53.1	48.5	43.3	2004
58.7	65.0	65.6	62.4	58.3	59.4	2005
74.4	73.1	63.9	58.9	59.4	62.0	2006
74.2	72.4	79.9	86.2	94.6	91.7	2007
133.4	116.6	103.9	76.7	57.4	41.0	2008
64.1	71.1	69.5	75.6	78.1	74.3	2009
76.4	76.8	75.3	81.9	84.1	89.0	2010
97.2	86.3	85.6	86.4	97.2	98.6	2011
87.9	94.2	94.7	89.6	86.7	88.3	2012
104.7	106.6	106.3	100.5	93.9	97.6	2013
103.6	96.5	93.2	84.4	75.8	59.3	2014
50.9	42.9	45.5	46.2	42.4	37.2	2015

COMMODITIES 🇺🇸 GOLD $US/OZ LONDON PM MONTH CLOSE

	JAN	FEB	MAR	APR	MAY	JUN
1970	34.9	35.0	35.1	35.6	36.0	35.4
1971	37.9	38.7	38.9	39.0	40.5	40.1
1972	45.8	48.3	48.3	49.0	54.6	62.1
1973	65.1	74.2	84.4	90.5	102.0	120.1
1974	129.2	150.2	168.4	172.2	163.3	154.1
1975	175.8	181.8	178.2	167.0	167.0	166.3
1976	128.2	132.3	129.6	128.4	125.5	123.8
1977	132.3	142.8	148.9	147.3	143.0	143.0
1978	175.8	182.3	181.6	170.9	184.2	183.1
1979	233.7	251.3	240.1	245.3	274.6	277.5
1980	653.0	637.0	494.5	518.0	535.5	653.5
1981	506.5	489.0	513.8	482.8	479.3	426.0
1982	387.0	362.6	320.0	361.3	325.3	317.5
1983	499.5	408.5	414.8	429.3	437.5	416.0
1984	373.8	394.3	388.5	375.8	384.3	373.1
1985	306.7	287.8	329.3	321.4	314.0	317.8
1986	350.5	338.2	344.0	345.8	343.2	345.5
1987	400.5	405.9	405.9	453.3	451.0	447.3
1988	458.0	426.2	457.0	449.0	455.5	436.6
1989	394.0	387.0	383.2	377.6	361.8	373.0
1990	415.1	407.7	368.5	367.8	363.1	352.2
1991	366.0	362.7	355.7	357.8	360.4	368.4
1992	354.1	353.1	341.7	336.4	337.5	343.4
1993	330.5	327.6	337.8	354.3	374.8	378.5
1994	377.9	381.6	389.2	376.5	387.6	388.3
1995	374.9	376.4	392.0	389.8	384.3	387.1
1996	405.6	400.7	396.4	391.3	390.6	382.0
1997	345.5	358.6	348.2	340.2	345.6	334.6
1998	304.9	297.4	301.0	310.7	293.6	296.3
1999	285.4	287.1	279.5	286.6	268.6	261.0
2000	283.3	293.7	276.8	275.1	272.3	288.2
2001	264.5	266.7	257.7	263.2	267.5	270.6
2002	282.3	296.9	301.4	308.2	326.6	318.5
2003	367.5	347.5	334.9	336.8	361.4	346.0
2004	399.8	395.9	423.7	388.5	393.3	395.8
2005	422.2	435.5	427.5	435.7	414.5	437.1
2006	568.8	556.0	582.0	644.0	653.0	613.5
2007	650.5	664.2	661.8	677.0	659.1	650.5
2008	923.3	971.5	933.5	871.0	885.8	930.3
2009	919.5	952.0	916.5	883.3	975.5	934.5
2010	1078.5	1108.3	1115.5	1179.3	1207.5	1244.0
2011	1327.0	1411.0	1439.0	1535.5	1536.5	1505.5
2012	1744.0	1770.0	1662.5	1651.3	1558.0	1598.5
2013	1664.8	1588.5	1598.3	1469.0	1394.5	1192.0
2014	1251.0	1326.5	1291.75	1288.5	1250.5	1315.0
2015	1260.3	1214.0	1187.0	1180.25	1191.4	1171.0

* Source: Bank of England

GOLD $US/OZ LONDON PM MONTH CLOSE

COMMODITIES

JUL	AUG	SEP	OCT	NOV	DEC	
35.3	35.4	36.2	37.5	37.4	37.4	**1970**
41.0	42.7	42.0	42.5	42.9	43.5	**1971**
65.7	67.0	65.5	64.9	62.9	63.9	**1972**
120.2	106.8	103.0	100.1	94.8	106.7	**1973**
143.0	154.6	151.8	158.8	181.7	183.9	**1974**
166.7	159.8	141.3	142.9	138.2	140.3	**1975**
112.5	104.0	116.0	123.2	130.3	134.5	**1976**
144.1	146.0	154.1	161.5	160.1	165.0	**1977**
200.3	208.7	217.1	242.6	193.4	226.0	**1978**
296.5	315.1	397.3	382.0	415.7	512.0	**1979**
614.3	631.3	666.8	629.0	619.8	589.8	**1980**
406.0	425.5	428.8	427.0	414.5	397.5	**1981**
342.9	411.5	397.0	423.3	436.0	456.9	**1982**
422.0	414.3	405.0	382.0	405.0	382.4	**1983**
342.4	348.3	343.8	333.5	329.0	309.0	**1984**
327.5	333.3	326.5	325.1	325.3	326.8	**1985**
357.5	384.7	423.2	401.0	383.5	388.8	**1986**
462.5	453.4	459.5	468.8	492.5	484.1	**1987**
436.8	427.8	397.7	412.4	422.6	410.3	**1988**
368.3	359.8	366.5	375.3	408.2	398.6	**1989**
372.3	387.8	408.4	379.5	384.9	386.2	**1990**
362.9	347.4	354.9	357.5	366.3	353.2	**1991**
357.9	340.0	349.0	339.3	334.2	332.9	**1992**
401.8	371.6	355.5	369.6	370.9	391.8	**1993**
384.0	385.8	394.9	383.9	383.1	383.3	**1994**
383.4	382.4	384.0	382.7	387.8	387.0	**1995**
385.3	386.5	379.0	379.5	371.3	369.3	**1996**
326.4	325.4	332.1	311.4	296.8	290.2	**1997**
288.9	273.4	293.9	292.3	294.7	287.8	**1998**
255.6	254.8	299.0	299.1	291.4	290.3	**1999**
276.8	277.0	273.7	264.5	269.1	274.5	**2000**
265.9	273.0	293.1	278.8	275.5	276.5	**2001**
304.7	312.8	323.7	316.9	319.1	347.2	**2002**
354.8	375.6	388.0	386.3	398.4	416.3	**2003**
391.4	407.3	415.7	425.6	453.4	435.6	**2004**
429.0	433.3	473.3	470.8	495.7	513.0	**2005**
632.5	623.5	599.3	603.8	646.7	632.0	**2006**
665.5	672.0	743.0	789.5	783.5	833.8	**2007**
918.0	833.0	884.5	730.8	814.5	869.8	**2008**
939.0	955.5	995.8	1040.0	1175.8	1087.5	**2009**
1169.0	1246.0	1307.0	1346.8	1383.5	1405.5	**2010**
1628.5	1813.5	1620.0	1722.0	1746.0	1531.0	**2011**
1622.0	1648.5	1776.0	1719.0	1726.0	1657.5	**2012**
1314.5	1394.8	1326.5	1324.0	1253.0	1204.5	**2013**
1285.3	1285.8	1216.5	1164.8	1282.8	1206.0	**2014**
1098.4	1135.0	1114.0	1142.4	1061.9	1060.0	**2015**

FOREIGN EXCHANGE

	JAN		FEB		MAR		APR		MAY		JUN	
	US / CDN	CDN / US	US / CDN	CDN / US	US / CDN	CDN /US	US / CDN	CDN / US	US / CDN	CDN / US	US / CDN	CDN / US
1971	1.01	0.99	1.01	0.99	1.01	0.99	1.01	0.99	1.01	0.99	1.02	0.98
1972	1.01	0.99	1.00	1.00	1.00	1.00	1.00	1.00	0.99	1.01	0.98	1.02
1973	1.00	1.00	1.00	1.00	1.00	1.00	1.00	1.00	1.00	1.00	1.00	1.00
1974	0.99	1.01	0.98	1.02	0.97	1.03	0.97	1.03	0.96	1.04	0.97	1.03
1975	0.99	1.01	1.00	1.00	1.00	1.00	1.01	0.99	1.03	0.97	1.03	0.97
1976	1.01	0.99	0.99	1.01	0.99	1.01	0.98	1.02	0.98	1.02	0.97	1.03
1977	1.01	0.99	1.03	0.97	1.05	0.95	1.05	0.95	1.05	0.95	1.06	0.95
1978	1.10	0.91	1.11	0.90	1.13	0.89	1.14	0.88	1.12	0.89	1.12	0.89
1979	1.19	0.84	1.20	0.84	1.17	0.85	1.15	0.87	1.16	0.87	1.17	0.85
1980	1.16	0.86	1.16	0.87	1.17	0.85	1.19	0.84	1.17	0.85	1.15	0.87
1981	1.19	0.84	1.20	0.83	1.19	0.84	1.19	0.84	1.20	0.83	1.20	0.83
1982	1.19	0.84	1.21	0.82	1.22	0.82	1.23	0.82	1.23	0.81	1.28	0.78
1983	1.23	0.81	1.23	0.81	1.23	0.82	1.23	0.81	1.23	0.81	1.23	0.81
1984	1.25	0.80	1.25	0.80	1.27	0.79	1.28	0.78	1.29	0.77	1.30	0.77
1985	1.32	0.76	1.35	0.74	1.38	0.72	1.37	0.73	1.38	0.73	1.37	0.73
1986	1.41	0.71	1.40	0.71	1.40	0.71	1.39	0.72	1.38	0.73	1.39	0.72
1987	1.36	0.73	1.33	0.75	1.32	0.76	1.32	0.76	1.34	0.75	1.34	0.75
1988	1.29	0.78	1.27	0.79	1.25	0.80	1.24	0.81	1.24	0.81	1.22	0.82
1989	1.19	0.84	1.19	0.84	1.20	0.84	1.19	0.84	1.19	0.84	1.20	0.83
1990	1.17	0.85	1.20	0.84	1.18	0.85	1.16	0.86	1.17	0.85	1.17	0.85
1991	1.16	0.87	1.15	0.87	1.16	0.86	1.15	0.87	1.15	0.87	1.14	0.87
1992	1.16	0.86	1.18	0.85	1.19	0.84	1.19	0.84	1.20	0.83	1.20	0.84
1993	1.28	0.78	1.26	0.79	1.25	0.80	1.26	0.79	1.27	0.79	1.28	0.78
1994	1.32	0.76	1.34	0.74	1.36	0.73	1.38	0.72	1.38	0.72	1.38	0.72
1995	1.41	0.71	1.40	0.71	1.41	0.71	1.38	0.73	1.36	0.73	1.38	0.73
1996	1.37	0.73	1.38	0.73	1.37	0.73	1.36	0.74	1.37	0.73	1.37	0.73
1997	1.35	0.74	1.36	0.74	1.37	0.73	1.39	0.72	1.38	0.72	1.38	0.72
1998	1.44	0.69	1.43	0.70	1.42	0.71	1.43	0.70	1.45	0.69	1.47	0.68
1999	1.52	0.66	1.50	0.67	1.52	0.66	1.49	0.67	1.46	0.68	1.47	0.68
2000	1.45	0.69	1.45	0.69	1.46	0.68	1.47	0.68	1.50	0.67	1.48	0.68
2001	1.50	0.67	1.52	0.66	1.56	0.64	1.56	0.64	1.54	0.65	1.52	0.66
2002	1.60	0.63	1.60	0.63	1.59	0.63	1.58	0.63	1.55	0.65	1.53	0.65
2003	1.54	0.65	1.51	0.66	1.48	0.68	1.46	0.69	1.38	0.72	1.35	0.74
2004	1.30	0.77	1.33	0.75	1.33	0.75	1.34	0.75	1.38	0.73	1.36	0.74
2005	1.22	0.82	1.24	0.81	1.22	0.82	1.24	0.81	1.26	0.80	1.24	0.81
2006	1.16	0.86	1.15	0.87	1.16	0.86	1.14	0.87	1.11	0.90	1.11	0.90
2007	1.18	0.85	1.17	0.85	1.17	0.86	1.14	0.88	1.10	0.91	1.07	0.94
2008	1.01	0.99	1.00	1.00	1.00	1.00	1.01	0.99	1.00	1.00	1.02	0.98
2009	1.22	0.82	1.25	0.80	1.26	0.79	1.22	0.82	1.15	0.87	1.13	0.89
2010	1.04	0.96	1.06	0.95	1.02	0.98	1.01	0.99	1.04	0.96	1.04	0.96
2011	0.99	1.01	0.99	1.01	0.98	1.02	0.96	1.04	0.97	1.03	0.98	1.02
2012	1.01	0.99	1.00	1.00	0.99	1.01	0.99	1.01	1.01	0.99	1.03	0.97
2013	0.99	1.01	1.01	0.99	1.02	.098	1.02	0.98	1.02	0.98	1.03	0.97
2014	1.09	0.91	1.11	0.90	1.11	0.90	1.10	0.91	1.09	0.92	1.08	0.92
2015	1.21	0.82	1.25	0.80	1.26	0.79	1.23	0.81	1.22	0.82	1.24	0.81

Source: Federal Reserve: Avg of daily rates, noon buying rates in New York City for cable transfers payable in foreign currencies

US DOLLAR vs CDN DOLLAR
MONTHLY AVG. VALUES

FOREIGN EXCHANGE

JUL		AUG		SEP		OCT		NOV		DEC		
US / CDN	CDN / US	US / CDN	CDN / US	US / CDN	CDN / US	US / CDN	CDN / US	US / CDN	CDN / US	US / CDN	CDN / US	
1.02	0.98	1.01	0.99	1.01	0.99	1.00	1.00	1.00	1.00	1.00	1.00	1971
0.98	1.02	0.98	1.02	0.98	1.02	0.98	1.02	0.99	1.01	1.00	1.00	1972
1.00	1.00	1.00	1.00	1.01	0.99	1.00	1.00	1.00	1.00	1.00	1.00	1973
0.98	1.02	0.98	1.02	0.99	1.01	0.98	1.02	0.99	1.01	0.99	1.01	1974
1.03	0.97	1.04	0.97	1.03	0.97	1.03	0.98	1.01	0.99	1.01	0.99	1975
0.97	1.03	0.99	1.01	0.98	1.03	0.97	1.03	0.99	1.01	1.02	0.98	1976
1.06	0.94	1.08	0.93	1.07	0.93	1.10	0.91	1.11	0.90	1.10	0.91	1977
1.12	0.89	1.14	0.88	1.17	0.86	1.18	0.85	1.17	0.85	1.18	0.85	1978
1.16	0.86	1.17	0.85	1.17	0.86	1.18	0.85	1.18	0.85	1.17	0.85	1979
1.15	0.87	1.16	0.86	1.16	0.86	1.17	0.86	1.19	0.84	1.20	0.84	1980
1.21	0.83	1.22	0.82	1.20	0.83	1.20	0.83	1.19	0.84	1.19	0.84	1981
1.27	0.79	1.25	0.80	1.23	0.81	1.23	0.81	1.23	0.82	1.24	0.81	1982
1.23	0.81	1.23	0.81	1.23	0.81	1.23	0.81	1.24	0.81	1.25	0.80	1983
1.32	0.76	1.30	0.77	1.31	0.76	1.32	0.76	1.32	0.76	1.32	0.76	1984
1.35	0.74	1.36	0.74	1.37	0.73	1.37	0.73	1.38	0.73	1.40	0.72	1985
1.38	0.72	1.39	0.72	1.39	0.72	1.39	0.72	1.39	0.72	1.38	0.72	1986
1.33	0.75	1.33	0.75	1.32	0.76	1.31	0.76	1.32	0.76	1.31	0.76	1987
1.21	0.83	1.22	0.82	1.23	0.82	1.21	0.83	1.22	0.82	1.20	0.84	1988
1.19	0.84	1.18	0.85	1.18	0.85	1.17	0.85	1.17	0.85	1.16	0.86	1989
1.16	0.86	1.14	0.87	1.16	0.86	1.16	0.86	1.16	0.86	1.16	0.86	1990
1.15	0.87	1.15	0.87	1.14	0.88	1.13	0.89	1.13	0.88	1.15	0.87	1991
1.19	0.84	1.19	0.84	1.22	0.82	1.25	0.80	1.27	0.79	1.27	0.79	1992
1.28	0.78	1.31	0.76	1.32	0.76	1.33	0.75	1.32	0.76	1.33	0.75	1993
1.38	0.72	1.38	0.73	1.35	0.74	1.35	0.74	1.36	0.73	1.39	0.72	1994
1.36	0.73	1.36	0.74	1.35	0.74	1.35	0.74	1.35	0.74	1.37	0.73	1995
1.37	0.73	1.37	0.73	1.37	0.73	1.35	0.74	1.34	0.75	1.36	0.73	1996
1.38	0.73	1.39	0.72	1.39	0.72	1.39	0.72	1.41	0.71	1.43	0.70	1997
1.49	0.67	1.53	0.65	1.52	0.66	1.55	0.65	1.54	0.65	1.54	0.65	1998
1.49	0.67	1.49	0.67	1.48	0.68	1.48	0.68	1.47	0.68	1.47	0.68	1999
1.48	0.68	1.48	0.67	1.49	0.67	1.51	0.66	1.54	0.65	1.52	0.66	2000
1.53	0.65	1.54	0.65	1.57	0.64	1.57	0.64	1.59	0.63	1.58	0.63	2001
1.55	0.65	1.57	0.64	1.58	0.63	1.58	0.63	1.57	0.64	1.56	0.64	2002
1.38	0.72	1.40	0.72	1.36	0.73	1.32	0.76	1.31	0.76	1.31	0.76	2003
1.32	0.76	1.31	0.76	1.29	0.78	1.25	0.80	1.20	0.84	1.22	0.82	2004
1.22	0.82	1.20	0.83	1.18	0.85	1.18	0.85	1.18	0.85	1.16	0.86	2005
1.13	0.89	1.12	0.89	1.12	0.90	1.13	0.89	1.14	0.88	1.15	0.87	2006
1.05	0.95	1.06	0.95	1.03	0.97	0.98	1.03	0.97	1.03	1.00	1.00	2007
1.01	0.99	1.05	0.95	1.06	0.95	1.18	0.84	1.22	0.82	1.23	0.81	2008
1.12	0.89	1.09	0.92	1.08	0.92	1.05	0.95	1.06	0.94	1.05	0.95	2009
1.04	0.96	1.04	0.96	1.03	0.97	1.02	0.98	1.01	0.99	1.01	0.99	2010
0.96	1.05	0.98	1.02	1.00	1.00	1.02	0.98	1.02	0.98	1.02	0.98	2011
1.01	0.99	0.99	1.01	.098	1.02	0.99	1.01	1.00	1.00	0.99	1.01	2012
1.04	0.96	1.04	0.96	1.03	0.97	1.04	0.96	1.05	0.95	1.06	0.94	2013
1.07	0.93	1.09	0.92	1.10	0.91	1.12	0.89	1.13	0.88	1.15	0.87	2014
1.29	0.78	1.31	0.76	1.33	0.75	1.31	0.76	1.33	0.75	1.37	0.73	2015

FOREIGN EXCHANGE

U.S. DOLLAR vs EURO
MONTHLY AVG. VALUES

| | JAN | | FEB | | MAR | | APR | | MAY | | JUN | |
	EUR / US	US / EUR	EUR / US	US / EUR	EUR / US	US / EUR	EUR / US	US / EUR	EUR / US	US / EUR	EUR / US	US / EUR
1999	1.16	0.86	1.12	0.89	1.09	0.92	1.07	0.93	1.06	0.94	1.04	0.96
2000	1.01	0.99	0.98	1.02	0.96	1.04	0.94	1.06	0.91	1.10	0.95	1.05
2001	0.94	1.07	0.92	1.09	0.91	1.10	0.89	1.12	0.88	1.14	0.85	1.17
2002	0.88	1.13	0.87	1.15	0.88	1.14	0.89	1.13	0.92	1.09	0.96	1.05
2003	1.06	0.94	1.08	0.93	1.08	0.93	1.09	0.92	1.16	0.87	1.17	0.86
2004	1.26	0.79	1.26	0.79	1.23	0.82	1.20	0.83	1.20	0.83	1.21	0.82
2005	1.31	0.76	1.30	0.77	1.32	0.76	1.29	0.77	1.27	0.79	1.22	0.82
2006	1.21	0.82	1.19	0.84	1.20	0.83	1.23	0.81	1.28	0.78	1.27	0.79
2007	1.30	0.77	1.31	0.76	1.32	0.75	1.35	0.74	1.35	0.74	1.34	0.75
2008	1.47	0.68	1.48	0.68	1.55	0.64	1.58	0.63	1.56	0.64	1.56	0.64
2009	1.32	0.76	1.28	0.78	1.31	0.77	1.32	0.76	1.36	0.73	1.40	0.71
2010	1.43	0.70	1.37	0.73	1.36	0.74	1.34	0.75	1.26	0.80	1.22	0.82
2011	1.34	0.75	1.37	0.73	1.40	0.71	1.45	0.69	1.43	0.70	1.44	0.69
2012	1.29	0.77	1.32	0.76	1.32	0.76	1.32	0.76	1.28	0.78	1.25	0.80
2013	1.33	0.75	1.33	0.75	1.30	0.77	1.30	0.77	1.30	0.77	1.32	0.76
2014	1.36	0.73	1.37	0.73	1.38	0.72	1.38	0.72	1.37	0.73	1.36	0.74
2015	1.16	0.86	1.14	0.88	1.08	0.92	1.08	0.92	1.12	0.90	1.12	0.89

Source: Federal Reserve: Avg of daily rates, noon buying rates in New York City for cable transfers payable in foreign currencies

US DOLLAR vs EURO
MONTHLY AVG. VALUES

	JUL		AUG		SEP		OCT		NOV		DEC		
	EUR / US	US / EUR	EUR / US	US / EUR	EUR / US	US / EUR	EUR / US	US / EUR	EUR / US	US / EUR	EUR / US	US / EUR	
	1.04	0.96	1.06	0.94	1.05	0.95	1.07	0.93	1.03	0.97	1.01	0.99	**1999**
	0.94	1.07	0.90	1.11	0.87	1.15	0.85	1.17	0.86	1.17	0.90	1.11	**2000**
	0.86	1.16	0.90	1.11	0.91	1.10	0.91	1.10	0.89	1.13	0.89	1.12	**2001**
	0.99	1.01	0.98	1.02	0.98	1.02	0.98	1.02	1.00	1.00	1.02	0.98	**2002**
	1.14	0.88	1.12	0.90	1.13	0.89	1.17	0.85	1.17	0.85	1.23	0.81	**2003**
	1.23	0.82	1.22	0.82	1.22	0.82	1.25	0.80	1.30	0.77	1.34	0.75	**2004**
	1.20	0.83	1.23	0.81	1.22	0.82	1.20	0.83	1.18	0.85	1.19	0.84	**2005**
	1.27	0.79	1.28	0.78	1.27	0.79	1.26	0.79	1.29	0.78	1.32	0.76	**2006**
	1.37	0.73	1.36	0.73	1.39	0.72	1.42	0.70	1.47	0.68	1.46	0.69	**2007**
	1.58	0.63	1.50	0.67	1.43	0.70	1.33	0.75	1.27	0.78	1.35	0.74	**2008**
	1.41	0.71	1.43	0.70	1.46	0.69	1.48	0.67	1.49	0.67	1.46	0.69	**2009**
	1.28	0.78	1.29	0.78	1.31	0.76	1.39	0.72	1.37	0.73	1.32	0.76	**2010**
	1.43	0.70	1.43	0.70	1.37	0.73	1.37	0.73	1.36	0.74	1.32	0.76	**2011**
	1.23	0.81	1.24	0.81	1.29	0.78	1.30	0.77	1.28	0.78	1.31	0.76	**2012**
	1.31	0.76	1.33	0.75	1.34	0.75	1.36	0.73	1.35	0.74	1.37	0.73	**2013**
	1.35	0.74	1.33	0.75	1.29	0.78	1.27	0.79	1.25	0.80	1.23	0.81	**2014**
	1.10	0.91	1.11	0.90	1.12	0.89	1.12	0.89	1.07	0.93	1.09	0.92	**2015**